GROWING WITH CANADA

Arts Insights showcases current research in the social sciences, humanities, and social work.

An initiative of McGill's Faculty of Arts, Arts Insights brings together research in the Social Sciences, Humanities, and Social Work. Reflective of the range of expertise and interests represented by the Faculty of Arts at McGill, Arts Insights seeks manuscripts that bring an interdisciplinary perspective to the discussion of ideas, issues, and debates that deepen and expand our understanding of human interaction, such as works dealing with society and change, or languages, literatures, and cultures and the relationships among them. Of particular interest are manuscripts that reflect the work of research collaborations involving McGill faculty and their colleagues in universities that are part of McGill's international affiliation network.

Arts Insights will publish two titles a year in English. The editors prefer original manuscripts but may consider the English-language translations of works that have already appeared in another language.

1 *Projecting Canada*
Government Policy and Documentary Film at the National Film Board
Zoe Druick

2 *Beyond Wilderness*
The Group of Seven, Canadian Identity, and Contemporary Art
Edited by John O'Brian and Peter White

3 *Mordecai Richler*
Leaving St Urbain
Reinhold Kramer

4 *Women in Power*
The Personalities and Leadership Styles of Indira Gandhi, Gold Meir, and Margaret Thatcher
Blema Steinberg

5 *The World and Darfur*
International Response to Crimes Against Humanity in Western Sudan
Edited by Amanda F. Grzyb

6 *Growing with Canada*
The Émigré Tradition in Canadian Music
Paul Helmer

Growing with Canada

The Émigré Tradition in Canadian Music

PAUL HELMER

McGill-Queen's University Press
Montreal & Kingston • London • Ithaca

ISBN 978-0-7735-3581-7

Legal deposit fourth quarter 2009
Bibliothèque nationale du Québec

Printed in Canada on acid-free paper that is 100% ancient forest free (100% post-consumer recycled), processed chlorine free

This book has been published with the help of a grant from the German Information Centre USA, Embassy of the Federal Republic of Germany, Washington, DC.

McGill-Queen's University Press acknowledges the support of the Canada Council for the Arts for our publishing program. We also acknowledge the financial support of the Government of Canada through the Book Publishing Industry Development Program (BPIDP) for our publishing activities.

Library and Archives Canada Cataloguing in Publication

Helmer, Paul, 1938–
Growing with Canada : the émigré tradition in Canadian music / Paul Helmer.

(Arts insights ; 6)
Includes bibliographical references and index.
ISBN 978-0-7735-3581-7

1. Music – Canada – 20th century – History and criticism. 2. Immigrants – Canada – History – 20th century. 3. Immigrants – Canada – Interviews. I. Title. II. Series: Arts insights 6

ML205.5.H478 2009 780.971'0904 C2009-904291-6

Typeset by Jay Tee Graphics Ltd. in 10.5/13 Sabon

Contents

Foreword

In his work, *Growing with Canada,* Professor Helmer has fashioned a compelling narrative of how some 120 musicians confronted European totalitarianism during both National Socialist and Soviet Communist regimes – and lived to contribute magnificently to Canada. The story begins in Berlin, not far from the Brandenburg Gate pictured on the German Information Center logo, and circles around two remarkable musicians, Arnold Walter and Helmut Blume, who began their careers in that great city. Forced to leave Berlin, they and many others from Germany and neighbouring countries displayed personal tenacity and courage in the face of adversity, not knowing that their journey would eventually take them to Canada. This book documents the significant contributions that these musicians made to their adopted homeland and is a fitting tribute to their achievements of which Canadians are the continuing beneficiaries. It is with great pleasure that I commend this important study to a wide audience both in Canada and in Europe.

Jörg Metger
Consul General of the Federal Republic of Germany

Acknowledgments

The publication of the present work was made possible by generous donations from the Arts Insights Series of McGill University and the Federal Republic of Germany. I am very grateful to both. I am indebted to the Social Sciences and Humanities Research Council of Canada for financial assistance in the research for this study. I owe a great debt of gratitude to Helmut Kallmann, creator of the superb Music Section of Library and Archives Canada, an indispensable starting point for research on Canadian music. Helmut Kallmann has been personally supportive of my work; Jeannine Barriault and Maureen Nevins have been extremely helpful on the many occasions I required their assistance. Thanks are also due to staff members of many other libraries and archives: Adelheid Iguchi (Universitätsbibliothek Tübingen), Lisa Rae Philpott (music reference librarian, University of Western Ontario), Janet Toole (Provincial Archives of New Brunswick), Birthe Joergensen (Joan Baillie Archives, Toronto), Marian Spence and Martha Tuff (Upper Canada College Archives, Toronto), Rhianna Edwards (music librarian, Acadia University, Wolfville), Paul von Wichert (Eckhardt-Gramatté Foundation, Winnipeg), Cynthia Leive (music librarian, Marvin Duchow Music Library, McGill University, and her ever-helpful assistants David Curtis and Gail Youster with John Black and Melanie Preuss in the audio department), Gordon Burr (senior archivist, McGill University Archives), Frances Fournier and Enid Britt (Simon Fraser University Archives). I am also indebted to Veronica Platts (Vancouver), David Duke (Vancouver), and Catherine Pye (Halifax). Rachel Anderson and Katharine Neufeld, as students in my seminar devoted to the topic, conducted interviews with a number of musicians. I owe a very great debt to Ruth Pincoe who, as editor, had the most difficult task of turning raw material into a meaningful narrative. I am also indebted to John Zucchi, of McGill-Queen's University Press, who never flagged in his determination to the see the project through to completion. The photograph of Arnold Walter (figure 4.1) is reprinted through the courtesy of Upper Canada College Archives, Barbara Barrows Collection. The essay, "Music in the University" (Appendix C) by Arnold Walter is reprinted through the kind permission of Margot Sunter, Community Foundation of Ottawa.

References to the musical life of cities and musicians are taken primarily from the first edition of *Die Musik in Geschichte und Gegenwart,* 1989 reprint edition. The second edition of this magnificent work has also been copiously cited. The numerous citations from the second edition of the *Encyclopedia of Music in Canada* (1992) and its updated online version are a testament to the importance of that bibliographic source. Translations, unless otherwise indicated, are my own.

Figures and Tables

FIGURES

TABLES

Abbreviations

ORGANIZATIONS AND INSTITUTIONS

ABRSM	Associated Board, Royal Schools of Music
BA	Bachelor of Arts degree
BMus	Bachelor of Music degree
CAMMAC	Canadian Amateur Musicians/Musiciens amateurs du Canada
CAPAC	Composers, Authors and Publishers Association of Canada Ltd.
CBC	Canadian Broadcasting Corporation
CC	Companion of the Order of Canada
CM	Member of the Order of Canada
COC	Canadian Opera Company
DMus	Doctor of Music degree
LAC	Library and Archives Canada
MMus	Master of Music degree
OC	Officer of the Order of Canada
RCM	Royal Conservatory of Music
TSO	Toronto Symphony Orchestra
TCM	Toronto Conservatory of Music

GROWING WITH CANADA

Introduction – Meanings of Exile: A New Perspective

On 27 February 1933 the Reichstag, Germany's guarantee and symbol of parliamentary democracy, was set on fire by Dutch national Marinus van der Lubbe.[1] The following day, using the fire as a pretext for a supposed Communist insurrection, the National Socialists proclaimed a national state of emergency and assumed unprecedented powers allowing the indiscriminate arrest of those whom Hitler classified as ideological opponents: social democrats, Communists, and Jews. The legal means for a large-scale persecution of unwanted "political enemies" was achieved by means of a succession of *Ermächtigungsgesetze* ("Enabling Laws") beginning on 23 March 1933, followed by a civil service law of 7 April that gave legal justification for a purge of non-Aryans from all government positions, including state employees in cultural institutions. The result was an immediate exodus of intellectuals, academics, writers, journalists, publicists, and artists from Berlin and other German cities; the academic haemorrhage of faculty from universities and research institutions was to cost Germany and eventually Austria their pre-eminence in many fields of human endeavour, including the social sciences, the natural sciences, and the arts.[2] Overall, Germany lost 39% of the faculty of its universities and academies. Entire research institutes were dismantled. In the first few months of 1933 the academic bloodletting in Berlin alone was completely unprecedented as social democrats, the first to bear the brunt of Nazi proscription, began to leave, and were followed by those who fell under the restrictions of later laws.[3] Some were re-established in North America; for example, in 1933 the *Institut für Sozialforschung* in Frankfurt with Max Horkheimer and Theodor

Adorno – a pioneer in social and economic theory – found a new home at Columbia University in New York, becoming, in effect, the New School for Social Research. These successive waves of émigrés resulted in a profound transformation of the artistic, economic, and academic life of the many nations through which these individuals passed and in which they eventually settled. Canada was a destination for many.

I have been able to identify 121 musicians who were forced to flee their homelands between 1933 and 1948, the cut-off dates for this study. The term "musician" is used here in its widest sense to include not only vocal and instrumental performers, teachers and educators, conductors, and composers, but also music administrators, musicologists, ethnomusicologists, lexicographers, broadcasters, managers, and music patrons. I have interviewed some thirty musicians (or in some cases surviving family members) and have supplemented their personal accounts of their experiences during these tumultuous years in Europe with archival material related to their careers held at university, provincial, and national institutions. Brief biographies of the musicians included in this study are given in appendix A (247–88); complete transcripts of the interviews are in the possession of the author.

Individually or in groups these musicians have, at one time or another, been referred to as Holocaust survivors, political exiles, deportees, self-exiles, refugees, voluntary exiles, expatriates, abductees, displaced person (DPs), "damned foreigners," expellees, escapees, asylum seekers, "enemy aliens," friendly aliens, emigrants, immigrants, landed immigrants, or new Canadians. Had their lives not been interrupted by political turmoil and war, they would undoubtedly have pursued successful musical careers in Europe. As it was, however, had they remained in Europe, their lives would have been in danger. Once their home countries refused them the right to participate as full and equal citizens, and in many cases, threatened their lives, these musicians were forced to accept the consequences of a failed political system that was unable to provide for its minorities, even when those minorities were, in many cases, the finest representatives of their respective societies. Emigration, or exile, was the only reasonable alternative. These musicians were active in the rich Austro-German musical tradition that was so radically tested during the 1930s and 1940s. Indeed, those who believed that artistic endeavours were independent of politics were sadly disappointed when new regimes proceeded to redefine the role of the state in artistic matters in a way that was inimical to the freedom most musicians feel is necessary. Certainly music has always provided a firm support for church and state authority – history provides countless examples – but now secular authorities inserted new racial or economic ideologies based not on voluntary cooperation but on forced compliance. This new enslavement of art to political ends was the frightening day-to-day reality for all citizens. Those who were part of the proud cultural heritage of central Europe were forced to either bow to new and threatening masters or seek a homeland elsewhere.

The musicians who came to Canada were only a small proportion of a much larger exodus of artists, intellectuals, and business elite to all parts of the globe. The United States likely benefited more than any other single country from this influx of human capital, and it is probably one of the principal reasons that America, originally disinclined to become involved on the world stage, was, by the force of events, catapulted onto the international scene and established global superiority in many areas. American scholars point to the resulting de-provincialization of the American mind while upholding the virtues of assimilation into the American melting pot as their yardstick.[4] Paradoxically this emigration brought about a much more robust presence of Austro-German culture in non-Austro-German countries than could possibly have been imagined before the Second World War. By December 1941, when the United States entered the war, the academic and artistic elite of Europe had immigrated to America and had congregated for the most part in New York, leaving most European capitals only shadows of their former selves. New York by default became the cultural centre of the world and retained that position for many years. Friedelind Wagner (1918–1991), who was forced from Bayreuth by her brother Wieland Wagner, left Germany in 1939 and became a US citizen in 1945; she later commented that she felt at home in New York because there were so many immigrants from Bayreuth living there. For her New York was "die bayreuthischte Stadt der Welt."[5]

Who could have predicted the chain of events sparked by a single fire back in 1933? Political developments through the 1930s and 1940s had led to the formation of a number of totalitarian regimes that gradually coalesced into two major and ideologically opposed regimes: National Socialism in Germany and Communism in the

Soviet Union. Both involved a profound disregard for human rights. The contrast between democracy and totalitarianism involves means and ends: in a democracy the means are the ends, but in a totalitarian state the ends justify the means. Democracies generally focus on the means by which decisions are made, whereas totalitarian states focus on the characteristics of an ideal state and ideologies may be temporarily sacrificed for political expediency, as in the case of the German-Soviet Friendship Pact of 23 August 1939 that allowed Germany to attack Poland with impunity from the west and at the same time permitted the Soviet Union to attack from the east only nine days later. On an ideological level, the two were sworn enemies, and the battle of Stalingrad is sometimes seen as the ultimate contest. Hermann Göring's address to the troops on 30 January 1943 highlights the Armageddon-like quality of this struggle:

> And from all of these epic battles, the battle for Stalingrad, rises up like a gigantic, monumental building. This will become the most significant battle in our entire history ... We know a heroic song from a battle without equal, it was called "The Battle of the Nibelungen." They too stood in a hall consumed with fire and slaked their thirst with their own blood – but fought and fought until the end. Such a battle is to be fought today, and every German in the next thousand years will speak the word Stalingrad with a holy terror and remember that Germany there set its stamp on the final victory.[6]

Göring's allusion to the *Nibelungenlied* was prophetic: neither the Nibelungen nor their latter-day counterparts survived. The assumption that all opposition, presumed or real, must be eradicated necessarily required the elimination of an opposing totalitarian regime, rendering mutual annihilation inevitable. But while their ideologies diverged, there were also remarkable similarities. Whether or not we agree with Hannah Arendt's thesis that both regimes were cut from the same cloth,[7] it cannot be denied that for many individuals it did not matter under which system they suffered. Among this group were citizens of those countries caught between the German fascist and Soviet Communist forces, particularly Hungary and Ukraine. Pianist Charles Reiner pointed out that, in a climate where a change of regime seemingly entailed little more than a change of shirt, one might face the same official first as a Nazi and then as a Communist: "Just before the end of the war when I came back to Hungary ... the same people who sent me to the camp [Mauthausen], the Nazis, were changing the colour of their shirts and were now Communists – I recognized them!"[8] Violinist Eugène Husaruk concluded that ideology of whatever stripe was simply an excuse for oppression: "The Germans executed 10 percent of my relatives but the Communists 40 percent; they were ruthless."[9]

The turmoil continued long after the cessation of hostilities in May 1945 as the Soviet Union solidified its hegemony over Eastern Europe – the Baltic States, Poland, Ukraine, Romania, Hungary, Czechoslovakia, and East Germany – and Soviet forces filled the power vacuum created by retreating German troops. When all remnants of a democratic government were purged from Czechoslovakia in February 1948, a second exodus ensued: when the Soviet Union quelled democratic tendencies in Hungary in 1956 and in Czechoslovakia in 1968, tens of thousands were again forced to flee. For the purposes of this study, however, I have concentrated on those who fled their homelands between 1933 and 1948.

What were the circumstances under which these musicians left their countries? What put them on their guard? When friends were abused by Gestapo or Communist thugs? When their apartments were searched? When they heard of close friends being questioned at the police station? Some were forewarned; others acted on their own, realizing the tragic consequences the worsening political situation would have on their livelihoods and indeed their lives. All were forced to confront the limits of their allegiance to the state, to make a difficult choice between remaining in their homelands, where their lives and careers were at risk, and leaving everything behind to begin anew somewhere else, whatever the cost might be.

The musicians who came from major central European and Baltic metropolitan centres – Berlin, Vienna, Prague, Budapest, Warsaw, Riga (see figure 1.1) – had many personal and professional contacts with leading musicians and theatre personnel, and they brought with them treasured memories of great performers. Some brought social democratic ideals that would flourish in their new homeland. Some came from established families with considerable social prestige. Others were socially and economically less fortunate.

Jacques Cartier, who sailed to Canada in 1534 and on his return to France reputedly said, "I am rather inclined to believe that this is land that God gave Cain,"[10] was perhaps the quintessential

European in his reaction to the vast expanses of bleak terrain that he encountered. A similar vision of Canada emerged in the literary fantasies of Karl May and Jack London. From the initial responses of the musical émigrés who arrived from war-torn Europe, it would seem that little had changed in four centuries. Composer Oskar Morawetz commented, "All the pictures I had seen of Canada were of vast, barren lands, with horses. It seemed to me like going to the wilderness, with no musical culture."[11] On landing in Canada, Peter Newman, now a well-known author on matters Canadian, was surprised to discover that the country was in colour: "I remember the moment I first sighted Nova Scotia from the ship's bow, surprised that the trees were green and the soil brown, since in the few newsreels I had seen of Canada, the land – like the film – had been black and white."[12] Pianist John Newmark knew Canada from school texts as "this country ... that ... was an enormous, a huge pink mass in my atlas, [where] there were bears, Indians, and trappers, and of course, the Royal Mounted Police. The biggest river was the St Lawrence. Some of the Great Lakes were in Canadian territory. Oh yes, Niagara Falls."[13]

Another possible reason for such reactions is that prior to the Second World War Canada did not have a reputation as a refuge for the dispossessed. While the émigrés were probably happy enough to have reached Pier 21 in Halifax harbour, there was no statue of liberty to welcome them. For some, desperate times dictated desperate actions; if there was no chance of pursuing their lives in England, the United States, South Africa, Australia, Shanghai, or Cuba, Canada was better than nothing. Some came involuntarily when Britain, in a panic, sent "enemy aliens" as far away as possible. For others, the choice was pure serendipity; a least one musician chose Canada when he found the US embassy closed for lunch. While a number of musicians initially came to Canada but continued their careers south of the border, many who had begun their North American careers in the United States moved north to make Canada their permanent home.

CANADIAN IMMIGRATION POLICY AND PRACTICE

This study of European musicians reveals that once the émigrés had decided to immigrate to Canada they faced no real impediments because of race, religion, or nationality. Paul Heller's remarkably courteous and efficient interview with immigration officer William Little in London in 1940 is noteworthy as an example of immigration procedures for European entrepreneurs wishing to come to Canada. In spite of advice from a business associate in Budapest that if they wanted to go to Canada they should get baptized first, Heller and his brother were undeterred.

> I met Mr Little, the chief of immigration in London and I never forgot the visit, believe me. He was charming because there was a friend of ours who had sent a recommendation for us to the High Commissioner, Vincent Massey. He wrote a letter, and based on that Massey passed it on to Mr Little and I got a telephone call inviting my brother and myself to an appointment at nine o'clock the next morning. We sat down for about fifteen minutes. Very nice. The moment my brother mentioned something about having an orange grove in Palestine, he asked "Are you Jewish?" He picked up some forms for us to fill out and these were sent to Ottawa and that was that. A few months later when we got the basic permission, my brother went to Canada House to get some information. Mr Little was passing by and he said "How did you manage to get permission?" My brother said, "Are you asking me? You are the chief of immigration!" We had to transfer a certain amount of money to ensure that we would be establishing a business in Canada; that was normal procedure.[14]

With the exception of pianist Lubka Kolessa (who came with her diplomat husband, Tracey Philips, and did not need a special visa) and the "Camp Boys" (who arrived as "guests" of the British Home Office), the thirty-eight musicians who arrived in Canada prior to 1942 did so through an order-in-council.[15] The normal procedure for refugees who did not have relatives or contacts within Canada to sponsor their immigration was to apply for landed immigrant status from a Canadian immigration office. In the early twentieth century the Canadian National Railway and the Canadian Pacific Railway had established a number of European control points for Canadian agents in order to canvass Europe for prospective colonists. In spite of major cuts due to economic conditions, this elaborate network was still in place during the late 1930s, with Canadian Immigration offices in London, Liverpool, Glasgow, Belfast, Paris,

Rotterdam, Hamburg, Antwerp, and Gydnia (Danzig). Jewish cantors Szalam Klamka, Jacob Kozaruk, Zelman-Gudek Srebrnik, and Iwan Tomaszewski from Poland were likely processed through the Canadian consular office in Gydnia. After September 1939 the offices in Hamburg and Gydnia were closed; in 1940, as the conflict widened, the Paris, Antwerp, and Rotterdam offices were shut down. The offices in Liverpool, Belfast, and Glasgow were later closed as well, leaving only London through the remainder of the war.[16]

Applications for a number of orders-in-council were made within Canada by individuals who had obtained visitors' visas abroad; they are designated as residing in Canada "under non-immigrant status." Such applications were made by Lotte Brott, Hugo Burghauser, Ida Halpern, Leon Koerner, Thea Koerner, Iby Koerner, Greta Kraus, Trudi Le Caine, Giuseppe Moschetti, Anna Katherina Schultze, Eric Schaeffer, Ernesto Vinci, and Arnold Walter.

In the cases I have been able to trace, applications were approved quickly, sometimes within weeks, as communications between Europe and Ottawa were usually carried out by cablegram. Some of the émigrés are listed as music teachers, cantors, organists, or music students; others were children of professionals or industrialists who would later take up music as a profession. Interestingly, although at least two were known to be practicing Jews, none were designated as such on the relevant permits, although their Jewish heritage could be implied by professions such as "Hebrew cantor," or "organist in Hebrew synagogue."

Estimates of the number of Jewish refugees who entered Canada during this period vary widely from zero to more than 100,000. In the preface to the 1982 edition of *None Is Too Many* Irving M. Abella and Harold Martin Troper state that fewer than 5,000 Jewish refugees were accepted into Canada between 1933 and 1945. The 2000 edition of this book states that "after the war until the founding of Israel in 1948, [Canada] admitted 8,000 more. That record is arguably the worst of all possible refugee-receiving states." Elsewhere Abella and Troper give an estimate of 4,000[17] with the comment that it "is impossible to specify the exact number of refugees of all classes, or Jewish refugees in particular," but that "Canada stood virtually alone in the niggardliness of her contribution." The figure of 4,000 was subsequently accepted in the scholarly literature.[18] A conference held at the Smithsonian Institute in Washington DC in February and December 1980 gave rise to several conflicting statements. One speaker maintained that "one of the most depressing cases during the refugee crisis of the 1930s was that of Canada, which literally closed its doors to Jewish refugees," while Abella and Troper revised their estimate downward to 3,500.[19]

Some authors imply that no Jewish refugees were allowed into Canada during this period. Donald Kerr and Deryck Holdsworth state that Canada's "denial of entry to European Jews fleeing Nazism is a particularly shameful aspect of Canada's record" and Paula Draper maintains that "Blair had been working for many years to bar Jews from Canada."[20] In 1990 Harold Troper stated that "Canada's doors remained closed to Jews. As a result, Canada had arguably the worst record among all the Western states in granting sanctuary to Jewish refugees from Nazi persecution."[21] It is not clear how Malcolm Proudfoot, who provided the number on which Abella and Troper based the estimate in their oft-quoted study, arrived at this figure. There are higher estimates. For example, Stephan Stompor provides a more sanguine assessment: "[Canada] accepted approximately 60,000 immigrants from 1933 on of which 80 percent were Jewish; another 200,000 immigrants followed until July 1935."[22] The implication is that more than 100,000 Jewish individuals, presumably refugees, were admitted. Statistics from the *Canada Year Book* and the annual reports from the Immigration Branch give 23,160 as the number of "Continental European Jews" who immigrated to Canada between 1 April 1933 and 31 March 1948, but it is unclear how widely or narrowly the category "Continental European Jew" was defined.[23] Was there latitude on the part of individual officers to interpret this official definition in their own way? Judging by Otto Joachim's experience it would seem that Canadian immigration officials were able to turn a blind eye to regulations when the occasion demanded. Joachim had a visa that allowed him only a brief stay in Canada on his way to Brazil and it had expired. He spoke excellent English to the officer who processed him. The official asked Joachim, "Is anybody bugging you?" Joachim replied "No." So he stamped Joachim's papers. That was all there was to it! After wandering the world for fifteen years in search of a homeland, he was finally free to stay in Canada. We can also imagine the consternation in the mind of the immigration official who dealt with pastor and musicologist Ulrich Leupold when he arrived in 1939 by way of Toledo, Ohio. Leupold's German passport undoubtedly bore the tell-tale designation "Israel" informing all and sundry that by the provisions of the Nuremberg Race Laws the bearer was Jewish. Since his mother was Jewish, the German authorities would consider him to be full-blooded Jewish. However, Leupold had become a member of the Confessing Church (a Christian movement opposed to the National Socialists) and had received training as a pastor in the Lutheran Church in Switzerland. He had accepted a position as pastor of St Matthew's Lutheran Church in Kitchener, Ontario, and was proceeding to accept the call there.

Much as we would like to know the answer for comparative purposes, it would be myopic to reduce the topic of European immigration to Canada between 1933 and 1948 to the question of how many Jews entered Canada. What is much more pressing is to determine the effect on Canada of this major migration of elite Europeans in the intellectual, artistic, scientific, and economic fields. To do this we must look at the contributions of all émigrés – both Gentile and Jewish. A number of émigrés told me that they considered themselves German rather than Jewish. As assimilated or emancipated Jews, they had taken their identity from the prevailing German culture around them.

In the absence of a coherent refugee policy, Mackenzie King's Liberal government left everyday decision making to the Immigration Branch. During the pre-1945 period, Director Frederick Charles Blair proposed a definition of refugees as "all who, because of political, religious, racial or economic troubles actual or threatened, have been forced or induced to move."[24] In his report for 1940–41, he stated that "some thousands of refugees were admitted to Canada from Europe during the fiscal year under review," neglecting to mention the fact that the emigration of persons who were citizens of countries "under enemy domination" was illegal.[25] Realpolitik trumped policy when the emigration of large numbers of qualified Europeans to Canada was at stake. If the present study is any indication, Canadian immigration authorities were able to transform a grim situation into a window of opportunity for Canada.

LIMITATIONS OF PRESENT EXILE STUDIES: THE EXILE AS ÉMIGRÉ

Within the last few decades "exile studies" (*Exilforschung*) has become an important academic field on both sides of the Atlantic, linking the work of scholars in a variety of disciplines including literature, art, dance, music, theology, film, and science.[26] The term reflects a European perspective – of émigrés as "lost" from Europe rather than "gained" by North America. Current research on musical émigrés has resulted in conferences at the Folkwang Hochschule in Essen in 1992 and at Harvard University in 1994.[27]

What happened to the musicians who went to our neighbour to the south? The United States had many well-established musical institutions, conservatories, and university departments specializing in performance and academic studies that offered career opportunities to established European expatriate musicians. The year 1933 marked the arrival of a number of well-known figures, including Arnold Schoenberg, Eric Hornbostel, Heinz Werner, Igor Kipnis, and Hugo Leichtentritt. The US quota of 25,957 German immigrants per year[28] may have encouraged this immigration, as did a provision that allowed entry to academics who had obtained appointments from American universities. A number of academic institutions took a proactive role in seeking out and hiring European artists and academics. The New School for Social Research became a haven for many European artists and academics;[29] other examples include the Princeton Institute for Advanced Study (Abraham Flexner), Mills College (French refugees) in California, and Black Mountain College in North Carolina (arts). The "Emergency Committee for Foreign Displaced Scholars" helped many find employment, and the National Committee for Refugee Musicians, chaired by Mark Brunswick, who had close links to many European musicians, actively sought out positions in the United States for refugees.[30]

One of the weaknesses of present-day studies of prewar émigrés is a narrow concentration on municipal, provincial, or national boundaries.[31] The history of Central Europe through the first half of the twentieth century demonstrates that national borders were extremely fluid. During the 1930s the German language, with its associated literary and musical achievements, was not confined to geographical Germany but served as the lingua franca of Central and Eastern Europe and the Baltic States. George Adams (the stage name of Adam Gutman, a Polish-born musician who survived several years in Auschwitz-Birkenau), stated that "as a Pole you had to learn German: German was the language of culture. At the time Germany was the most cultured country in the world."[32] The Austro-German musical repertoire that formed the basis for our musicians was a shared heritage among many nations; the core repertoire of operas and symphonies performed in Berlin were also those performed in Vienna, Prague, Budapest, Breslau, Leningrad, Moscow, and many other European cities. Certainly there were nationally inspired Slavic operas and instrumental works – strongly complemented by a concerted effort in collecting the traditional musics of many nationalities that began during the nineteenth century and continued into the twentieth – but this repertoire was restricted to a particular country or ethnic region. The common repertoire was much more universally recognized and appreciated. This meant that musicians had less difficulty than émigrés in language-oriented disciplines such as literature since verbal expression was less important. While music is an "international language" only in a qualified sense, performance of standard repertoire would not vary from country to country; verbal skills and other conceptual national or local idiosyncrasies come to the fore only with a move into teaching or administrative roles.

Previous research has concentrated primarily on politically motivated (usually German-speaking) emigration of the pre-war era;[33] the postwar period, which is qualitatively and quantitatively much more significant, has been little studied. The much longer period of Soviet hegemony over Europe insured that a dispassionate look at the topic could never be assayed while relevant materials were unavailable for study and politically conformist regimes were in power. Now that the Iron Curtain has been lifted, scholars can study the period without hindrance.

One of several definitions for the word "exile" given in the *Canadian Oxford Dictionary* is "a person expelled *or long absent from his or her native country*" (the italics are mine).[34] Certainly none of the cases examined in this study fit the classical definition of exile – a person banished from her or his homeland as punishment for committing a crime. The fascist or Communist totalitarian regimes never saw themselves bound by such juridical scruples; moreover, none of the musicians in the present study were actually subject to a court hearing or forced expulsion. They left not because they were physically forced to but rather because of the certainty that if they remained they would have been subject to serious mental and physical constraints; their exile was a pre-emptive action taken to avoid possible – or probable – loss of liberty and life. Hans Walter broadens the distinction between "racial" and "political" refugees as used by the Nazis: "racist [refugees] were those persons who, even without having been politically active, simply from the fact the of the racial-political policy of the NSDAP, feared the loss of their existence and with the accession to power of the National Socialist movement feared pogroms." Political refugees were those who "in any way were politically active before 1933 in the political chaos of the German Empire," including "all those German-speaking persons ... irrespective of nationality or race, who left Germany and the states that were later annexed by Germany (Austria, Czechoslovakia) because of the actual or intended accession to power of the Fascists and who could not or did not want to return there, as well as all those who in any foreign country directly or indirectly took a position in a political, journalistic or artistic form against German Fascism" (my translation).[35]

In 1963 the International Rights Committee in Paris defined a refugee as "any person who, because of political events that occurred in the country in which he or she was a subject, voluntarily or involuntarily left that territory and did not assume a new nationality or enjoy the protection of any national state." None of these definitions take into consideration the political dimension of the race issue, but both were inextricably linked; art itself, and indeed all aspects of an individual's existence, came to be politically relevant. Performers of traditional musical repertoire do not expose themselves politically to the same extent that writers might, yet the simple act of packing up and leaving because they feared their lives were in jeopardy can also be considered a political act. Composers subject to abuse because of the avant-garde tendencies of their compositions might leave in order to pursue their creative lives more freely elsewhere. In all cases the act is voluntary: the preconditions for exile do not exist. Is a political refugee necessarily an exile? If refugees do not live in the consciousness that they are in a state of exile, then presumably they are not. The consciousness of living in a state of exile would seem to be a precondition for consideration as an exile.

The musicians with whom I have had contact had difficulty in applying the term "exile" to themselves. Asked whether he considered himself an exile forced to leave his native country, composer Istvan Anhalt replied, "No, no. I was dying to leave. I couldn't wait. I left at the first moment I was able."[36] By putting the emphasis on an act taken by choice in order to preserve life and liberty, Anhalt was able to preserve human free will in a situation that would normally be considered to be determined exclusively by circumstances. Each émigré faced the need to make an existential decision that would determine a future life. By allowing themselves to put the past behind, they were able to release their creative energies, unhampered by the need to undo past wrongs. Obstacles now became opportunities.

The present study proposes a new model to which I have been led by the testimonies of informants, a model that might be called the "exile as émigré" model. Here the exile is seen as an émigré who has made an existential choice at a stage in life when he or she can say "I have had enough, I can do better." In that moment the "exile" transforms himself or herself into an émigré, thereby freeing himself or herself from tyranny, and a new life becomes possible. Each time this occurs it is a victory for humanity, a victory that we can all applaud. Freedom of choice accrues to the individual not through in any way discounting the terror or danger arising from the external threat but by accepting the fact that the indomitable human spirit of these individuals is somehow able to rise above the situation. The present study celebrates this epiphany, the eureka moment experienced by each émigré or by the parents of those who were still children.

The decision to become an émigré can be made only on an individual basis, never collectively. It may be taken at various points in an émigré's life – sometimes earlier, sometimes later – depending on individual character and external conditions. Even in instances where all members of a family were confronted by the same danger, individual family members would choose a route to take. For composer Oskar Morawetz the decision came so late that it almost cost him his life. As a Jewish citizen of a Czechoslovakia, a country that no longer existed, his position was indeed precarious. In March 1940, seven months after war was declared, his family had safely immigrated to Canada, but Morawetz had still not yet made the decision to come to Canada.[37]

Everyone is to a greater or lesser degree constrained by circumstances, but external events alone are not sufficient to explain why people react the way they do. Such a view would lead us to a deterministic universe in which free will, let alone chance or coincidence, had no place. In certain cases the "exile-as-exile" paradigm seems appropriate. For example, conductor and composer Alexander

Zemlinsky (1872–1942) had delayed his departure from his beloved Vienna, but finally left for Prague in the autumn of 1938, travelling via Amsterdam to New York, where he arrived on 26 December 1938, a broken man, unable, after a magnificent career in a city and country he dearly loved, to adopt to a new homeland.[38] It was a tragic case.

Often the choice to emigrate is taken in the émigré's country of origin at a time when he or she has only the vaguest notion of which country might offer a new homeland. Each person faced three choices: to stay, come what may; to stand and fight; or to leave, that is, to become an "exile." This study includes examples of all three. The parents of two émigrés in this study chose to stay in Germany but sent their children to safety on the Kindertransport. The parents perished. Sophie-Carmen ("Sonia") Eckhardt-Gramatté chose to stand and fight. Faced with the loss of her right to work she challenged the German bureaucracy and succeeded in winning back her professional dignity (see appendix D). The 121 musicians who came to Canada decided at some point in their career to leave their totalitarian homeland in spite of the cost and become émigrés. It is their stories that will engage us here.

AN OVERVIEW

The present study is divided into seven chapters, preceded by this introduction, and followed by an epilogue. The first chapter sets the scene in Europe – the political situation during the 1930s and 1940s – and examines the artistic community in which these musicians studied and, in some cases, began their professional careers. It traces the routes they took, around the world in some cases, to reach Canada. The second chapter includes a discussion of the eleven men sent from Britain to Canada along with thousands of other "enemy aliens" and prisoners of war and the "Eden" behind barbed wire that they created in the backwoods of New Brunswick and Quebec. These internees had certainly left Europe but they had not yet entered Canada. Chapter 3 is a brief survey of the musical landscape that these musicians found when they came to Canada in terms of individual musicians, music institutions, and music organizations. The next four chapters discuss the careers and contributions of émigré musicians. Chapter 4 examines the structural changes that occurred during the postwar years and later in

Canada's two largest music faculties – the University of Toronto and McGill University – and the significant roles played by Arnold Walter and Helmut Blume in these transformations. Chapter 5 deals with the establishment of opera in these two universities and in several other Canadian centres. Chapter 6 outlines the contributions of Arnold Walter and Helmut Blume in attracting some of the finest European and Canadian musicians to their respective institutions. Chapter 7 is devoted to the many freelance central European musicians who were active in centres across the country. The epilogue tells the stories of émigrés who attempted to come to terms with their past on visits to their former homelands.

Links among these musicians in European cities such as Berlin, Vienna, Prague, Budapest, and Warsaw were re-established in Canada. For example, during the 1930s Gerhard Kander, a brilliant child violin virtuoso, was to have made a concert tour of Germany with Hans Neumark (John Newmark) under the auspices of the Jüdischer Kulturbund. The tour did not come about, but ten years later they met and began performing behind barbed wire in the backwoods of New Brunswick. After their release, these two "Camp Boys" appeared on concert stages across Canada and the United States.

Most of the musician-émigrés who came to Canada arrived as young students or professionals on the threshold of their careers. A small number came as children, with or without their parents; three were sent to England with the Kindertransport, a humanitarian initiative that provided sanctuary in Britain for about ten thousand German-Jewish children under ten, billeting them with English families – at the cost of separating them, sometimes permanently, from their families.[39] Almost all the émigré musicians went on to spend the major portion of their creative lives in Canada. Istvan Anhalt (who coined the term used in the title of this book) spoke of "growing with Canada," reflecting his consciousness of coming to a country as a student and being given the opportunity to develop his talents in a musically accepting environment. A few had established careers in Europe long before coming to Canada, and their Canadian experiences are understandably marked with bitterness: examples include conductor Heinz Unger and pianist-conductor-teacher Alfred Rosé, who had reached significant high points in their lives before they arrived and could not find opportunities to match their experience and expectations.

This is the story of the sometimes confrontational, sometimes fruitful meetings of musical traditions of Central Europe and Britain. Canadians, buttressed by an immigration policy that clearly differentiated between British subjects and "aliens" (those who were not British subjects) were often wary of these newcomers, occasionally curious, and in some cases quite welcoming. Bearing wounds from the past but putting the best face on the present and the future was a quality that gradually endeared many émigrés to their new hosts.

As a student, a pianist, or a colleague, I have been personally acquainted with many of the musicians who are subjects of this study. In most cases I knew them as musicians long before I was aware of their European backgrounds; they never dwelt on past experiences and at the time I did not press the point. The discovery of what they had endured before reaching Canada impressed me all the more in hindsight. When I began the study I was looking forward to the challenge of interviewing the émigrés and recording their stories. Unfortunately, for many, my work began too late. Hans Gruber arrived on his motorcycle for an interview on a snowy day in March 2001; he died in early August of the same year, unable to correct the final version of his transcript. A proposed interview with Franz Kraemer was postponed because of health issues, and ultimately never came about. As of July 2009, fifteen of the musicians I interviewed had passed away. When death precluded an interview, I turned to accounts from spouses, siblings, and children, and to secondary sources.

This work is also a tribute to the Canadians who cared for, hired, and supported our central European musicians at a time when help was hard to come by. Typical of these are Kaspar and Lois Fraser, who sponsored the unknown twenty-one-year old Mannheim violinist Gerhard Kander as their fiftieth birthday present to one another: Mrs Fraser commented, "I wanted to prove to some of my anti-Semitic friends that Christians and Jews could live peacefully together." Kander, whose parents had perished in concentration camps, said of the Frasers, "They adopted me, for God's sake."

PART ONE

Europe

1

Facing Totalitarianism: Journeys and Refuges

The European musicians who found their way to Canada came from a rich network of master–student and collegial relationships with some of the finest musicians and musicologists on the European continent. They came from central Europe and the Baltic States and had participated in the musical and intellectual life of Europe during a period when social and cultural life in the many cities was at a pinnacle (see figure 1.1).

The musicians arrived in Canada in three waves (see figure 1.3). The first wave consisted of about forty individuals[1] who fled National Socialism in Germany, Austria, and Czechoslovakia between 1937 and 1940 and travelled directly to Canada, often by way of England. A further eleven reached Britain before war broke out, but in 1939 were classed as "enemy aliens." In June 1940 they were interned in England and then sent to Canada. The "Camp Boys," as they called themselves, were released through 1942 and 1943 as Canadian sponsors were found for them; approximately 1,000 Canadians posted the equivalent of thirteen million dollars to secure their release.[2]

A second wave of about seventy émigrés arrived after 1945. Paradoxically, Germany and Austria became safe havens for many long before the military authorities in Berlin capitulated in 1945. A collapsing Reich was preferable to subjugation under the Red Army. After April 1944, refugees from the Baltic States, Poland, Ukraine, Romania, and Hungary chose the uncertain western trek rather than remaining to face the approaching Communist menace from the east. Thus the escape routes of some twenty-five émigrés included a sojourn in Germany and Austria. In the absence of a peace treaty

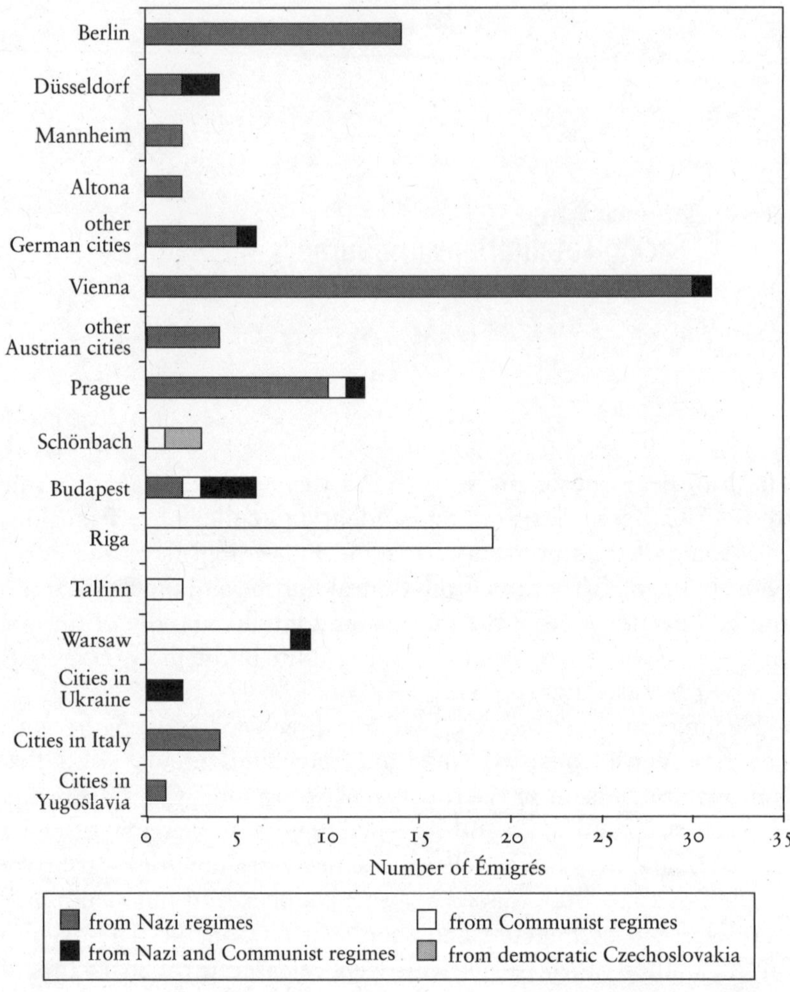

Figure 1.1 Cities of origin: numbers of émigrés who came from or were closely associated with specific European cities

after the official cessation of hostilities in early May 1945, the Allies continued to jockey for position.[3] Europe was overwhelmed by more than thirty million refugees[4] as the Soviet Union asserted its presence in Eastern Europe and the Baltic States. Most of the musicians from the Baltic States who had fled from the advancing Red Army along with the retreating German armies in 1944 wound up in United Nations displaced persons camps in Germany awaiting resettlement – a preferable alternative to the "repatriation" proposed by Soviet authorities in 1948 and 1949.[5] After failing to come to a political agreement with the Soviet Union on the repatriation question, the Western Allies carried the burden alone. The Soviets insisted on forced repatriation of their citizens (often with tragic consequences) whereas the West preferred to leave the choice up to individual refugees. The United Nations established refugee camps under the aegis of the United Nations Relief and Rehabilitation Administration (and after 1947, the International Refugee Organization) to house, care for, and support the refugees, and eventually help them to find countries to which they could immigrate. The Western world did not include refugees from Communist regimes under their definition of "displaced person." For example, The United States Displaced Persons Act of 1948 defines "Displaced persons" as those who were victims of Nazi, fascist or "quisling" regimes, Spanish Republican and other victims of the Falangist regime in Spain, or those who, for reasons of race, religion, nationality, or political opinion, had been deported from or obliged to leave their country of nationality or former habitual residence before the outbreak of the Second World War.[6]

Mariss Vetra and Armas Maiste, however, fled by boat to Sweden. A number had confronted the "Russification" of Latvia, the Czech putsch of late February 1948, or the domination of Hungary by hard-line Communists in the same year. With prospects for a free and democratic, if socialist, Eastern Europe after the war fading quickly, many moved further and further west in an effort to stay as far away as possible from the "Stalinification." Others who had fled to the United States before the war chose to continue their careers in Canada; a fourth group arrived by way of Shanghai, a sanctuary for European Jewish refugees during the war years but no longer safe once the Communists overran the city in 1949.

The third wave of émigrés consists of nine musicians who arrived between 1956 and 1987 after extensive sojourns in the United States, New Zealand, or Europe. Surprisingly, a number of musicians emigrated from democratic states in order to preserve their individual liberty.

The many and varied escape paths of these musicians indicate they were certain of the countries they wished to leave, but not of the countries where they might find permanent refuge. Only sixteen musicians came to Canada directly, of whom two (George Adams and Karel Ančerl) spent time in Nazi concentration camps. The rest

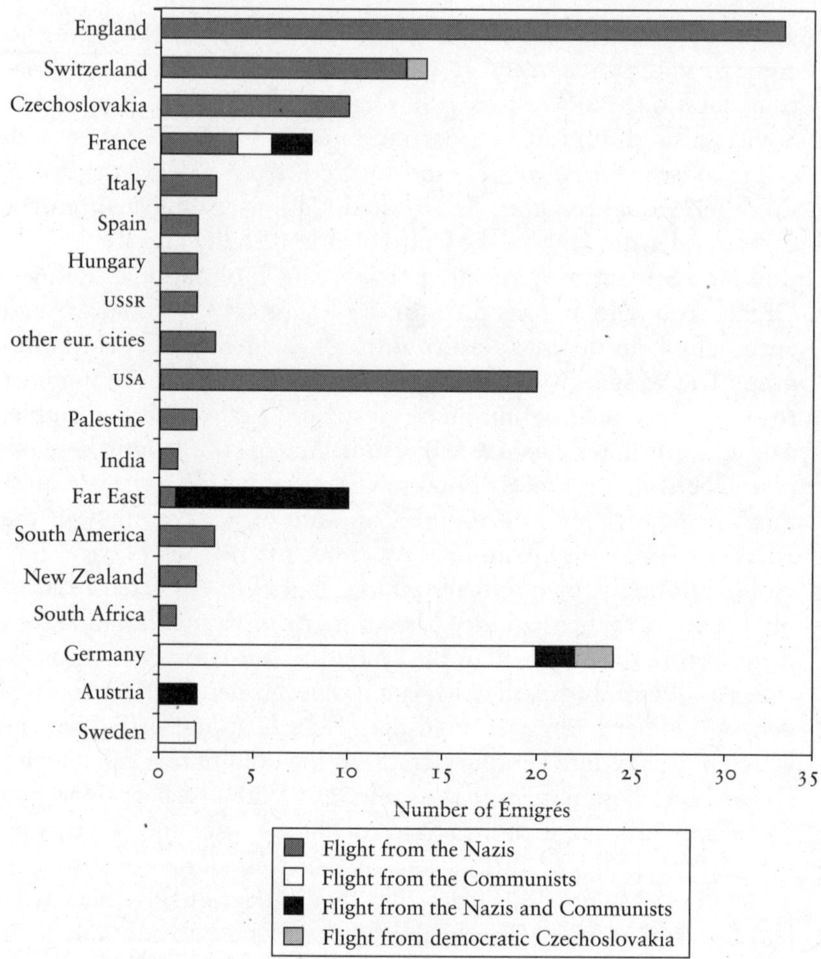

Figure 1.2 Temporary havens: countries in which émigrés spent at least several months after fleeing their homelands

spent time in at least one other country before coming to Canada (see figure 1.2). England was the most popular choice (32) but by 1948 all (with the exception of Walter Susskind) had left; there were few good employment opportunities for musicians in Britain. The United States was the next most popular destination (20) and émigrés remained there for varying periods of time. It is important to note that the total number of countries of sojourn (148) exceeds the total number of émigrés (121): seventy-three musicians lived in one intermediate country, twenty-three in two countries, six in three countries, and three in four countries. Perhaps none surpassed the odyssey of Walter Joachim, who wandered the world for eighteen years, travelling from Germany to Czechoslovakia, Kuala Lumpur, Shanghai, through the United States, and in 1949 back to Germany, where he tried to re-establish a career that had been abruptly terminated sixteen years previously. In 1951 he finally accepted an invitation from his brother Otto Joachim (ever his brother's keeper) to come to Montreal to fill a vacant cello position in the Montreal Symphony Orchestra. Outrunning the totalitarian menace was often frustrating. Those who fled to the Orient in hopes of leaving the political turmoil of Europe behind were sadly disappointed when British-governed India and Singapore imposed the Empire-wide internment of "enemy aliens." Shanghai proved a safe haven for some years, but conditions changed when the Chinese Communists captured the city; a number of these émigrés found their way to Canada by continuing the eastward trek to British Columbia in 1947.

The majority of the musicians in this study – eighty émigrés – fled Nazi regimes in Germany, Austria, and other countries overrun by German forces, but as early as 1944 Germany and Austria became countries of refuge for millions of Europeans fleeing westward to escape the advancing Soviet forces; twenty-six musicians fled the Communists, and another fifteen were persecuted by and fled from both totalitarian regimes. The musicians who sought haven in Shanghai (with the exception of Ida Halpern, who left in 1939) fled both European Nazism and Asian Communism. Three musicians (Otto Joachim, Walter Joachim, and Herbert Ruff) lived in several countries in the Far East. Under certain circumstances, democratic regimes could also produce political refugees. Two émigrés from Schönbach bei Eger (Anton Wilfer and Ewald Fuchs) were expelled from Czechoslovakia by the democratic government under the Beneš decrees and found a temporary haven in Germany; thirteen years previously Germans had fled in the opposite direction. The long hand of Soviet Communism forced several Latvian émigrés to reconsider their chances of security in postwar France. Communists who had been in the Resistance persecuted emigrants from Baltic countries as pro-fascists because they had the audacity to flee from a "socialist" state. The eleven "Camp Boys" arrived in July 1940, but although they pursued active musical activities in the camps, they did not engage with Canadians and Canadian music institutions until their release in 1942–43; for this reason they are counted in the 1942 column. Of the musicians who came to Canada, nine went on to careers in the United States: six conductors (Carl Bamberger, Otto Klemperer, Thomas Mayer, Leo Müller, Walter Susskind, and Bruno Walter), one bassoon player (Hugo Burghauser), one pianist (Béla Böszörmenyi-Nagy), and one stage director (Felix Brentano). It is understandable that a large number of conductors would move on since conductors' appointments with individual orchestras are rarely permanent; these emigrations are not shown on the table. The postwar arrivals of refugees from Communist regimes began in 1947 as Baltic musicians were released from displaced persons camps in Germany. Other postwar arrivals include refugees from Czechoslovakia and Hungary in 1948 and from Shanghai in 1949. A few émigrés arrived sporadically after 1960. If we were to include musicians who fled to Canada during the Soviet invasions of Hungary in 1956 and Czechoslovakia in 1968, the total number of musicians who fled for political reasons from the Nazis would be approximately equivalent to the number who fled from Communist regimes.

European expatriates in Canada were not always thrown entirely upon their own resources: identifiable communities of interest include the Latvians in Halifax, the Troppau group in Toronto, the Schönbach group in Montreal, and the camaraderie of the "Camp Boys." But for the most part, geographical constraints in Canada led to the establishment of a number of musical "islands" that had little contact with one another. For example, many musicians in Toronto were unaware of musical developments in cities no further away than Kitchener or London, Ontario. On the other hand, other émigrés such as Arnold Walter made it their business to be concerned with musical happenings throughout the country.

VIENNA AND THE EUROPEAN MUSICAL MILIEU

"I heard all the finest violinists in Vienna," Hansi Lamberger remembered. "Hubermann was teaching at the Academy, Erica Morini, Váša Přihoda [husband of Alma Rosé], Mischa Elman, Fritz Kreisler, Nathan Milstein, and Joseph Szigeti. The Beethoven Violin Concerto played by Huberman was an unforgettable experience and, of course, we were always in the standing room section in the Musikvereinssaal. I remember a performance of *Der fliegende*

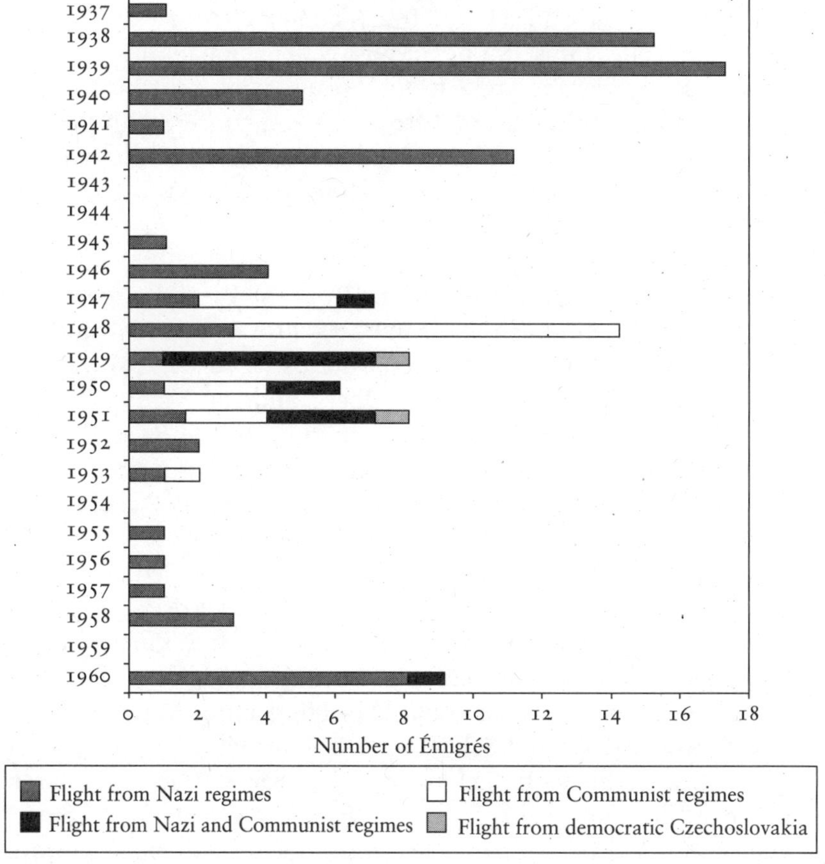

Figure 1.3 Arrivals in Canada: number of émigré musicians arriving in Canada

Holländer which impressed me very much. I also went to hear the *Ring of the Nibelungen* – Bruno Walter, Karl Böhm, all the finest conductors were there."[7] German violinist Bronislav Huberman was also an important figure in the career of Lorand Fenyves.

Nicholas Goldschmidt likewise revelled in the brilliant musical life of Vienna, home to many of Europe's most respected musicians.

> Karajan was a schoolmate of mine in Vienna; he went to Franz Schmidt and I went to Joseph Marx. I knew them all. And Bruno Walter conducted Beethoven's Missa Solemnis in the centenary year of his death, 1927. I was there with Elisabeth Schumann, Richard Meier, and I heard the famous *Rosenkavalier* with Lotte Lehmann, Maria Olszewska, and Elisabeth

> Schumann. I heard Richard Strauss conduct *Tristan* and *Rosenkavalier* himself. I heard Elisabeth Schumann in an all-Strauss program, and Richard Strauss played the piano. That was unforgettable. I heard Toscanini's first concert with the Vienna Philharmonic. These are the things that you don't forget ... I can't live without it and you actually can't pass it on. You can only pass on the result of it.[8]

Alfred Rosé, a son of the illustrious Rosé family and a nephew of Gustav Mahler, found himself at the centre of Vienna's musical comings and goings. His father Arnold Rosé (1863–1946) was concertmaster of the Vienna Court Opera and the Vienna Philharmonic, concertmaster in Bayreuth, founder of the Rosé Quartet, and a teacher at the Music Academy in Vienna.[9] Alfred's sister Alma Rosé, also a successful violinist, later married Váša Přihoda, perhaps the most brilliant Czech violinist of the period. In 1943 she was transported to Auschwitz-Birkenau where she led a women's orchestra; she perished there in 1944.[10] Alfred Rosé's autograph books indicate that such musical luminaries as Hans Pfitzner, Pietro Mascagni, Umberto Giordano, Alfredo Casella, Gian Francesco Malipiero, Ernst von Dohnányi, Paul Hindemith, Maurice Ravel, Igor Stravinsky, Arnold Schoenberg, Alban Berg, Elisabeth Schumann, Leo Slezak, Lotte Lehmann, Felix Weingartner, Fritz Busch, Bruno Walter, and Arturo Toscanini were guests at the Rosé home.[11] Pianist Anton Kuerti's family were members of Vienna's cultural and social elite.

> My mother's family had lived in Vienna for a very long time. My father was a physicist and mathematician. Before he emigrated, he worked at the *Radiuminstitut* in Vienna. He knew many of the leading scientists; I have a letter from Einstein recommending him on the basis of his scientific work which he had sent to him. My mother had a doctorate in botany. Her uncle was the publisher and associate of Karl Kraus,[12] her other uncles were quite prominent, one was a doctor, another a chemist, also apparently a very fine amateur pianist, always had music in his house and curiously enough apparently Hitler attended one of his musicales once, I suppose way back in the teens. My mother sang in the Vienna Philharmonic Choir. My father's mother came from quite a well-to-do family from

> Hamburg. They were smart; they left in the early 30s. One became a very wealthy man in the oil business in New York.
>
> My mother went to lectures that were given by Webern. Any cultured Viennese Jew went to concerts, theatre, as much as they could afford. My father was at one time a great devotee of Karl Kraus. My mother had the complete *Fackel* and later would sell it. It's been reprinted so it's no longer such a rarity. They would go when Kraus was giving his famous lectures and even singing. One of my father's aunts ... accompanied Karl Kraus on the piano at a couple of his events. They were very much involved both culturally and politically with the social democrats – other members of my family even more so.[13]

A number of the musicians who came to Canada were closely associated with leading members of the Viennese dodecaphonic school. Franz Kraemer studied with Alban Berg in 1934,[14] and the following year was associated with Aloys Haba and the music festival in Prague held in September 1935. Karl Steiner was acquainted with several members of the avant-garde Viennese circle. In 1932 he became a pupil of Olga Novakovic who introduced him to members of Schoenberg's circle, including Hans Erich Apostel, Hanns Jelinek, and Josef Polnauer. Steiner also studied conducting with Ludwig Zenck, who had been a pupil of Anton Webern, and for five semesters studied musicology at the University in Vienna (1931–34) with Robert Lach, Egon Wellesz, Erwin Ratz, and Alfred Orel.

Ida Halpern became a close confidant of Egon Wellesz when she was a university student. "As a professor he was the most stimulating lecturer in the Vienna University music department ... the incomparable great musical scholar without whose research and discovery it can rightly be said that musicology would not have advanced to the place where it now stands." Halpern had wanted to do her dissertation with Wellesz but he advised against it; "She should not, he warned, make things difficult for herself by becoming a student of the one member of the institute disliked, even resented, by Lach."[15] In the end, her thesis was supervised by Robert Haas. "We were brought up with this new idea in music and knew personally the three great masters [Schoenberg, Webern, and Berg]."[16]

Pianist Lubka Kolessa came from an illustrious Ukrainian family that counted a well-known ethnomusicologist and a composer among its members.[17] She studied with Emil Sauer in Vienna and thrilled audiences across the continent as much for her commanding stage presence as her insightful interpretations. Kolessa also gave many concerts in Sweden, in the Netherlands, and in the Soviet Union (1931–32); she toured South America in 1938. She performed and recorded concertos with Germany's finest orchestras under Karl Böhm, Wilhelm Furtwängler, and Herbert von Karajan (who, years later, fondly remembered her).

BERLIN AND THE ACADEMIC WORLD

In the academic sphere of the Friedrich Wilhelm University in Berlin young students sat at the feet of Europe's most revered musicologists, including Arnold Schering, Hermann Abert (until his death in 1927), Curt Sachs, Johannes Wolf, and Erich von Hornbostel. Ethnomusicology, a discipline pioneered in Berlin and known at the time as "Vergleichende Musikwissenschaft" [comparative musicology], fell victim to Nazi suppression in 1933 when Hornbostel's Phonogramm-Archiv was silenced; Hornbostel fled to the United States to teach at the New School for Social Research in New York, a haven for many refugee European scholars. At the Berlin Hochschule für Musik Curt Sachs was writing on world musics and had assembled an extensive collection of musical instruments. Sachs was also forced to leave and he subsequently obtained an appointment at New York University in 1937. These scholars and others were the musical and intellectual mentors of a number of émigrés including Arnold Walter, Ulrich Leupold, Mieczslaw Kolinski, and Walter Kaufmann, and it is possible that they might have met during their years in Berlin. Arnold Walter, a student at the University of Berlin during the 1920s, studied with Johannes Wolf, Hermann Abert, Robert Lach, Friedrich Blume (who was appointed Lektor in 1923), Georg Schünemann, and Curt Sachs. Mieczyslaw Kolinski studied with Erich von Hornbostel, Hermann Abert, Arnold Schering, and Curt Sachs, and he also served as Hornbostel's assistant (1926–33) at the Phonogramm-Archiv, undertaking field trips to the Bavarian Alps and the Sudeten. During the mid-1930s Kolinski transcribed collections of Surinamese, Dahoman, Togonese, Ashanti, Haitian, and Kwakiutl music for Northwestern University and Columbia University.[18] Helmut Blume studied with Paul Hindemith[19] from 1934 to 1938 at the Berlin Hochschule für Musik.[20]

Companionships formed among many of the émigrés during their student years in Germany were later renewed abroad. Gerhard Kander knew Lotte Brott (née Goetzel) as a child: "We used to go bicycling together [in Mannheim]. Her parents were friends of my parents ... I was supposed to do a tour with John Newmark with the Kulturbund.[21] I did the tour but he didn't." The tour eventually came about on another continent under circumstances that neither could have foreseen. Kolinski and Walter met years later at the University of Toronto where Walter hired Kolinski for the first ethnomusicology position in Canada, possibly because he had known him from their student days in Berlin. Walter and Blume, forced out of Europe by political events in Germany, eventually became close personal and professional colleagues in Canada.

THE DECISION TO LEAVE: PATHS OUT OF EUROPE

As the clouds of totalitarianism began to form, these musicians confronted a growing menace – a threat sensed at different times and in different places; each reacted according to their personal beliefs, ideals, and inclinations.

Arnold Walter was the first of the émigré musicians in this study to leave. On 27 February 1933, the night of the Reichstagsbrand, Walter was in his office working on a review when he received a telephone call from a friend who said, "Don't go home tonight, the Reichstag is in flames, things are fishy." His friend warned him to leave Berlin immediately; as a social democrat, his life was now at risk. Walter remained to see his colleagues from *Vorwärts* "lined up against the wall with their hands up" and learn that the editors of *Weltbühne*[22] had all been sent to concentration camps before he left in a hurry, travelling on an expired Czech passport, first to Belgium then on to Paris. Although he was assured that he was safe in France, he proceeded to Mallorca to study Spanish traditional music at l'École internationale des Baleares (1934–36). Spain, however, was soon engulfed in a deadly civil war between republicans and monarchists – a struggle between socialists and fascists – that became a prelude to a more deadly Europe-wide conflict. Because Walter's name was on an "Izquierdista" (a list of social democrats), he was "liable to be put in prison, or shot ... For the second time I lost all my possessions." Criminal proceedings had been launched against Walter, presumably because he had left Germany illegally. From personal documents it appears that Walter's wife Josephine (née Hoerberger) had managed to make her way to France with Walter's passport; a Czech consul issued Walter a temporary passport, enabling him to take a boat from Palma di Mallorca to Marseilles on 11 August 1936. From France he finally made his way to England, having obtained, on 4 August, a letter from the Society of Friends (Quakers) arranging for him to study folk music at the Cecil Sharp House in London. He was reunited with Josephine, who managed to pass him the requisite £10 he needed in order to land. He remained in England for a year.[23]

Otto Joachim had been leading a small orchestra in a café on the Königsallee in Düsseldorf until the night they were told, "No Jews allowed," and they lost their jobs. "All the Düsseldorf cafés were famous for their little orchestras which played jazz, reduced symphonies, chamber music, whatever ... I went to the Königsallee, there was a little gathering of twenty people. So they said, 'There is a Jew inside.' And I said, 'But he is not Jewish.' So they said to me, 'If you don't keep your mouth shut, we will throw you in the river!'"[24] In 1934, after a number of similar episodes, Joachim finally decided to leave; he was advised to do so without reporting to the authorities. His mother had seen a newspaper advertisement that read, "Jews and foreigners wanted for a band in the Far East, Bombay," and there was a saxophone position available. Otto did not overestimate his talents as a saxophone player but nevertheless he applied. At first he was turned down, but then he received a communication asking him to leave the following day. When a neighbourhood policeman guided him to the Düsseldorf railway station there was an SA group singing the Horst-Wessel Lied ("Die Fahne hoch, die Reihen fest geschlossen!"). His friend bought him a copy of *Der Stürmer* (an anti-Semitic comic strip) and instructed him to bury himself in it until he reached the border. The train stopped briefly in Dachau.

Hans Neumark (John Newmark), a self-confessed "non-practising Lutheran,"[25] had met violinist Szymon Goldberg[26] in 1925 and in 1934–35 undertook two concert tours with him in Spain (Madrid, Seville, Salamanca, San Sebastian, Alicante, Zaragoza) playing works by Beethoven, Mozart, Handel, Hindemith, Reger, Chausson, and Falla. Newmark likely made his decision to leave Berlin after the infamous Kristallnacht (9 November 1938); the sound of breaking strings of five Steinway grand pianos and a dozen uprights, thrown out of windows by a gang of Nazi thugs, was unforgettable.[27] He left Germany illegally on a fishing boat bound for Holland and arrived in England on his birthday, 12 June 1939.

Ulrich Leupold found himself in the bizarre situation of being in danger from the authorities both because he was Jewish and because he was Christian. His "non-Aryan" mother, opera singer Gertrud Igel, had been warned by her landlady that the Gestapo had come looking for her while she was at church. She immediately went into hiding for the duration of the war. In 1935, after completing musicological studies, Leupold had joined one of the five seminaries of the Bekennende Kirche (Confessing Church), which in its confession of faith – The Barmen Declaration of May 1934 – had set itself in direct opposition to the officially sanctioned Reichskirche (German Lutheran Church) and was subject to increasing persecution.[28] Leupold also distributed pamphlets about activities of the seminary. When the Gestapo searched his apartment they found nothing to incriminate him, but nevertheless he was on the "list." He made arrangements to leave, travelling first to England and then the United States.

For those émigrés in this study who were children during the political turmoil of the 1930s, the decision to leave was taken by their parents. Hans Gruber's father was a textile industrialist and the family maintained homes in Vienna and Brno, where the textile mills were located. In 1935, shortly after returning to Vienna from a two-day visit to Berlin, he announced that they were leaving Europe. He had already arranged to send his family to Britain with staff members who were to look after the London branch of the business. Young Hans was sent to a school in Champéry-sur-Montreux in the Swiss mountains. He was picked up by a chauffeur and driven to Paris to join his mother. By December 1938 all the immigration matters had been taken care of, and the family sailed for Canada in 1939.[29] Mario Duschenes spent the war years at the Conservatoire in Geneva: "There were superb artists, lots of good conductors. It was a good place to be and we were protected from the horrors of the war. We didn't have much to eat, but it was a lot better to spend the war there than any place else."[30]

Erika Nalos (later Kurth) was one of many who watched the entry of German troops into Prague with deep sadness: "I saw the Nazis invade Czechoslovakia on 15 March 1939. I was walking to school, it was snowing with wet snowflakes, soldiers in motorcycles drove past, one red-faced; I was sorry for him, he must have been cold. Our Czech teacher warned us students that now we could no longer trust anyone anymore." Lotte Goetzel (later Brott) was in Mannheim where she was to appear as a soloist in a Vivaldi cello concerto with her school orchestra. As she entered the concert hall a school official informed her that the Gauleiter was in attendance and no Jews were allowed on stage, let alone as soloists. Hurt and infuriated, she told her parents "I'm leaving, I'm going away. I cannot stand the humiliation."[31] Her parents agreed to send Lotte and her sister Lena to a "Pensionnat pour jeunes filles" in Neuchâtel, Switzerland, while they cast about for a future home; they finally decided on Montreal, in Canada.

Following Kristallnacht the families of Walter Homburger and Gerhard Kander were thrown on their own resources. The two families had become good friends and the Homburgers allowed the Kanders to stay with them after they had been forced from their apartment in Mannheim. Both Walter Homburger and Gerhard Kander were sent to England with the Kindertransport. Gerhard never saw his parents again. Other children on the Kindertransport include Rudolf Lowenstein and Helmut Kallmann.[32]

Nicholas Goldschmidt benefited from the advice of his uncle Paul Hymans, a Belgian statesman and diplomat. Hymans warned Goldschmidt to get out of Europe while there was still time to do so safely.[33] Goldschmidt left for the United States late in November 1937. Greta Kraus said that, "Even after the Nazis had taken over and the persecution had begun Mother wouldn't believe that things were as bad as people were saying. After being harassed by a group of Nazi thugs, things changed. I went home and said, 'Now Mother, you must listen to me!' I told her how dangerous the situation was, and something in her snapped."[34] A relative in the chemistry faculty at the University of Vienna arranged for Kraus to come as his secretary to Hawkesbury, Ontario, where he had received a position with the International Paper Company. A short time after her arrival in Canada, she accepted a job (brokered for her by Arnold Walter) as a music teacher at Havergal College in Toronto.[35] Karl Steiner was arrested shortly after Kristallnacht; he left from the Westbahnhof amid goodbyes from his colleagues Hans Erich Apostel and Olga Novakovic and was sent to the Dachau concentration camp where he was held for four months of *Umerziehung* ("re-education"). After his release he was refused entry into France, but managed to obtain passage to Shanghai.[36]

Mieczyslaw Kolinski made several attempts to flee the National Socialists, only to find that their relentless subjugation was spreading throughout Europe.[37] "As no Jews were allowed to leave [Germany] I had to get an official permit to make an already-planned field trip to the Sudeten. When I finished the field trip, I sent the recordings back to the Archive but I stayed in Czechoslovakia." Kolinski contacted American anthropologist Melville Herskovits, who was on the faculty of Northwestern University in Evanston, Illinois, and received grants from the Carnegie and Rockefeller Foundations for his transcriptions of Surinam and West African folk music, which were essential for Herskovits's anthropological studies. By 1938, when the political situation became critical, Kolinski had obtained a tourist visa to Belgium, stopping off in Paris to discuss the possibility of an appointment at Northwestern University with Herskovits. Kolinski remained in Belgium and in August 1939 received notice of his appointment, but emigration became impossible when war broke out in September.

> On 15 May 1940, just before the Germans took Brussels, the Belgians jailed me for being a German and then, when the Nazis came, they freed all the "Germans" including me. Then came the decree that all Jews had to register. Ninety percent of us, like myself, were so stupid as to register, thinking it would be better to be law-abiding and avoid trouble. But every month there were new decrees, new curfews, new restrictions. Finally in 1942 we received summonses to report for deportation to a "labour camp" in France. What we didn't realize was that from there they sent people to Auschwitz. I was all ready to go and report but a friend of mine told me I was out of my senses and convinced me to try to hide with an anti-Nazi Christian family. So, I spent more than two years at the home of a young lady, the assistant of a professor I knew, and her mother, a widow. After the Liberation, I married the young lady and since then, we've lived ... happily ever after.[38]

Paul and Edwina Heller remained in Warsaw, enduring the early stages of the Blitzkrieg, until 4 September 1939 when they left with their parents and seven-year-old nephew: five people in a sports car that seated only four. Their housekeeper put some furs, food, and a few other small things in a hat box. Everything else they left behind. They planned to drive to the Rumanian border, but were cut off by the Russian army; they eventually crossed the border into Hungary through the forest and mountains on 17 September with consular passports. A number of cities were bombed along the way.

In Hungary Lorand Fenyves came face to face with threats to Jewish musicians. An ugly incident gave him some idea of what was to come:

> One day as we were rehearsing, a group of about twenty students from another faculty completely (that was always the way, they took people from somewhere else so you didn't know who they were) broke into the room with briefcases filled with stones and began asking everyone for their identification papers. Strangely enough all of my friends seemed to produce the correct papers without any difficulty. I was very young and naive at the time. The janitor took me by the arm, took me down the hall into the girl's washroom and locked the door. It saved me from harm, because a friend of mine who was not so fortunate was beaten up and we had to take him to the hospital. That decided it for me that I could not stay in Hungary so I began to look around for somewhere to go.[39]

OPPOSING FORCES IN THE BALTIC STATES

Once war erupted between Germany and Poland, the Baltic States were sacrificed to Soviet Communism. For about five years two totalitarian regimes overlapped each other, grinding any countries caught between as the tides of war shifted back and forth. By "eliminating" the upper classes ("exploiters"), intellectuals, educators, and officials through deportations, the Communists created the "vacant" spaces that made "Russification" possible. The Soviets also deported women, children, and the elderly, often separating families. The "Russification" of the Baltic States in 1940 was a brutal affair involving the deportation of selected resident nationals. According to Jānis Kalejs "not long after the occupation began wholesale arrests and deportations were begun, as many as 30,000 people being deported between the hours of two and eight o'clock in the morning of a single day – thousands were routed out of their beds and driven to the railway stations where they were packed in freight cars (smaller than the Canadian type) forty to fifty to a car, and the doors locked."[40] Robert Dambergs remembered that "the Russians 'cattle-carred' the Latvians and shipped them off, not just intellectuals, anyone, old people, women, children, there was a massive shipment out. They came in the night and told you 'Collect what you can carry.' They took the whole family, then they separated husbands from wives and later on they separated mothers from children."[41] There were three waves of Soviet deportations in the Baltics. The first, in late 1940, included about 35,000 Latvian "non-proletarians." In 1945–46 a further 105,000 were deported. In a third wave in March 1949, with the forced introduction of collective farming, deportations amounted to 70,000 (approximately 5.5% of the population), including anyone who could have been a potential opponent of the regime. Most of these presumably perished in the Soviet gulags of Russia and Siberia. In addition, some 65,000 Latvians fled to Germany and Sweden in advance of the Red Army in 1944.[42] The toll in Estonia and Lithuania was equally devastating.

Nick Dambergs, husband of dancer Mirdza Dambergs, was director of a textile factory in Riga. When Communist officials replaced him, his employees refused to work until he was reinstated. The KGB interior minister forced Dambergs to return to his former job, saying: "Either your brains will be on this paper, or your signature." In June 1940 Dambergs foiled a deportation order with a desperate move, shouting to a group of drivers that the KGB had just ordered a new round-up, telling them to start their engines and get away. The trucks fled, but after this the Dambergs were no longer safe. Later, at a demonstration ostensibly in support of the Communists, Dambergs made signs saying "Death to the enemies of the state" and marched defiantly past the National Theatre where the government officials were seated. Under the Communist regime, as Mirdza Dambergs was to discover, any display of Latvian nationalism was repressed:

> Once they wanted me arrested for dancing a particular piccc about autumn in Liepaja, composed by Jānis Kalniņš's father, [about] a kind of historic Latvian young man going to the war with a very old shield and a Latvian girl in a Latvian costume.

> He put his hand on her and led her out on the stage. There was a war, he fought, and then he fell down and died. Then the Latvian girl came out with red and white roses (red and white are the colours of the Latvian flag). The Communist party members who had been in the audience rushed backstage, and said "We want her arrested immediately." They eventually talked them out of it; I took the red and white roses on purpose. I had been dancing it all the time. I took a chance.[43]

On 22 June 1941 the Germans launched "Operation Barbarossa," a six-month campaign to invade Soviet Russia along a 3,000 kilometre front. The German forces that occupied the Baltic States must have appeared as liberators of sorts, freeing these countries from Soviet bondage, and many Latvians were induced to serve on the German side. Three years later, when the tide turned and Germany was in retreat, many Latvians who had experienced Soviet occupation feared the worst and fled with the retreating German troops before the advancing Red Army. Making their way toward Germany they eventually wound up in refugee or displaced persons camps. For those who were able to utilize any opportunities afforded them, the years in these camps were by no means lost. Musicians and other artists had a great deal of freedom to participate in educational and cultural activities and to further their careers in the German-speaking world around them. Accounts given during interviews indicate that language groups were placed together; Latvian and Estonian newspapers were published and contacts maintained between camps.

Between 1944 and 1948 Jānis Kalniņš was at camps in Germany at Haffkrug and Bad Segeberg. With the permission of the British Military Government[44] he conducted concerts in Lübeck, and on 15–16 February 1946 he accompanied violinist Olafs Ilzins. A review of 20 June 1948 refers to Kalniņš conducting the Lübeck Civic Orchestra in performances of his Symphony in C minor and his Violin Concerto with soloist Jānis Kalejs,[45] describing the two works as "clear structural statements, creations of a romantic temperament." The personal tie with Kalejs was renewed in Canada when Kalniņš recommended Kalejs for a position at Acadia University. Kalejs noted that he had lived under three Communist regimes: in 1917–18 he experienced the Russian Revolution as a youth in Bobruysk (a small Russian city southeast of Minsk); in 1940 he was in Latvia when the country was overrun by the Communist Red Army; in 1945 he fled from the Soviets near Leipzig, and only reached the American sector "under great difficulties."[46] When he and his wife Felicita Kalejs arrived in Oldenburg in 1946, the area was occupied by Canadian forces; together with other Latvian musicians, they gave recitals for the Canadian troops, for Germans, and for other displaced persons camps. During the five years he spent in German displaced persons camps Jānis Kalejs was able to continue his career by performing on British Army radio network broadcasts in Hamburg; however, his beloved violin, made by Curt Jung, was stolen.

Other Latvian musicians who passed through German displaced persons camps and arrived in Canada around 1948 include Lína Karlsone (Montreal), Erike Freimane-Plampe (Toronto), Edíte Timermane-Ozala (Toronto), Jānis Niedra (Toronto), Jānis Cirulis (Toronto), and Victor Kviesis (Saskatoon). Alfred Strombergs was in displaced persons camps in Braunschweig and Holzminden: "I got together with a group of Latvian artists, a coloratura soprano, a cellist, and a violinist and did a number of concerts in the communities."[47]

Imant Raminsh's family also fled Latvia: "My father was certainly on a list of people to be arrested since he was a forester, a guardian of the land and a respected member of society. Anyone with an education at that time was suspect to the Soviets as a potential opponent. Through sheer luck he avoided the first wave of deportation. We fled – probably everyone who could leave left – and we ended up in a refugee camp in northwestern Germany in the British Sector, as far away from the Soviets as possible."[48] Feeling they were still too close to the Communist peril, the family moved even further into the British zone, to camps including Wildflecken, Würzburg, Meerbeck, and Fallingbostel (an Emigrant Transit Camp). Raminsh's childhood memories include Christmas celebrations in the camps, walks in the countryside, the "yellow peril" (rations of corn soup), and the stories told by his father illustrated with quick hand-drawn sketches. There was no question of returning to Latvia after the war. One branch of the family came to Canada, another moved to the United States, and a third branch immigrated to Australia. "Those who came were the lucky ones, they had stories to tell. Those who couldn't get out, their stories will never be heard."

Udo Kasemets ended up in a large Estonian camp at Geislingen-an-der-Steige, a town south of Stuttgart, in a former warehouse barracks.[49] "The IRO had virtually taken over this little industrial town where nice houses were built for the workers. These buildings were given to displaced people to live in. There was a huge congregation of Estonians; there were all kinds of cultural activities." Kasemets stayed in this camp until 1951 and remembered the flourishing cultural traditions carried on by his countrymen. Choruses from other camps joined forces for a choral festival in Augsburg. Estonian theatre directors and actors presented demanding productions. "It was the first time I saw – naturally in a translated form – *The Glass Menagerie*." Kasemets also took advantage of the opportunity to pursue further education outside the camps. Resuming his studies first at the Hochschule für Musik in Stuttgart, and later at the Kranichstein Institut (founded in 1948, now the Darmstadt International Music Institute)[50] in Darmstadt, he encountered a bizarre situation: owing to the political situation during the 1930s and 1940s and extensive war damage, his mentors at the academy had little knowledge of contemporary music. "Any kind of modern thought had been naturally banished or burned and was not available. The teachers didn't know anything. The only person who came at that time was Hindemith." Kasemets was fascinated by the burgeoning cultural life in postwar Germany; new theatres and new creative enterprises were springing up and there was a pervasive curiosity for new things.

> Unfortunately the teachers had no clue, they couldn't inform you, they were just as curious as you were. My real awakening came when I got to Darmstadt in the summer of 1950, the Kranichstein summer courses. There I met Varèse, Krenek. I worked with Krenek and he introduced me in a real sense to twelve-tone music. New music was really brought back to Europe by the exiles. Those who were in the forefront were forced to leave for the States for a while then they returned to Europe to pick up where they left off.[51]

The US military forces played a role in setting up the Kranichstein-Darmstadt courses and other events in postwar Germany. It would be interesting to study the American influence on postwar western European contemporary music; in a sense one might view avant-garde music as a gift of the United States to Western Europe, considering that Nadia Boulanger and Darius Milhaud returned to Paris after their American exile. Hindemith and Krenek returned to Europe but Schoenberg, Stravinsky, and Bartók remained in America. Kasemets also enrolled in a conducting seminar with Hermann Scherchen, who had spent the war years in Switzerland. "There I heard my first Schoenberg, *Survivor from Warsaw*, and Varèse's *Ionisation*." At the end of the performance "a couple of these German youths walked out and banged the door, Scherchen stopped the applause and said, 'I gather that some of the people didn't understand this piece. I think we should play it again.'" Kasemets also heard compositions by Webern: "That changed my whole life completely. And when I came to Canada that following February, when the boat was approaching Halifax the sun was shining and I though to myself – 'This is a new land, one can start with this new stuff, it's a new beginning, and so in many ways it was.'"[52]

Ironically, musicians from the Baltic States who sought refuge in France found themselves harassed by those who were sympathetic to socialism. Robert Dambergs described the problems faced by his family:

> There were Communist cells in the Resistance. Since we were Balts, Latvians, we had to be fascists because we ran away from "heaven on earth." At one point, when my brother and I were six or seven years old and were surrounded by the local Communist family children and held in a field for several hours until finally they pulled an air-filled ball out that I had been playing with, slit it open with a knife and said. "This is what we are going to do to you." This happened around 1952, 1953 ... We would get phone calls in southern France, "Oh your father isn't home yet, are you sure he is not lying in a ditch somewhere?" So we moved to Paris hoping we could put some distance between [ourselves and this] and it ended up getting worse. We got phone calls "Your grandmother isn't home yet; maybe she is taking a swim in the Seine." We were pursued and the pursuit was controlled out of Moscow as we later discovered. My father felt we had to put an ocean between ourselves [and this].[53]

Talivaldis Kenins knew it was impossible for him to return to Latvia because his father had been prominent in the Latvian Republic formed after the First World War. However, he found that France was also precarious:

> I got a scholarship to the Conservatoire but was forced to play in third-class dance halls to make some money. I was an exile. I couldn't get a regular job. After five years residency I would have been eligible for French citizenship (they didn't count the years I had previously spent in France). With papers, I would have been eligible to teach at a provincial conservatoire. In France after the war, however, there was a strong Communist presence and they began to dictate [things]. The police were Communistic; those who had been in the Resistance became adverse to immigrants from the Soviet Union, but de Gaulle later cleaned this up.[54]

An unexpected visit from Arnold Walter, who was now a Canadian music administrator, provided him with an opportunity to leave behind this harassment and immigrate to Canada.

JOURNEYS FROM CZECHOSLOVAKIA AND HUNGARY

By early October 1938 Nazi Germany had annexed the Sudetenland under the terms of the Munich Agreement[55] and was threatening to invade Czechoslovakia. Those of Jewish background were immediately put on alert. The families of Oskar Morawetz, Hans Gruber, Erika Kurth, and the Koerners found their lives in serious jeopardy and each took measures to escape the impending menace. The Czech government, which included Edvard Beneš and Jan Masaryk, left for London where they established themselves as the government-in-exile, and a number of Czech émigrés followed them there.[56]

When Germany annexed the Sudetenland, all persons living there were classified as German citizens. This gave rise to a bizarre situation: a number of important German opera houses in Czechoslovakia employed German musicians and singers, many of whom had left Germany in 1933 after the promulgation of the race laws: – now they were again at risk. According to the Nazi ideology, Jews could not be Germans even if they were the finest protagonists of German culture. Provincial opera houses in Reichenberg (Liberec), Gablonz (Jablonec), Aussig (Usti nad Labem), Troppau (Opava), Teplitz-Schönau (Telpice-Samov), Brüx (Most), and Eger (Cheb) were in jeopardy, as was the famous German Opera in Prague, a centre of which Oskar Morawetz had fond memories. Four other Canadian émigrés – Thomas Mayer, Herman Geiger-Torel, Nicholas Goldschmidt, and Walter Susskind – were also forced to leave. The last performance in that illustrious house was on 25 September 1938; four days later the Munich Treaty came into effect.[57] The Czech Republic remained under German authority as the Protectorate of Bohemia and Moravia throughout the war.

Aloys Fogl – a violin maker and a confirmed Czech patriot and social democrat – was Czech but his father-in-law, Anton Wilfer, was Sudeten German. Wilfer had been drafted into the German army in 1934 (at age forty-three) and by 1945 he was in Italy; after surrendering to the British he spent about a eighteenth months in prisoner-of-war camps. Under the provisions of the 1946 Beneš Decrees, all Sudeten Germans were expelled from the Czech Republic. When Wilfer and his close associate Ewald Fuchs (who was also a son-in-law) were forced to leave the country they went to Mittenwald, Germany. Thus, the Beneš Decrees spelled the end of a centuries-old violin-making school in Schönbach that had been an essential part of the lives of three émigrés, Aloys Fogl, Ewald Fuchs, and Anton Wilfer. On 24 February 1948, the day of the Communist putsch, Fogl's wife and his mother-in-law crossed the border into Germany, and the family was reunited in Mittenwald. Mrs Fogl recalled: "We were on a truck. The border guard said the baggage could go through the front of the station, but we would have to go behind the station. And that in spite of the fact that we had to pay to leave! As people we had to go illegally."

Fogl's exit was not so smooth: "I left Czechoslovakia in June 1948 after being in prison for three months. They caught me trying to cross the border in Franzenbad. I was an active member of the social democratic party when the Communists took over; since I was on the 'right' wing of the party rather than the 'left,' I was considered *persona non grata.*" Under the new regime, moderate social democrats were just as suspect as National Socialists. The left faction of the social democratic party had aligned itself with the Soviet Union, but the right wing was more moderate. "Unfortunately the Communists won." Fogl was expelled from all his social democratic positions, ostensibly for crimes against the state, and he was arrested by his best friends within the party.[58] His escape from the Czech Republic was hair-raising. He had been drafted into the Czech army but had been able to postpone his military service from the fall of 1947 to 1 April 1948. He was arrested on 24 February and imprisoned in Eger, but was released on 21 June 1948 under a decree from president Klemens Gottwald (1896–1953) granting political amnesty to 1,250 prisoners. As a law-abiding citizen he reported for military service, which he expected would begin in October 1948.

> Instead of transferring to Prague, I stayed on the train to Asch, the border town on the most westerly point of the Czech Republic. My friend said I could take my suitcase with me. It was the only thing I had – a bag with my personal documents, a hat, a few pairs of socks. That night there was a torrential rain. I knew the border by heart, because while I was in prison, all those who had tried to escape exchanged stories to figure out what might be the best way of getting out. We knew in our minds what the border looked like, how they were caught and so on. I knew the railway tracks were the border between the Czech Republic and Germany (Bavaria). It was already after midnight, so I jumped down and for two or three minutes ran as fast as I could and then lay down in a potato field which was quite high at that time. I knew that Czech border guards had been running behind others who had fled and pulled them back. I listened whether someone was running after me. Then I looked around. Perhaps I would be taken to a jail somewhere. I saw a light and followed it, it was a farmhouse. The farmer came in his nightgown with axe in hand – after all it was the middle of the night and near the border. I offered him what I had to let me stay until the morning. Next morning, US jeeps passed by and I was brought to a collection point in Moschendorf. There I experienced real hunger. We ate exactly what Germans ate in 1945 – in other words, nothing. A piece of bread for three days, some dirty water in the morning, sleeping on military cots – it was cold. From Moschendorf we came to Schwabach, then to Ludwigsburg which was already under IRO jurisdiction.[59]

In Istvan Anhalt's case, military service, which lasted from 1 December 1942 to 16 March 1944, was a labour camp in Bereck (now in Rumania), in which hard physical work completely sapped his strength. On one occasion Anhalt collapsed from exhaustion.

The sergeant-major of the company, "who was not totally devoid of all humanity," had given a lemon to Keleman, one of his favourites, who was also from Transylvania and was one of Anhalt's comrades. Seeing Anhalt lying on the ground, Keleman gave him half of the lemon. Anhalt recounts that never before had he experienced such a reaction to food; the lemon acted like an injection of adrenaline, energizing him and restoring his flagging spirit. Without it, he is sure he could not have continued. There were also several escapes.[60]

Violinist Arthur Garami was in the same camp.[61] One memorable event in this camp was a performance of the Brahms Violin Concerto with Garami as soloist and Anhalt playing an orchestral reduction on the keyboard of an accordion; two men held the accordion on a crate and activated the bellows! The unit, consisting of about 1,200 men, was divided into four companies of about 300: Garami was in the third company and Anhalt was in the fourth.

On 16 March 1944 Anhalt's battalion was taken to Stanislav in Poland. Here they worked under mixed Hungarian-German control and were considered prisoners-of-war. Several of Anhalt's comrades died of hunger or exhaustion. During the retreat of July 1944, military guards killed about 10 percent of the battalion for attempting to escape or for falling behind due to exhaustion. Anhalt had developed wounds on his feet, so he took the risk of escaping in the knowledge that if he were caught he would be shot. Peasants accepted him into their home where he lay for three days; then he was taken to a hospital. He stayed in hiding, with false documents, from the beginning of August until 1 December 1944 when he finally reached Budapest, but on 24 December Russian troops surrounded the city. Anhalt found refuge first in the monastery of St John Bosco (masquerading as a young priest with the generous help of the Pater Antal Rákospalota) and later at the home of Jenö de Kerpely, a professor at the Conservatory. When the Russian troops entered Budapest on 21 January 1945 Anhalt was captured and held on suspicion of being a former German or Hungarian soldier. In spite of his protests he was imprisoned in a house with German SS. He later learned that they were all to be sent to Russia as prisoners of war. But once again Anhalt succeeded in escaping.

Arthur Garami also wound up in a military labour camp in December 1942. The hard, rough work placed a great strain on his hands, but after he complained about the conditions, he was reassigned as a doctor's assistant so his hands could be spared. Nevertheless, to his deep regret, he was unable to play the violin for two years. On one occasion, when the battalion entered Poland, Garami and his comrades had to sleep out in the open in frigid temperatures, sharing a single blanket among several men. One morning they discovered to their horror that the man on the edge of the blanket had frozen to death. On another occasion he was forced at gunpoint to enter a body of water – ostensibly to be killed. The experience left him with a deep fear of large bodies of water, and in later years he refused to go near lakes or swimming pools. Garami was reluctant to talk about his time in the labour units, referring to it only as "the army." He believed he was saved from starvation and kept alive by his mother who sent him tins of goose grease and bread; the food often arrived moldy but it was eaten nevertheless. When the Russians "liberated" Poland in 1945 Garami returned to his native Hungary on foot; totally exhausted and suffering from tuberculosis, he found his way to the former Keletis estate (the family of one of his friends) and collapsed. Over the next three months a friendly doctor nursed him back to health, but he was for a time a broken man.[62]

At age twelve Charles Reiner wanted to enter the Franz Liszt Academy but was rebuffed.[63] "Zero for Jews. That was all! My professor said 'You just come in the back door, they don't have to see you. You come up.' And I did. Nobody ever saw me." Like his fellow Jews, Reiner was forced into Nazi labour brigades where he witnessed horrific atrocities.

> I had to work, to do all kinds of stupid shovelling. I remember – this is a very sad story – a group of old, old people were led to the same pass as I was, shovelling sand. One old man collapsed in front of me; he just couldn't go on. The brigade leader shot him in front of my eyes. And he said "You. You pick him up and put him in the Danube." And I said to myself, "If I don't do this immediately, he will kill me too." And I shovelled this old man, with the leader's help, in the Danube. He shot him once more. I was sick for three days and I vomited all the time. And I couldn't help it. This is one part of my story which is not too easy to talk about. I had to forget that.

In 1944–45 Reiner was interned in the concentration camp at Mauthausen, Austria. When the train he took from Budapest left for

Germany, Reiner had to get on the end of the train. It turned out that the first part of the train was sent straight to the gas chambers and the second ended up in limbo, but the last part eventually reached Germany.

Lorand Fenyves decided to leave Hungary after he was severely harassed by Nazi thugs. In 1934 the well-known violinist Bronislav Huberman came to Budapest and Fenyves played for him. "I was prepared for anything, but he placed some orchestral excerpts in front of me and asked me to play them. I did as well as I could with these and left it at that." Soon after this, Huberman asked Fenyves and his sister, who was also a violinist, to join the Palestine Symphony Orchestra. At this point, Fenyves already had an offer for the position of concertmaster of the Stockholm Symphony Orchestra. His father advised him to take the position in Sweden because he had agreed to it. Fenyves also played for Adolf Busch, "a real gentleman." Not knowing what to do, he finally went to see Felix Weingartner, the assistant conductor of the Vienna Philharmonic. (Fenyves admired Weingartner greatly and had played Weingartner's Violin Concerto in Vienna with the composer conducting.) Weingartner advised him that if he went to Sweden he would soon be the head of the orchestra, have a wonderful salary, probably marry a pretty Swedish wife, and would not know "which end of the bow is up and which end is down." "You *must* go to Palestine!," he told me. "We can discuss this with the orchestra in Sweden; they will understand." The position in Palestine was only for one year. Fenyves arrived in 1936. "I remember the first program, conducted by Toscanini: Brahms's *Second Symphony,* Mendelssohn's *Sommernachtstraum,* Rossini's Overture to *The Italian in Algiers* – just the pieces that Hubermann had asked me to play for him in Budapest!"[64]

However, politics followed the young violinist to Palestine. The orchestra was composed of players from many different countries. "There was a good esprit de corps in the orchestra in Palestine. The Germans in the orchestra tried to set the tone, but the Poles and Russians were a counterweight to them. The Hungarians, there were only four of us, were sort of caught in the middle." After Kristallnacht, works by Wagner were withdrawn from the orchestra's repertoire. Fenyves also witnessed a confrontation between Jascha Heifetz and an irate citizen who was incensed that Heifetz had programmed Richard Strauss's Violin Sonata. Heifetz was physically attacked on his way to the concert and had to shield himself with his violin case.[65] Palestine became a haven for some 75,000 Central European Jewish refugees, including several musicians who eventually came to Canada. When his year-long position ended, Fenyves returned to Hungary, then returned to Palestine to spend the war years as concertmaster of the Palestine Symphony Orchestra." Eli Kassner, who had fled to Palestine from Vienna, discovered his love for the guitar while living in Palestinian kibbutzes.

HAVENS IN THE FAR EAST

As the political situation in Europe became increasingly unstable, some European musicians sought sanctuary further afield. One of the best options was the Orient: for a time, India, Hong Kong, Singapore, and even Shanghai seemed far away from danger.

Walter Kaufmann left Berlin for the presumed safety of Prague in 1933, only to confront the same threat in his native Czechoslovakia a few years later. He enrolled as a student at the German University in Prague, studied with Franz Becking and Paul Nettl, and graduated with a dissertation on Gustav Mahler. "As a political statement he refused to accept the degree because the *Ordinarius* (Franz Becking) was the leader of the Nazi youth group in Prague."[66] Kaufmann decided to leave Europe altogether and fled to India in 1934. As a British colony, India was closely linked to British foreign policy, and with the outbreak of war adopted British restrictions concerning "enemy aliens." On 3 September 1939, 850 Germans (out of a total of some 1500) were arrested and interned. (This move alarmed Britain since the High Commissioner for Refugees of the League of Nations felt that the aggressive Indian policy would hinder the reciprocal treatment of British citizens in Germany.)[67] Eventually some 600 were released. As a Czech citizen, Kaufmann was not affected by these measures.

Kaufmann's time in India was extremely productive; he enjoyed twelve years of uninterrupted composition and ethnomusicological research in a non-Western cultural milieu that was to provide him with a substantial ethnomusicological vocabulary. On his arrival in 1934 he immediately obtained employment as a composer for Bhavnani Films[68] and Information Films of India. From 1937 to 1946 he was director of music for All-India Radio in Bombay (now Mumbai). Two months after he arrived in Bombay he organized a string quartet in which he played the viola. He also founded the Bombay Chamber Music Society, which presented weekly concerts in the homes of Society members who had large rooms and a piano (a rarity in Bombay). Occasionally these performances involved a small orchestra that included Zubin Mehta's father. Kaufmann wrote a number of chamber compositions for the Society and his first piano concerto was also premiered by this group with Kaufmann as soloist. A performance of the concerto by Edith Kraus and Heinrich Swoboda was broadcast on Prague Radio on 17 January 1937,[69] and music critics remarked on the strong Indian influence in the work. In addition to performing and composing, Kaufmann lectured at Sophia College, Bombay University, and began collecting Nepalese traditional music, which he described as "a strange combination of Indian, Tibetan and Kashmiri music." He learned Indian and Urdu notation, and began to incorporate Oriental elements in his own compositions. His research into Indian traditional music led to several important publications on the ragas and the music of ancient India.[70]

It is not clear what prompted Kaufmann to leave India. Escalating riots between Hindus and Moslems and uncertainty regarding the move to independence from British rule, may have prompted a decision for political considerations. In a letter to pianist Edith Kraus, who had remained in Prague throughout the war, he mentions the possibility of a position at the Prague University and asks her advice as to whether he should pursue it, but he finally decided not to return to his homeland.[71] By this time he had become a British citizen, and in 1946 he left for England, where he spent the next year as guest conductor of the BBC and a film composer for J. Arthur Rank Films. The position as head of the piano department of the Halifax Conservatory must have seemed a rather large step down for such a multi-talented individual. Kaufmann was in close contact with Dr Srul Laufer, now established in Halifax, who may have been involved in persuading this brilliant musician to continue his career in Canada.

Otto Joachim escaped from Germany in 1934[72] and had obtained a contract as a saxophonist in a band at the Adelphi Hotel in Singapore. Two months later he was hired as a band leader at the well-known Raffles Hotel, where he stayed six years. He remembers his time at the Raffles as idyllic, "It was hot, of course. You got a fantastic salary, you lived like a king. We ate with all the guests: you had two menus – one cold, one hot – you got international cheeses, international fruit." Joachim also played concerts at the Victoria Hall with François Dahane, a pianist from the Dutch East Indies; their programs included Beethoven's Violin Sonata in A major, op. 47 ("Kreutzer"), and a violin sonata by Ferruccio Busoni. As head of the Refugee Committee he organized concerts with the help of organist Werner Behr, and he played a role in bringing a number of Jewish musicians to Singapore. He found a job for his brother Walter Joachim in Kuala Lumpur in 1937 and eventually managed to get his parents out of Germany as well. Since Kuala Lumpur was only 300 miles from Singapore he had good contact with his brother and family until 1940.

Joachim had also become close friends with Sir Alexander Small, a British official in Singapore, and was sometimes driven to their palatial home in an open Rolls Royce to play chamber music with Small's wife. In August 1940 Small informed Joachim that according to regulations he was required to either intern him or send him either to Australia (where, it was rumoured, detainees were set to hard labour building roads) or to an equally uncertain future in Shanghai. Otto chose Shanghai, one of the few refuges left in the world. In order to leave Singapore legally he needed a one-year extension to his passport from the Japanese authorities; when he embarked on the *Hakusanmaru,* a Japanese official greeted him with the words, "Mister Joachim? Bon voyage!" Small had likely advised the Japanese to let Otto Joachim leave without any difficulties, but on the ship the Japanese showed some anti-Semitism.

Shanghai was, for a time, an important haven, since it was one of the few remaining places that did not require a visa for entry. For the sum of $540 a refugee could board a ship from Genoa or Trieste and sail relatively unhampered through the Suez Canal or around the Cape of Good Hope to Bombay, continue by way of Singapore and Hong Kong, landing about four weeks later in Shanghai.[73] Refugees who arrived in the mid-1930s were assured of a welcome reception because Jewish relief organizations had established social institutions to integrate newcomers. However, these facilities were strained by an influx of about 17,000 European refugees after November 1938 and a year later refugee aid stopped completely. Refugees could choose to live in the International Settlement, the French sector, or Japanese-controlled Hongkew, a desolate sector seriously damaged by the Japanese bombardment of 1937 and the destruction of the retreating Chinese armies. Parts of the city took on a decidedly central European flair as professionals, artists, and musicians recreated many of the cultural features of their former milieu in European cities such as Vienna or Berlin. There were five German-language newspapers, and some sixty German-language theatrical productions were given; operas, operettas, and orchestras competed with one another for the attention of a highly educated public. In 1942, however, once the war in the Pacific began in earnest, conditions deteriorated. In 1943 a square mile of Hongkew was designated as a restricted, ghetto-like area into which 16,000 refugees and 100,000 Chinese were cramped. Walter Joachim was one of the fortunate people who were allowed to pursue their professions outside this area. Renata Berg-Pan describes a performance of Brahms's String Quartet in c minor, op. 51, no. 1, that was interrupted by a bomb hitting the top floor of the building.[74] The camaraderie developed during these years of duress is documented in numerous books on and by the Rickshaw Group, which sponsors frequent reunions.[75]

Ida and George Halpern arrived in Shanghi in 1939, just after Ida Halpern had completed her dissertation on Schubert at the University of Vienna. George's sister Fanny G. Halpern, who had a degree in psychiatry, had established herself in Shanghai in 1933 and founded China's first modern psychiatric hospital, the Shanghai Mercy Hospital for Nervous Disorders.[76] George Halpern considered opening a pharmaceutical company while Ida Halpern taught music history and psychology of music (in English) to Chinese students at the University of Shanghai, but the couple were also making plans to leave.[77] Following unsuccessful efforts to enter Australia and Argentina, the Halperns arrived in Vancouver on 7 August 1939 on the *Empress of Asia*.

Karl Steiner came to Shanghai after his release from Dachau, presumably by way of Marseilles. Erwin Marcus, who came directly to Shanghai from Vienna in 1938, taught composition and piano at the Shanghai National Conservatory, conducted the Grand Opera and the International Choral Society, and also taught for a year at the Provincial Government Music College of Fukian. Andreas Barban left Vienna for Shanghai in March 1939 with his wife Betty (née Berljawsky) and her parents. Betty opened the first wedding photography shop in Shanghai while Andreas taught piano. Herbert Ruff arrived in Shanghai by way of Hong Kong.

Otto Joachim came to Shanghai from Singapore; Walter Joachim came by way of Kuala Lumpur. Both brothers had been teaching and playing in orchestras and at night clubs. In Shanghai Otto Joachim opened a radio shop, enjoyed access to news of goings-on in the city, and set about continuing his experiments with electronic instruments. He made a set of electronic string instruments with a foot control for dynamics and condenser mikes for amplification, but the instruments suffered under the extreme humidity. Since he had been in the Orient for seven years, Otto obtained permission to work in the city and was allowed to live outside Hongkew, the area assigned to Jews. Any available teaching work, either private or at the conservatory, was at a minimal level. The program for a concert for the Alliance française given at the Lyceum by Walter Joachim and Erwin Marcus included a Hindemith cello sonata.

> In the intermission just before I played it, we heard soldiers pounding on the door with rifle butts. They wanted to know what was going on. They didn't know what a concert was. I opened the door and saw dear knows how many of these soldiers and tried to shush them up. Me telling the army to shut up! So I let them in and got them to stay quiet. The soldiers didn't have any shoes on, Chinese soldiers wear slippers. And they all sat in the aisle, quietly listening to Hindemith![78]

In 1949 Shanghai was attacked by Communist forces under Mao Zedong, who eventually drove out the Chinese Nationalists under Chang-kai-Shek. When Shanghai proved inhospitable, Karl Steiner, Erwin Marcus, Andreas and Betty Barban, Herbert Ruff, and Otto Joachim continued their odyssey, travelling east across the Pacific Ocean to Canada. When Otto Joachim came to Canada, his original plan was to wait for a passage to Brazil, his preferred destination, but he finally decided against South America. Walter Joachim remained in Shanghai for another two years before he finally left in 1951.

CHOOSING CANADA

The musicians I have traced in this study spent time in at least one intermediate country before they arrived in Canada (see table 1.2), making provision for their personal security according to constantly shifting changing political situations in Europe and elsewhere. These decisions to come to Canada, like their decisions to leave their homelands, were personal. Having confronted political regimes that threatened life and liberty and made the decision to leave, many discovered that the countries to which they had fled were no more than temporary havens that would prove inhospitable if not dangerous.

England, the destination of choice for the majority of the émigrés because of its democratic heritage, was seen as a bulwark against totalitarianism, but once the "phony war" became horrifyingly real in May 1940, the situation in Britain changed. Most countries in the British Commonwealth were involved in the internment of "enemy aliens" at various points during the war. By 4 September 1939, based on local denunciation records, Canada had interned some 837 persons,[79] and similar actions in Singapore, Kuala Lumpur, and Hong Kong forced musicians who had sought haven to move yet again. Mass internment in Britain began in May–June 1940, when fears of a possible German invasion forced the government's hand, a measure that affected the lives of thousands who had sought asylum in England.[80] This dragnet swept up eleven musical émigrés who were sent by the British War Office (presumably in consultation with the Home Office) – along with hundreds of others – to internment camps in Canada. Their story is told in chapter 2.

Few of the musicians who came to Canada had any idea of what the country was like before they arrived. It was by no means an inviting prospect for cultivated central Europeans, most of whom chose Canada because there few other alternatives. For example Walter Goetzel (Lotte Goetzel's father) chose Canada more by default than design in casting about for a suitable country in which to pursue his business interests. The Hellers had arrived in Budapest, where they knew no one, in September 1939. Shortly after their arrival they ordered a suit for Paul from a tailor's shop. After one of the fittings, the manager said, "There's a gentleman who wants to meet you, someone in the lumber business." This gentleman advised the Hellers to go to British Columbia, the centre of the lumber industry, stating that his best friends – the Koerners – had left the previous year for Vancouver. "But," he added, "if you go there you should get baptized and only then apply." Word had spread that Jews were not welcome in Canada. The Hellers procured an Aryan certificate through the good offices of the Polish consul in Budapest and with this were able to secure a transit visa through Italy. By December 1939 they were in London, where they applied for emigration to Canada. They arrived in Montreal in 1940, and by 1941 had made their way west to Vancouver.

Leopold Bloch-Bauer had visited the Rockies for a hunting and hiking tour in 1937 and chose Canada because he was favourably impressed by the country and its people.[81] Bloch-Bauer probably convinced the Pick family to emigrate as well. The Bloch-Bauers fled first to Zurich and then London where they received permission to emigrate in August 1938. Other members of the family followed later.[82] When Hugo Simons (Jan Simons's father) decided that it was no longer safe for the family to remain in Holland, he first thought of moving to the United States, and went to the American consulate to complete the formalities. Finding it closed for lunch and feeling this was not merely a coincidence, he walked further down the street to the Canadian consulate which happened to be open and initiated the move to Canada.

The United States served as a temporary haven for a number of musicians, but when career opportunities opened north of the border, some – including Ernesto Vinci, Alfred Rosé, Ulrich Leupold, Ernesto Barbini, Lothar Klein, and Nicholas Goldschmidt – were ready to move north, even to a country they knew little about.

2

Life in Jurisdictional Limbo

STATELESSNESS

One issue that surfaced during the course of several interviews was that of statelessness. For most émigrés in the first wave, changing citizenship from the country of origin to the country of adoption involved an onerous process but these difficulties pale against the problems confronted by those who had remained in Europe and were finally forced to leave their countries without proper papers. Being at the jurisdictional mercy of a host country was a profoundly unsettling experience: immigration to Canada, facilitated by individuals or by organizations, offered one way out of the dilemma.

Rolf Duschenes, who came to Canada as a "Camp Boy" was able to sponsor his brother Mario Duschenes, who had spent the war years studying in Geneva but had no papers. Mario Duschenes recalls:

> I played recorder in the Ars Antiqua in Geneva for three years. It consisted of recorder and a group of gambas, viols, and harpsichord; we traveled around Switzerland and appeared also in France and Belgium. It was difficult for me to travel over borders because I was stateless and didn't have a regular passport. My brother arranged my emigration to Canada. He had been here for eight years before that and figured that I would have a fairly good chance of making a living here and he became my sponsor. You had to have someone who would guarantee looking after you financially if things turned out badly, so he applied for my immigration papers. I left Switzerland to come to Canada in 1948.[1]

Istvan Anhalt ended up in Paris:

> We spent three days in a transit center ... in Vienna ... I went to the opera twice: one was a wonderful performance of *Don Giovanni,* conducted by Josef Krips from the harpsichord, and the other performance, again conducted by Krips I think, was *Othello* ... [A]fter a few days I was taken with dozens of others by lorry into the night, we didn't know where we were going to be taken, but we found out that we were taken into Germany, just over the border, to a place called Ainring, which was near Berchtesgaden ... I lived in this camp which housed hundreds and hundreds of DPs ... and I just stayed there not knowing what would happen next, perhaps five weeks ... Eventually it was a French Jewish UNRRA officer who heard me play the piano (there was a piano in the camp) and finding out that my aim was to move to Paris to study music, he said one day "I'm going to go on a leave, by car, by jeep, if you want you may come with me to the border." I said indeed I would be very grateful, so he took me in his jeep ... And finally the jeep pulled up in front of the railway station in Strasbourg, and this kindly UNRRA officer bought me a ticket to Paris, on the night train, and bought me a copy of a French newspaper, to bury myself in and hide behind, because I had no French whatever, I couldn't converse. Soon I boarded a train and the next morning we pulled into the Gare de l'est, and I was in Paris, in mid-March, a beautiful spring morning ... [W]ithin one week I had a *carte d'identité,* I was admitted as an *auditeur* at the Conservatoire, and also I was admitted to the Cité universitaire as a resident, and I also obtained a monthly stipend from the union des étudiants juives, a few thousand francs, which was just enough to pay the rent for the room and buy lunch and buy some baguettes ... I discovered within days, that Stravinsky, with whom I wanted to study, was in California, but I attended a lecture at the Sorbonne on him given by Nadia Boulanger, all that within the first three weeks ... Boulanger was just a name to me, but I went to the lecture and what I was able to understand from it, I was impressed, and I spoke with her after the lecture, and she immediately accepted me as a private student ...
>
> I had no passport because I left Hungary illegally ... I had no one to sponsor me, but the Hebrew Immigrant Aid Society

> officer, a Canadian lady, Lottie Levinson, came to a year end's concert where I conducted, as part of the year end's work in the conducting class, and what she saw or heard was enough for her to think of me and one day she called me to her office to tell me that there was a new foundation in Montréal, the Lady Davis Foundation that sponsored some displaced intellectuals who might want to come to Canada, and she advised me to apply. Well, I did apply but I had very little hope that I would be selected, but I was selected. I was telegrammed saying that I was awarded a Lady Davis Fellowship with an appointment at McGill. Oh yes, the two came together.[2]

For George Fiala the lack of papers meant that "one of the most productive periods of my life" in Belgium would come to an abrupt end.[3] His contacts in that country, virtually untouched by the war, included the elite of Brussels society and his works were regularly performed by leading Belgian musicians.

> I was still stateless – if you don't live ten years officially in Belgium, you cannot obtain Belgian citizenship, which would have given me permission to work there. My sister had married and left for England and my father's second marriage was to a Belgian, Germaine Leclercq, who was the daughter of a deputy in the Belgian parliament, so he was allowed to stay. His French was quite good and he became an architect in Charlerois, where my uncle continued to live. I continued as long as I could, writing music, but it couldn't last for ever.

Through the efforts of a Ukrainian-Canadian organization Fiala was allowed to come to Canada in 1949. "I didn't know much about Canada before I came here, just that it was a big, beautiful country and had a large Ukrainian population. In 1948 they offered to sponsor me to come to Canada. The IRO paid for my passage and I came on the same boat as Istvan Anhalt in January 1949."

BRITISH INTERNMENT OF "ENEMY ALIENS"

The mass internment of "enemy aliens" in England during May and June 1940 and their subsequent deportation to the "colonies" seems to be a blot upon that country's tradition of democratic freedom. Even Canadian immigration authorities have come under censure for a perceived lack of understanding of the situation and a seeming reluctance to release the "Camp Boys" – as they came to be known – into civilian society viewed as an egregious oversight. However some records pertaining to this period, including the correspondence between the British War Office and the Canadian Immigration Branch, are not yet available. The entire exercise may have been the result of the prodding of Lord Beaverbrook (Maxwell Aitken of Newcastle, New Brunswick), a prominent Canadian in high office in England. Beaverbrook's newspapers, including the *Daily Express*, forcefully advocated mass internment, and Beaverbrook joined Churchill's war cabinet in May 1940.

During the Second World War Britain incarcerated 27,200 Austro-German men and women – among them businessmen, academics, and artists – who had fled from Europe to England before 1939 to escape the Nazis.[4] In 1939 the British government had no intention of repeating the error made during the First World War when mass internment of "enemy aliens" created a logistical and personal nightmare for some 30,000 unfortunates. As late as 24 October 1939 Viscount Cobham indicated that the government would not call for mass internments and Home Secretary Sir John Anderson insisted on a "liberal internment policy." On 4 September 1939, however, an internment policy involving tribunals was announced: internees would fall into one of three classes:

> Class A – those who would presumably help Germany – were to be interned immediately
> Class B – a compromise category for individuals such as German businessmen who might pose a risk – were to be subject to reporting restrictions
> Class C – those subject to oppression by the Nazis on racial, religious, or political grounds, and those who had thrown in their lot with Britain – were allowed to remain at liberty.

It is unclear who actually gave the order for internment, since interdepartmental wrangling between the Home Office and the War Office led to confusion about jurisdiction.[5] If the War Office, acting under the War Cabinet, had decided in favour of internment, Beaverbrook would have participated in the decision. The Joint Intelligence Committee also spoke of a potential "fifth column" of "refugees of dubious loyalty abroad in Britain who might provide support to the Germans if they landed in England," and therefore urged the internment of all aliens. By this time Canada had arrested more than 800 Austro-Germans.

On 7 May 1940 Neville Chamberlain lost power and Winston Churchill, who had a decidedly tougher stand on the internment issue, became prime minister. Germany had occupied Denmark and Norway in April and was now poised to overrun the Netherlands, Belgium, and France. The War Office, the Foreign Office, the Chiefs of Staff, the Joint Intelligence Committee and the more clandestine MI5 all pressured the Home Office for large-scale internment. On 10 May the order went out to intern all "enemy aliens" in areas where German parachute troops were likely to land (east and southeast England).

The arrests began at 8:00 a.m. on Saturday, 11 May 1940. Gerhard Kander recalled that he had been arrested on Whitsunday (12 May). By 17 May the first internees had arrived in Huyton, near Liverpool; by 29 May others had been sent to the Isle of Man. These internees represented a cross-section of groups opposed to the National Socialists: rabbis, Lutheran pastors of the Confessing Church, social democrats, Communists, Jesuit priests, Anglican ministers, assimilated Jews, and baptized Jews. The Isle of Man camp hosted artists Kurt Schwitters and Egon Wellesz as well as violinists Siegmund Nissel and Norbert Brainin (who later formed the Amadeus Quartet). Ralph Vaughn Williams was chosen to chair a committee that subsequently recommended the release of "persons of eminent distinction who had made outstanding contributions to art."

On 30 May 1940 Viscount Caldecote asked Vincent Massey, Canada's high commissioner in London, if Canada would accept a number of internees. The Canadian Cabinet discussed the issue on 5 June and replied to Britain that the undertaking would be difficult. Churchill was not amused, and sent a renewed request to Massey on 7 June; the British Cabinet stated that the internees were "potentially dangerous" and that Britain was extremely vulnerable. In reply to Massey's request for numbers and types of internees, Caldecote stated that there were 2,633 Class A internees, 1,823 prisoners of war, and 1,500 Italian fascists. The Canadian government agreed to take 4,000 internees and 3,000 prisoners of war, and requisitioned ships that had been earmarked to take soldiers to

India to transport the internees abroad. The announced embarkation date was 24 June. Details of the ships that transported prisoners of war and internees to Canada and the numbers of prisoners of war and internees that arrived in Quebec in the summer of 1940 are given in table 2.1.

On 21 June 1940 Britain announced mass internment, more than a month after arrests had begun, in three stages since there was insufficient accommodation for the expected 25,000 internees. By the end of June, 27,200 individuals had been detained. The whole operation was under the jurisdiction of Home Secretary Sir John Anderson, and internees, even abroad, were to remain wards of the Home Office, a fact that greatly hampered their subsequent release. Moreover, on 2 July, the *Arandora Star*, a ship carrying more than 1,200 German and Italian internees, was sunk off the Irish coast by a German torpedo; more than 600 lives were lost.[6] Following this tragedy, there was fierce debate on the internment policy. Three government White Papers proposed a total of twenty-one release categories to replace the previous A, B, and C classes, and those who had been sent to Canada and Australia were given an opportunity to return to Britain. By the end of February 1941 about 15,000 internees had been released. Some 1,300 returned from Canada to help the British war effort and serve in the Pioneer Corps. It is horrific to realise that it took the loss of life on the *Arandora Star* to bring public attention to the basic injustice of interning class B and C "enemy aliens." If the British internment policy had been allowed to proceed, it is likely that 75,000 German and Austrian men, women, and children in Britain might have been arrested. As it was, the policy of shipping enemy aliens to the colonies deprived Britain of the services of talented and highly motivated émigrés for the war effort. However, a considerable number were not picked up, including Emmy Heim, who put her musical talents to work for the crown for the duration of the war:

> During the past seven years [I] have repeated throughout England what I did in Vienna during 1914–8; singing for the wounded and the prisoners. At Oxford and Cambridge Universities, I sang also for the men taking army courses, and in London took part in the concerts for war-weary Britishers arranged by Dame Myra Hess during the "Blitz." Again and again I sang for Red Cross and similar charities in Britain. But I don't want

> to talk of the time every evening that indescribable sound of the sirens sounded in London and we had to go to the shelters. We took a little bag with us – just a pair of shoes and maybe one photograph we wanted with us to the end. And there we were supposed to sleep but not many of us could. The noise of explosives was continuous; unbelievable the courage and kindness of every single fire-watcher and air-raid warden. I cannot praise them enough or express how grateful we were to them. In the day we all tried to live as normally as possible and we turned to Schubert and Bach with more intensity than ever.[7]

THE "CAMP BOYS" – MUSIC BEHIND BARBED WIRE

Just as Europeans were preparing to face the darkest years of the war the "Camp Boys," albeit within a perimeter of barbed wire, were embarking on an intellectual, artistic, and cultural experience that might have been described as the envy of the civilized world. They enjoyed access to some of the best European art, music, and literature, including works unavailable to their European compatriots, – including Gotthold Ephraim Lessing's *Nathan der Weise* and Alban Berg's *Wozzeck*. At a time when most Canadians were subject to rationing, internees were treated to Viennese delicacies with whipped cream, prepared by fine old country chefs. Interviews with the musician "Camp Boys" reveal that most of them viewed their period of internment as an educational opportunity of a lifetime that they used to full advantage. Friendships formed during their time in the camps endured throughout their professional lives and their mutual camaraderie extended to a surviving network of personal contacts throughout Canada and the United States that they sill maintain.

Several thousand "Camp Boys" – including eleven musicians who began their Canadian careers behind barbed wire in the backwoods of New Brunswick, Quebec, and Ontario – found themselves in jurisdictional limbo: they had left Europe but they were not actually "in" Canada. The list of the camps for prisoners of war Canada in table 2.2 includes nine that were used to house internees.[8] The eleven musicians in this study who were brought to Canada as internees were held at five of these camps: Camp A (Farnham, Ontario), Camp B (Ripples, near Fredericton, New

Table 2.1.a. Ships transporting internees to Canada, 1940; estimations from sources by Eric Koch and Peter and Leni Gillman

Ship	*Embarkation port and date*	*Arrival in Quebec*	*Classification of internees*	*Koch*	*Gillman*
Duchess of York	Liverpool	29 June	Class A internees	2,112	1,700
	20 June		prisoners of war	535	500
*Arandora Star**	Liverpool	sunk 2	Class A internees	473	–
	1 July	July	Italian internees	717	–
Ettrick	Liverpool	13 July	Class B and C	1,308	1,700
	3 July		internees	405	900
			Italian internees	785	
			prisoners of war		
Sobieski	Greenock	15 July	Class B and C	982	1,000
	4 July		internees	548	550
			prisoners of war	–	400
			Single Italian		
			internees		

*According to Koch, when the *Arandora Star* sank on 2 July 1941, 146 Class A internees and 453 Italian internees were drowned; according to Draper, the boat sank on 1 July and 603 lives were lost. According to Stent, the boat left on 30 June and 175 of the Germans and 486 of the Italians drowned. Helmut Blume was scheduled to sail on the *Arandora Star,* but since it was full he was put on the next boat.

Table 2.1.b. Numbers and classifications of internees arriving in Quebec, June–July 1940; estimations from sources by Eric Koch, Paula Jean Draper, and Peter and Leni Gillman.

Classification	*Koch*	*Draper*	*Gillman*
Class A internees	2,112		1,700
Class B and C internees	2,290	2,284	2,700
Italian internees	405		400
Nazi prisoners of war	1,868		1,950
Totals	6,675		6,750

Sources:

Draper, Paula Jean. "'The 'Camp Boys': Interned Refugees from Nazism," in Franca Iacovetta et al., *Enemies Within: Italian and other Internees in Canada and Abroad* (Toronto: University of Toronto Press, 2000), 172.

Gillman, Peter, and Leni Gillman. *"Collar the Lot!" How Britain Interned and Expelled its Wartime Refugees* (London: Quartet, 1980), 169–71, 204.

Koch, Eric. *Deemed Suspect: A Wartime Blunder* (Toronto: Methuen, 1980), 262.

Stent, Ronald. *A Bespattered Page? The Internment of "His Majesty's Most Loyal Enemy Aliens"* (London: Andre Deutsch, 1980), 104.

Brunswick), Camp N (Newington, near Sherbrooke, Quebec), Camp Q (Monteith, Ontario), and Camp T (Trois Rivières, Quebec).

While internment was certainly far from pleasant, and was for some a terrifying experience, many of the internees – particularly those who were younger – survived quite well. It is not at all clear

Table 2.2. Internment camps in Canada. Camps where musical émigrés were held are highlighted.

Camp location	Number / letter	Province	Inception date	Release or closure date	Internees held
Angler	101	Ontario	10 Jan. 1941	29 July 1946	German POWs
					from June 1942 on 650 Japanese internees
Bowmanville	30	Ontarip	12 Apr. 1945	12 April 1945	750 prisoners of war
Chatham	10	Ontario	May 1944	Nov. 1946	600 internees and prisoners of war
Cove Fields	L	Quebec	June 1940	Jan. 1941	internees, German prisoners of war
Espanola	21 / E	Ontario	July 1940	30 Nov. 1943	1,400 soldiers
Farnham	40 / A	Quebec	Oct. 1940	Jan. 1942	500 refugees
				May 1946	officers and marines
Grand Ligne	44	Quebec	June 1943	May 1946	700 officers
Gravenhurst	20	Ontario	30 June 1940	June 1946	500 officers and soldiers
Hull	32	Quebec	Aug. 1941	Mar. 1947	communist sympathizers, then German prisoners of war
Île-au-Noix	41 / I	Quebec	July 1940	Dec. 1943	300 internees
Île-de-St-Hélène	S	Quebec	3 July 1940	Nov. 1943	350 (including 50 Italian merchant marines)
Kingston	31 / F	Ontario	Sept. 1939	Dec. 1943	125 internees
			June 1940		600 (including 300 officers)
Medicine Hat	132	Alberta	1 Jan. 1943	Dec. 1946	2,000 Afrikakorps prisoners of war
			1944		additional thousands of German prisoners of war
Mimico	22 / M	Ontario	19 July 1940	Apr. 1944	up to 700 merchant marines and prisoners of war
Monteith	23 / Q	Ontario	14 July 1940	Dec. 1946	internees and merchant marine prisoners of war
			Jan. 1942		2,000 German officers
Newington	42 / N	Quebec	Oct. 1940	1941	700 internees
(Sherbrooke)			1942	June 1946	700 German officers
Neys	100 / W	Ontario	13 Jan. 1941	Dec. 1943	500 officers and soldiers
			Aug. 1944	April 1946	500 Nazi officers
Ozada (Lethbridge)	133	Alberta	May 1942		300 German prisoners of war
			Sept. 1942		more than 12,000 German prisoners of war

Table 2.2 continued

Camp location	*Number / letter*	*Province*	*Inception date*	*Release or closure date*	*Internees held*
Petawawa	33	Ontario	Sept. 1939	March 1946	600 German citizens
			Autumn 1941		Japanese merchant marine prisoners of war
			Feb. 1944		1,600 officers and soldiers
Red Rock	R	Ontario	July 1940	Oct. 1941	1,150 refugees, merchant marines
Ripples (Fredericton)	70 / B	New Brunswick	Aug. 1940	July 1941	500 German and Italian civilians
			July 1941		700 officers
SeeBee-Kananaskis	130	Alberta	Sept. 1939	June 1946	650 internees, merchant marines
			1942		German officers and soldiers
Trois-Rivières	T	Quebec	June 1940	Sept. 1940	717 prisoners of war
Wainwright	135	Alberta	Dec. 1944	June 1946	500 Nazis

whether any of these internees had actualy considered immigrating to Canada beforehand. During the war the internees were the wards of the British Home Office, and the camps were under the jurisdiction of Canada's Department of National Defence.[9] Release into civilian life under a sponsorship program initiated by the Immigration Branch likely gave younger internees an opportunity to experience the hospitality offered by individual Canadians and doubtless played a role in their decision to apply for landed immigrant status when this option was offered at the end of the war. Students whose education in England had been interrupted by their internment were the first to be released under the program and went straight to university. The Canadian government classed the internees as temporary visitors (refugee classification); those who were released were given temporary permits pending the conclusion of the war. A number of internees returned to Britain and Germany to resume work in family businesses, and about thirty socialists returned to Europe to live in the German Democratic Republic. Many, however, chose to remain in Canada.

The internees displayed remarkable initiative in establishing an active social and cultural life almost as soon as they arrived, under military escort, in Quebec City. In the camps where they were eventually placed they organized concerts and launched newspapers. Music, poetry, drama, literature, art exhibitions, and culinary pursuits served to mitigate the harsh realities of the physical situation in which they found themselves. Letters written by internees were restricted to a single sheet of paper and were subject to censors in Ottawa. Return addresses consisted of the number or alphabetical letter designating the camp so as not to reveal a geographical location. Each camp published a newspaper, generally reproduced on carbon copies and distributed by hand.[10]

What was life like behind barbed wire? The days began with a bell for wakeup at 6:00 AM; at 6:30 everyone went outside in groups of twenty for roll call. The commanding officers did the count then went for breakfast. Since the dining room held only 250 men, there were three sittings, each lasting fifteen minutes; the same held for lunch, and for dinner, which began at 5:00 PM. At 7:00 PM there was another inspection, after which the internees were allowed to walk inside the compound for an hour. At 8:00 PM everyone returned to the barracks. The day ended with lights out at 9:00.[11]

In addition to using whatever opportunities he could to further his career as a pianist, performing frequently and arranging concerts for other camp musicians, Helmut Blume made efforts to obtain his release, writing to the authorities in May 1941. Blume found the camp ritual boring, and commented that "one killed time as best one could." Like Blume, John Newmark found camp life difficult, not least because of the adverse living conditions. He chafed under the idea that he was already advanced in years and that the Nazis had robbed him of his career:

> The endless uncertainty of what would become of us and the complete isolation with hardly any news from families and friends left behind in Europe and its bombings were very hard to endure. To walk along barbed wire six times a day, the difficult nights in overheated and cramped quarters with 35 double bunks in each hut, the snoring and the nightmarish outcries in dreams left and right, and, worst of all, the utter lack of privacy, twenty-four hours of forced company, mostly detested, sometimes comforting, but rarely enjoyable. All this had a deep and long lasting effect on all of us. It was not surprising under these circumstances that some of the elder camp inmates cracked up and had spells of deep depression. They were in and out of the hospital, being treated with tranquilizers and sedatives. More than a few of them had had shattering experiences behind them, fleeing first from the Russians, then being persecuted by the Nazis, escaping to Holland or Belgium and then across the Channel to England, losing most of their belongings and often, worst of all, their families in their eternal exodus.[12]

On 9 October 1941 K. Hellman of Camp N (near Sherbrooke) wrote to Myron Taylor, the vice-chair of the Evian Conference, requesting a review of the status of the internees, and citing the Canadian order-in-council that had reclassified the internment camps as "refugee camps" and the prisoners of war as "refugees."[13] This inquiry resulted in some improvement in living conditions. A number of students had been released in Canada and some internees had been released for employment in the war effort, but many still remained in the camps.

At Christmas and Chanukah 1942, the internees received a message from the Central Committee for Interned Refugees, a body composed of representatives from the United Jewish Refugee and War Relief Agencies and the Canadian National Committee on Refugees that reviewed the measures taken on their behalf. Those who had first-degree relatives in Canada were released. However, the US government continued to hold a firm anti-admission policy. Even those who had registered under the quota system in Britain before their internment and those who had relatives living in the United States were barred from entry.[14] The Central Committee also outlined efforts for improving the educational and recreational facilities in the camps, including the provision of "libraries, films, sports equipment, newspapers, magazines, music, musical instruments, radios, toiletries, provision for the writing of examinations, materials for handicrafts, paintings, games, clothing, and optical, dental, and medical equipment."[15] The Church of the Brethren donated pianos, gramophones, recordings, and musical instruments for an orchestra.[16] Jerome Davies of the YMCA commented that the organization's aim was to provide the internees with educational facilities similar to those available at an American college or university.[17]

Hans Kaufman spent his camp time profitably, not only playing and teaching violin but also practising his occupation of choice – tailoring – learned years earlier in Vienna, keeping a scrupulous record of his clients, requests for services, payments, and dates. At his release on 17 June 1941 he was showered with good wishes from his compatriots, expressing their admiration for his abilities.[18]

Charles Cahn had been a student at Oxford when he was interned; he was sent with his father and brother first to Camp Q (Monteith), and later to Camp A (Farnham), east of Montreal. Cahn remembers that at first the internees had to wear big red circles on their backs and red stripes on their trousers, but later they were allowed to wear their own clothes. Music, sports, lectures, and a school were organized in the camp: "We were behind barbed wire until October 1941, classified according to the Geneva Convention as 'Prisoners of War, class 2, civilian internees' ... Bill Heckscher directed the school, I was secretary." Many years later Heckscher received an honorary degree from McGill University, presented by Walter Hitschfeld, who had also been one of the twenty or so students in the camp school and was now vice-principal of McGill. Paul Hugo Meyer also commented on the educational opportunities during his camp years:

> What made the internment such a great experience for the younger ones among us was that we were able to live in a congenial

> and fairly homogeneous human environment where strong and lasting ties could be formed – the kind of ties that others of our generation formed at school, college, or in the army, and eventually the disadvantages of prison life were almost forgotten among the intellectual stimulation, the creature comforts (regular cafés at Camp B . . .) and the human warmth. Eventually, certainly, most of us got married and lived happily ever after. What is much more significant is that whenever I visit some American or Canadian university, I am likely to find an "Old Camp Boy" on the faculty, and this creates a human tie even after forty years.[19]

Education facilities in the camp itself were coordinated by the War Prisoners' Aid Committee of the YMCA chaired by Ernest MacMillan, who had personal experience of internment during the First World War. He had just completed a visit to Bayreuth to see performances of Wagner's music dramas when Britain declared war on Germany in September 1914. He was interned in Germany as an enemy alien and spent the war years in a prison camp at Ruhleben, near Berlin. Macmillan regarded his experience in the German camp as an example of the flourishing artistic and intellectual life that could be possible behind barbed wire.[20] While MacMillan's experience at Ruhleben gave him useful background for work with the Committee, which was responsible for arranging study, recreation, and worship opportunities for German prisoners of war in Canada, this experience also led him to downplay difficulties experienced by the internees. For example, he later countered Newmark's complaints by saying "My dear boy, there is not too much wrong with living in a detention camp, I spent my time in Ruhleben getting my master's degree in music via correspondence with the Royal Academy of Music in London, by writing a string quartet."[21] In communications with Frederick Charles Blair, however, MacMillan did attempt to speed the release of the internees, unfortunately with little success.

While the physical facilities at the camps may not have resembled those of an American college there is no doubt that the teaching faculties could have rivalled any Ivy League institution. The most elaborate educational system was likely that at Camp N (Newington, near Sherbrooke), where many internees from Camp B (Ripples, near Fredericton, New Brunswick) were transferred in June 1941.

(For the remainder of the war, Camp B was used to intern German and Italian prisoners of war along with a number of Canadians.) Since Camp N was close to Montreal, some men were able to complete university level courses at McGill University.

Life in camp was not always Spartan. The recreation hall at Camp B (Ripples) boasted a café where Continental pastries were served. Internees could enjoy *Apfelstrudel* piled high with *Schlagobers* (whipped cream) – a rarity in wartime Canada – prepared by Viennese chefs, while listening to music played by Willy Amtmann and other European musicians.[22] John Newmark fondly remembered "a smorgasbord of sweets, over ten different cakes, pies, cookies, patisseries, together with coffee and whipped cream."[23] Franz Kraemer became the camp spokesperson because of his ability to negotiate,[24] and Walter Homburger, as secretary, spent his time typing with two fingers.[25]

The recreation hall at Camp B also had a radio, so musicians could listen to the Saturday afternoon broadcasts of the Metropolitan Opera. They also heard CBC broadcasts, one of which was a Toronto broadcast of Greta Kraus and Arnold Walter playing one of J.S. Bach's concertos for two harpsichords. John Newmark was probably not aware that these two musicians were émigrés, but he was so startled to hear there were *two* harpsichords in Toronto that he determined to go there immediately after his release. The broadcast was one of a series of six featuring a string orchestra conducted by Ettore Mazzoleni playing concertos by C.P.E. Bach, J.S. Bach, Handel, Corelli, Rameau, and Mozart.[26]

On 21 July 1940, eight days after their arrival, pianist Helmut Blume and violinist Hans Kaufmann made their Canadian debuts in a variety show reviewed by a critic whose pseudonym was "XYZ."

> Sunday night's performance made history in the annals of this camp. For the first time a well-thought-out and properly organized cabaret was presented to an enthusiastic audience, which was augmented by the Camp-Commander and numerous officers ... But to come to the actual performance, which many, though unfortunately not all, of us were privileged to witness on Sunday. It was compiled and arranged by Edward Hahn in a manner wholly admirable. It was obvious that it had been put together with infinite care and it had been rehearsed untiringly.

Ernst Sawady opened the proceedings after a short overture at the piano by Hans Cohn. Mr Sawady left no doubt in our minds after his first few words that the job of compering [sic] the show was in the best of hands. In fact he won the hearts of his audience without difficulty from the very first moment.

Jack Kahnow sang "Abschied von Sorrent" (Goodbye to Sorrento) in a pleasing manner and thereby set the ball rolling. He was followed by Toscanelli the juggler, who showed his skill in no uncertain manner.

Next on the program came "Loeffler and his Accordeon [sic]." A misleading statement, because his presentation in this case was 99 percent Loeffler and only 1 percent accordeon, though we all know, of course, [that] he actually is a wizard on that instrument. Loeffler, a born comedian, proved to be a popular favourite.

One good thing follows another and Hans Kaufman played on his violin to everyone's satisfaction. Here we have a really brilliant artist in our midst who, I hope, will give us many hours of pleasure in the future. He has now shown that his abilities are not confined to the classics, but also include a fluent rendering of lighter music. He opened with Toselli's "Serenade," followed by Kreisler's "Liebesfreud." This was again followed by "Lovely Rosmarin," also by Kreisler, and lastly by "Old Folks at Home," a Kreisler arrangement of "Swanee River."

Then we had a couplet by Mr Sawady which brought the house down, and deservedly so. To the tune of "Bolle" he passed amusing and delightful comment on our misfortunes from the day of our internment right up to the present.

The second half was opened by Edward Hahn singing two songs: one from [Albert] Lortzing's [opera *Der*] *Waffenschmied* and Tosti's "Serenata." He sang the former with a full resonant voice and the latter, an Italian air, was exceptionally well received. There followed the "Volksliederchor," a choir, which sang "Heidenroeslein" and "Wenn alle Bruennlein fliessen." This had been well rehearsed and the listeners were well satisfied with the harmonious rendering of these popular folk songs.

Max Kalischer provided a humorous interlude the highlight of which was an imitation of a motor-car; when he left the platform rather prematurely the audience called him back to sing "Krumme Lanke" with his usual sang-froid.

> Then came the undoubted high spot of the evening: Loeffler, Kaufmann and Rudi Highieak presented a medley of popular tunes. The last mentioned has a very pleasant tenor voice and his singing of "O sole mio" was quite excellent. Later his rendering of the old Viennese melodies found undoubted favour in the audiences' ear ... An encore given by [Loeffler and Kaufmann] took the form of an ultra-modern jazz-medley which I should like to see performed in a proper theatre. I have no doubt that it would bring the house down just as it did Sunday night. The idea of jazzing up the violin is not new, but the combination of violin and accordeon is surely original and the final effect was absolutely brilliant. To finish we were invited to sing "John Brown's Baby" [sic] and everybody joined in with tremendous enthusiasm.
>
> In conclusion I would like to mention the valiant efforts of the two pianists who miraculously managed to overcome the handicaps of the instrument at their disposal and who permitted us to forget the fact that it is really abominably out of tune. Hans Cohn gave us some excellent interludes of popular music. Helmut Blume accompanied the more serious parts with equal success. The performance ended with the Canadian anthem and God Save the King.[27]

Helmut Kallmann's article, "Music in the Internment Camps," which traces the early career of John Newmark, is one of several sources documenting the impressive concert activities carried out behind barbed wire. Newmark partnered violinists Gerhard Kander (eleven concerts) and Viennese-born Willy Amtmann (three concerts) in sonatas by Handel, Mozart, Beethoven, Franck, and Brahms, and he also appeared as a soloist playing Beethoven's Piano Sonata in A flat major, op. 26. Many internees were undoubtedly delighted to have a live concert artist in their midst. Kallmann, speaking for the internees, said: "We admired and took pride in Johnny. His performances provided eagerly craved spiritual nourishment: furthermore, since camp commanders were invited to concerts and plays, his artistry might convince the authorities that the refugees had a contribution to make to Canada and should be treated as desirable immigrants."[28]

Helmut Kallmann arrived at Camp T (Trois Rivières) in July 1940. A piano was delivered to the camp on 27 July and on 3 August he heard his first Canadian concert: the program included John Newmark accompanying actor Otto Diamant-Admandt in a dramatic reading of Rilke's "Die Weise von Liebe und Tod des Cornets Christoph Rilke."[29] In early August, Kallmann's group was transferred to Camp B, where they were soon joined by a group of internees from Camp Q (Monteith, Ontario) including violinist Willy Amtmann, with whom Newmark was to give many concerts.

Camp B finally received an upright piano in early November 1940. Gerhard Kander (who had obtained a violin from fellow internee Lothar Sandler) and John Newmark picked up where they had left off in Germany; in the 1930s the pair had been booked for a series of Jüdischer Kulturbund concerts. On 14 November 1940 Kander and Newmark presented a program of two Mozart violin sonatas (K 304 in E minor, and K 454 in B-flat major); years later, Kander recalled that Newmark played this first concert at sight. A repeat of this recital a week later included Willy Amtmann, with Walter Homburger as page turner. Homburger put his experience as page turner to good use on stage at Town Hall in New York, when Kander and Newmark made their New York debut, on 11 February 1947.[30] Three Camp Boys in Town Hall! "There was supposed to be a page turner there," Homburger modestly remembers, "and when he didn't turn up Jonny said, "Can you turn for me?" I had done it before but I don't read music. But I know when it goes up or goes down. So the only thing Jonny had to do was this [nod] ... My parents were in the audience, they practically dropped dead. I didn't tell them before."[31] A number of musicians were excused from outdoor work in order to practise and rehearse. Kander had been released from tree-cutting duties by a doctor who looked forward to hearing his concerts, and spent much of the winter in the warm boiler room practising for future engagements in the Canadian backwoods.[32] The activities of Camp B are now commemorated in a museum in Minto, New Brunswick. Years later Homburger was invited to Governor General Adrienne Clarkson's residence for a reception in Alfred Brendel's honour (he had brought Brendel to Canada for his first tours). Clarkson told him that she had recently visited the Ripples museum and was astonished to realize that during her broadcasting career she had worked with several people who had been in that camp, including Franz Kraemer and John Newmark.[33]

In June 1941 some of the internees from Camp B, including Helmut Kallmann, were transferred to Camp A (Farnham, Quebec) while others, including Newmark, were sent to Camp N (Newington, near Sherbrooke). In January 1942 the internees from the Camp A (Farnham) camp were also taken to Camp N so Kallmann was again able to enjoy Newmark's performances. He noted three recitals in particular: a program of sonatas by Bach, Mozart, and Brahms with violinist Willy Amtmann; a performance of Mozart's Piano Concerto in D minor, K 466, with an orchestra consisting of two violins, one viola, one cello, and two flutes; and a program that included Schubert's Fantasy in F minor for piano four hands, D 940 performed by John Newmark and Helmut Blume.[34] Newmark was released in October 1942.

One notable musical creation of these years was Freddy Grant's song "You'll Get Used to It." Grant, a songwriter and pianist, was born in Berlin, studied in Germany, and came to London in the mid-1930s. This song, written in response to the tedium of life as an internee, became a hit on both sides of the Atlantic and was taken up by various Canadian luminaries including Wilf Carter and the Happy Gang; it also became a popular feature of *Meet the Navy*, a show that toured throughout the war years and afterward.[35] Grant's lyrics capture the quintessential Canadian non-heroic, grin-and-bear-it attitude in the face of adverse circumstances, and the ironic, jaunty, march-like tune in E flat major struck a sympathetic note among internees, armed forces, and the general populace alike. The original text, bemoaning the monotony and daily drudgery of camp life, appeared in the November 1941 edition of the Camp A (Farnham) newspaper.[36] A revised version in C major with a new text by "Victor Gordon"[37] describing general wartime difficulties and deprivations was published by Gordon V. Thompson in 1942.

There were other songs in a similar vein. Ernest K. Sawady's *Canadian Diary 1940–41: Mehr oder Weniger Heitere Erinnerungen an die Internierung in Canada* has song texts in both English and German, including: "Don't Let It Get You Down!," "Bolle's Reise nach Canada" (with the refrain "Aber trotzdem hab'n wir alle uns köstlich amüsiert" / "But still it was quite pleasant – we had a lot of fun"), "Freut Euch des Lebens," "Trampsong," "I Want to Be Alone," and "Yes Sir," a spoof on the ritual of daily roll call.[38] Vernon Brooks later characterized camp life as a fairyland-

surrounded by a thick fog, rather like "Brigadoon."[39] One camp poet [probably Alfred Becker] wrote a sonnet pointing to a brighter future.

The day will come when all of us
Will love and joy recover,
Just see that you keep grinning.
And if you do,
You'll find it's true:
Life's worth a new beginning.[40]

When John Newmark was released in October 1942 he went to Toronto, in part to thank his sponsor.[41] That winter he gave concerts with Helmut Blume and Gerhard Kander in a number of centres including Ottawa and Kingston. After his release in August 1943 Helmut Kallmann also went to Toronto, where he got a job as an audit clerk. When he was looking for a rooming house, Newmark suggested he try the Barthas, Hungarian refugees who ran a house on Lowther Avenue. But several months later, the house was sold, and the rent became prohibitively expensive. In October 1943 he moved, again on a recommendation from Newmark, to a residence run by a Mrs. Schuster, who wanted a boarder who could play the piano.[42]

Gerhard Kander achieved his integration into Canadian society with remarkable ease, due to the efforts of his sponsors Kaspar and Lois Fraser.[43] Kander's sponsorship amounted to $1,000, half from the Frasers and half from an unknown donor. In January 1942 Kander was sent a first-class train ticket to Montreal, where he was feted at a party given by a Dr Illiewitz and his wife, who also wished to sponsor the violinist.[44]

A number of Canadians, some of whom were recent immigrants themselves, reached out to help the internees in the camps. Jan Simons remembered the close contact his family had with Max Stern, who had fled Nazi Germany via Paris and London, and came to Canada in 1941 as an internee. Jan's father, Hugo Simons, visited Stern and other internees in Camp A (Farnham) during the war and brought food on a regular basis.[45] In 1942, soon after his release, Stern began a long association with the Dominion Gallery in Montreal;[46] Jan Simons worked for him there shortly after the war, and the art dealer sent large fruit baskets to the family each year in thankful acknowledgement of their support.

As Montreal musicians learned more about the internees, they contributed to and participated in recreational and educational efforts on their behalf. Lotte Goetzel and Alexander Brott (who were married in 1943) gave a number of concerts for the internees in Camp A (Farnham). Rose Goldblatt, who had come to know the plight of the internees through a friend who was the director of the Farnham camp, discovered that among the German civilian prisoners were a number of pianists looking for music scores. "I was among the interested Montrealers who sent music to the camps, including the Sherbrooke camp where John [Newmark] was interned."[47] Newmark was overwhelmed with the response: "Thanks to those donations I was even able to give an entire recital of bad music, mostly Victorian trash, which was literally a 'roaring' success!"[48]

The exceptional educational opportunities provided by internees themselves, some of whom were among the finest European scholars, stimulated brilliant students, a good number of whom went on to become academic, artistic, scientific, and industrial leaders in Canada and the United States. This resulted in some interesting encounters. Charles Cahn completed medical studies at the University of Toronto and became an intern at the Toronto General Hospital. In April 1946 he was appointed as a commissioned medical officer in the Royal Canadian Army Medical Corps. One of his first assignments was on the *Queen Mary*, which had served as a troop ship through the war and in September 1946 was being used to bring 700 war brides, some with their babies, from Southampton to Canada. During the voyage Cahn was examining a sick baby when the captain of the ship, the colonel of the RCAMC, and several elderly gentlemen in civilian clothes came in. "Good afternoon, doctor," the captain said, "I'd like you to meet Sir John Anderson." Anderson was the man to whom Cahn owed his internment!

> It suddenly struck me that in 1940 when I crossed the Atlantic Ocean going west for the first time I was his guest (so to speak); and six years later when I crossed the Atlantic going west for the second time he was my guest! Should I speak to him about the irony of this event? I was tempted to test his sense of

humour, but then remembered that he had lost his job as Home Secretary during the London blitz in October 1940, having been criticized for taking away our freedom without due process of law. So I said nothing, not wanting to remind him of a dark period in his political career.[49]

Once the internees were given an opportunity to decide for themselves, the vast majority chose Canada. After the war it would have been possible for many of them to return to newly established democracies in their homelands. Both Germany and Austria initiated an elaborate program for financial compensation of losses suffered because of political circumstances (*Entschädigungsgesetze*). Helmut Kallmann commented that some returned to families in Great Britain, and about thirty others, mainly young idealists of a leftish bent, returned to East Germany with a desire to rebuild their country.[50] It seems that the internees who chose to remain in Canada rather than returning to Europe gradually came to view this country as their adopted homeland. For example, on their release in 1942 Charles Cahn and his brother Peter, who had been interned with their father on 25 June 1940, returned to England in 1946, but by 1948, disillusioned by European politics, they had decided that their future seemed brighter in Canada.[51] Hans Kaufman went back to Vienna with his wife in 1967, but finding working conditions inhospitable, he returned to live in Canada permanently. The fact that many internees felt they had been betrayed by Britain also worked in Canada's favour. They were much more willing to commit their energies to a country that, even if unprepared for their arrival, at least did not deliberately frustrate the legitimate aspirations of this most highly qualified group.

The persecution of intellectual and artistic minorities in totalitarian regimes throughout Europe created a formidable and motivated opposition force that was extremely well qualified to play a part in the struggle against those who had treated them so harshly. Émigrés placed their language skills and extensive knowledge of customs and culture in their former homelands at the disposal of Canadian military and media authorities in Canada. Some served in Ottawa as censors for prisoner-of-war mail. Others composed music to raise the morale of Allied troops and presented concerts on behalf of the war effort. Still others worked on propaganda broadcasts beamed into Nazi- or Communist-occupied Europe.[52]

In the summer of 1944 the Department of External Affairs set up a "provisional psychological warfare committee" in Ottawa to prepare German anti-fascist broadcasts for distribution in Europe on the Voice of America.[53] Three Camp Boys – Helmut Blume,[54] Karl D. Renner,[55] and Charles Wassermann[56] – were encouraged to participate in this effort. Blume later hired Eric Koch for the project and when Blume left for McGill in 1946, Koch succeeded him as head of the German section.[57] Koch recalled recording messages from prisoners of war to be sent to their families in Germany; the messages were limited to twenty-seven words and had to pass the censors. "One prisoner, believing the message was live-to-air, suddenly abandoned his prepared script and shouted "We will win the war. Long live Hitler!"[58] Blume also hired Mario Duschenes on several occasions: "Once in a while I got an engagement to read in German for the International Service – parts from plays about Canada. I was given the part of reading the voices of younger fellows."[59] Parts in these radio sketches were also distributed amongst other internees; the intention was to demonstrate how the expression of different points of view and critical thought were acceptable in a democratic society.[60]

PART TWO

Canada

3

Musical Life in Canada: An Overview of the Interwar Years

Canada was far from the wasteland of ice and snow envisioned by European romantics. By the time the first émigrés in this study began to arrive during the interwar years, Canadians had developed a vibrant and multifaceted musical life. This chapter will examine the musical landscape that these émigrés found across the country. They may well have wondered what they would encounter. How did the musical life compare to what they had left behind in Europe. Was a new orientation required? Who were the musicians they needed to meet? What sort of institutions would they find? What did they need to learn before they could begin to contribute in their own way? Would the environment be an accepting one? Although the musical landscape of Canada was indeed isolated and to a large extent dominated by British-Franco traditions, the brief survey that follows reveals a number of influences and contacts from Continental Europe.

It might have been cold comfort to learn that Canada's musical life was bifurcated in a manner that reflected its history: there was an anglophone community oriented towards London and Edinburgh, and a francophone community oriented toward Paris, with Montreal serving as the geographical synapse of the two.[1] Many of the music teachers and performers in anglophone Canada had been either educated in Britain or taught by British-trained musicians, and their attachment to England was still strong. Perhaps the finest example of a Canadian reared under these conditions was Ernest MacMillan (1893–1973).[2] Born in Mimico, he completed his musical education in Edinburgh and London, and became a major figure in Toronto's musical life as conductor of the Toronto Mendelssohn

Choir (1942–57),[3] principal conductor of the Toronto Symphony Orchestra (1931–56), principal of the Toronto Conservatory of Music (1926–42), and dean of the Faculty of Music of the University of Toronto (1927–52). In his spare time he was an organist of note and made significant contributions to educational and musical publications. A superb musician and a consummate gentleman, MacMillan was a prime example of the British domination of the musical scene in Toronto and to some extent across Canada. His annual performances of J.S. Bach's *St Matthew Passion* at Easter and Handel's *Messiah* at Christmas, conducted from memory, were staples for concertgoers through the 1920s, 1930s, and 1940s.

Montreal-born Wilfrid Pelletier (1896–1982)[4] can be seen as MacMillan's francophone counterpart. After studies in Paris he worked his way up the musical ladder at the Metropolitan Opera in New York from rehearsal pianist to conductor, working alongside Canadian tenor Edward Johnson, who was general manager of the Metropolitan Opera from 1935 to 1950. Pelletier became one of the regular Metropolitan conductors and in that capacity founded the "Metropolitan Opera Auditions of the Air" to give aspiring singers a venue to display their talents. Several prominent Quebec families persuaded him devote some of his musical activities to Quebec. The Société des concerts symphoniques de Montréal, which later became the Montreal Symphony Orchestra, was formed in 1934 and Pelletier soon became the artistic director. He played a major role in the establishment of the Conservatoire de musique de Montréal, which was founded in 1943, and in 1951 he became artistic director of the Québec Symphony Orchestra. Pelletier also made a significant contribution to the Montreal Festivals, an organization that sponsored summer musical and artistic performances at venues throughout Montreal (1939–65).[5]

MUSIC EDUCATION

In the early twentieth century salon music was still a popular self-generated home entertainment. Canada's flourishing piano and organ manufacturing industry and robust music publishers supplied instruments and sheet music that catered to the tastes of both urban and rural populaces.[6] The ubiquitous presence of keyboard instruments in Canadian parlours created a large pool of students requiring a correspondingly large pool of music teachers. While the advent of radio and motion pictures marked a decline in musical entertainment in the home, these teachers laid a strong foundations for both private and public music education in Canada, and teaching remained a an important source of income for many musicians. For example, schools run by the Roman Catholic Church, not only in Quebec but in other provinces, included music as an essential part of their curriculum.

Non-publicly funded music education was provided across Canada by a multitude of private music teachers who, banding together, formed conservatories or academies according to British or French models. In some cases these organizations affiliated themselves with universities and became full-fledged schools of music, preparing students for university degree examinations. Teachers remitted a percentage of their fees to cover administration charges and studio facilities but little was done to ensure employment security. The wide variation in quality and standards of instruction in these conservatories was offset by systems of examinations established by local conservatories to ensure more uniform and recognizable levels of achievement. By the time the European émigrés arrived, conservatories, academies, and music schools had become established in cities and university towns across Canada.

In 1898 Edward Fisher established an examination system for the Toronto Conservatory of Music (TCM). The Ottawa Ladies' College organized a conservatory for which graduation required the performance of a number of set test pieces, including works such as Schumann's *Kreisleriana*, Thalberg's Variations on *Home Sweet Home*, op. 72, and Chopin's Ballade in F minor.[7] In 1895 the Associated Board of the Royal Schools of Music (ABRSM), a British institution, initiated a system of examinations. This system, based on an Old Country model became established in several centres, in some cases over local opposition. In his history of the Royal Conservatory of Music Ezra Schabas describes a battle over examination jurisdiction waged in Toronto in 1898–99 between teachers who advocated the ABRSM examinations and those who preferred the TCM system.[8] McGill University worked jointly with the ABRSM from 1902 to 1909, but then set up its own examination system. The ABRSM subsequently became established in the Maritimes and through the western provinces; by 1930 British examiners were testing about 3,500 candidates across Canada. In the TCM (after 1947, the Royal Conservatory of Music, RCM) examination system, which gained national significance, examination repertoire and studies were neatly packaged into a series of ten graded books published by the Frederick Harris Music Publishing Co. The culmination of the system was the ATCM (later ARCT), a diploma that confirmed a student's achievement and carried the privilege of attaching these four coveted letters after their names. Through the mid- to late 1930s in Ontario the CBC (Canadian Broadcasting Corporation) broadcast TCM examination test pieces performed by Toronto music teachers.[9] The TCM's extensive national system of graded repertoire and examinations touched the lives of thousands of young musicians across Canada. Gifted teachers working in private studios produced not only generations of students who would appreciate and enjoy music for the remainder of their lives, but also a few star pupils who went on to brilliant careers.

The British tradition of competitive music festivals – undoubtedly a novelty to the émigrés – were another important feature of Canada's musical landscape. In these sporting affairs, sponsored by local service organizations, youngsters faced off against one another in front of an audience of well-wishing parents. Adjudicators with droll "old country" accents passed judgement, and hearts rose or fell as the marks were read out.[10]

Music studies at the University of Toronto were often carried on extra mures (outside the classroom) according to an Old World tradition that relied heavily on a student's personal initiative in obtaining an education. Harvey Olnick described the typical British attitude toward music as one of benign neglect, in which music was treated as a gentlemanly pursuit, but not something one would take seriously. "Musicians were considered on a level with people in trade."[11] The university curriculum in music was geared to British organists who needed to study harmony and counterpoint, and courses were few and far between. John Beckwith's description of his student days in the postwar 1940s supports this picture:

> On Thursdays ... [we would go] in threes and fours to Healey Willan, who blew pipe smoke at you, told witty anecdotes about English notables of the turn of the century, and called you "old man." Mondays you went in similar convoys to Leo Smith, who stroked his white pencil-like moustache, caressed the piano keys, and called you "dear boy." Examinations included such questions as "What do you know about Tchaikovsky" and cen-

> tred on a true appreciation of counterpoint gleaned from a study of the *48*, eschewing Bartók, Stravinsky, or anything smacking of newer trends.[12]

Healey Willan (1880–1968) was born and educated in London, England. He arrived in Toronto in 1913 to head the theory department of the Toronto Conservatory of Music. His compositions reveal a penchant for modal and contrapuntal writing in the Anglo-Catholic tradition. Leo Smith (1881–1952) was born in Birmingham, England, and educated in Birmingham and Manchester. He came to Toronto in 1910 to teach at the TCM and the Faculty of Music. During the 1930s he was principal cellist of the Toronto Symphony Orchestra. In 1945 there were twenty-one music students in the bachelor of music program and twenty-eight in the bachelor of arts program. The sole requirement for the doctoral degree in composition was an hour-long symphony, and studies were done extra mures.

Through the first half of the twentieth century the position of music studies within McGill University was tenuous. When a proposal was put forward in 1922 to add music as an elective to the arts program, Dean Cyrus Macmillan responded by asking, "Since when has Music been among the Arts?"[13] By 1946 McGill University, like the University of Toronto, had adopted the British structure: a faculty of music offering a bachelor of music degree geared toward the writing of fugue and counterpoint. The University was affiliated with the performance-oriented McGill Conservatorium that offered an associate diploma and a two-year licentiate diploma.

During the 1930s the only full-time position in the McGill Faculty of Music was that of the dean who was simultaneously director of the Conservatorium. This dual office, which survived through to the 1960s, spared McGill much of the jurisdictional faculty–conservatory wrangling that occurred in Toronto in the 1950s. (When MacMillan resigned as principal of the TCM in 1942, the practice of single individual serving as both TCM principal and the dean of the Faculty of Music at the University of Toronto was discontinued.) From 1939 to 1955 British-born Douglas Clarke held the position of dean, assisted by part-time staff members: Claude Champagne (from 1932 to 1941) and later Marvin Duchow (from 1944) and Alexander Brott (from 1939). In April 1937 a consultative Subcommittee was struck with a mandate to investigate the offerings of the Faculty and to discuss possible residency requirements for the bachelor of music degree.[14]

Francophone Canadians were decidedly oriented toward Paris, and serious music students did not consider their education complete without an apprenticeship at the Paris conservatoire. The "Prix d'Europe,"[15] instituted by the Quebec government in 1911 and modeled on the Prix de Rome in Paris, gave qualified Quebec music students a chance to study abroad: the list of recipients constitutes a "who's who" of Quebec artists, including Noël Brunet, Kenneth Gilbert, Clermont Pépin, Jacques Hétu, and Chantal Juillet. There was no corresponding grant program in anglophone Canada.

The first music school in a francophone university was l'École de musique, created at Université Laval in 1922.[16] The first class of students included Arthur LeBlanc (1906–85) a well-known Quebec violinist who completed his studies in Paris with Georges Enesco and Jacques Thibaud. Claude Champagne (1891–1965) returned to Montreal after studies in Paris full of enthusiasm to undertake musical and administrative duties. He taught at McGill University from 1932 to 1941 and was a major proponent in the founding of the Conservatoire de musique de Montréal. Throughout his career he played a major role in both public and private music education in the province; unfortunately this left relatively little time for composition. The Conservatoire de musique de Montréal, founded in 1943, was the first entirely state supported music institution for higher learning in North America. It was modeled on the Paris conservatoire; professional instruction is provided through a system of excellent teachers, standardized repertoire, and examinations, a no charge to students. Today there are seven such institutions distributed throughout the province of Quebec. Wilfrid Pelletier, one of the founders, remained director until 1961.

The Halifax Conservatory was directed by Ifan Williams, Sr (1889–1957), who taught string instruments and formed an orchestra composed of Conservatory students. He supplemented this ensemble by recruiting wind players from a Dutch contingent stationed in Halifax whom he paid out of his own pocket.[17] Beginning in 1935 the Conservatory sponsored a competitive festival that attracted budding musicians from the entire province. The Maritime Academy of Music was founded in 1934 by Harry Dean, an expatriate Englishman, active in the city as organist, conductor, pianist, and music administrator. In 1954 the Halifax Conservatory merged with the Academy to form the Maritime Conservatory of Music.

Up to 1956, the School of Music at Acadia University in Wolfville, Nova Scotia, which was established in 1927, offered the only undergraduate degree programs in performance and composition available within a school of music in Canada. Requirements for Acadia's bachelor of music in performance program included five works of an advanced character, and substantial repertoire from the four major historical style periods as well as theoretical and historical work and studies in harmony, counterpoint, and history, ensemble performance, and three arts and science courses. Edwin Collins, dean of the School of Music was English-born and had studied under Charles Stanford before immigrating to Canada in 1926. String classes were taught by members of the Halifax Conservatory – Jean Fraser and later Ifan Williams (1889–1957).

Sackville, New Brunswick, was home to one of the oldest music schools in Canada: Mount Allison Conservatory, founded in 1885. In addition to a bachelor of music program that dates back to 1917, Mount Allison University offered licentiate degrees with artist's and teaching specialties.

Calgary was fortunate to have the Mount Royal College of Music, a superb music school founded in 1910 and affiliated with the University of Alberta. The Mount Royal orchestral program provided the city with the foundation for the Calgary Symphony organized by Clayton Hare in 1949.

ORCHESTRAS, CONCERTS, AND OPERA

In the early decades of the twentieth century many musicians across Canada were employed in theatres accompanying vaudeville shows and silent movies, but with the advent of the "talkies" in 1928 and the economic downturn of the 1930s, many musicians found themselves out of work, and began to form ensembles that might replace their income. In Europe there was a centuries-old tradition of private and state support for cultural organizations, but in Canada musicians were forced to become entrepreneurs in their quest to establish themselves and receive remuneration for their services. During the interwar years, professional orchestras in Canada were few and far between. By 1930 the Toronto Symphony Orchestra

(TSO), conducted by Ernest MacMillan, was some sixty-four members strong, and presented a regular season of concerts playing repertoire ranging from Brahms and Sibelius symphonies to a highly successful Wagner series performed by an expanded orchestra.[18] In 1939, just as Canada was about to go to war with Germany, MacMillan advocated the continued performance of German music for the listening public, emphasizing that art should not be sacrificed for political expediency.[19] With the support of a women's auxiliary committee, presentation of children's concerts, a riotous "Christmas Box" program, and eventually pop concerts, MacMillan's TSO weathered the storms of the Second World War and the subsequent postwar period.

The Montreal Orchestra, founded by Douglas Clarke in 1930, was disbanded in 1941. The Société des concerts symphoniques de Montréal, founded in 1934 and seen as more oriented toward the francophone community, continued throughout the war years. In 1942, the Société symphonique de Québec (which appeared in public in 1902 and was incorporated four years later) joined with the Cercle philharmonique de Québec to form the l'Orchestre symphonique de Québec. The McGill String Quartet, founded by Alexander Brott in 1939, was gradually transformed, under the direction of Lotte Goetzel, into the McGill Chamber Orchestra.

During the 1930s the eighty-member Vancouver Symphony Orchestra, conducted by Allard de Ridder, presented a series of seven concerts in Vancouver and two in Victoria, providing a solid foundation for west coast orchestral music. Orchestras had been formed in Winnipeg, Regina, Edmonton, Moose Jaw, and Calgary but pressures on personnel during the First World War led to their demise.

Although there were a number of attempts at establishing opera performance on a regular basis in Quebec City, Montreal, and Toronto during the early twentieth century, success was not possible without the presence of a critical mass of musicians – conductors, singers, stage directors, voice teachers and students – all supported by public and private means, as finally came about in Toronto at mid-century. Earlier operatic initiatives include the Opera Guild in Montreal, founded by Pauline Donalda in 1942, which gave annual presentations of operas for twenty-eight seasons. Donalda had studied in Paris and after her performing career, became a notable teacher, returning to Montreal in 1937.[20]

Touring groups in Canada through the 1920s and 1930s include the New York-based San Carlo Opera Company, which made regular visits to Vancouver, Winnipeg, Toronto, and Montreal, and some smaller centres such as Hamilton and Winnipeg. Operetta was also very popular: few anglophone towns were without performances of works by Victor Herbert or Gilbert and Sullivan, while francophone communities enjoyed light operas by Jacques Offenbach, André Messager, Charles Lecocq, and Robert Planquette.[21] The "opera houses" or even "grand opera houses" found in many towns and cities were mainly multi-purpose theatres suitable for vaudeville and travelling minstrel shows. During the 1920s and 1930s, many of these buildings also served as movie houses and, until the advent of "talking" movies, hired musicians on a relatively regular basis.

Canada's somewhat parochial attitude toward opera, encountered by many of the émigrés, stemmed from a long and prevailing British tradition. In 1942 CBC general manager Gladstone Murray commented: "The Anglo-Saxon temperament does not on the whole take to the themes and declamatory style of grand opera. The Briton, on the whole, prefers musical comedy or light opera with its simple emotions, catchy tunes and words that can be appreciated."[22]

Large music festivals were an important feature of the Canadian musical scene. Through the late 1920s and early 1930s summer musical fare was presented in the Canadian Pacific Railway (CPR) hotels strung along the railway from the Chateau Frontenac in Quebec City to the Empress Hotel in Victoria. These CPR festivals, organized primarily by John Murray Gibbon with the assistance of a number of well-known Canadian musicians, were elaborate affairs featuring Canadian musicians, composers, and artists as well as a wide variety of Canadian folk music ensembles; some CPR hotels employed musicians throughout the year.[23]

Wind bands were a popular form of music-making.[24] Bands associated with religious, civilian, and military organizations performed both indoors and outside in the band shells found in most Canadian towns of any size; Salvation Army brass bands were particularly prominent in smaller towns and urban centres.[25] Permanent military bands employed professional musicians, who in turn formed a rich network of music education and performance, and provided wind and brass sections for local orchestras.

Community Concerts Associations, a system of community organizations affiliated with Community Concerts Inc., owned by Columbia Artists management in New York, provided communities with an opportunity to hear touring national and international artists in their own town or city, in whatever venues were available, including movie theatres, school gymnasiums, and churches. Although this system had serious drawbacks, it broadened the musical palette available to smaller municipalities. By 1955 some 75 local concert associations were in existence.[26]

The Women's Musical Clubs were yet another important feature of the Canadian musical scene. These organizations, founded with the purpose of encouraging the knowledge of music and performances by members, spread across Canada with clubs in Halifax, Québec, Montreal, Ottawa, Toronto, Hamilton, Winnipeg, Regina, Saskatoon, Lethbridge, Calgary, Edmonton, Vancouver, and Victoria, among others. Eventually Women's Musical Clubs began to organize concerts on a professional basis, hiring local, national, and international performers. Many of these concert series still flourish today.[27]

Canadian artists were not unknown on the international stage during the first half of the twentieth century. Examples include tenor Edward Johnson (1878–1959) who had a successful international career before he was appointed general manager of the Metropolitan Opera in New York in 1935. Pianist Ellen Ballon (1898–1969) studied in New York and Vienna and enjoyed a respectable career in the United States. Kathleen Parlow (1890–1963), who studied with Leopold Auer in St Petersburg, also had an international career, and later returned to Canada to teach.

ETHNOMUSICOLOGY

Canada was one of the first countries in which phonograph recordings of indigenous musics were made. Much of this research involved European scholars.[28] As early as the 1890s James Teit, a member of the Museum Branch of the Geological Survey of Canada, recorded songs and tales among the Salish nation in the Thompson River area as well as songs of other first peoples in British Columbia. A number of these recordings were submitted to the Berlin Phonogramm-Archiv (administered by Erich von Hornbostel and Otto Abraham) and were published in the *Boas Anniversary Volume*

(1906).[29] Franz Boas, a German-born anthropologist who taught at Columbia University from 1896 until his death in 1942, did field work among the Inuit of Baffin Island and the Chinook and Kwakiutl nations in the 1880s. In 1914 he met Canadian anthropologist Marius Barbeau, who had been recently hired by the Museum Branch of the Geological Survey of Canada, and inspired Barbeau to pursue his collection and study of both indigenous and traditional music.[30] In the course of his career Barbeau collected some 13,000 original texts including 8,000 tunes; his transcriptions are accompanied by meticulous documentation. An archive devoted to French-language traditional music was founded at Université Laval in 1944. Ango-Saxon traditional repertoire was also the subject of numerous studies, including Helen Creighton's collection of some 4,000 songs from the English, French, Gaelic, Micmac and German communities[31] and English folklorist Maud Karpeles's two-volume collection of traditional songs from Newfoundland in 1934.

COMPOSITION

Much of the music created in Canada during the interwar years was still quite conservative and in many cases, rather strongly influenced by late nineteenth- and early twentieth-century British or French styles, but even in the 1930s there were rumblings of change as new sounds and new compositional techniques began to appear. Canadian composer John Weinzweig had gone to the United States to study at the Eastman School of Music (1937–38), which offered courses in twentieth-century music.[32] On his return, he began to pass these new ideas along to his colleagues and composition students at the Toronto Conservatory of Music, and later, at the University of Toronto.

Claude Champagne, writing in Montreal during the 1940s, followed the French tradition of Fauré, but his music was also touched with modal and folk song inflections. In the early postwar years a wave of francophone composers, along with a few anglophones, travelled to Paris to study with Nadia Boulanger;[33] Talivaldis Kenins and Istvan Anhalt were also students of Boulanger in Paris. Other Canadian composers studied in Paris with Vincent d'Indy, Darius Milhaud, or Olivier Messiaen.

RADIO BROADCASTING

The establishment of radio transmission during the interwar years created a sense of national identity equal in importance to the ribbons of steel that forged a transportation link from coast to coast in the later decades of the previous century. Music broadcasts kept Canadians in touch with one another and played a prominent role in communication.[34] By 1929 a transcontinental network had been established and TSO concerts were broadcast across the country. A number of Canadian composers, including Claude Champagne, W.O. Forsyth, Clarence Lucas, and Ernest MacMillan were well represented in these programs. During the 1920s the Canadian National Railway and the Canadian Pacific Railway both supported radio dissemination of serious music through their own stations and networks, but radio broadcasting of music began in earnest with the establishment of the Canadian Broadcasting Corporation (CBC) in 1936 as a crown corporation with contractual links to a network of private stations. The CBC was probably the most important source of employment for many musicians, and it also supported a number of Canadian composers. The live broadcasts of the New York Metropolitan Opera on Saturday afternoons, which began in 1931, also remained a staple for generations of opera lovers.

MUSICAL FAMILIES WITH TIES TO THE OLD WORLD

A number of musical families who had a strong influence on the Canadian musical scene during the first half of the twentieth century also had ties to Britain and Europe. The Adaskin family,[35] who settled in Toronto in the early twentieth century, were of Latvian origin. Composer and violinist Murray Adaskin married Frances James, a well-known soprano. Cellist John Adaskin also became a conductor, CBC producer, and promoter of Canadian music. Violinist Harry Adaskin, a member of the Hart House Quartet, also became a broadcaster and married pianist Frances Marr.

The Hambourg family,[36] who came to Toronto in 1910, were of Russian origin. The most prominent family members were pianist Michael Hambourg and his three sons: violinist Jan Hambourg, cellist Boris Hambourg, and pianist and jazz musician Clement Hambourg. The Hambourg Trio (Michael, Jan, and Boris) appeared with a number of Canadian artists including Alberto Guerrero, Elie Spivak, Reginald Stewart, Norah Drewett, and Géza de Kresz, while the Hambourg Conservatory boasted a large faculty of local and international teachers and became a centre for visual artists, writers, and performers.

The Massey family,[37] who made their fortune in the manufacture of farm implements, supported the musical community of Toronto by providing two important venues: Massey Hall, which opened in 1894 and had superb acoustics for orchestral concerts; and Hart House, a student centre (until 1972 restricted to men) at the University of Toronto that housed a theatre and a large hall where many concerts featuring well-known musicians were presented. The Hart House String Quartet,[38] established in 1924 with funding from the Massey family, gained international recognition and toured North America and Europe until the end of the Second World War. The first violinist, Géza de Kresz, was born in Hungary and had been concertmaster of the Berlin Philharmonic before coming to Toronto in 1923, and cellist Boris Hambourg was a member of the Quartet throughout its existence. Vincent Massey had a lasting influence on music in Canada: as Canada's High Commissioner in London during the Second World War, he played a crucial role in the lives of a number of musical émigrés, and after the war, as chair of the Massey Commission, he did much to influence public policy towards the arts.[39]

Prominent musical families in Montreal included the Masellas, an Italian family that included three horn players, three clarinetists, two violinists, a harpist, a bassoonist, and an oboist. In 1947 clarinetist Rafael Masella became the first Canadian to win a prize at the Geneva International Competition. Many more Canadians would follow.[40] The musical salon maintained by Hélène and Michel Hirvy in their Westmount home served as a launching pad for Walter Joachim. "I saw Klemperer, Pelletier, the critics of all the papers. I also met John Newmark."[41] Other prominent musical patrons in Montreal included Louis Athanase David and his wife. Madame Athanase David was a founder of the Montreal Orchestra in 1930 but she grew disenchanted with Douglas Clarke as conductor and in 1934 threw her resources behind the founding of the Société des concerts symphoniques de Montréal in 1934. Louis-Athanase David, who was provincial secretary at the time, obtained a grant to start the project and Mme David was undoubtedly instrumental in enticing Wilfrid Pelletier to accept the position of conductor. Athanase David and his wife were also among the founders of the Montreal Festivals, a concert series that presented many Montreal and Canadian premières.

OPPORTUNITIES FOR IMMIGRANT MUSICIANS

Canadian efforts at identifying and recruiting central European artists and academics for conservatory teaching positions during the interwar years were sporadic. Two prominent Canadian musicians who were based in New York at the Metropolitan Opera – Wilfrid Pelletier and Edward Johnson – were well aware of the influx of superb musicians arriving in the United States,[42] but did little to assist European artists in coming to Canada, presumably because employment opportunities for musicians were limited. Canadian administrators who did hire central Europeans include Terence MacDermot at Upper Canada College (Arnold Walter), Watson Kirkconnell at Acadia University (Felicita and Jānis Kalejs), and Ifan Williams at the Halifax Conservatory of Music (Ernesto Vinci in 1939, Walter Kaufmann in 1948, and many Latvian émigrés in the postwar years).

Ernest MacMillan was well aware not only of the standard of central European musicians[43] but also of their plight; he played a role in finding jobs for Ernesto Vinci at the Halifax Conservatory,[44] Hans Gruber in the Victoria Symphony (1942), and Hugo Burghauser in the Toronto Symphony (1938). He also knew Emmy Heim well.[45] Whatever plans MacMillan may have had for revitalizing the TCM and the Faculty of Music at the University of Toronto did not include an influx of Austro-German musicians: the above appointments were for positions outside Toronto and Arnold Walter's appointment as head of the Senior School was made in 1944, two years after MacMillan left the TCM. Perhaps his experiences with Heinz Unger, whom he had engaged to conduct the Toronto Symphony in 1937 and 1938, had made him wary of newcomers; there is some evidence of rivalry between the two conductors.[46] The Conservatoire system initiated by Pelletier in Québec was not established until 1944, and employment opportunities there came only in the 1950s.

While MacMillan, Pelletier, and Johnson could likely have done more to provide opportunities for European musicians during those crucial years, it appears that in centres where music institutions existed, émigrés musicians were able to respond to local needs as teaching positions, vacancies in performing ensembles, and other music positions became available.

Needless to say, during the 1920s and 1930s musical life in Canada differed greatly from that of Europe. It is true that aspects of this difference made it difficult at first for many immigrants to adapt to the musical institutions and organizations they found in their new country. It also made it difficult for Canadians to understand their new colleagues. It is also true, however, that Canada presented wonderful opportunities for these musical émigrés, many of whom were relatively young, with the bulk of their careers ahead of them. Canada, in turn, had much to gain from this remarkable group of musicians. It is literally impossible to imagine the second half of the twentieth century without their high levels of talent, skills, and experience, their administrative gifts, and their continued patronage of music.

4

Rebuilding Canada's Post-Secondary Music Education System

By the time the Victorian brick building at the south-west corner of College Street and University Avenue that housed the Royal Conservatory of Music and the Faculty of Music of the University of Toronto met the wrecker's ball in the early 1960s[1] the Anglo-Saxon music tradition that had prevailed inside was also in shambles. A similar drama unfolded in Montreal's Square Mile, as the nineteenth-century homes once occupied by mainly Scottish barons of industry fell or were converted for use by McGill University; Workman House, which housed the McGill Conservatorium, was demolished in 1952.[2] The battle was not between outside forces – the "Prussians," as they were sometimes called, against the British establishment that held sway in these two central Canadian universities – but oddly enough between members of that establishment itself; this group essentially destroyed itself and most of the actors left the stage. In one sense, the fall of British influence in these two centres parallels the demise of a Canadian immigration policy that was originally designed to protect British privilege. It is the story of two men – Arnold Walter and Helmut Blume – both educated in interwar Berlin, and the role of music in the university; their careers dominate the next three chapters of the present study. They were responsible for creating administrative structures that would allow music to flourish at a level comparable to that which they had known in Europe. Much would change as Berlin encountered London and Edinburgh on the university campuses of Toronto and Montreal.

Arnold Walter and Helmut Blume can justifiably be credited with establishing the two musical institutions around which so much of Canada's musical life now revolves – the faculties of music at the University of Toronto and at McGill University. (In 2004 the Fac-

Figure 4.1 Arnold Walter ca. 1930. Reprinted through the courtesy of Upper Canada College Archives, Barbara Barrows Collection.

ulty of Music at McGill University became the Schulich School of Music). Most musicians today probably take these schools for granted, but in the first decade following the Second World War, when our émigrés set to work, the outcome was very much in doubt. Granted these two faculties existed long before the émigrés arrived on the scene, but left to their own devices, it is doubtful whether they would have survived. Arnold Walter's battle in Toronto began earlier and was more protracted. Blume, working in Montreal, was able to build on ideas and programs already in place in Toronto. Both Walter and Blume began their Canadian careers as cogs in the music education apparatus, and gradually transformed existing structures from the bottom up. They had little or no support from senior administrators.

In the Europe that Walter and Blume knew, music in the universities was based on an intellectual pedigree that dated back to classical Greek writers (such as Plato), medieval Latin authors (such as Boethius and Aurelian of Réomé), and continued through the Renaissance to the present day, dedicated to the pursuit of knowledge primarily in verbal form. Music scholarship was an intellectual enterprise that sought to understand the multifarious aspects of music in a historical sense – how things change over time – and in a systematic sense – what does not change over time – aspects of music that are universally valid, such as acoustics, aesthetics, and theory.[3] By the second decade of the twentieth century central Europe also had a vast system of post-secondary schools of music (Hochschulen, Konservatorien, Akademien) in which musical performance was cultivated, usually with a smattering of theoretical subjects. Music performance was carried on in places such as churches and concert halls, but not in universities. This separation of academic and professional aspects of music was rooted in the system: the two disciplines were housed in different buildings where mental attitudes were carefully nurtured to preserve autonomy. (In North America the distinction was made between departments of theory and departments of performance or applied music.) Europe of the 1920s saw a breakdown of this rigid separation when historical performance practice came to be recognized as a scholarly topic.[4] Elements of performance, such as tempo, pitch, ornamentation, dynamics, phrasing, articulation, and instrumentation were now seen as changing aspects of lost or forgotten traditions that could be rediscovered through a systematic study of treatises, manuals, handbooks, artistic representations, period instruments, paleography, and other documents of the period. History was now overlapping performance; the two disciplines were seen as complementary to one another. Description on the side of the musicologists was transformed into prescription for performers. Both disciplines were winners in a new rapport that was to bear considerable fruit in the later decades of the twentieth century.

ARNOLD WALTER AND THE UNIVERSITY OF TORONTO

As a newcomer, Walter had earned his spurs in a seven-year stint of teaching at Upper Canada College and became acquainted with

Toronto's musical establishment through events at the Heliconian Club, the University Women's Club, the Vogt Society, the Home Service Community Centre, and the Royal Canadian Institute. He also served as president of the Society for Contemporary Music with Healey Willan as vice-president. In 1944 the University of Toronto appointed Walter as vice-principal of the TCM, with a mandate to establish a Senior School as an upper-level performance wing. (In August 1947 the Toronto Conservatory of Music became the Royal Conservatory of Music. For the remainder of this chapter it will be referred to by the abbreviation RCM). It has been said that "Everything [Walter] undertook seemed geared to the unfolding of a master plan for music in Canada, a plan conceived in the first few years after his arrival,"[5] but this is highly unlikely. Walter had a social democratic penchant for state support of the arts in higher education but any "master plan" would have been hampered by the realities of the situation he encountered in his new position. He soon found himself embroiled in a struggle between two opposing concepts: a central European orientation, and solidly entrenched British tradition. He must have been frustrated at every turn, continually forced to rethink and re-adjust. Walter did, however, have an uncanny ability to assess and work within a given situation, and Edward Johnson, chair of the RCM board, must have sensed Walter's valuable administrative abilities. Walter's academic record was also impressive: he had been registered simultaneously at the universities of Prague in the law faculty and Berlin in the music faculty. He held a doctorate in law, had attended seminars taught by Europe's pioneering musicologists, and had taken two semesters of medical studies.

Walter set about the task of creating the Senior School with his usual vigour and astute political acumen. In an initial memorandum of 1 October 1944 followed by a more complete version of 1 December he addresses the Board of Governors of the University with the request that the proposal outlining the establishment of the Senior School be forwarded to the provincial government.[6] He describes an "advanced School of Music within the framework of the Conservatory" for which a special appropriation of $50,000 from the provincial government is requested in order to hire full-time salaried staff. With these funds, he argues, an institution could be established that would provide professional music education for performers and avoid the "flight of native talent to the United

States and Europe." He notes also that Ernest Hutcheson, director of the Julliard School of Music in New York, had prepared a similar report for the Conservatory in 1937. (2) The RCM was to be the "most prominent national establishment for the training of Canadian musical talent," and Walter advocated establishing a "strong graduating and professional department, leading either directly to active professional occupation or to the advanced courses of the University." (3) Such a system would eliminate the perceived shortcomings of the RCM: the lack of a rounded music education and poorly paid teachers with little interest in the institution. Although the proposal maintained a fee structure, Walter pointed out that free instruction was offered not only by schools such as Curtis and Julliard in the United States but also by the newly-formed Conservatoire provincial de musique et d'art dramatique in Montreal, which had a budget of $79,600 that was soon to be increased to $100,000. (4)

> We desire to emphasize how important it is for the Province of Ontario to meet competitively the situation created by new developments in Quebec. The most recent step in the encouragement given the arts in Quebec was the establishment a year ago of the Institute of Music (La conservatoire de musique et d'art dramatique), dedicated to the free teaching of all branches of music: instrumental, vocal, and composition. Under the direction of Wilfred [sic] Pelletier of the Metropolitan Opera Company and Claude Champagne, free instruction is open to British subjects living anywhere in Canada. The only stipulation placed on this free musical education is that the candidate must pass a matriculation examination. Not only is free instruction given. Pupils unable to provide musical instruments have been supplied when they enter the school. The instruments are given to them outright on successful completion of the course ... In contrast, it may be noted that direct and indirect grants from the provincial treasure of Ontario, to promote music, are very limited.

The wealth of detail in the report suggests that Walter was in direct contact with Pelletier himself. Walter recommended hiring full-time staff to teach piano, violin, voice, theory, organ, woodwinds, and brass; the cost was to be partially offset by a student fee of $250, so that with the operating grant, the junior division could operate without a deficit. (5) Walter's proposal was accepted. Armed with letterhead proclaiming him Director of the Senior School, replete with a University seal, he set to work.

The "new school of music for advanced study" was announced in July 1945 by Conservatory director Charles Peaker on the editorial pages of the *Globe and Mail*.[7] Details included sixteen new scholarships as well as new departments for piano, headed by Lubka Kolessa, and violin, headed by Kathleen Parlow; programs in singing, composition, and church and organ music were to be initiated the following year. The scholarships were financed primarily by the RCM along with a CAPAC scholarship of $750 and additional awards donated by Lucio Agostini, Neil Chotem, and Samuel Hersenhoren, prominent performing musicians in Toronto. A second *Globe* article about a year later announced a teacher's training course leading to a bachelor of music; Senior School graduates were to receive a Licentiate diploma from the TCM[8] and there were also plans for an opera school that would mount two productions each year.

The proposal and its subsequent actualization reveal Walter's ability to exploit the opportunities of a given situation like an astute politician. What Ontario official could fail to accept the challenge posed by a government-funded Quebec initiative? The Senior School, however, was an imperfect response. The basic problem was that the Conservatory already had a performance function and was unwilling to cede any aspect of its jurisdiction to an entity that seemed to be encroaching on its turf. The Senior School was initially conceived as an upper stratum of the Conservatory (the letterhead printed for the Senior School confirms this) but it immediately came into conflict with the Conservatory's existing Licentiate program in performance. The struggle for meaningful reform of the performance component of the Conservatory became a struggle between a synthesis of European-American music schools and a British system of music teaching personified by two talented, energetic, and willing defenders of the status quo, Ernest MacMillan and Ettore Mazzoleni,[9] who had been educated at Oxford University, had taught at Upper Canada College, and in 1945 had been appointed principal of the TCM.

Walter's most significant achievements during 1946 were the creation of the Opera School and a bachelor of music program in school music. For the degree program, which was based on US

Table 4.1. Music programs and degrees at the Toronto / Royal Conservatory of Music and the Faculty of Music, University of Toronto.

Stage	*Conservatory*			*University*		
A 1944	Licentiate			Mus. Bac.		B.A.
B	Senior School			Mus. Bac.		B.A.
C	Senior School	Licentiate		School of Music		
D 1945	Senior School	Licentiate		Mus. Bac.		B.A.
E 1946	Senior School	Licentiate	Opera School	School Music	Mus.Bac.	B.A.
F 1947	Senior School	Licentiate Course	Opera School	School Music	Mus.Bac.	B.A.
G 1948	Senior School	Licentiate Course	Opera School	School Music	Mus.Bac.	B.A.

This table is a slightly revised version of a chart in a position paper by Arnold Walter, typescript with handwritten revisions, 13 pp. LAC, Arnold Walter fonds (MUS 71), (uncatalogued) vol. 18.

models and intended to train secondary school music teachers, Walter hired two Eastman graduates – Robert Rosevear and Richard Johnston – to teach instrumental and choral performance and music theory in a manner closely oriented toward the US educational system, an initiative that had far-reaching effects on music education programs in other Canadian universities.

Two years later Walter took stock of the developments to date and he drew a pessimistic conclusion. In a position paper written in 1948[10] he alludes to his increasing frustration in trying to establish a distinctive identity for the Senior School that could hold its own against well-endowed US counterparts such as Curtis, Julliard, and Peabody by attracting the best Canadian talents, giving them the finest teachers, and offering degrees comparable to those available elsewhere. The paper includes a table outlining the changing features and relationships of the Conservatory and University music programs over the previous three years (see table 4.1).

In 1944 the Conservatory's Licentiate course had about eight students. The BA program at the Faculty of Music was originally designed as a school music course but was found unsuitable by the Ontario Department of Education. In 1944–45 there were twenty-eight students. The Senior School could have been organized either as the higher stratum of the Conservatory, incorporating the Licentiate program, or as a School of Music at the University, incorporating the existing Mus. Bac. and BA programs. By the time affairs had progressed to stage C (see table 4.1) neither the Licentiate course at the Conservatory nor the Senior School at the University seemed feasible, so the Senior School was set up as an independent two-year course linked to the Conservatory, with no connection to the Faculty of Music. By 1946 (stage D) There were plans to add the Opera School and a school music program to the Senior School. Since, as noted above, the school music course came under the jurisdiction of the Faculty of Music, the Faculty was considerably enlarged. In 1947 the Conservatory's Licentiate course was expanded to two years (stage F); the graduation requirements were practically the same as those for the Senior School. The next year (stage G), in response to the extension of the Licentiate course, the Senior School became a three-year course.

To Walter's regret, Mazzoleni had strengthened the RCM Licentiate program by adding a second year, thus making it an attractive alternative to the Senior School. This in turn had forced Walter to add a third year to the Senior School program. Enrolments for the Licentiate and Senior School programs were almost the same, as were graduation requirements.[11] It seemed that three years of Walter's work in establishing the Senior School had been wasted. The Faculty of Music, with MacMillan as dean, had grown to about fifty students, and the new school music program – pioneered by Walter and originally planned as a Senior School course – had been transferred to the faculty because "the University did not see its way to granting the Senior School the right of conferring degrees."[12] The new two-year RCM Licentiate program had 30 students, and the Senior School only twenty-nine "because of the wholly uncooperative attitude of the Conservatory teachers not employed in the Senior School." In practice, Walter notes, "the Senior School is still struggling to establish its identity at home, after about three years of unremitting hard work." No effort had been made to concentrate resources into one outstanding school, and "the existing organizations were apparently not to be changed in any way." Walter also draws attention to fundamental differences between the Senior School and the Conservatory. "Because of its size, the Conservatory stands for mass production. It caters to thousands of non-professional students, it employs (of necessity) hundreds of mediocre teachers. The Senior School, on the other hand, exists for the most gifted few." Walter set out three options: to merge the Licentiate program into the Senior School; to allow the Senior School to merge into the Licentiate; or to develop the Senior School into a degree-granting school of music similar to those in leading American universities. He concludes that "it is all but impossible to establish the new without changing the old" (11).

Although Walter made frequent references to prestigious music schools south of the border, it would be misleading to conclude that he was intent on following an American model in his reorganization proposals. While he undoubtedly wanted Toronto to have a musical institution equivalent in quality to the Curtis, Julliard, or Peabody schools, he was quite aware that financial resources were limited and that Torontonians could never the match the substantial endowments that supported these well-known American institutions. The fate of educational and cultural institutions left to the vagaries of the marketplace did not sit well with Walter's social democratic ideals. Harvey Olnick remembered,

> [Walter] said to me many times, if you can implant it in the university, it gets paid for by the state; if you leave it outside you're at the mercy of fund raising and fund raising and fund raising. As a matter of fact, Arnold Walter was dedicated to the proposition that outside people would not intrude in the university. This is the antithesis of the American system where you encourage the public and by the same token the fundraisers to get into the thing. He wanted it excluded and he wanted to raise the money straight from the university.[13]

In a paper prepared for his own use, likely that same year, Walter set out the basic incompatibility between his view of a professional music school and that of the existing powers – the Faculty with MacMillan as dean, and the Conservatory with Mazzoleni as principal:

> Sir Ernest MacMillan's point of view: The study of music through performance has no place in a university. The American university school of music is, for that reason, a bad example which should not be followed.

Mr Mazzoleni's point of view: Little change. The Senior School (a disturbing element for some years) should become a department among other departments of the Conservatory, subject to the authority of the principal, without any independence whatsoever, and co-existent with an expanded Licentiate course.

My own point of view: Both the music department of the university and the Conservatory should be changed a great deal. There should be only one advanced school of music under the university: one focal point to attract all available talent in English-speaking Canada. The courses now under the faculty of music would be included in such a school; the Conservatory would lose its newly expanded Licentiate course: otherwise it would remain what it always was – a vast collection of virtually independent studios. Of course, the Conservatory should be stripped of its power to resist all changes and innovations.[14]

The Senior School owed much of its prestige to its teaching faculty: Kolessa and Parlow filled that expectation admirably. Kolessa had been teaching at the TCM since 1942 and her success as a performer in New York heightened awareness of the Senior School. Parlow, a brilliant violinist with an impressive international career, had been a member of the TCM faculty since 1941.[15]

In 1949 Walter prepared a "Memorandum Respecting the Establishment of a School of Music of the University of Toronto."[16] This proposal, which may have been forwarded to the University of Toronto Board, builds on ideas expressed in his earlier "Report on the Senior School." Here he minces no words, pointing to the 1937 Hutcheson Report that castigated the TCM as "a clearing house for private teachers ... lacking a strong graduating and professional department." Hutcheson had recommended that the Conservatory be reduced in size and separated into a preparatory school and a graduate (senior or professional) school coupled with an increase in scholarship funds. Walter notes that the Senior School had been established on a rather "tentative and experimental basis" with the result that as of 1949, in addition to the Faculty's bachelor of music courses, which had been expanded considerably, there were two graduating departments in the Conservatory (Licentiate and Senior School). Walter recommends a university school of music that would integrate professional music training with general education so as to avoid the division between the education of scholars and that of performers that had its roots in outdated European models.[17] The school of music was to grant degrees in performance – an idea embraced by the National Association of Schools of Music in the United States: "It is rather an old-fashioned idea to consider the study of music through performance a form of manual training unsuitable for College credit." Moreover, all advanced performance training was to take place at the school of music, leaving the Conservatory as a junior or preparatory school. Such a structure would allow the Senior School to fulfil its original mandate as a degree-granting professional department of the Conservatory that included courses taken within the Faculty of Music. Walter also envisions a graduate department, and notes that the solution of this music education dilemma hinged on acquiring proper facilities, equipment, and a faculty of salaried teachers.

On 22 February 1950 Sidney Smith, president of the University of Toronto, convened a meeting with Edward Johnson, Ettore Mazzoleni, Ernest MacMillan, and Arnold Walter to make recommendations to the RCM Board regarding reorganization.[18] MacMillan outlined the prevailing system with British-type bachelor of music degrees in music education and in theory and composition and a bachelor honours degree, with performance provided in either the Senior School or the Conservatory. Mazzoleni suggested a fusion of university degree courses and Conservatory and Senior School diploma courses into a university school of music similar to models in the United States. Sidney Smith proposed a college of music similar to the University's four arts colleges and the college of education. Mazzoleni (with MacMillan's agreement) balked at this suggestion, stating that all college level training, including University degree courses, should be under Conservatory jurisdiction because of its long-established position in music education and the fact that Conservatory facilities, faculty, and equipment would be essential to all units. Smith argued that such Conservatory control would take "degree work away from the University." Mazzoleni replied that the proposed united graduating courses would still be controlled "nominally by the Senate of the University."

By 1952 matters had come to a head, as Sidney Smith continued attempts to obtain agreement for reorganization. A "Statement Approved Unanimously by the Board of Directors of the Royal

Conservatory of Music of Toronto,"[19] circulated in February 1952 outlines Smith's model and states that "in order for the new college of music [to preserve] all the prestige, influence and good-will that have been built up by the Royal Conservatory of Music over a term of years it was decided that the new college would be known as the Royal Conservatory of Music of Toronto ... This new and enlarged Royal Conservatory of Music will be divided into two parts: the School of Music (the former Conservatory) and the Faculty of Music." The School of Music, headed by a principal, was to continue the Conservatory's present programs, except for the Licentiate program, the current graded instruction, and the Opera School; a department of ballet and drama might eventually be added. The Faculty of Music, headed by a director, would be responsible for all degree programs as well as the Licentiate and Artist Diplomas formerly conferred by the Conservatory, since the degree and diploma courses involved common academic work. Smith envisioned the Faculty of Music students as a more compact group, most of whom would later pursue professional careers as performers, teachers, or supervisors. He asserted that the two heads (the principal of the School of Music and the director of the Faculty of Music) would be "on the same level," and would be supplemented by a council drawn from the teaching staff of both School and Faculty, functioning as a liaison between the two divisions and the University Senate. Mazzoleni was offered the position of principal of the School of Music with the added responsibility of the Opera School. The new Royal Conservatory of Music of Toronto "college," was to be headed by a dean, with Edward Johnson filling this position until an appointment was made. Smith also promised to work toward obtaining salary security and possibly retirement pensions for RCM teaching staff. Smith's plan was intended to preserve the prestige of existing diplomas and certificates, and he concluded with a plea for unity: "The Conservatory is larger than any individual and the cause to be served has greater national significance than any minor issues that have arisen in controversy during the past weeks."

The choice of dean was a significant bone of contention. Mazzoleni, supported by MacMillan, had designs on the position; Smith favoured seventy-three-year-old Edward Johnson for the job. When Johnson turned down the offer MacMillan pressured Smith on behalf of Mazzoleni and announced his resignation as dean of the Faculty of Music on 30 June 1952, when the reorganization would be complete. Mazzoleni in a huff resigned as Conservatory principal, but a few days later, without consulting MacMillan, withdrew his resignation and gave public support to the reorganization, leaving MacMillan to feel betrayed both by Mazzoleni and the University.[20]

Meanwhile an emissary had been dispatched to London, England to search for a suitable replacement, "preferably someone with a title."[21] Boyd Neel, O.B.E. a British-born medical doctor who had conducting experience but had never pursued music professionally, was appointed dean and given the unpleasant task of keeping the warring parties at bay.[22] The whole situation made the newspapers and became something of a cause célèbre. The public reaction to a performance of Godfrey Ridout's new oratorio *Esther* at Massey Hall in June 1952, conducted by Ettore Mazzoleni, was overwhelming.[23] Ridout, one of many British-influenced Canadian musicians, was the obvious darling of the crowd. Oskar Morawetz remembered the occasion: "When Ridout arrived on the stage, it was like the king had arrived. [The applause] was not so much for Ridout as against Walter."[24]

Sidney Smith, principal of the University of Toronto, did nothing to conceal his personal animosity toward Walter, describing him as having – "overwhelming ambition, Teutonic mentality, and an individualism to the extent of failing to work with others,"[25] and Smith's successor, Claude Bissell (whose brother Keith Bissell was a composer of note)[26] displayed a similar attitude toward the "outsider." Teachers at the Conservatory TCM were also united in their opposition to the newcomer.[27] To accomplish any meaningful change at the Faculty of Music in Toronto against such overwhelming odds is remarkable and the battle had its costs. Walter almost despaired of realizing his vision.

Harvey Olnick's description paints a vivid picture of the administrative situation: "Boyd Neel came here as ... the dean of the Royal Conservatory ... he never had any duties but one. He was told by Sidney Smith to sit with Arnold Walter and Mazzoleni at a meeting every Wednesday at ten o'clock and if they didn't agree, to cast the deciding vote."[28] Boyd Neel confirms Olnick's statement: "They both appeared and sat at the table with their backs to each other. By the end of the first hour the angle of incidence had decreased to forty-five degrees and, by the end of the first meeting, we were all facing the table! Having gained their confidence, I suggested that the three of us should meet every Wednesday morning, a custom we kept up for some ten years."[29]

In a very real sense Walter was not party to the reorganization undertaken by Smith and he remained aloof from the brinkmanship of MacMillan and Mazzoleni. He was, however, able to work with the administrative infrastructure that the university administration had left him and the next decade gave him the opportunity for substantial program building. It is a tribute to Walter's capable administration that he was able to make substantial modifications to the Faculty of Music while still retaining elements of the British system. The result was a rich palette of courses including a performance degree and graduate studies in musicology, music theory, music education, and performance. The fact that he never became dean likely did not bother him; he retained the title of director of the Faculty of Music until his retirement in 1968. In retrospect it is unfortunate that true peace was not maintained between Walter and the Anglo-Saxons. Walter had tried in his own way to ingratiate himself with that establishment. He had made beautiful music as a harpsichordist with the Oxford-educated Mazzoleni conducting, his symphony had been performed by the TSO with MacMillan conducting, he had served on an executive with Healey Willan, and he had taught recorder to the children of the privileged at Upper Canada College, again as a colleague of Mazzoleni.

By 1956 Mazzoleni had become reconciled to the existence of the Senior School. Although the RCM's Associateship examinations offered successful candidates the priviledge of adding ARCT to their names, he knew that there was little more that the Conservatory could offer to advanced performers.[30]

Walter often alluded to developments in music education south of the border and noted Howard Hanson's view that degrees in performance were becoming more essential, but there is no evidence that Walter intended to copy a particular American model: "Our main task must obviously consist in evolving a Canadian pattern in co-existence with the US."[31] It is ironic that the majority of models that Canadians often refer to as American actually follow European patterns in which there is a distinct separation between the academic and performance functions. The variety of post-secondary music education in the United States includes strictly academic music faculties (Columbia and Harvard), universities that physically separate academic studies from performance (Yale), and the wide range of endowed schools of music specializing in performance, with or without a preparatory department (Peabody, New England Conservatory, Julliard, Curtis). Private donors take the place of state support. There are also examples of combined facilities in Midwestern universities and music schools that exist primarily for supplying bands for recreational and sports events. There was no US model for the Opera School; instead, the Opera School was conceived as a replication of a provincial European opera house. Walter's achievement was to create a Canadian model that differed significantly from the British, European, and US paradigms. It seems that the slow genesis of music education in Toronto was based not on one particular model but was rather the result of Walter's ability to build upon the situation as he found it, incorporating elements from all three traditions.

Following the 1952 upheaval – in which Walter played virtually no part and through which his British rivals had unwittingly left him a free hand – Walter set out to accomplish some serious institution building. In 1954 he created the first musicology chair in Canada and hired Harvey Olnick to establish a program.[32] Robert Rosevear, Walter's assistant, briefed Olnick on the local scene, "trying to put the best face on Toronto in the 50s – a formidable task." Impressed by Walter's learning, Olnick enquired about the state of the music collection. "Walter neatly side-tracked that by observing that the library was temporarily closed. I later learned that he had a master key. In time I understood why."[33] After complaining about the poor state of the faculty's holdings, Olnick convinced the chief librarian that a music collection for the entire university would be desirable, and proceeded to obtain financial and administrative backing for the project. In time this music library became the finest music resource in Canada.

The Edward Johnson Building was planned by a building committee chaired by Boyd Neel, but it must be seen as the physical evidence of Walter's goals for university-level music education in Toronto: it had classrooms, rehearsal rooms, a library, a concert hall for solo and chamber music (that after the mid-1970s included a two-manual, tracker-action Casavant organ) and a magnificent theatre, eminently suitable for opera productions, with one of the largest stages in Toronto and a hydraulic orchestra pit that could accommodate sixty musicians. Walter's lecture on the occasion of the dedication of the Edward Johnson Building in 1962, entitled

"Music in the University"[34] (see appendix C), reveals his keen awareness of the position music education played in Europe and America and the model he pioneered for Canada. He points with pride to the fact that performance had taken its rightful position alongside academic music studies in a state-supported structure similar to the European Hochschulen or American schools of music, and he alludes to the necessity of educating musicians – rather than training technicians – as a process that can best be achieved within an academic framework.

The transformation of the Faculty of Music went through several stages. In 1953, the extramural general music program was disbanded and the bachelor of music programs in composition and history and literature of music were instituted. In 1954 masters programs in composition, musicology, and music education came into being.[35] In 1965 the Senior School was replaced by a four-year bachelor program in performance, completing the goal of bringing post-secondary performance into the university. That same year a doctoral program in musicology was instituted. In 1968 the Faculty of Music was divided into four sections – composition, history and literature, music education, and performance – and the groundwork was laid for hiring Canadian-born and -educated John Beckwith as dean in 1970. The Opera School had been relocated to the newly built MacMillan Theatre in 1963 but remained under the administration of the Conservatory. Mazzoleni held the position of director until 1966. In 1969 the Opera School became the opera department of the Faculty of Music. (See table 4.2 for a comparison of course and program changes in the music faculties of the University of Toronto and McGill University.)

Under Walter the Faculty of Music in Toronto established Canada's first institutional electronic music studio in 1959, with assistance from Hugh LeCaine of the National Research Council. Walter also introduced the Orff method to Canada, first by supporting Doreen Hall's studies in Salzburg, and in 1955 hiring her to teach Orff classes at the faculty.[36]

Walter was also active in musical matters on the national scene. In 1965 he was a co-founder, with Helmut Blume, of the Canadian Association of University Schools of Music (CAUSM, after 1971 the Canadian University Music Society, CUMS).[37] While Blume had organized the initial meeting of university representatives in July 1964, Walter gradually assumed a leadership role and served as the

Table 4.2. A chronology of course and program developments in the faculties of music at the University of Toronto and McGill University, 1944 to 1987

Date	*University of Toronto*	*McGill University*
1944	Walter hired to initiate Senior School	
1946	Walter initiates Opera School; Walter initiates Music Education program and hires Robert Rosevear and Richard Johnston	Blume hired as piano instructor
1949		Anhalt hired
1952	Re-organization into School and Faculty of Music, with Mazzoleni as principal of the School and Walter as director of the Faculty	
1953	Boyd Neel appointed as Dean	
1953–54	BMus degree in composition and in history and literature of music initiated	
1954	Walter hires Harvey Olnick as musicologist; MMus degrees in composition, musicology and music education initiated	
1955		Clarke leaves; Duchow, Brott, and Blume (triumvirate) appointed; Duchow appointed Acting Dean Opera School initiated
1956		BMus degrees in performance, school music, and composition initiated in a 4-year program many new appointments Denis Stevens appointed dean, Nov.
1957		Stevens's appointment rescinded, June Duchow continues as acting-dean
1958		Artist Diploma and Concert Diploma
1959	Electronic music studio established	Anhalt presents electronic music concert
1962	Edward Johnson Building inaugurated	
1963	BMus program extended to four years	Duchow resigns as acting-dean; Blume appointed acting dean
1964		Blume appointed dean; electronic music studio established
1965	Senior School dissolved; BMus in Performance (four-year) initiated; PhD in musicology initiated	

Table 4.2 continued

1966	Kolinski hired as ethnomusicologist	BMus degrees in theory and history initiated
1968	Walter retires; Faculty reorganized into four divisions: composition, history, music education, and performance	MMA degrees in composition and musicology initiated
1969		Israel Katz hired as ethnomusicologist
1970	John Beckwith appointed dean	MMA degree in theory initiated
1971		Strathcona Building inaugurated
1975		Pollack Hall inaugurated
1976–77		MMus degrees in performance and composition renamed; MA degrees in theory and musicology renamed; Paul Pedersen appointed dean
1978		BMus and MA degrees in School Music initiated
1979		MMus program in Sound Recording initiated
1981		BMus in Jazz performance initiated
1988		PhD program in musicology, theory and school music initiated

first president in 1965–67. István Anhalt was one of McGill delegates to the conference.[38] The role of CAUSM was to facilitate dialogue between administrators and teachers of music at the university level, propose minimum standards for music degree programs, and encourage the professional development of both institutional and individual members. Now affiliated with the Learned Societies it has become an integral part of the Canadian academic mosaic. Walter served as president of the Canadian Music Council and the Canadian Music Centre, and was chair of the editorial board of the *Canadian Music Journal* (1956–62), a short-lived but valiant foray into the area of serious music criticism in Canada. Two of his essays – "Education in Music" (1955) and "The Growth of Music Education" (1969) – present excellent summaries of the development of music education in Canada. The introduction of "The Growth of Music Education" states: "All these migrations, peregrinations, and pilgrimages are based on the assumption that foreign schools are better than even the best Canadian ones ... Are they really better? Not in Europe." Walter praises Gilles Lefebvre for his efforts in bringing serious music to many students and communities through Jeunesses Musicales, and he also stresses the role of organizations such as CAMMAC and the Banff School of Fine Arts as well as CBC radio and television broadcasts of serious music.[39] On the international stage Walter served as president of the International Society of Music Educators and the Inter-American Music Council.[40] His social-democratic ideals, learned in his student days, stood him in good stead as he continued to use the international forum to plead for continued and ongoing state support for music education.

Walter sometimes used his formidable knowledge of art and music to intimidate or to provide valuable guidance. At his oral examination, Walter Kemp (who had previously incurred Walter's wrath by neglecting to ask his permission before performing Bach's Brandenburg Concerto no. 5 with a student orchestra) was faced with the question, "And what do you know about the theories of Johannes Kepler?"[41] Walter seemed equally "frightening" and "remote" to Edward Laufer, who had moved from Halifax to study at the University of Toronto because Toronto was the musical centre of Canada.[42] On their arrival in Toronto, Laufer and his father, Dr Srul Laufer paid a visit to Walter. Dr Laufer spoke German with Walter. Edward Laufer understood their conversation, knowing German from his youth. He passed the dreaded "Viva Voce," facing a group of examiners led by Walter, with flying colours, giving ample evidence of his knowledge of the required work (Bartók's Piano Concerto no. 3) and discussing at length Mahler's Symphony no. 6, a work that was virtually unknown in Toronto at that time (Laufer had only recently obtained a score). Laufer also remembers well a consultation in which Walter assured the young student that he should utilize every hour of the day to the maximum.

Walter would occasionally fraternize with students in the Conservatory cafeteria. Most first-year Artist Diploma students who were required to take Walter's history course were in awe of this man who seemed to know so much, but Walter would point to scholars such as Donald Francis Tovey, who could not only cite the page of a book on which a particular detail could be found, but also tell you the particular stack, shelf, and in the British Museum where this book was kept. Asked by a graduate student how a distinguished composer such as Gustav Mahler could come from such an unimportant town, Walter replied that many other important people also came from insignificant towns; then he sat down at the piano and immediately played Wagner's Prelude to *Tristan and Isolde* from memory.

Years later Alan Gillmor remembered in vivid detail how Walter, in a gentle manner, led him to his epiphany. He had been shunted from one thesis advisor to another and was at a standstill with his dissertation:

> I recall my first meeting with him, sitting in his office peering up at him seated behind a large desk, the light from a west window in a late winter afternoon pouring in behind him onto me like a spotlight, while he sat smoking a cigarette, smoke curling around his face; and then a voice breaking the silence with: "*Sagen Sie mir, kennen Sie Deutsch?*" Fortunately, I did know a little Deutsch and that seemed to please him. Anyway, my fears came to nought. He was a marvelous advisor. We would meet frequently, sometimes in his book-lined home, and he was a fund of knowledge and sound advice. One of his favourite techniques was to casually slide a book across his desk and say, "You might want to have a look at this." It could be anything from the works of Hermann Hesse (*The Glass Bead Game*) to Poggioli's *Theory of the Avant-Garde* ... It was the Poggioli book that finally broke a log jam for me. I believe I was Arnold's last doctoral student, for he died not long after my defence. I owe him a very great deal. Here's a man who simply did not allow his musical prejudices to get in the way.[43]

Walter was a father figure in Helmut Kallmann's career. Kallmann had been sent to England on the Kindertransport (both of his parents perished in the Holocaust) and had come to Canada as a "Camp Boy," On release from the Sherbrooke camp in 1943, he went immediately to Toronto: "I found that they had a music library on College Street. I went there and this was August and unfortunately the sign said that the Music Library was closed during the month of August and so I could hardly wait until the library opened ... there were stacks and stacks of books about music ... It was a gold mine."[44] In Toronto he met Arnold Walter and his wife and for six months did household chores in their Rosedale home in return for free room and board and the use of a grand piano. "When they had company I would be asked in and sit with them. This was ... like out of a novel by Thomas Mann. These were strictly nineteenth century, upper-crust, aristocratic, highly educated women who read Goethe all the time and listened to Hugo

Wolf songs." Walter advised Kallman to take the new bachelor of music course in school music because he did not play piano that well. Kallmann began the program in 1946, the first year it was offered. His teachers were Leo Smith ("He had never studied the *Harvard Dictionary!*"), Healey Willan, and Walter, whose course on music history from Wagner to the present particularly captured Kallmann's interest.

Perhaps Harvey Olnick, in his inimitable manner, best summarized Walter's achievements:

> "[Walter] was the one person who could have started things going here. Everybody else blew their mouth out, but he did it, and what his faults were, what the hell, they're not important. It's what he did that is important, and I respected him from the moment I met him to the moment he died."
>
> I fought with him, and you had to fight with that guy because he had fixed views, but I think he respected me as he didn't do many others. Because I think I was the only one who was invited to his home for dinner, a private dinner, and who was there – before either of these people had any acclaim at all. One was a literary critic, Norry Frye, and the other was the TV man, Marshall McLuhan. Marshall McLuhan that evening, at dinner, gave out already one of his crazy things and Nory Frye assassinated him, demolished him from top to bottom. But Walter knew them, he thought I should know them, so he was an astute guy.[45]

In 1972 Arnold Walter was invested into the Order of Canada and a portrait of him by Artin Cavouk hangs in the foyer of the Edward Johnson Building. He died in Toronto on 6 October 1973.

HELMUT BLUME AND MCGILL UNIVERSITY

What background could have prepared Blume to keep a steady hand on the tiller when the wind and the waves were against him at McGill University? Blume was a native Berliner, born on Easter Sunday, 1914. His father was a respected psychologist who continued his practice in Berlin through the Second World War apparently without hindrance. During his years at the Hochschule (1932–38) young Blume studied with Paul Hindemith,[46] and continued to correspond with Hindemith until the 1940s. To earn extra money after he graduated from the Hochschule in 1938, Blume accompanied singers, ballet troupes in Berlin, and ensembles on tours throughout France.[47] At one such performance he found himself playing the national anthem, rather shakily he later admitted, for a presentation at which Adolf Hitler was present. On another occasion he performed with a ballet troupe when Joseph Goebbels, a lover of ballet, was in the audience. Aware that the political situation was deteriorating quickly and that he was at risk (his grandmother was Jewish),[48] he made plans to leave Germany. While serving as an accompanist for a Berlin ensemble on tour in France, he secured a commitment from the École russe de musique in Paris that he would be allowed to study there so that he could obtain a valid visa to leave Germany. In September 1938, however, he was called to serve his obligatory eight-week military training in Küstrin (now Kostrzynin).[49]

> I survived seven weeks but then could not take it any longer and feigned a schizophrenic attack, running around shouting that if the spirits came I was going to shoot my commanding officers. I was then sent to Berlin to the doctor in charge (*Oberarzt*) for a consultation. Awaiting my rendezvous with the doctor at home, I was arrested at 3:00 a.m. on a charge of desertion (*Fahnenflucht*); I still remember the charge being yelled out at the top of the officer's voice. I spent a night in prison, but the charge was dropped when my father forced me to undergo an (unneeded) appendectomy, necessitating a seven-day period of recuperation in the hospital. This allowed me to fulfill my eight-week requirement. Then, with letter in hand from the École russe de musique in Paris stating that I could study there, I received my passport and visa and left Germany legally. I went from Paris to Canterbury, England, in 1939 where I began to teach piano.[50] On Sunday May 1940 I, along with several thousand other "enemy aliens," was arrested and sent to a detention camp in Huyton to await deportation abroad. I was scheduled to board the *Arandora Star* but since that boat had already been filled with detainees, was forced to await the next boat. The *Arandora Star* was sunk by a German torpedo on 2 July. I boarded the SS *Ettrick* for an adventurous voyage across the ocean, not knowing where I was headed.[51]

Blume may have had aspirations of becoming a concert pianist but although he continued to perform in eastern Canada with former "Camp Boys," he turned to other career choices. His release from camp was sponsored by Lady Hamilton, a patron of the arts who had studied music in Leipzig in 1888 and knew Brahms and Clara Schumann[52] so Blume went directly to Toronto to thank her and her architect husband. This grande dame was over eighty at the time; she rented out her coach house to Blume and gave him a beautiful Steinway grand that is still in the possession of his widow, Ljerka Blume.[53] Blume stayed in Toronto from 1942 to 1944; he was head of the piano department at the Hambourg Conservatory and he studied with Alberto Guerrero at the TCM. In 1944 he moved to Ottawa to work with the Wartime Information Board and in December of that year moved to Montreal to begin a long career with the CBC as head of the German-language section of the International Service.

Blume's stint as propaganda and music director for the CBC International Service in Montreal earned him great respect among his colleagues, and the administrative skills he gained through these years were put to good use in his dealings with the administration at McGill University. Eric Koch described him in official capacities, as "always calm and diplomatic. He had nerves of steel, and like a mole, stuck to his guns."[54]

When Blume first came to McGill University in 1946, as a part-time piano instructor, paid at an hourly rate with no benefits, he likely had no idea that his efforts there would result in a radical transformation of music education at McGill University, the premier anglophone music institution in Quebec. In retrospect it appears as if the pieces of the music puzzle fell inexorably into place, but Blume and his colleagues encountered a myriad of obstacles, many of them linked to the British system and musicians committed to defending the status quo. As in Toronto it was a slow and sometimes awkward process for a central European to shape an advanced institution that could train the finest musicians in a variety of fields.

In 1946 the McGill Faculty of Music (now the Schulich School of Music) was geared to training organists in fugue and counterpoint. The Faculty was affiliated with the performance-oriented McGill Conservatorium of Music, which offered Associate and Licentiate diplomas. A bachelor of music degree required about two years of study but there were no residency requirements and few courses were offered.[55] The calendar states that the "Conservatorium offers courses leading to the degree of bachelor of music through the faculty."[56] In the early postwar years there were fifteen to twenty students and the Faculty had only one full-time position: the dean, who was also director of the Conservatorium. This dual appointment, which continued through the 1960s, spared McGill the faculty/conservatory jurisdictional wrangling that occurred in Toronto. Douglas Clarke (1892–1962), a British-born and educated musician, had been appointed director of the Conservatorium in 1929 and dean of the Faculty of Music in 1930. Part-time staff members included Claude Champagne (from 1932 to 1941), Alexander Brott (appointed in 1939), and Marvin Duchow (appointed in 1944). Istvan Anhalt came to McGill in 1949 on a three-year Lady Davis Fellowship,[57] and when this ended, Clarke hired him to teach piano and a course on analysis. In 1956 Duchow appointed Anhalt as assistant professor. Anhalt recalls that the Faculty "was really going from year to year on life support ... It was a dying faculty of music. Douglas Clarke was presiding over a mere corpse."[58]

The 50th anniversary of the McGill Conservatorium, celebrated with a series of concerts through November and December 1954, proved to be Clarke's undoing. The concerts were auspicious enough – a program of Anhalt's compositions, a piano recital by Blume, and an orchestral concert, played by professional musicians conducted by Clarke in a program that included Vaughn Williams's Sea Symphony and Saint-Saens' Piano Concerto in G minor with Ellen Ballon as soloist. The orchestral concert was a financial disaster. Anhalt commented, "I had a feeling that McGill wanted to get rid of the man and didn't know how, but by accusing him of having lost so much money on these concerts they somehow used that as leverage to give him early retirement. So he retired at age 61 or 62, married Octavia Wilson who was a former student of his, and mine too, and they went to live in England."[59] Clarke died in England in 1962.

Clarke's departure in 1955 marked a turning point. The University struck a Principal's Committee chaired by Marvin Duchow (in charge of theoretical subjects), with Alexander Brott (in charge of orchestral instruments and related instrumental subjects and performances), and Helmut Blume (in charge of keyboard, radio, TV, opera, and vocal subjects).[60] This triumvirate hoped to get things moving. On 5 April 1955 they submitted a twenty-five-page "Report by the Principal's Committee on Plans for the Reorganization of the Faculty and the Conservatorium of Music of McGill University" to Cyril James, principal of McGill University.[61] In the words of the University archivist, "Cyril James's term as Principal of McGill ... opened an era of greater control by his office over all aspects of the administration of the University. His Principalship was marked by the expansion of the university's commitment in a number of traditional fields as well as its involvement into new ones."[62] This is certainly true with respect to the affairs of the Faculty of Music. While rumours within the faculty concerned the possible closure of the music faculty, this report and a later report in December spoke of "expansion" and "increase." The Faculty of Music was to become a "centre" for music in McGill University and in anglophone Montreal. The concept of "professional training" outlined in the April document also represented a marked change of direction. Marvin Duchow wrote the section on theoretical subjects (4–8), and Alexander Brott the section on orchestral and instrumental subjects (9–14). The innovative proposals in Helmut Blume's section on "keyboard, radio (television), opera, and vocal subjects" (15–21) reveal his continued interest in music technology gained from his work at the CBC. He proposed the purchase of a harpsichord and suggested that Greta Kraus be hired as a teacher (16). He recommended the establishment of a radio and television music school (17) with courses in recording, microphone technique, and programming of music broadcasts. He also recommended an opera school (17–8), modelled on the RCM Opera School and on the CBC Opera Company, along with courses in opera history, opera repertory, and coaching sessions. "An eighteenth-century opera not involving more than three or four roles and a small chamber orchestra might be contemplated for production at the end of the second year." Other proposals included a schola cantorum modelled on Celia Bizony's "Musica Antica e Nuova,"[63] and a summer music school incorporating George Little's experience with the Otter Lake camp (18–19).

At a meeting on 6 July 1955 to discuss these proposals James questioned "whether the training of brilliant performers was the function of the University?" and added that "performers were not taking the full university courses and therefore were not eligible for scholarships."[64] He suggested that students interested only in performance should enrol as partials. In his view, the music department had three goals: to train outstanding musicians, to train outstanding teachers, and to acquaint the University population with music. "The only basis for the Faculty of Music is to do what the Conservatoire cannot do." Mindful that in Montreal performance students would always be attracted to the completely state-supported Conservatoire de musique de Montréal, James felt McGill needed to offer a much broader education if it were to continue to attract performance students.

An interim report of December 1955[65] points to progress made. Marvin Duchow, now acting dean, had expanded the theoretical and arts courses in the bachelor of music program, and instruction in radio, opera, and harpsichord had begun. A proposed music education program to train instrumental teachers for the Protestant school system was also being developed, and twenty-seven additional instructors had been hired for theoretical and practical subjects. It was undoubtedly Blume who made the contact with Montreal musicians and could gradually extend part-time Conservatorium positions to full-time Faculty positions once the administrative structures allowed for this.[66] The past year had indeed been a turning point. Many of the new faculty members hired in 1955 stayed at McGill for the next twenty to thirty years, including a number of émigrés from Central Europe: Mario Duschenes, Arthur Garami, Walter Joachim, Erwin Marcus, Charles Reiner, and Luba Zuk. Canadians who joined the faculty include Kelsey Jones, who made his harpsichord available to students (Greta Kraus could not be persuaded to move from Toronto), Carl Little, who was to teach broadcasting studio techniques and production, and Neil Chotem, who taught composition and arranging for radio, television, and film. Attempts at establishing a music library also were undertaken. Unfortunately proposals for a ballet and drama school were withdrawn in January 1957.[67]

Enrolment in these years remained unsatisfactory. István Anhalt, chair of the theory department, remembers strategy sessions in which full-time faculty members Alexander Brott and Marvin Duchow would protest to Blume that they could not admit a particular student because she or he did not have the proper qualifications. "We accused him of roping in students from Sherbrooke Street. 'Never mind,' Blume would reply, 'he (or she) is a very enthusiastic person,' and adding 'If you don't have students, you have no school.'" So the faculty was obliged to work with the students that Blume was able to find.[68] It was a trying time for all. In some years there was no orchestra for Alexander Brott to conduct, but Blume threw himself into the task. Anhalt commented that Blume was "really a partner in building up the theory department, before performance. Strength came first in the theory and composition department because McGill was quite willing to pay the salaries of musicologists and composers, but not performers. But in the 1970s, Blume was able to sell the idea of full-time positions for performers."[69]

Since performance had always been affiliated with the faculty of music through the Conservatorium, Cyril James was not opposed to performance per se, but he did have reservations about performance as part of the Faculty of Music, arguing that "performers don't publish," and therefore could not earn academic status. Blume countered this objection by pointing out that "every time a performer goes on stage he or she submits him/herself to peer review in a public forum and hence, for all intents and purposes, publishes."[70] Blume's argument won the day and performance gained equivalent-to-academic standing, allowing him to hire full-time faculty in the performance area. The bachelor of music in performance, initiated in 1956 (the second such program in Canada)[71] saw its first graduate in 1959: Ann Bonathan. The possibility of fruitful cross-fertilization of the two complementary aspects of music – the analytical and the practical – now became a reality as the Faculty of Music entered a period of growth that could scarcely have been imagined in the 1950s.

Luba Zuk commented that Blume "put the McGill Faculty of Music on the map. In 1955, he started sending small ensembles to different functions, to play in Redpath Library, on the terrace, to play in front of Moyse Hall, to play at the Principal's receptions. He said 'They have to know we exist.'"[72] The community outreach undertaken by faculty members was an important aspect of the new approach. A McGill String Quartet (the third ensemble to bear that name) had been founded by Alexander Brott in 1939, and with some changes of membership, remained active until the early 1950s, presenting varied repertoire, often with guest artists; cellist Lotte Goetzel joined the quartet in the 1944–45 season. The McGill Chamber Music Society, formed in 1947 to sponsor the McGill Quartet concerts, began to include chamber orchestra concerts led by Alexander Brott and over the years the orchestra concerts increased in number. When the Quartet ceased activities in 1953, this orchestra of about fifteen players became the McGill Chamber Orchestra,[73] which continued to present a combination of classical and modern repertoire. Through the "interregnum" years (1955–63) the Faculty of Music presented the Ellen Ballon lecture series, which brought internationally-established musicologists, music educators, performers, and composers to Montreal. Recitals by faculty members also became a regular feature of McGill and Montreal musical life. Early-afternoon campus concerts presented by Faculty and Conservatorium students gave the general public an opportunity to keep abreast of musical developments within the faculty, and in the 1957–58 season McGill singers and orchestra musicians launched their first opera production.

When Clarke retired in 1955, Marvin Duchow had been appointed acting dean, but it appeared that British-Born Cyril James felt that the position of dean would best be filled by a British candidate. His choice – Denis Stevens – had a superb combination of academic and professional credentials: Stevens was a distinguished musicologist with an impressive publication record, an extensive performing background as conductor, and broadcasting experience at the BBC.[74] Bringing in an outsider can always create difficulties but James, who ultimately bore the responsibility for this decision, may have felt that not enough progress was being made on the local level and that only an external appointment from Britain would bring order to the Faculty of Music. In his history of McGill University, Stanley Frost notes that "an apparently brilliant appointment of yet another Englishman proved unpopular and he had literally to be paid not to come to McGill."[75] What Frost does not point out is that this appointment precipitated a sea change within the faculty. The Board of Governors who appointed Stevens as "Professor of Music and Dean of the Faculty of Music" at a meeting on 21 November 1956[76] would have had no idea that the end of this appointment, and of British domination at the music-administrative level at McGill, could be triggered by something as innocuous as recommendations for a lecture series.

Each year the McGill Faculty of Music organized a Faculty Lecture Series that presented distinguished international musicians to the Montreal public. The lecture series began in 1951 and was originally known as the Ellen Ballon Lecture Series. At a meeting on 29 January 1957 it was decided that the series for the next year should consist of six lectures: four musicologists (series A) and two lectures of a more popular nature (series B). Stevens, as the new dean, was asked to suggest names for Series A, and the inaugural lecture of the four was to be given by Stevens himself. Ellen Ballon, possibly the most distinguished McGill music graduate from the first half of the twentieth century,[77] was to propose speakers for Series B.

At the following Faculty meeting, held on 27 February 1957, Duchow presented Stevens's objections to Ballon's nominations. Duchow remarked that "Present as an invited guest was Dr Ballon, whose arguments tended to stray from a defense of her nominees to a vindication of the popular lectures as such." (Ballon had proposed Ernest Ansermet and Thomas Schippers). In a letter to Stevens, who was still in England, of 5 March 1957, Duchow noted that the lecture series was divided between scholarly and popular presentations and that the popular lectures had an "earlier function of creating favourable public interest in – and, it is hoped, support of – the activities of this Faculty." He also recommended that Stevens include a French scholar because of the provincial orientation toward France, and concurred with Stevens's choices of Friedrich Blume and Egon Wellesz.

In a letter to Duchow of 10 March 1957, Stevens outlined his conditions for the nominations for lecture series B, "expressing fear lest the tone of the series as a whole be impaired by any untoward element in popular lecturing." Stevens insisted that all nominations for Group B should be submitted to him. In a further letter to Duchow of 26 March 1957 Stevens agreed to deliver the inaugural lecture on the condition that his address be slated as one of the two lectures comprising Group B. Duchow's letter of 8 April 1957 to Ballon indicates that the dean-elect was eager to nominate the candidates for series B himself. On 18 April 1957 Duchow again wrote to Ballon, reminding her that Stevens wanted "all arrangements for the next session's lecture series completed within the next few weeks" and stated that unless he had heard by the end of the month, Stevens would "submit to Faculty, through [Duchow] some likely names to fill this gap." Duchow's letters to Ballon reveal that he was caught between the two: he did not want to antagonize a Faculty benefactor but at the same time, he wanted to accede to the wishes of the dean-elect. When Ballon did not submit her nomination to Stevens by the end of April, Stevens nominated Denis Matthews, a decision with which Duchow concurred. In a letter to

Ballon of 10 May 1957 he pleads that "this is, as you know, my terminal period of office during which it is quite impracticable for me to inaugurate further correspondence to ascertain the acceptability of your candidates to Mr Stevens," and mentions that he had received Ballon's nomination of Igor Stravinsky in a letter of 25 April. Had Duchow not passed on Ballon's suggestion?

In a letter to the principal of 16 May 1957 Duchow summarized the sequence of events over the last month. A week later (23 May) a bombshell arrived in the form of a letter from Stevens as "Dean-Elect of the Music Faculty" addressed to "All Members of the Faculty," on the subject of "Special Lectures." Among other statements the faculty read that "Miss Ballon's first-rate incompetence in administrative procedure allied to her second-rate social antics and her third-rate piano-playing has already brought McGill's Faculty of Music into grave disrepute in Europe and America, as is well known. If you as a body intend to encourage her in her follies and disregard my advice, given to you as from a professional musician and scholar as well as from incoming dean, you must suffer the consequences, which I can assure you will be serious."[78] Stevens added that because of his heavy concert schedule he would not have time to deliver the inaugural address. Four days letter the faculty replied in kind, and on 30 May they conveyed the following points to the principal. Stevens's reply:

(a) flouts the authority of the faculty in disregarding its unanimous decision in the matter of the inaugural address;
(b) represents a libelous attack upon a distinguished graduate of the University;
(c) contains what might be interpreted as a punitive threat against members of the staff, thereby seriously encroaching upon their freedom of opinion and expression;
(d) is characterized throughout by a tone and spirit which is autocratic and offensive in the extreme and is incompatible with the democratic process of discussion; and
(e) is proof of Mr Stevens's incompetence to discharge an important function of the dean of a University faculty, namely the wise and tactful handling of personal relationships.

One can imagine that Blume took a spirited part in this discussion since his background had prepared him well for countering authoritarian threats, although he was probably surprised at the direction from which they came; Dorothy Morton would have fiercely defended one of McGill's own. This document must be considered the most important stepping stone in the development of the Faculty of Music. The assembled members of the faculty, the vice-principal, Dean Fieldhouse, Acting-Dean Duchow, Prof. Blume and Mrs Dorothy Morton vowed to submit their resignations "to take effect the day of Mr Stevens's assuming office."[79] At a meeting later that day the University Statutory Selection Committee concluded that Stevens's "conduct has affected adversely the general well-being of the University." On 20 June the principal informed Stevens in Surrey, England, that his appointment as Dean had been rescinded by the Board of Governors the previous day.[80] The flurry of airmail letters was at an end; Duchow remained as acting dean[81] and the Faculty of Music came of age.

As we shall see the "wise and tactful handling of personal relationships" on the part of the dean would become a touchstone of Blume's tenure in that office. An additional earmark would be the "democratic process of discussion." Blume knew how precious that legacy was and he had every right to insist upon it in a North American university. By May 1957 the music faculty had its charter of rights and subsequent rebuilding would take place under that motto.

By 1958, in spite of Blume's best efforts, things were at a low ebb. McGill's vice-principal of finance complained that music was the smallest faculty in the university and yet he had to pay the salary of three "deans" – Duchow, Stevens, and Blume![82] The dean's report of 23 June 1958 (written by Duchow) notes important improvements to the bachelor programs in performance, composition, and music education.[83] Duchow describes the performance program as "something of a radical departure in Canada ... the plan is still the subject of considerable controversy in professional circles in the United States where it originated," and mentions the Eastman School of Music where such a program "has been successfully implemented." "Merit," he continues, "lies in the fact that it seeks to combine the aims of the traditional conservatory ... with those of the liberal arts music course." (1) Duchow may have been worried that the performance aspect of music was becoming too prominent within the University. Eastman (Duchow's own alma mater) was affiliated with the University of Rochester, but Howard Hanson's "radical departure" took place in a school of music that kept itself at a "safe" distance from the university. Sub-specializations at McGill included choirmaster, opera, oratorio and lied, accompaniment, instrumental or vocal pedagogy, radio production, and a planned conducting option. Duchow could boast that McGill "offers a wider range of choices than does any other Canadian university with the possible exception of Toronto." The improved composition program, developed by Istvan Anhalt and Kelsey Jones, was intended to overcome inadequacies inherited from the older British model. "[That model] failed to recognize that certain important aspects of extra-curricular musical training which in England or the Continent would, in the course of events, be acquired in the church, the school, or even in the home, are not normally accessible in this country. The present curriculum, designed to fill these lacunae, is like that of Toronto based upon patterns evolved in American universities." The music education program resembled Toronto's pioneering efforts of 1946. Graduate programs in musicology, composition, school music, and theory, following 1954 Toronto models, were also proposed.

Duchow's 1958 report emphasizes the increasing profile of McGill's music program, with quotations from Ernest MacMillan and Arnold Walter. Indeed, Walter, who was struggling with the Conservatory–Faculty jurisdictional problems, pointed enviously to the McGill model in his 1969 article, "The Growth of Music Education": "[McGill] cut the Gordian knot by discontinuing the licentiate and associate diploma; by changing the conservatory in such a way that it became in effect a preparatory department." Walter congratulated Blume by quoting the rationale behind such a move: "The level of attainment in the Associate was a very junior one and did not justify the conferring of a row of impressive letters after the name of the successful candidate. We ... felt that the public may be misled into believing that the holder of such a diploma has, in fact, attained a professional standing when actually he has barely passed the preparatory stage."[81]

In spite of all this activity, the McGill administration seemed intent on closing down the Faculty of Music; McGill historian Stanley Frost was convinced that the University was quite willing to let it quietly expire.[85] In the mid-1960s the Faculty of Music had about fifty students, which was regarded as an enormous growth. McGill retained two consultants to study several schools and faculties and make recommendations for the next phase of University development. Their report (which Anhalt claims never to have seen) concluded that every department in the Faculty of Arts and Science except music was going to grow, and recommended that the Faculty of Music be closed. A few years previously, McGill had eliminated the studio portion of the fine arts program, and only maintained the Art History program, so there was a precedent. But Blume and the rest of the faculty refused to capitulate. Anhalt remarked, "We all worked like hell, and we started to get better students, like John Hawkins and Bill Benjamin, and the rest. I was able to build up a composition class. The critical mass came together and by the late sixties, we were able to host a student composer's symposium; our students showed up very well in relation to Toronto and the New England Conservatory."

Blume was appointed acting dean in 1963 and dean in 1964. It is clear from Blume's own reports that he did not institute changes without first discussing the issues with the staff members concerned and obtaining their agreement. This collegial demeanour was a legacy of his European background, and went a long way toward establishing a relationship of trust with local teaching staff, even while he was making radical modifications to existing programs. Blume gave particular support to the establishment of an electroacoustic studio at McGill. This project was initiated in 1964 by István Anhalt with equipment supplied and maintained by the National Research Council. Anhalt had spent time at National Research Council during the summers of 1959–61 and in 1961 he visited the Columbia-Princeton Centre in New York and the Bell Telephone Laboratories in Murray Hill, New Jersey; he had also worked with Pierre Schaeffer in Paris. While Blume was unable to provide funding, he offered the coach house behind 3500 Redpath Street to house the venture. "There were absolutely no strings attached; McGill was able to do what it wanted with the equipment."[86] Blume's efforts also managed to save the music program at Marianopolis College and simultaneously provide well-trained students for McGill's music degree programs. Sister Mary O'Neill, a long-time member of Marianopolis music faculty, recounts that in the late 1960s the College was considering giving up its music program because of the difficulty in hiring qualified teachers.[87] Blume suggested that College students take some music courses at the McGill Faculty of Music, participate in ensembles, and share resources such as the music library – a mutually beneficial arrangement that continues to this day. Other achievements of the faculty under Blume's deanship include the opening of the Strathcona Music Building in 1971 and Pollack Concert Hall, a major Montreal venue for solo and chamber music concerts, in 1975. Graduate programs in musicology, theory, music education, and composition were instituted during his tenure, as well as a much more robust orchestral and choral training program.[88]

In 1976 the Canada Council commissioned Blume to prepare a study of music education in Canada, particularly with regard to training professional orchestral musicians. Blume conducted interviews with music educators in schools across Canada and examined a number of pertinent problems of music education. His report, "A National Music School for Canada" (1978)[89] recommended the creation of a national school, built on the existing facilities in the Banff Centre in Alberta, with an estimated enrolment of ninety-six orchestra players, twenty-four singers, sixteen conductors, sixteen stage designers, and eight pianists, all graduates of university music schools. Like the National Theatre School in Montreal, this school was to be almost totally state subsidized. Since education is a provincial jurisdiction, and Blume himself hinted that Québec would likely block the proposal, the report was shelved.

No other Canadian city benefitted from the thorough reorganization of post-secondary music education that took place in Toronto and Montreal, but a number of émigrés established themselves at other Canadian universities and began on a more modest basis to build a framework for music education corresponding to the needs of the individual institution and to their own interests. Some of the émigrés had completed degrees in musicology and published dissertations in Europe (Ida Halpern, Mieczslaw Kolinski, and Ulrich Leupold); others had undertaken substantial musicological studies but had not achieved degrees (Walter Kaufmann, Arnold Walter, Erwin Marcus, and Karl Steiner). By about 1930 musicology had been established as a new discipline at Cornell University and Columbia University, and an influx of trained musicologists from Central Europe found their way to the United States where they formed the backbone faculty on many campuses.[90] In Canada, however, until the early 1950s, there were no teaching positions for musicologists. The next section will examine the contributions of a number of émigrés in other Canadian universities.

WATERLOO LUTHERAN UNIVERSITY

Ulrich Leupold, a musicologist and a Lutheran pastor, played an important role in Canadian Lutheranism, while continuing his cultivation of church music in performance, writing, and teaching. Leupold was born in Berlin and completed his musicological studies at Friedrich Wilhelms University (1927–34); he also studied theology at the University of Zürich and was associated with the Confessing Church. Fleeing from the Nazis, he reached England in 1939, and after a brief time in Toledo, Ohio, arrived in Waterloo, Ontario, late that same year. He served as an assistant pastor at St Matthew's Church in Kitchener. Soon he was also teaching church music courses at Waterloo College, and Greek and New Testament theology at Waterloo Lutheran Seminary. His column "Musical Echoes" in the *Canada Lutheran*, in which he discussed both musical and theological topics, appeared regularly from 1941 to 1947, and sporadically until 1968. Leupold was also active as an organist, performing frequently, and serving as a consultant for the design and purchase of organs. In 1945 Leupold introduced the first music course in the Seminary and established a church music program leading to a certificate in sacred music. This program, combined with music courses offered in the faculty of arts and science, formed the basis of the music department of Waterloo Lutheran University.[91] Leupold also encouraged Walter Kemp, whom he had met in England, to come to Waterloo Lutheran University in 1965 to set up the music department. Kemp remained at the University until 1976 and he also conducted the university choir.[92] Leupold gave valuable guidance to a number of students, including Elmer Iseler, who was studying English at Waterloo College and sang in Leupold's choir. Convinced that Iseler was in the wrong faculty, Leupold persuaded Iseler's parents (his father was a pastor in Preston) to allow their son to study music in Toronto, necessitating a move away from home.[93] Iseler went on to become one of Canada's foremost choral conductors.

In addition to his work at the university Leupold served on numerous Lutheran and Lutheran-Catholic councils contributing to new service books; he was a co-editor of the 1958 *Service Book and Hymnal* and editor of *Laudamus* (1970), a work of hymnody that occupied his final years.[94] His translation of Luther's writings on liturgy and hymns was published in an edition of the collected works of Luther, and one of Leupold's hymns, "Er ist erstanden, Halleluja" is published in the current German hymnal, the *Evangelisches Gesangbuch*.[95]

UNIVERSITY OF NEW BRUNSWICK

Plans were underfoot to establish a music school at the University of New Brunswick with Jānis Kalniņš as director. Albert Trueman, the president of the university, was a singer and had designs on founding a music department to compete with Mount Allison in Sackville.[96] Funds for Kalniņš's appointment had been secured from the University's benefactor, Lord Beaverbrook. On 14 March Trueman announced a beginning in the development of instruction in music and in the enrichment of musical activities at the University, with the appointment of Kalniņš as director of music "to develop a mixed choir, male choir, quartets and an instrumental ensemble, a course of lectures on the history and appreciation of music will be added to the University curriculum. The creation of a department of music will depend upon – among other things – the interest which may be shown in the work which Mr Kalniņš undertakes."[97] A further announcement two weeks later in the *Brunswickan* that Kalniņš would be appointed director of music and would "take charge of musical activities on the campus in September," seemed to point to an imminent decision, but there was no department of music. Nevertheless, Trueman noted a "steadily growing interest in music" in Fredericton and "undoubtedly at the University itself among the students a wide variety of talent," and praised Kalniņš highly: "We are extremely fortunate in having a man of Mr Kalnins's attainments in Fredericton. A highly trained musician, and experienced and skillful conductor, he will be able to lay the foundations of a new and enriched musical life at the University."[98] To seal the appointment, on 17 November 1949 Trueman and Kalniņš gave a concert together in St Paul's Church. Since Kalniņš's had originally been appointed organist at St Paul's United Church in 1948, he was aware of the musical literacy in Fredericton. The November concert was subtitled "Music for Organ by Contemporary Composers." The program presented Hindemith's Sonata no. 1, a fugue by Arthur Honegger, Messaien's *Le banquet céleste*, and Stravinsky's *Berceuse and Finale*. After the intermission, those audience members who remained were offered more traditional fare. Trueman sang two arias "Come Away, Death," by Thomas Arne, and Kalniņš continued with Liszt's transcription of the "Pilgrim's Chorus" from Wagner's *Tannhäuser* and the Scherzo from Alexandre Guilmant's Organ Sonata no. 5, op. 80. Trueman sang two arias from *The Magic Flute* ("O Osis and Osiris" and "Within These Sacred Dwellings,"), and the evening ended with Kalniņš playing his own Five Chorale Preludes. This auspicious and challenging program must have raised more than a few eyebrows.

What happened to the appointment that Trueman announced so enthusiastically? The problem was not a lack of financial support – Lord Beaverbrook, the University Chancellor, himself offered to underwrite the cost of the project[99] – but rather a reluctance to embark on such an ambitious undertaking. A minute from the University Senate meeting for February 1949 reads: "The Arts Faculty recommends the establishment of a Department of Music. The President said that the time is not ripe for a separate department. He recommends that one course be taught in music history at a salary of $500–$1,000. One could find some local musician such as Mr Kalniņš to do this." In May 1949 the President of the University of New Brunswick announced that "J. Kalniņš would supervise for 1949/50 [sic] to teach a mixed choir, an instrumental group at a salary of $10/hour for the period of two hours of instruction per week. Approved." By 1951 the idea for a music department seems to have evaporated. A minute from February 1951 notes that "Mrs Daughey had talked about organizing a School of Music but said we couldn't do it at this time despite His Lordship's generous offer of assistance." There were likely too many academic and administrative problems to be solved in fashioning a music department *ex nihilo*. Kalniņš preferred to accept the security of an appointment at the Teacher's College, and he remained there until his retirement in 1971. A director of music was hired to oversee the Creative Arts series and provide a band for football games, but the first full-time music appointment did not come until 1962 when a resident musician was hired with funding from the Canada Council.[100]

UNIVERSITY OF BRITISH COLUMBIA

Ida Halpern created a stir in the fledgling music program at the University of British Columbia soon after her arrival in Vancouver in

1939. In 1940 she gave the University's first classes in music appreciation and gleaned good local coverage in both the university publication UBSSEY and the *Vancouver Daily Province*.[101] The courses lasted until 1961. Halpern's important contributions to Canadian ethnomusicology are discussed in chapter 7. The music program development at UBC, however, was substantially the work of Welton Marquis, an American musicologist who was appointed head of the Music Department in 1958 and remained until 1971. The extent to which his work might have been modeled on that of Toronto or Montreal has not yet been investigated.

CONCLUSIONS

Undoubtedly the most significant achievement of the émigrés in this study was the radical transformation of post-secondary music education in Canada. While the bachelor of music programs offered at the University of Toronto and McGill University when the émigrés arrived might have served well enough to train organists these courses did little to prepare students for the increasingly diversified challenges facing musicians and music academics in the second half of the twentieth century. Walter at the University of Toronto and Blume at McGill – two Berlin-educated refugees from Nazism – proceeded to remake their respective institutions, helping them to grow into the two premier anglophone post-secondary music schools in the country. To state that they merely followed US models is belittle their achievements. There were several different US models, and although both were well aware of developments in music education south of the border, there is no evidence that either Walter or Blume had a particular school or faculty in mind. They also knew all too well that Canada could never call upon the extensive private funding that American music schools enjoyed. In a sense the schools in Toronto and Montreal were in competition with one another, but Walter and Blume knew also that they were engaged in a common enterprise to improve post-secondary music education in Canada. Both men initially worked within an entrenched British system, befriending as far as possible the numerous musicians committed to that system. Without ruffling too many feathers they gradually nudged, cajoled, persuaded, and pressed for change until music performance became a part of the academy with a breadth of humanistic, theoretical, and creative musical offerings to round out the programs. It is a tribute to their diplomatic and administrative skills that they managed to create a distinctively Canadian structure. Walter's description of Toronto also holds true for McGill: "Toronto ... is organized basically [on American lines] ... but even in the States there are few Universities which offer as wide a spectrum of music studies as Toronto does. Some specialize in performance, others in music education, still others in musicology. We provide for all three on an equal footing. Research in electronic music is found in Columbia and Princeton only; our opera school (a department of the Royal Conservatory and affiliated with the Faculty) is the envy of many."

The most dramatic developments in the field of post-secondary music education in Canada were made during the third quarter of the twentieth century. Walter and Blume changed these institutions from the inside out; the new degree courses and programs were a by-product of their goal to establish a new symbiosis between the intellectual and professional aspects of music as a discipline. The physical aspect of the faculties also changed.

How did the respective university administrations fare in this struggle? The appointment of deans is the prerogative of principals and presidents. Although they were justly proud of the British heritage of democratic institutions, they failed to recognize the musicians who had fled Nazi persecution as true democrats. These two émigrés had to contend with administrators who did not comprehend the drastic changes required to equip future professional musicians with the skills and knowledge to face the challenges of the twentieth century. One of the more serious problems created by the entrenched pro-British bias was that a perception that the dean of a music faculty should be British-trained if not British-born led to the fiasco with Denis Stevens at McGill and poisoned the atmosphere at the University of Toronto for many years. But the grain of sand, the foreign matter grinding against the smooth interior surface of the oyster, gradually produces a beautiful pearl. In the end, the powers that be could not hinder the work undertaken by these two émigrés whose love for music transcended personal ambition.

5

Opera in the University

"BUT I THOUGHT YOU WERE ONLY INTERESTED IN SERIOUS MUSIC!"

The ground for opera in Toronto and Montreal may not have been a desert, but it was admittedly fallow[1] when Arnold Walter and Helmut Blume took up the task of establishing this great central European art form in Canadian universities.

Opera began as an aristocratic genre in Italy in the early seventeenth century and gradually became a commercial enterprise that allowed the bourgeoisie an opportunity of aping the aristocracy. The genre also added significant prestige to royal houses as the rays of the sun king in Versailles spread across Europe and lesser potentates in the German states began cultivating the art. In the nineteenth century aristocratic and royal patronage of opera fell on hard times. Although individual composers such as Richard Wagner still received support on a grand scale, the tide was turning. By default municipal and regional governments took up the slack, providing for public opera houses administered by entrepreneurs and staffed by local artists. There was an elaborate apprenticeship system where singers, instrumentalists, and conductors could learn their trade from the bottom up and, depending on their abilities, might graduate to national opera houses. These provincial opera houses were an excellent training ground for budding conductors, and the craft learned in the daily grind of the orchestra pit could also be applied to the concert stage. Most European conductors were thus proficient in both operatic and symphonic repertoire.

But how could opera be cultivated in the absence of such training possibilities? Walter began by putting the educational aspect of opera in place. Since opera is a profession that must be learned, this aspect of the process could be offered by the university in a legitimate academic program. In Canada, funding would need to come from the university since the state seemed to be unaware of opera. The next step was to assemble a group of central Europeans with experience in operatic singing, staging, and production who could be induced to work together in a common enterprise. If these two conditions – operatic expertise and university support – were not fulfilled (as happened in London and Halifax) the initiative would fail. In return for a rigorous training program in voice, acting, theory, and history, along with a set of standards evaluation, the university would provide the facilities and the full-time appointments needed in order to plan for the education of opera singers on a long-term basis. The only problem was that the University of Toronto was opposed to any such endeavour. The manner in which Walter prevailed and in doing so not only helped to create the premier professional opera company in Canada but also planted seeds that were to influence operatic endeavours across the country, is the subject of this chapter.

UNIVERSITY OF WESTERN ONTARIO

The first educational institution in Canada to promote the study and performance of opera in the postwar years was the University of Western Ontario in London, Ontario. In the summer of 1946 Dr Harvey Robb, director of the Western Ontario Conservatory of Music (which operated under the auspices of the University), invited conductor Alfred Rosé, then living in Cincinnati, to hold an opera workshop,[2] which resulted in a performance of opera excerpts in late August. Two years later Rosé moved to London to teach at the University. Working with local singers and piano accompaniment over several seasons, Rosé built this summer workshop to substantial proportions. Concerts and productions included excerpts from *Martha, Tannhäuser, Mignon, Il trovatore, The Prince of Pilsen*, and *Countess Maritza*.[3] In 1953 they mounted a complete production of *The Magic Flute* in Convocation Hall, but the initiative was lost when Rosé's enthusiasm began to wane. Opera cannot be maintained without a supporting cast.

THE UNIVERSITY OF TORONTO

Canadian tenor Edward Johnson, general manager of the Metropolitan Opera in New York (1935–1950) and also chair of the TCM board, encouraged Arnold Walter to proceed with plans for an opera school that could provide advanced opera training for Canadian singers. Walter had heard about Rosé's 1946 workshop performances, and offered this "fellow Austrian" the position of director for the proposed school. By 18 September 1946, when they were unable to reach an agreement on salary,[4] Walter immediately contacted Henry Levinger, the editor of the *Musical Courier* in New York, to ask his help in finding someone for the job. Levinger was an old friend of Nicholas Goldschmidt:

> Everyone knows the story of how I was hired in Toronto. I was at Steinway Hall to see a friend of mine, Henry Levinger, whom I hadn't seen for over twenty years and whom I knew from Vienna. I just went to him to tell him "I am now here in New York after being employed San Francisco and New Orleans and I want to open a studio because I have many students. I said, "In case you hear of something, anything, where I can be myself, my own boss, where I can develop things and do pioneer work particularly in opera, let me know, I'll give you my telephone number." Then I said, "I'm going to visit a friend of mine from Vienna, Thea Dispeker, the agent, she's still around," and I went across the hall to visit her. Within a few minutes, Levinger called me back and said "I just got a telephone call from Toronto, from Arnold Walter; they are planning to establish an opera department there." And that happened in one minute. My whole life depended on that moment.[5]

On 26 September 1946, eight days after Rosé had turned down his offer, Walter confirmed Goldschmidt's appointment and made arrangements for his immigration.[6] Goldschmidt arrived in early October, in time for the beginning of the fall term. Walter's network of connections with people of influence outside Toronto has scored its first triumph. Beginning with Goldschmidt he set about hiring experienced émigré musicians from central Europe, some of whom already had begun careers on European stages.

Did Walter know whom he had hired? Probably not. His initial attempt to find an opera director had failed and he was fishing for names. His call to Levinger was on speculation and Goldschmidt just happened to drop in to see Levinger; when Walter called, Levinger immediately thought of his old friend from Vienna. Goldschmidt had used the war years to good advantage. A letter of introduction from his uncle Paul Hymans (a Belgian statesman and diplomat) to Nicholas Murray Butler, the president of Columbia University in New York, opened the door of the music department for several productive years of opera at Brander Matthews Hall.[7]

> I was appointed to Columbia between 1942 and 1944. I was asked to do the opera department, and also lecturing, but lecturing was not my main activity. I took on the musical direction of the Columbia University Opera Department. I don't think it was an opera department – it was more concerned with developing opera productions. There was a famous small theatre there, the Brander Matthews Theatre, a charming little theatre. The first thing I did was *The Village Barber* (*Der Dorfbarbier*) by [Johann Baptist] Schenk. Then I did a new work by Ernest Bacon, the first performance by Hugh Thompson, a baritone. He became very well known at the Met. He started at Columbia University with me.

A second letter to former US president Herbert Hoover led to an appointment to produce operas at Stanford University.[8] Goldschmidt also worked with the San Francisco Conservatory and later the New Orleans Opera.

Finding a stage director for the opera school did not go so smoothly. Again relying on old world contacts Walter hired Viennese-born Felix Brentano, a student of theatre director Max Reinhardt. Brentano had followed Reinhardt to New York in 1937, had produced Broadway plays and musicals, and had worked with choreographer George Balanchine. Brentano's first two years at the Opera School were fairly good but a crisis erupted during the 1948 production of Gluck's *Orpheus and Eurydice:*

> There is one of the most wonderful recitatives before [the aria "Che farò senza Euridice?"] the famous recitative which was the revolution, really a dramatic thing, not the Monteverdi style any

more. And he wanted to cut the recitative because [he felt it was] too long . . . And I just refused, absolutely refused. I was so furious with Brentano, Arnold had to put down his foot."[9]

The way was open for hiring Herman Geiger-Torel. The combination of Goldschmidt and stage director Geiger-Torel, both of whom had worked in the provincial opera house in Troppau, was a major coup for Walter and the Opera School. "I didn't do it alone, because Herman Geiger-Torel [assisted;] he had great merit, but I brought him here. That for me is the most important thing because without me, he would have never come. No one knew him. I learned a lot from him in the provincial theatre."[10] Geiger-Torel played a significant role. He was given carte blanche to set up a curriculum that included general repertoire, stagecraft, role interpretation, classes in diction, body movement and improvisation, and the occasional lecture on the history of opera ... a gruelling timetable. "We were starting from scratch. This was the best way I knew to do it."[11]

Did Walter know any more about Geiger-Torel than what Goldschmidt told him? Probably not.[12] From 1928 to 1930 he was assistant stage director of the Frankfurt Opera, and in 1930 he was Lothar Wallerstein's assistant at the Salzburg Festival. Posts as stage director followed in Aussig, Czechoslovakia (1930–31) and Bremerhaven, Germany (1931–32). But Geiger-Torel was Jewish. Trouble began in 1934 when he lost a contract with a German opera house. Like others in his predicament, he found refuge in Czechoslovakia. He worked with Goldschmidt during his years at the Troppau opera house in Moravia (1934–37); a program from those years for a production of Puccini's *Girl of the Golden West* still survives.[13] Before and during the war Latin American countries that had a tradition of European opera attracted many émigrés. The Teatro Colón in Buenos Aires had an opera season that could rival Dresden or Vienna and became home to conductors such as Fritz Busch, Erich Kleiber, Otto Klemperer, and Felix Weingartner.[14] Thomas Mayer, another Canadian émigré, also spent fruitful years in Latin America. Geiger-Torel staged six operas (including *La Traviata* and *Manon Lescaut* with Claudio Muzio) at the Teatro Colón in Buenos Aires. In 1943 Geiger-Torel moved to Montevideo, Uruguay, to take a position as chief stage director for opera; two years later he became stage director of the Teatro Municipal in Rio de Janeiro. During his Latin American sojourn he was also active in Cuba, Guatemala, and

Brazil. When Juan Perón came to power in 1946 many Germans were forced to leave Argentina; Geiger-Torel moved on to New York. Two years later Goldschmidt gave him the opportunity to come to Toronto to replace Franz Brentano. Geiger- Torel's enthusiasm for opera knew no bounds and his background had prepared him well for the challenges he would meet in Toronto. In an essay on "Stage Direction," he outlines his dramatic philosophy:

> Opera is undoubtedly theatre. Opera should never preserve traditions which thirty years later become unconvincing and even ridiculous. Gustav Mahler once said: "Tradition is sloppiness." This is the reason why opera became unpopular on this continent, especially among the youth . . . Opera consists of more than the high E flat of the coloratura-soprano or the high C of a "troubadour"-tenor. Opera is today (and should be always) a highly interesting and appealing union of the most diverse art-forms: musical composition, poetry, and scenic design. It is the distinguished and graceful duty of the stage director of today to transform opera into musical drama, to eliminate, in close co-operation with the conductor and company's manager, the antiquated star-system ... Opera acting, and with it the whole production, must always be above all inspired by the music, i.e. by musical form, harmonies, and dynamic accents, then by the text and the period of the story.[15]

Speaking of his appointment, Goldschmidt commented that Walter knew "if you come from Europe you know what opera is all about. My goal was to get the best out of the students. Give them instruction on the basis of what I learned abroad and give them the discipline which they had to, shall we say, be aware of, and without which we would never have any opera singers. It's not haphazard; if you are going to sing opera, you have to learn it."[16] Goldschmidt's goal was to have opera sung by Canadian singers for Canadian audiences: "I can claim rightly, that I started opera activities within Canada, by Canadians in 1946. I conducted twenty-six Canadian premieres for the CBC Opera Company."

What models could Goldschmidt draw on for the Opera School? During his apprentice years working in municipal and provincial European opera houses he had gained valuable experience, particularly in Troppau. "In some way, I replaced the small municipal, provincial theatres [with] the Opera School. I knew what you had to learn, I had to do everything. You had to play percussion in the orchestra, or conduct the chorus backstage or tell the stagehand to put on the electronic gunshot. I had to know what it's all about, and therefore I could tell people. That's how it started."

During these years Walter began to forge the personal alliances he knew were essential to promote and support opera in the community. Accepting the fact that the Canadian situation was unlike central Europe, he held the first meeting of the executive of the "Opera and Concerts Committee" in his office at the RCM on 11 March 1947; a second meeting was held a week later in the Conservatory's crowded and dingy cafeteria in the basement of 135 College Street – a favourite meeting spot where students rubbed elbows with soon-to-be-famous musicians.

Once the Opera School was underway Walter could arrange public appearances with his students singing operatic excerpts, making the contacts vital to obtain the social and financial support required for operatic productions. For example, Walter was the guest of honour at a gala Christmas reception of the Canadian Club at the Royal York Hotel on 15 December 1947, presenting a program by students from the newly formed Opera School. On the back of the program, he noted his guests for a New Years' Day breakfast: Greta Kraus and husband, Erwin Dentay, Floyd and Jean Chalmers (who became important music patrons in Toronto and nationally), Peter Askonas, and Emmy Heim.[17] He also established the Five O'Clocks, a series of informal concerts given in the Recital Hall of the RCM building on College Street.[18]

Helmut Kallmann commented that Walter encountered some opposition in Toronto: "There were people who objected to the central European influence of Walter, Goldschmidt, and so on, and they said that somebody like Weldon Kilburn could have done a wonderful job starting an opera school. I don't know but I think the European influence was definitely an advantage."[19] Oskar Morawetz was astonished by the attitudes of some of his Toronto colleagues: "When Dr Walter started this, some teachers who were quite prominent said, 'This will be the end of our vocal department.' So I said, 'What do you like?' 'Lieder.' Everything was Lieder. I remember when he did the first few performances, the teachers almost boycotted it. And when I told them that I love opera, they said, 'But I thought you were only interested in serious music!' But the person who was most against opera was [George] Lambert. He was the teacher of Jon Vickers, a person who hated opera!"[20] (Vickers, however, was grateful to Lambert for not exposing him to opera too soon. Lambert gave the upcoming heldentenor a steady diet of oratorio before allowing him to move on to music drama.) Toronto musicians had difficulty comprehending the central European tradition that considered opera and Lieder of equal worth with singers who were proficient in both genres.

Goldschmidt conducted many of the early Opera School productions himself but when this became too onerous, additional conductors, most of whom were émigrés with experience in European operatic pits, were found. Ernesto Barbini came from Italy by way of the Metropolitan Opera in 1953. Goldschmidt noted that Barbini conducted "mainly the Italian repertoire and he was quite successful ... He was, I would call it, a typically resident, routine conductor. He got the results, but not beyond."[21] Alfred Strombergs had apprenticed at the Liepaja Opera House in Latvia and played a major role in operatic productions in Halifax before moving to Toronto in 1957. He was head coach of the Opera School from 1960 to 1971 and also worked with the Canadian Opera Company.[22] Walter Susskind came to Toronto in 1956 as conductor of the TSO, but because had been assistant conductor to George Szell at the German Opera in Prague and also had years of operatic conducting in Britain, he was also very well qualified to assist the Canadian Opera Company.

The CBC Opera Company was created in 1948 through the cooperative efforts of Arnold Walter, Nicholas Goldschmidt, Geoffrey Waddington, Hermann Geiger-Torel, Charles Jennings (general supervisor of radio programming), and Terence Gibbs. Realizing the high quality of singers in Toronto, Gibbs proposed the creation of a permanent ensemble using the prestigious CBC Wednesday Night as its venue.[23] Four operas were broadcast in the first season (1948–49) and five the next. An advertising brochure for the first season lists a production of *La bohème* on 20 October 1948: "The first of four operas to be performed on CBC Wednesday Night during the season by the specially formed CBC Opera Company – Mary Morrison, James Shields, Edmund Hockridge, Andrew MacMillan ... conducted by Nicholas Goldschmidt." Careful mention is made of the auditions for lead roles: "twenty-six singers were auditioned. The fact that 50 percent of those finally chosen were associated with the Conservatory is indicative of the work it has done in developing operatic talent."[24] The Canadian premiere of *Peter Grimes* in October 1949 was an outstanding national music event that garnered rave reviews and received the 1950 Best Music Program award in the Canadian Radio Awards competition.[25] The CBC opera series ended in 1955.

Walter outlined his hopes for Canadian opera in a brief to the Massey Commission in 1949.[26] True to his social democratic ideals, he reviewed the progress already made in the Toronto opera scene and stated that with government support much more could be done. "In these circumstances it will soon be necessary to form a Canadian Opera Company, which should work in close collaboration with the Opera School and yet not be identical with it. Such a company will automatically share the economic problems of every other opera company in the world; it will not be self-supporting, and will, therefore, depend either on private contributions or on support from Governmental sources." This may well be the first official reference to the Canadian opera company that materialized in 1958.[27] Early on, it seems, Walter sensed the unease of the University of Toronto regarding its sponsorship of opera performances. The Opera School began as a division of the TCM, fulfilling both educational and production functions. The University's refusal to continue support for the production portion of the School's activities in 1950 led to the establishment of the Toronto Opera Festival Association, a professional production entity that eventually became the Canadian Opera Company (COC).[28] Goldschmidt remembered the break with the university:

> We were challenged at that time [by the university.] "Unless you have $25,000 cash by the coming weekend [it was Tuesday to Saturday,] a general manager, and incorporated" [you will not be able to continue]. And we got it incorporated in 24 hours by a great friend, Senator Godfrey; he did it with his law firm. And then some benefactors, I don't know who they were, brought in this $25,000, and the general manager of the Royal Alex, Ernest Rawley and Geiger-Torel the stage director, and I was the music director.[29]

Geiger-Torel's tenure at the Canadian Opera Company lasted until 1975, a year before his death. Although he was severely criticized for poor casting choices and unsuccessful productions[30] as well as "under-rehearsed ensembles and the enormous debt left behind at his retirement in 1975,"[31] few would deny his importance in the Toronto opera scene. Four months before he died he told the COC Board "If you, Metro Toronto, and the Arts Councils had given assistance which, for instance, the late Mr Pompidou, Prime Minister of France, gave the general director of the Paris Opera ... I would have given you the best opera company in the world. Well, there is hope that in the coming years enough irrigation can be created to transform the Canadian operatic desert into a land of operatic fertility."[32] One of Geiger-Torel's goals was to produce the complete Wagner Ring cycle; this was finally realized in September 2006 in the magnificent new Four Seasons Centre for the Performing Arts designed to house the COC and the National Ballet. Walter, Geiger-Torel, and Goldschmidt would all have been very pleased. For Geiger-Torel, however, the situation in the mid 1970s seemed bleak:

> My ambition was to give my successor a minimum of headaches and a maximum of artistic and financial security. I fear he will inherit all of my headaches. However, I know I have built a strong contingent of Canadian talent in opera; that I am able to hand over to him an opera company which has developed a style of its own, a homogenous ensemble of fine performers, a highly efficient technical and administrative staff and an organization well-trained and disciplined; that I have been able to build a loyal and knowledgeable audience. I have done the pioneer work of what may be termed "laying the lyric cornerstone" in Toronto. I think I have given Lotfi Mansouri a good foundation on which to build. Twenty-six years is time enough for pioneering. It is time to move forward. Mansouri will be able not only to maintain the reputation of the COC as a very fine opera company, but also to raise it into the ranks of the greatest in the world.[33]

The rehearsal room of the University of Toronto Opera Division has been named in Geiger-Torel's honour, and his annotated opera scores are held by the Music Library of the University of Toronto, located in the building named for Edward Johnson; and Torel's deeply-furrowed green leather chair is kept at the Joan Baillie Archives of the Canadian Opera Company.

Obviously efforts at establishing opera in Toronto could not be based solely on the efforts of singers, conductors, and stage directors. Voice teachers who had knowledge and experience with operatic literature played a vital role. The first émigré to revitalize the vocal faculty was Ernesto Vinci, who arrived in Halifax in January 1939 by way of Germany, Italy, and Halifax.

Vinci was born Ernst Wreszynski in Gnesen, Prussia (now a part of Poland). He used the surname Wygram professionally during his time in Germany and in Milan, Italy, and evidence suggests that he adopted the surname Vinci as a professional name in Italy in order to distinguish his singing persona from his medical career in North America. It is doubtful that he used the names Vinci or Wygram to disguise a Jewish background.[34] Vinci was educated in Berlin where he studied at the Berlin Hochschule für Musik; he also studied law and medicine at Friedrich Wilhelms University before he fled Germany for Milan in 1933. In Milan he earned a second medical degree and continued voice training. By 1936 was employed as a professional baritone in Italy and Switzerland. In 1938 he left Europe for New York. Wilfrid Pelletier referred him to the Halifax Conservatory to head the vocal department, a position he held until 1945.[35] In Halifax he was a vocal coach for Portia White,[36] one of the foremost Canadian singers of her generation, and during the war he also appeared in some 256 concerts organized by Hugh Mills on behalf of the Canadian war effort.[37] On 3 December 1942 MacMillan accompanied him in a recital at Eaton Auditorium in Toronto, and he also participated in freelance opera productions of *The Marriage of Figaro, The Abduction from the Seraglio, Martha,* and *Dido and Aeneas*, (some of which were performed in air force hangars) for army, navy, and air force troops.[38] Vinci lectured on vocal repertoire at Dalhousie University and the Pine Hill Divinity Hall and taught voice at the Halifax Ladies College. In 1945 Walter's long arm plucked him from his productive role in Nova Scotia and brought him to Toronto. Vinci was appointed head of the TCM voice department and was soon swamped by students who enrolled in the newly-formed Opera School the following year. Goldschmidt remembered: "I knew him very well; we were very good friends. He started at 8:15 in the morning and stopped at 10 o'clock in the evening with a very short lunch or dinner break and half-hour lessons every day. I was there. Sometimes I played the piano for him when no one was around. He was an institution like George Lambert."[39]

Vinci also thrilled Toronto audiences with performances of Brahms's *Die schöne Magelone* and Schubert's *Die schöne Müllerin.* John Kraglund, not known for verbal exuberance, was ecstatic: "Dr Vinci's rich baritone voice, both singing and speaking, carried the audience to the delightful happy ending."[40] In a recital with harpsichordist Greta Kraus, he introduced Toronto audiences to songs and arias of the seventeenth and eighteenth centuries.[41] Vinci taught summer courses in Winnipeg (1945–48) and at the Banff School of Fine Arts (1949–69) where he was the head of the vocal (later opera) department and touring company, and where in 1958 he coproduced Trevor Jones' opera *The Broken Ring.* He continued to perform and present concerts until the mid-1960s, and contributed articles on voice production and related subjects to *Opera Canada* and the CBC *Times.* His numerous pupils include John Arab, Maurice Brown, Glyn Evans, Marguerite Gignac, Robert Goulet, Elizabeth Benson-Guy, Joan Hall, Andrew MacMillan, Joan Maxwell, Mary Morrison, Sheila Piercey, Roxolana Roslak, and Bernard Turgeon.

Jan Rubes was a graduate of the Prague Conservatory. After his debut in 1940 as Basilio in *The Barber of Seville*, he became a lead singer in the Prague Opera. On his arrival in Toronto in 1948 he baffled his Toronto colleagues by asking about opera. "What opera?" they replied. He made his North American debut on 30 January 1949 in a concert managed by Walter Homburger at Eaton Auditorium, and he appeared as Betto in Puccini's *Gianni Schicchi* with the Royal Conservatory Opera on 30 March and 4 April of that same year. His next break was a starring role in a Canadian film, *Forbidden Journey* (1950, directed by Richard Jarvis and Cecil Maiden). His co-star Susan Douglas was also a Czech refugee. (She had picked her stage name at random from a telephone directory.) The two discovered they had grown up in the same neighbourhood in Prague; within three weeks they were married. Susan Douglas went on to found Young People's Theatre in Toronto, and was also head of CBC Radio Drama. Rubes found Canadian audiences wonderful because he knew that many were seeing opera for the first time, and predicted that opera would become established as "a love of the Canadian people."[42] From 1949 to 1958 he was a soloist with the CBC Opera and was very grateful to the CBC for its role in supporting Canadian singers during the 1950s and 1960s: "Without the CBC I would have died."[43] Rubes appeared as host and singer in *Songs of My People*, a CBC radio program devoted to a central European musical diet. The program was originally conceived in 1954 as a summer replacement but lasted for ten years. In addition to his vast repertoire, comprising some ninety roles in six languages, he also worked as a stage director. When he was appointed touring director for the Canadian Opera Company in 1974, Geiger-Torel described him as "one of the most versatile artists in our city, perhaps in our country – one of those rare singers who has a brain. It is high time we make use of his abilities as stage director, actor, producer, and educator, as well as performer. His appointment is an enormously sensible addition to our program and development. He might bring drastic changes for the good of our company, which I welcome very much."[44] Rubes's innovations for touring included an orchestra of twenty-three musicians and set designs consisting of projected scenery and lighting effects. Rubes worked as an actor in the 1980s and developed a major career in Canadian and US television and feature films.

Irene Jessner was born in Vienna and spent the early part of her career in Austria and Czechoslovakia. She joined the Metropolitan Opera in 1936 at the invitation of Edward Johnson, who, in 1952 brought her to Toronto.[45] She was past her prime as an operatic performer but her extensive knowledge of vocal technique and operatic repertoire ensured her status as an exemplary teacher. Students who passed through her studio in the course of three decades on the vocal faculty of the Opera School include Stephanie Bogle, Martha Collins, Roxolana Roslak, Nancy Hermiston, Linda Bennett, Jean MacPhail, Mark Dubois, Bruce Kelly, and Patrick Timney.

MCGILL UNIVERSITY

The genesis of the Opera Studio at McGill came about through the efforts of Helmut Blume, who was intent on replicating the successful Opera School in Toronto; Blume laid out much of the groundwork in his section of the 1955 proposals for reorganizing the McGill Faculty of Music:[46]

> It is suggested to start the McGill Opera School on a modest basis, as an Opera Seminar, at the beginning of the next session, with courses in Opera History, Opera Repertory, and piano

> coaching sessions. An eighteenth-century opera not involving more than three or four roles and a small chamber orchestra might be contemplated for production at the end of the second year, if the Conservatory has by then been converted into a small theatre. Sets and scenery to be made in conjunction with the Fine Arts Department. Instructors in stage-deportment, production, direction, and coaching to be appointed on a part-time basis. There are several artists in Montreal who would fill the necessary requirements.[47]

To run the program he hired Edith and Luciano Della Pergola, two talented and experienced opera singers who had distinguished careers on European opera stages in Milan, Vienna, and Naples. Edith Della Pergola (née Leb) sang in the Naples premiere of Schoenberg's *Von Heute auf Morgen* under Hermann Scherchen. Since both were Italian (Edith by marriage to Luciano), they had come through the war unscathed. Edith remembers the first meeting with Blume in Montreal in 1955. Her sister, who had already moved to Montreal, knew that Blume was looking for teachers to expand the offerings at McGill and suggested she and Luciano contact him. Luciano remembered the first meetings with Blume, who spoke French with "an obvious German accent." They attended meetings with émigré Bernard Diamant, Rhea Lensens, Jean Millar, and an operatic coach (whose name Edith Della Pergola could not recall). The future course of what was later to become the Opera Studio was laid out from the beginning. To well-meant but wayward suggestions of the locals, Blume replied "The purpose of this meeting was to introduce the Della Pergolas as voice teachers and future colleagues of yours, and to inform you that they will be in charge of the productions of operas in the future, that's all."[48] Basta! Della Pergola's motto for McGill Opera was "Ne sutor ultra crepidam" (Do not presume to judge without knowledge, or literally, No cobbler is above the sandals.).[49] Blume would stand behind the Della Pergolas with their stunning operatic credentials.

In the inaugural season, 1956–57, the Della Pergolas produced Pergolesi's *The Maid as Mistress (La serva padrona)* and Purcell's *Dido and Aeneas*. During their thirty-four-year tenure with the McGill Opera Studio, they presented forty-eight complete opera productions – including Debussy's *Pelléas et Mélisande,* Mozart's *The Marriage of Figaro,* and Verdi's *Rigoletto* – and more than 160 excerpts. Under the Della Pergola successors, Bill and Dixie Neill, the program, now known as Opera McGill, gained an international reputation attracting singers from Canada and the United States. Opera McGill's major production in January is eagerly awaited by opera lovers in Montreal, and graduates of the program are taking their rightful places on international stages. The second phase of the proposed building schedule for the Schulich School of Music includes an opera hall. For Blume and McGill this is a remarkable achievement.

HALIFAX

Efforts at establishing opera in Halifax grew out of the work of Mariss Vetra and Teodor Brilts at the Halifax Conservatory. By 1948–49 a number of Latvian conductors, opera singers, voice teachers, and former ballet corps members from the Riga opera had come to settle in Halifax. The occasion was the bicentennial celebration of the city of Halifax; the means was a city grant to launch an opera sponsored by the Halifax Men's Press Club (an organization that had previously devoted its energies to the Miss Halifax pageant); the venue, unfortunately, was the Dalhousie University gymnasium. Vetra, Brilts, and Alfred Strombergs mounted a production of Mozart's *Don Giovanni* with an all-Canadian cast, teaching the music to the singers number by number. The challenges and rewards of working with non-professional singers inspired Vetra to undertake this project, knowing that mounting such a work with the resources available in Halifax would require hard work and long rehearsals. In the program notes he wrote:

> For the first time in my life I am working with artists who do not belong solely to their art. They spend many hours each day at their own daily jobs, at office work, banks, newspaper, and even heavier manual work. Each day I admire more the fortitude of these people who come from a full day's work and are still able to rehearse with me until late at night. One of my singers lives so far away that he must come by plane ... and is it not a wonder that the well known fog of the Halifax airport has never stopped his arrival? Never has he complained about the inconvenience or expense. Another, who belongs to an important office in the city, has for months sacrificed his family

life on account of rehearsals. The third, a lady, is virtually spending her honeymoon at rehearsals. Is this not enjoyable?[50]

The success of *Don Giovanni* led in 1950 to the formation of the Nova Scotia Opera Association, which mounted annual productions in the Capitol Theatre (now demolished) in Halifax; operas include *Tales of Hoffmann* (1950), *Countess Maritza* (1951), and *Madame Butterfly* (1952). Vetra proudly noted that the fourteen soloists required to mount the *Tales of Hoffmann* showed "that Nova Scotia is able to supply even such a large number of singing artists."[51] Strombergs used that program to appeal for a permanent orchestra that would present regular orchestral concerts, rather than hiring musicians on a freelance basis to "accompany" the opera: "We shall be able to have a first-class orchestra that, working with the Opera Association and kindred organizations, will make Halifax the Eastern fortress of Canadian culture and art. I hope that the public will respond with enthusiasm to this prime necessity – a symphony for Halifax!"[52] Strombergs's dream became reality a few years later with the formation of the Halifax Symphonette, which in 1955 became the Halifax Symphony Orchestra under Thomas Mayer; the ensemble continued under various names and guises as a permanent ensemble in the city. For the years when there was a critical group of former members of the Riga opera living in Halifax, productions were successfully mounted. Had an opera school program been brought into the university – the only way of ensuring long-term stability – the story might well have been different. However, Vetra left Halifax for Toronto in 1953, and Strombergs followed in 1955. The Halifax- based opera company envisioned by these musicians, with the Halifax Conservatory as its launching pad, did not survive their departure.

VANCOUVER

Opera in Vancouver became a reality in the 1950s through a cooperative effort of local patrons and émigrés. Dr Norman (Larry) Mackenzie, president of the University of British Columbia, began a summer opera program and hired Nicholas Goldschmidt to introduce University of British Columbia students to the repertoire. The first session ran from 3 July to 12 August 1950.[53] In addition to producing opera, Goldschmidt also introduced singers to major choral and Lieder repertoire. In spite of poor facilities, enthusiasm for staging opera began to gain momentum. Productions through the mid-1950s included *The Magic Flute* (excerpts, 1953), Menotti's *The Consul* (1955), Mozart's *Cosi fan tutte* (1956), and a double bill of Menotti's *The Medium* and Puccini's *Gianni Scicchi* (1957). Building on the many musical and administrative contacts that Goldschmidt had established during the summer sessions, plans for a more extended arts festival began to materialize, culminating in the Vancouver International Music Festival of 1958, in which opera played a significant part.

The genesis of the Vancouver Opera in 1959 was due to the cooperation of a number of Vancouver arts patrons, among them Paul and Edwina Heller. The first production – the Vancouver premiere of Bizet's *Carmen* – was a very successful event.[54] During intermission a friend of the Hellers approached them, annoyed that he had not been asked to contribute. Paul replied "Nobody gave money, ten of us just guaranteed a thousand dollars each; that was enough." The patrons even took sandwiches down for the artists. "We started with three operas, now there are four."[55]

Canada's musical émigrés must be given credit for bringing opera in its finest form to Canada and establishing it on a firm foundation. Toronto's magnificent new opera house, the Four Seasons Centre for the Performing Arts, is a tribute to the vision of Arnold Walter who knew and cherished that great European art form and was willing to set about making it a reality within an inhospitable environment. He established the educational basis for opera in 1946 by bringing the European provincial opera house structure into the university, by means of the TCM Opera School; here singers could learn their trade. This task involved bringing together a critical mass of conductors, stage directors, and singing teachers, all of whom had experience on European stages. He set about organizing the administrative support and the infrastructure necessary behind the scenes. He also cultivated the all-important social contacts among Toronto's elite, building an audience and a pool of patrons from the top down. Talented local singers, the raw material of opera, he found in abundance, and he helped to found a permanent production facility, the COC, to provide a professional outlet for these singers, many of whom went on to international careers. The COC, currently operating at an audience capacity of 96 percent, is truly Canada's opera mecca.

In Montreal Helmut Blume established the educational basis for opera in McGill's Opera School, modelled on that of Toronto, but his goals were more modest and did not include a professional production facility. In London and Halifax, where an educational basis was not formed within the university, opera as an integrated educational-production model, did not take root.

Walter and his cohorts in Toronto succeeded where Handel in London had failed: he established a home for Italian – and French and German – opera in a British bastion. It is also important to note, however, that demographics were on the side of the émigrés, since postwar immigration brought a large influx of central Europeans to Toronto, tilting the national mix away from a British majority.

6

New Faculty Appointments Complete the Transformation of Music in the University

The present chapter examines the hiring of staff for the programs that Arnold Walter and Helmut Blume created at the University of Toronto and McGill University. "There was no search committee," Harvey Olnick recalled. "In those days everything was *ad hoc* purely at the discretion of Dr Walter."[1] With no full-time faculty there was neither time nor incentive for long-term planning; academic committees that could share the responsibility for appointments were an impossibility. Part-time staff hired from the conservatories for performance programs that were not yet academically accredited were not interested in spending extra hours on committee work with no recompense. For newly formed academic programs – such as the music education degree courses at the University of Toronto – Blume and Walter had to act completely on their own initiative.

UNIVERSITY OF TORONTO

Walter was well aware that a program is only as good as the people who staff it. He had known some of Europe's finest music scholars and musicians in his earlier days, and was eager to hire the best musicians available. His first academic appointments for the new music education program in 1946 were Robert Rosevear and Richard Johnston. These two graduates of the Eastman School of Music in Rochester, New York, had been trained in the pedagogical milieu focussed on equipping high school music teachers and had expertise in chorus, band, orchestra, and teaching techniques. Walter knew that they could bring invaluable musical and human resources to the faculty. Both made magnificent contributions to the music education course at the University of Toronto, and Johnston's later career also took him to the University of Calgary. The Faculty of Music, which for so long had been weighted toward Britain, was considerably enriched by these new faculty members from the United States.

For the Senior School the supplementary appropriation of $50,000 independent of RCM financing (requested in Walter's brief to the University board) ensured Walter a free hand to offer full- time positions to performing musicians, something that was unheard of at the TCM but taken for granted in European institutions.

Walter's first appointment was internationally renowned pianist Lubka Kolessa. Listening to her recordings today it is clear that she was undoubtedly one of the great pianists of her generation.[2] With her crystalline Scarlatti, endearingly quirky Schumann, and magisterial performance of Brahms's *Variations on a Theme by Handel* she created a magical tonal realm that was entirely captivating. Eric Koch has a vivid memory of hearing her play in Frankfurt in the 1930s.[3] Why, with her career as soloist with the finest German orchestras and conductors, including Karl Böhm and Herbert von Karajan, did she came to Ottawa? Not being Jewish, she could have continued her career in Europe, but in 1937 she moved to England and married Tracey Phillipps, a British diplomat whom she had met in Istanbul. Phillips acted as her manager for a tour of South America in 1938, and their son Igor was born in Canada in 1939.[4] In 1940 Philipps undertook a lecture tour in Canada on the "International Relations towards the Betterment of British and Foreign Understanding," sponsored by the National Council of Education of Canada; Kolessa's role was to perform and "render service to British art." However, the couple separated and soon divorced. Kolessa went to live in Ottawa at the Institut Jeane d'Arc, which was headed by Mother St Thomas, a piano teacher. The Grey Nuns cared for her and her child. In 1944 Kolessa came to Toronto as head of the piano department in the newly formed Senior School. Her success as a performer heightened awareness of the new school.[5] Through her students Kolessa was able to pass on some of the rich European heritage gained from her own teachers, Emil Sauer and Eugen d'Albert, both of whom had been pupils of Liszt. Kolessa's students include pianists Howard Brown, Richard Gresko, Ireneus

Zuk, conductor Mario Bernardi, and composers John Hawkins, Edward Laufer, and Clermont Pépin. Luba Zuk, who studied with Kolessa for a brief period in 1948, later recounted:

> When the Vienna Philharmonic came here for the first time in the late 1950s they played at the Forum with Karajan. Kolessa wanted to go to that concert but didn't want to go alone so she invited us to go with her. After the concert she said she wanted to go to talk to him after everyone else had seen him. Karajan was sitting in this concrete cell signing autographs, people were speaking to him – he was ashen, he had a stone-like complexion – "Yes," "No," "Danke schön." When everyone had gone, Kolessa said, "Now I will see him." She said something to him, he looked up, and I have not in my life seen a face change so much so quickly. Karajan broke into a smile, he suddenly had the happiest face on earth – it was like magic. They talked for a long time in German.[6]

The maestro had not forgotten. Kolessa's career in Toronto was a stormy one. Her liaison with Walter became public knowledge in late 1948.[7] Rumours swirled thick and fast, shocking Toronto's mid-century white Anglo-Saxon Protestant preserve. Regardless of the merits of the case, in what was decidedly the Senior School's loss, Kolessa's public life in Toronto was abruptly ended. She continued to teach privately at 112 Cluny Drive, where she lived for the rest of her life, and she continued to see Walter until his death,[8] but her public commitments shifted to Montreal. In 1952 she began commuting to Montreal to teach at l'École de musique Vincent d'Indy, the Conservatoire de musique, and – through the efforts of Helmut Blume – the Faculty of Music at McGill University.

Walter also hired a number of talented and brilliant Canadian musicians. Violinist Kathleen Parlow, a native of Calgary, had studied under Franco-Belgian violinist Leopold Auer in St Petersburg and went on to a widely-acclaimed European career. She came to the newly-founded Senior School in 1945 but continued performing in Canada. Her students included two young émigrés: Gerhard Kander and Hans Kaufmann. In 1952 Walter appointed John Beckwith to teach one of the music history courses, marking the beginning of Beckwith's magnificent life-long commitment to the Faculty of Music.[9]

Béla Böszörmenyi-Nagy, a suave Hungarian-born pianist who had studied at the Franz Liszt Academy in Budapest and taught there from 1937 until 1948 when he fled the Communist regime, arrived on the Toronto music scene to take Kolessa's place at the Senior School. Nagy's arrival in 1948 was undoubtedly brokered by his Hungarian colleague Géza de Kresz, who had returned to Toronto in 1947. "Dr B," as he became known, joined the teaching staff at the RCM. A typewritten transcript of a talk given to the Conservatory staff in halting English shortly after his arrival reveals not only his urbane manner, steeped in the central European traditions, but also his appreciation of his new homeland. He pays tribute to the generosity of those who welcomed him to Canada, "your free, strong and so lovely country." Deflecting curiosity about his opinions on the current political situation in Europe, he states that, "we musicians, painters, and writers, generally artists can choose much more better our political standpoint, if we can remain perfectly unpoliticians. [sic] Our ideals, our principles are established by such prime-ministers of the artist's country government like Bach, Mozart, or Beethoven and their work, I think, is the most reliable and the most authentic code for everybody who has moral sense in all countries or in all systems." He discusses musical life in Budapest and in Hungary, with descriptions of the Budapest Opera House, Hungarian musical repertoire, and a defence of Béla Bartók against charges of mechanical technique.[10]

Böszörmenyi-Nagy's performance repertoire included Beethoven's *Diabelli Variations* and Bach's *Goldberg Variations* – heavy fare for postwar Toronto audiences. He appeared throughout Ontario, toured the Maritimes on a number of occasions, and appeared with the TSO; his interpretation of Beethoven's Piano Concerto no. 4 elicited warm critical praise.[11] Always urbane, polite, well-groomed, a brilliant thinker, Dr B was an inspiration to his students: Canadian musicians who studied with him Paul Helmer, Gordon Macpherson, Paul McIntyre, Earle Moss, Charles Reiner, Bruce Vogt, Lorne Watson, and Robert Weisz. In addition to his studio at the RCM, he taught several sessions at the School of Fine Arts in Banff, passing on his artistic credo: "Sentiment is when you overdo feelings that are not true."[12] He spoke of the modern school of Gieseking, Cortot, Fischer, Solomon, and Bartók as "not attractive" but better able to "bring out the composer's ideas," and contrasted the entertainer, who comes down to the level of the audience, with the artist, who attempts to bring the audience up to his or her level.[13] His final session at Banff on 15 August 1952 included a talk on modern music – introducing students to Wagner, Debussy, Schoenberg, Britten, Prokofiev, and Shostakovich – and a performance of Bartók's Piano Concerto no. 3 with pianist Sandra Munn – a heady mix! Dr B left Toronto in 1953 to accept a teaching position at the School of Music, University of Indiana.

The close tie between Greta Kraus and Arnold Walter eventually led to positions for both Kraus and Oskar Morawetz at the Faculty of Music. Greta Kraus came to Toronto from Hawkesbury[14] and soon became acquainted with Arnold Walter, who at that time was music master at Upper Canada College. Walter introduced her to the principal of Havergal College who immediately hired her to teach piano and recorder.[15] In Toronto Walter managed to procure two harpsichords, and soon Walter and Kraus were rehearsing double harpsichord concertos for a CBC broadcast with Ettore Mazzoleni as conductor.[16] Soon Kraus was in demand for regular CBC Sunday evening programs with guests including Ernest MacMillan and Healey Willan, and she was pleasantly surprised by a Toronto performance of J.S. Bach's *St Matthew Passion*: "Sir Ernest conducted it magnificently, Healey Willan played the recitatives very imaginatively on the piano, and I was amazed by the high level of the choral singing – much higher than in Vienna, where even the opera chorus stank."[17] Soon Kraus was asked to play the continuo part on a harpsichord, setting a Toronto tradition that lasted many decades. MacMillan engaged Kraus for everything that required a harpsichord.

Kraus's appointment at the TCM in 1943 marked the beginning of a long and fruitful relationship with the Senior School and the Faculty of Music at the University of Toronto. Her classes in Lieder and German diction became staples for all singers, and beginning in 1963 she directed the faculty's Collegium Musicum. Harvey Olnick remembered her as "the kind of teacher who taught with love and imitation. She was old fashioned in her sense of style, so the new ideas on the Baroque [eighteenth-century performance practice] that came out were foreign to her."[18] Kraus became close friends with a number of musical émigrés, including Oskar Morawetz, whom she introduced to Arnold Walter.[19] Kraus and Edward Laufer shared an interest in Heinrich Schenker, and Laufer did a number of interviews with Kraus on Shenkerian analysis; Kraus had taken private lessons with Hans Weisse (1924–30) and was one of the few students who had group lessons with Schenker (1931–33).

Kraus also performed frequently with flutist Robert Aitken, who remembers that "for fifteen or twenty years, Greta and I played together every Thursday afternoon, sometimes for six or eight hours without a break." In later years she rediscovered the piano: "Her performances, with Lois Marshall of Schubert's *Die schöne Müllerin* in 1979 and songs by Hugo Wolf in 1981 are the best-remembered products of that reborn love." Lois Marshall said of Kraus "She has a great spirit, a great heart."[20] Greta Kraus died in Toronto in March 1998.

Oskar Morawetz arrived in Toronto in 1940[21] and continued his music education at the Faculty of Music, where he studied with Alberto Guerrero and Leo Smith; he received a BMus degree in 1944, and a DMus in 1953. His first recognition as a composer came with CAPAC awards in two successive years (his first string quartet in 1945 and *Sonata Tragica* in 1946). He taught at the TCM from 1946 to 1952, and from then until his retirement in 1982 at the University of Toronto. He had a remarkable knowledge of the standard orchestral and chamber repertoire, and could quote musical passage on demand or identify works by looking at a page or two of the score. As a composer he was largely self-taught, and while he was certainly influenced by the canon he knew so well, he had an original voice. He commented that *Carnival Overture* (1946), an early work that had become popular, was "very much in the style of what Slavic composers did at the end of the last century, like the *Carnival* by Dvořák; you know, I didn't have it in mind. But if I write something sad it's never typically Czech, and if I write something happy, it's never typically Dvořák. It's just a mixture."[22]

A number of his works are based on twentieth-century figures who became symbols of the struggle for freedom from tyranny and oppression. The text of *From the Diary of Anne Frank* (1970, scored for soprano and orchestra), taken from the well-known diary of a Dutch Jewish girl in hiding during the 1940s, expresses the range of emotions experienced by this child in fear for her life; the setting features extreme chromaticism and a tortured vocal line. During the Communist regime in Czechoslovakia Morawetz wrote a Czech translation of the work for a radio broadcast in Prague, but a member of the radio staff asked him to consider instead a translation she had prepared. Morawetz was quite upset: she had changed some of the words so that text underlay no longer fitted the music. "She mixed it all up. The important words were mutilated. I said, 'Thank you very much but I really can't accept it like it is." [Anne wrote] 'My God, why did all this happen to me?' and [the translator] changed it to something like 'Oh fate.' ... This destroys the whole meaning of the work." But the translator replied, "Mr Morawetz, you don't understand. I just wanted to help you. If you leave it the way it is, our Communist committee would never accept it. You can't give so much importance to God!"[23] *Memorial to Martin Luther King* (1968) began as a vehicle for Russian cellist Mstislav Rostropovitch; Boris Berlin, a Russian émigré who came to Canada in the 1920s, had written to Rostropovitch hoping to put him in contact with Morawetz. Rostropovitch asked Morawetz to write a work, "something that is on a completely different subject, a different form, different orchestration." Morawetz set the cello part as a musical symbol of King's struggle for racial equality, culminating in the famous statement, "Free at last, thank God I'm free at last!"

Walter can also be credited with luring John Newmark to Toronto, at least for a short time. The Recreation Hall at Camp B in Ripples, New Brunswick had a radio; among the various broadcasts Newmark heard during his time there was the series of six concerts from Toronto featuring Greta Kraus and Arnold Walter, both playing harpsichords.[24] Walter had undoubtedly induced Mazzoleni (his colleague at Upper Canada College) to explore some nice pre-Classical repertoire. Newmark was so delighted to discover that there were *two* harpsichords in Toronto that he determined to go there immediately after his release. In Toronto he also met his sponsor Lady Hamilton as well as Adolf and Gwendolyn Koldofsky.[25] Newmark studied conducting with Ettore Mazzoleni and made enquiries about joining the Musician's Union in Toronto so that he could once again appear professionally (he was now forty years of age). Incensed to hear that he would be required to spend at least a year in Toronto before he could be admitted to the union, he left for Montreal where he sought out the Musician's Guild office; after telling his story he was immediately accepted into membership. Newmark remained in Montreal for the rest of his life.[26]

Talivaldis Kenins had been originally destined for a career in the diplomatic service, following in his father's footsteps, and to this end had studied at the Lycée Champollion in Grenoble, France.

Returning to Latvia, he studied piano and composition at the State Conservatory in Riga from 1940 to 1944, when he fled the Communist advance into Latvia. After a short period in Germany, he moved to France in 1951 to continue his music education at the Paris Conservatoire.[27] The premiere performance of his Sonata for Cello (1950) played by French cellist Maurice Gendron resulted in a UNESCO fellowship. This work reveals a strong compositional hand well versed in the neo-classical tradition with a particular penchant for contrapuntal writing. It also reveals Kenins's predilection for concertante writing: "The concertante style is the dominant part of my musical speech, and after having studied and taught the technique of counterpoint for so many years, the canonic and fugal devices were such a part of my musical expression that sometimes I wasn't even aware of their presence."[28]

Walter, who was the Canadian representative on the UNESCO board and happened to be in Paris for the 1951 board meeting, contacted Kenins about a position at the Faculty of Music.[29] Since the St Andrews Lutheran Latvian church in Toronto was looking for an organist, the stars seemed to be aligned. Kenins's memory of the snowy day he arrived in Toronto, 18 November 1951, was particularly clear because it was the anniversary of the short-lived Latvian republic; he was the new organist hired to play special services commemorating the occasion at the St Andrews Lutheran Church. The following year he joined the faculty of the RCM (where he was enthusiastically greeted by Edward Johnson); soon after he joined the Faculty of Music at the University of Toronto, where he taught until his retirement in 1984. He joined CAPAC and served for a time as treasurer and then president. His activities in the Latvian community include the founding of the St Andrews Latvian Choir and in 1959 the Latvian Concert Association of Toronto. His works have been extensively performed at Latvian music festivals in Canada and the United States.

As a composer, Kenins used the harmonic vocabulary of extended chromaticism with bi-, pan-, and polytonality, and an occasional foray into twelve-tone technique (for example, the "Nocturne" from his *Concertino à Cinque*, 1969). His works for organ are particularly impressive. An accomplished organist himself, he wrote idiomatically, exploiting sonorities in a mid-twentieth-century French manner. His most diffuse and difficult work is probably the brooding orchestral *Beata Voces Tenebrae*.[30] Its dark tones reflect a sombre period in the composer's life when, shattered by the death of three friends, he was forced to contemplate his own mortality. The music threads along a tortured path toward a final epiphany with musical quotations from works that also deal with departure and death, including Liszt's *Funerailles*, the "Crucifixus" from Bach's Mass in B minor, Beethoven's Piano Sonata in E flat major, op. 81a ("Les Adieux"), and the "In paradisum" from Fauré's *Requiem*.

Kenins felt a need to rely on the structural dialectic of the sonata form, an aggressive primary idea pitted against a more lyrical, reflective one. The goal was to "build opposing elements into a cogent overall structure – the sonata form, with which I could identify my essential need for musical direction."[31] Many works employ the classic fast-slow-fast tripartite division of movements. Kenins's *Chants of Glory and Mercy* for vocal soloists, choir, and orchestra uses the Gloria from the Latin Mass as a counterpoint to a moving treatment of the words of Martin Luther King and a contralto voice in *Sprechgesang* reading a letter from a deportee to Siberia: "I still live with the nightmare of that dreadful hour when we were dragged out of our home in the middle of the night to start that long fateful journey,"[32] the fate of many of Kenins's fellow Latvians.

Few Canadian composers can boast a total of eight symphonies, all of them performed.[33] In addition to arranging a number of traditional Canadian songs, this Latvian expatriate found inspiration in First Nations mythology: works such as the chamber drama *Lagalai, Legend of the Stone,* (1970) and the symphonic cantata *Sawan-Oong, the Spirit of the Winds* (1973) are based on legends drawn from West Coast and Oji-Cree traditions respectively.[34] Kenins's last work, a concerto for viola, was performed in 2000 by Rivka Golani-Erdös in Vancouver with an orchestra conducted by Mario Bernardi. Talivaldis Kenins died in January 2008 at his Toronto home.

Walter was not involved in Emmy Heim's return to the TCM in 1946. Heim first came to Canada in 1934 to visit her brother Jules Heim in Montreal, and made her Canadian debut in Hart House Theatre at the University of Toronto on 16 October 1934, accompanied by Ernest MacMillan. Her partnership with MacMillan continued throughout her many appearances in Toronto until her death in 1954. Her first Canadian pupil was Frances James (later Adaskin), a noted Canadian soprano who studied with Heim at the

TCM in 1934. Heim settled permanently in Toronto in 1946: Students who came to her studio include Lois Marshall, Elizabeth Benson-Guy, Jan Simons, Joan Maxwell, James Milligan, and Mary Morrison. Jan Simons remembered her as "a wonderful teacher and human being, highly artistic but not very strong on vocal technique."[35] Canadian composer Paul McIntyre, who was Heim's studio pianist for three years, had the highest regards for her artistic abilities: Vocal technique as such had no place in her pantheon. Personality yes, but also a searing study of the meaning of the text, of what the text meant to the composer and how this was reflected in the music, of what the text and the music meant to the singer, and of how all this was to be conveyed to the listener. The greatest sin was to let escape even a single note that was not invested with maximum expression. It was a regimen that no student ever forgot.[36] For Nicholas Goldschmidt she was "one of the most wonderful women I ever met as a personality, as a teacher, she had a knowledge of everything." He spoke with awe of her knowledge of Lieder and remembered her introductory comments for his Hallmark recording, made in January 1954, accompanying himself in a group of Schubert songs:[37] "The Lieder composer expresses something beyond the words ... one must try to feel the mystery of the language through the colour of the voice." For MacMillan, Heim had "a personal magnetism that cast a radiance on us all ... She had that artistic conscientiousness that made every note in a song a matter of special study."[38] During her final illness, Heim corresponded frequently with Frances James; in a letter of 17 November 1952 she wrote: "Darling, I am so proud of you ... Now you are starting to grow. And in the right way too. Without conceit, but with joy and confidence. Once you have discovered that you as a personality can give personal things (no imitations) you will find more and more wealth in your soul that you can give to others. And that is what we are here for."[39]

Frances James also came under Walter's influence. In the early 1940s Walter introduced James to Hindemith's *Marienleben*. She studied this superb cycle with him and they performed it at the Heliconian Club in 1943 for the Toronto Society for Contemporary Music. At Walter's instigation, Hindemith was invited to Toronto to hold a class and a lecture at the TCM. After the lecture James sang the *Marienleben* for the composer during a musicale featuring Hindemith's works. Hindemith was impressed with her interpretation, and praised James for her performance.[40] Later in 1946 Hindemith invited James to perform the revised version. "This opened the door for all other contemporary things I did in Toronto, and led to my being looked upon as an expert in contemporary music.[41]

Pianist Anton Kuerti was lured to Canada as much by Arnold Walter and the University of Toronto as by Canadian politics.

> I abhorred the militaristic nuclear policies of the United States and particularly at that time the Vietnam War. I was a conscientious objector; I was acknowledged as such, so I didn't have to come to Canada to evade the draft, although I would have even if I had not been classed as a conscientious objector. I also refused to pay my taxes because about half of them were being used for military expenditures and I felt that the nuclear armaments were a crime against humanity ... I liked Canada very much on the occasions that I had been here.[42]

But Kuerti was no stranger to Canada; he gave his first Canadian concert in Winnipeg in 1956, and had also appeared with the CBC Winnipeg Orchestra under Eric Wild. He had met John Peter Lee Roberts (then a CBC music producer in Winnipeg) and the two became good friends. He made his TSO debut in 1961 as a replacement for Myra Hess on forty-eight hours notice. Shortly after he moved to Toronto he was appointed pianist in residence at the University of Toronto, and he remained at the Faculty of Music until 1989. Kuerti's contributions to Canada include the Festival of the Sound, held every summer in Parry Sound, Ontario, which he founded in 1980 and led until 1985. Kuerti continues to perform and is one of Canada's most internationally recognized pianists.

Kuerti has no difficulty in incorporating his political ideals with musical life; for him music should be cultivated with a view to its ethical value. He remains deeply committed to protesting social injustice, wherever that may occur in the world. A staunch advocate of human rights, he ran (unsuccessfully) as candidate for the New Democratic Party in 1988. His pragmatic solution to the problem confronting every pianist – poor tuning and servicing of pianos – was to do these jobs himself and to transport his Viennese Bösendorfer in his own truck. Kuerti is particularly noted for his performances of works by Beethoven and Schubert, and more recently Carl Czerny – three Viennese composers to whom he bears a close affinity.

The globe-trotting Lorand Fenyves arrived at the University of Toronto in 1966.

> Then in 1957 there was the possibility of going to Geneva. I looked forward to working with Ansermet ... Murray [Adaskin] wanted Isaac Stern to hear Andy [Dawes] and to recommend someone whom Andy could study with. It was the year Murray had a sabbatical and he went to Geneva. Stern recommended that Andy study with me in Geneva (that was in 1959 or 1960.) We already had one child, and the second was on the way. We thought it might be a good opportunity. The weather in Geneva was not very good, something like here, and in 1965 we came to Canada.[43]

Fenyves had been teaching at the Jeunesses Musicales Camp in Orford, Quebec, since 1963, and in 1965 he collaborated with Gilles Lefebvre in founding the Orford String Quartet: violinists Andrew Dawes and Kenneth Perkins, who had studied with Fenyves in Geneva, were matched with violist Terence Helmer and cellist Marcel St-Cyr to form a uniquely Canadian blend. The Orford Quartet flourished for more than twenty years and was probably the most successful international chamber music group that Canada had produced up to that time. Fenyves's other students include Adele and Otto Armin, Steven Dann, and Victor Martin. Fenyves held teaching and coaching positions at the University of Western Ontario, the Jeunesses Musicales World Youth Orchestra, the National Youth Orchestra, the Banff School of Fine Arts, Aldeburgh, the Cornwall International Seminar of Music, the Toho School in Japan, and beginning in 1985, once more in Hungary. He was still actively teaching at the time of his death in March 2004.

Since social context is axiomatic to ethnomusicological work, Mieczslaw Kolinski's ideas on musical analysis inevitably fell on fallow ground, but as one who had known the pervasive reach of totalitarianism, he could truly appreciate how music could be manipulated and distorted by a ruthless regime. Kolinski had been a victim of the dismantling of the Berlin Phonogrammarchiv by the Nazis in 1933 and had lost his job as assistant to Erich von Hornbostel "when the whole business started with Hitler. Otherwise, I'd probably still be there."[44] Comparative musicology was suppressed and its proponents forced to emigrate. Racial ideology had decreed that non-Western musics were lower forms of culture and not worthy of study.

Walter hired Mieczslaw Kolinski in 1966 to initiate ethnomusicological studies at the University of Toronto. Although Ida Halpern had taught a course in ethnomusicology at UBC from 1964 on, this first full-time appointment of an ethnomusicologist at a Canadian university represented a major step toward the accreditation in Canada of non-Western and indigenous musics as a serious discipline. Walter had undoubtedly known Kolinski from their student days at the University of Berlin. Kolinski had been a pioneer in the field, working with Curt Sachs and Erich von Hornbostel. Prior to coming to Toronto Kolinski had spent a number of years in New York. Kolinski's students include Beverley Diamond, Jay Rahn, and Bang-sŏng Song. Beverley Diamond praised his attempt to "develop analytical methods that were allegedly objective and free of socially formed values" and considered his classification of tonal structures based on the cycle of fifths "as useful as any."[45]

> As a victim of world events, he felt that any scholarship rooted in social values was polemical and capable of social misuse. Hence he developed an analytical system whose terminology and basic premises were unrelated to any music systems of the world. In the early 70s I scarcely understood that those "standing recurrent movements in the second degree nexus" related to that Belgian hiding place [in which Kolinski spent the years 1942–44] ... As we engage today with community collaborators, as well as transnational matters as contrasted as intellectual property and global commerce, on the one hand, and social injustice on the other, it is wise to remember that we also speak from very different positions, rarely as victims (as Kolinski did) but more often from the vantage of relative privilege.[46]

At his death Kolinski left a number of unpublished studies: the sequences of Adam of St Victor (566 pages), transcriptions and analysis of 117 French-Canadian folksongs (now at the Canadian Museum of Civilization), transcriptions of 152 Kwakiutl songs, transcriptions of 309 Haitian folksongs, and a major study of harmonic analysis entitled "Complete Chord Classification, Based on the Cycle of Fifths." A proper appreciation of Kolinski's contributions to the discipline must await a final assessment of these works,[47] but a common theme running through his career is an eloquent plea for a more encompassing perspective in academic studies.

> There is no difference between traditional Western music and the folk or classical music of other cultures. All mankind is the same animal – the brain and central nervous systems are the same for all mankind. This accounts for the fact that certain basic tonal and rhythmic structures can be found in the music of unrelated cultures. These features form a link to understanding. Otherwise, it would be impossible to understand anything, for example, of the music of the Indonesian gamelan. Music has universal roots and these can be used to build bridges between people and countries.[48]

Walter's role in Lothar Klein's appointment is unclear, since it took place in 1968, the year Walter resigned as director. Klein was born in Hannover, and came to the United States as a child when his family fled the Nazis in 1944. He received his musical education at the University of Minnesota and then returned to Europe (1958– 60) for additional composition studies at the Berlin Hochschule with Boris Blacher and Josef Rufer. He also studied with Luigi Nono in Darmstadt.[49] He taught at several American universities before coming to the University of Toronto. As a composer Klein has written a number of prize-winning works, and his music has been performed across Canada and in the United States.[50]

MCGILL UNIVERSITY

Helmut Blume took up the challenge of importing the academy into the university somewhat later but with as much zeal as Walter had done in Toronto. Luba Zuk, an émigré from Ukraine, recalls his early activities at McGill

> My memories of Helmut Blume are of the highest and warmest order. Some people didn't like his manner, but, in my opinion, he put the McGill Faculty of Music on the map. In 1955, he started sending small ensembles to different functions, to play in

Redpath Library, on the terrace, to play in front of Moyse Hall, to play at the Principal's receptions. "They have to know we exist," he said. He started sending out emissaries and said we had to be visible. He offered teaching appointments to me and other colleagues. He said, "I want to enlarge the Faculty. I want to get as many people on staff as possible. I want to make the University aware. Eventually I want to find musicians full-time jobs." I had been teaching privately, and he asked me if I wanted to come as a junior teacher. I agreed but he cautioned: "But you have to remember one thing. We might pay you less than you would get privately, but at least it is a position." My income was less at first, but he persisted as promised. Eventually I was appointed to a position with salary security.[51]

As a piano duo Luba Zuk and her brother Ireneus Zuk achieved considerable prominence for their performances of twentieth-century music. Works by George Fiala, Graham George, Bengt Hambraeus, David Keane, Donald Patriquin, Clifford Crawley, Gary Kulesha, and Ann Southam were commissioned for them, and they made a number of visits to Ukraine, performing and examining at local centres there.

Istvan Anhalt, one of Blume's early colleagues at McGill, gives an insightful view of the Faculty of Music during the 1950s.[52] Anhalt arrived in Halifax on 23 January 1949 to teach at the faculty at McGill on a three-year fellowship from the Lady Davis Foundation.

I was through with Paris; I was through with being a student. I wanted to start working. It was Canada that gave me this opening for which I am grateful to this very day ... Did I ever consider myself an exile, forced to leave? No, no. I was dying to leave. I couldn't wait. I left at the first moment I was able to do so. I wanted to strike out and look for a new life. Where, I had no idea. [My works were written] in response to what I sensed around me, and that was my attitude pretty well all along. To me Canada was a wonderfully exotic, interesting, exciting country full of opportunities, but I had to find "keys" for them, I had to respond to them. It didn't take me long to find out about the musical assets of this country ... I feel that I *grew* with this country. I had my modest baggage, baggage which I considered to be modest, but it had a potential. Right from the beginning I

> wanted to respond to what I found in this country. I was exhilarated by the openness and freedom of this country. It was not perfect: no environment is totally open and totally free and receiving, but there was enough openness, enough freedom, enough welcoming, so I felt I could find my niche. I could find my path, but it would be up to me to recognize what needed to be done and what I could possibly do.[53]

Anhalt's early career at McGill was marked by a desire to prepare Montreal audiences to accept music by twentieth-century composers, and thus provide a framework for newer works by Canadian composers including himself. In a concert at Moyse Hall on 20 January 1950, only a year after his arrival in Canada, he prepared and performed a program that included Bartók's Sonata for Two Pianos and Percussion and Stravinsky's Sonata for Two Pianos with pianists Jean-Marie Beaudet and Jeanne Landry and percussionists Louis Charbonneau and John Nadeau. Glowing press reviews noted that the performances were Montreal and possibly Canadian premieres.[54] The concert at McGill on 20 March 1952 was devoted to Anhalt's compositions. A concert on 6 December 1954, during the series celebrating the 50th anniversary of the McGill Conservatorium, also presented works by Anhalt played by some of Montreal's finest musicians, including Eugene Kash, Walter Joachim, Charles Reiner, George Little, and Maureen Forrester. This program included premieres of his *Fantasia* for piano (his first dodecaphonic composition) and *Comments*, a vocal work with text taken from three stories in the *Montreal Star*; Anhalt referred to *Comments* as his first Canadian piece, the first work composed as a response to the Canadian situation, but which at the same time was a reflection of past events.[55] Anhalt also organized what was likely the first concert of electronic music in Canada, presented at McGill on 30 November 1959. The program included John Bowsher's *Sonata pian' e forte,* several demonstration pieces by Hugh LeCaine, two works by Anhalt, and Stockhausen's classic *Gesang der Jünglinge* (1955).[56]

Anhalt moved conscientiously through the major twentieth-century techniques from his student compositions, through dodecaphony and music produced by electronic means to forge a personal style not specifically bound to any of the preceding idioms.[57] Anhalt's compositional career has been divided into four phases: a neo-classical period, influenced by Bartók and Stravinsky

(1941–53); a dodecaphonic phase (1954–58); an electronic phase (1959–74), and a consolidation phase in which he reworks and expands earlier styles and techniques.[58]

Anhalt's move to Kingston in 1971 as head of the music department at Queen's University was precipitated by the FLQ crisis in Quebec in October 1970, and he looked forward to the prospect of a peaceful and productive tranquility in the smaller Ontario city.[59] In Kingston he found stimulating contacts in a diversity of disciplines but he maintained contact with his Montreal colleagues. In 1984, the year he retired from Queen's, he completed two significant works: *Winthrop*, a mind-drama based on the English Protestant tradition; and a book, *Alternative Voices*, dealing with linguistic analysis and music-text relations in which he analyses a number of seminal works of the contemporary musical canon. On 11 January 2005 the Kingston Symphony presented the premiere of *The Tents of Abraham*, an orchestral work with a religious context dealing with the common roots of Judaism and Islam, Sarah, Hagar, and Ishmael.[60]

Early appointments brokered by Blume include Charles Reiner, émigré pianist from Hungary. Reiner had lived in Budapest from 1945 to 1947 and studied at the Franz Liszt Academy with Arnold Szekely and Béla Böszörmenyi-Nagy. In 1948 he fled the Communist takeover, and for the next year he studied at the Geneva Conservatory with Dinu Lipati and Louis Hiltbrand. After further travels he arrived in Montreal in 1951 with $20 in his pocket.[61] Since the Montreal Musician's Guild would not allow him to accept professional engagements until he had been a resident of Montreal for a year, his Canadian debut was delayed until 27 November 1952. The program for this recital, presented at the Ritz-Carlton Hotel (a wonderful 600-seat concert hall that also astonished Edwina Heller) included Bach's Partita in C minor, BWV 826, Beethoven's Piano Sonata in C minor, op. 111, Violet Archer's *Theme and Variations* (a new work based on the French Canadian folk song "Là-Haut sur ces montagnes"), and Liszt's *Mephisto Waltz*. The concert was a great success and opened many doors for the young pianist. Gilles Lefebvre, founder of Jeunesses musicales, introduced Reiner to violinist Arthur LeBlanc, with whom Reiner performed throughout the province.

In 1954 Reiner was hired on an hourly basis as a piano instructor at the McGill Conservatory, and with Blume's help soon received a full-time appointment. He subsequently formed an accompaniment class, and remained at the Faculty of Music until 1994. In 1954 Lefebvre offered Reiner a sixty-concert tour with Henryk Szeryng; this contract marked the beginning of their long association. The pair played about 900 concerts throughout the world – a tribute to Reiner's superb collaborative-pianist skills. The arrangements for Szeryng's recital with the Pro Musica Society in Montreal resulted in an amusing exchange. When Szeryng said his pianist would be Charles Reiner, he was told, "That's not possible; he is a local." Szeryng answered, "Madame, first of all he is international like me, we have made thirty-five records, and beside that, if he doesn't play for me I won't come."[62]

Reiner was able to leave his European experiences behind him and take advantage of the opportunities provided by his new homeland; his infectious sense of humour considerably enhanced the collegial environment at McGill. He was thrilled to be asked to be a judge at the Geneva International Competition. "Can you imagine what it feels like? You were a student and you are asked back as an international judge. Nine people from the whole world are asked to judge, and I was asked from Canada. It was fantastic."

Erwin Marcus had a brief appointment at the McGill Conservatory in 1955. Born in Vienna he studied musicology at the University of Vienna. He was active as a pianist and a coach during the interwar years, and from 1930 to 1934 was accompanist for Leo Slezak and Vera Schwarz. In 1938 he fled the Nazi regime and spent the next ten years in Shanghai working as a teacher and a conductor. In 1949 he came to Montreal, where he lived for the last seven years of his life. Unfortunately, his compositions never gained more than local recognition, but a number were broadcast on CBC, including a Quartet for Clarinet, Violin, Violoncello and Piano (broadcast 1955) a Piano Suite (broadcast 1956), and a Piano Sonata (performed by his friend Rose Goldblatt, broadcast 1957).[63] He also assisted Pauline Donalda in the Opera Guild (1949–50).

Viennese expatriate Karl Steiner taught at the McGill Conservatory from 1964 to 1989. He had spent a brief period of internment in the Dachau concentration camp in 1938 and after his release he fled to Shanghai where he lived until the Communist takeover in 1949.[64] He considered a return to Austria, but was dismayed by the horrific aftermath of the Nazi regime in which his entire family had perished. Instead, he chose Canada, landed in Vancouver, and travelled across the country to Montreal, where he lived until a few years before his death in 2003.

Steiner made it his mission to introduce atonal and twelve-tone music to Montreal students and audiences and to promote the work of pupils of the Second Viennese School: Hans Erich Apostel, Julius Schloss, Eduard Steuermann, and Hanns Jelinek. His recording of works by these composers, *Music of the Second Generation of the Second Viennese School*, is a pioneering achievement.[65] Owing mainly to his efforts, a number of these dodecaphonic pieces were accepted as test pieces for the curriculum at the McGill Conservatorium. Otto Joachim's *Twelve 12-Tone Pieces for Children* (1959) is a result of Steiner's efforts to have material in the dodecaphonic idiom available for beginning musicians: "When Karl Steiner came," Joachim commented, "he was a nobody, and here he established himself a little. I had him teach Davis, my son, and somehow my twelve-tone pieces were the result of Karl Steiner's insistence on my writing twelve-tone music for children, for my son."[66] Steiner's work was perhaps better known in New York and Vienna than in Montreal, and he felt he was not really understood in Canada.[67] He lectured at the University of Louisiana, Mannes College (New York), and the University of Toronto, as well as at McGill. A number of articles on Steiner have been published in the Austrian periodical, *Österreichische Musikzeitschrift*, and he was often cited in this journal.[68] He was a close friend of Vienna musicologist Hartmut Kronos and he corresponded with Hanns Jelinek regarding performances of Jelinek's works in Montreal.[69] He was a friend of Julius Schloss (1902–73), who had been Alban Berg's secretary. When Schloss eventually immigrated to the United States, he brought with him an important collection of material relating to the Schoenberg circle. After Schloss died, his widow sold a portion of the collection to the Marvin Duchow Music Library at McGill University. [70]

Baritone Jan Simons came to Canada as a child with his family who had fled the Nazis by way of Holland. He studied in New York in the 1950s with Emilio di Gogorza and Joseph Regneas, and his Montreal debut in Celia Bizony's Musica Antica e Nuova earned a rave review from Brian MacDonald, then music critic for the Montreal *Herald*. He joined the Faculty of Music at McGill in 1961. Simons gave many recitals with John Newmark in programs of mixed repertoire and the major Lieder cycles by Schubert

(*Winterreise*, *Die Schöne Müllerin*, *Schwanengesang*) and Schumann (*Dichterliebe*). "[Newmark] was pretty tough, very critical, which taught me a great deal. He was a very fine coach and always there with the words should you forget them. He often said that he was a frustrated singer and had a very rough voice, likely from heavy smoking."[71]

In the 1970s Simons was introduced to the Hussler technique, and worked with Yvonne Rodd-Marling in London. He was also a founding member of the Festival Singers of Canada (now the Elmer Iseler Singers). After his retirement, he continued to teach privately and lead a song interpretation class at McGill. His death in 2006 was mourned by many fellow musicians.

Simons's colleague Bernard Diamant was born in Amsterdam and studied in The Hague and in Berlin at the Hochschule für Musik during the 1930s. In 1945 he fled the Communist regime in Czechoslovakia, and lived in France until 1950. He arrived in Montreal on 20 August 1950 and quickly established himself as a leading voice teacher.[72] His best-known student was Maureen Forrester whom he taught in the 1950s at the beginning of her international career. (It is interesting to note that although Maureen Forrester was the first Canadian singer to have established an international career without having studied abroad (with the exception of a short period of study with Michael Raucheisen in Berlin in 1955), her two main teachers in Canada – Bernard Diamant and John Newmark – were both émigrés.) Diamant's other students at McGill University and École Vincent d'Indy include Rosemarie Landry, Joan Patenaude, John Boyden, and Anna Chornodoska. Diamant gave recitals across Canada and the United States with John Newmark and in the 1950s he joined Celia Bizony's Musica Antica e Nuova, performing repertoire ranging from Monteverdi to Hindemith.[73] In 1968 he began teaching in Toronto, and in 1972 he joined the Faculty of Music at the University of Toronto.

Armas Maiste came to McGill in 1974 after a multi-faceted career that embraced classical and jazz music. A refugee from Communist-dominated Estonia, Armas Maiste fled his native city Tallinn in 1944 and studied for six years at the State Academy in Stockholm.

> I studied first at the State Academy of Music in Tallinn (1940–44) but we left Tallinn when I was 15. We had lived under one occupational force and now it was the turn of some-

> one else. The entire city was levelled. Our house took a direct hit on 9 March 1944 (my birthday)! The bomb landed on the kitchen table and we were sent scurrying from the building. Everything was destroyed, all memorabilia, everything. My mother decided that that was enough of that. We would have to leave; we left only with the things we could carry with us.

Maiste arrived in Canada with his family in 1950; they initially lived in Sault St Marie where they had a distant relative,[74] but an Estonian friend advised Maiste to move to Montreal where there were more professional opportunities. Maiste is noted both as teacher and performer for his proficiency in classical and jazz repertoire. He participated in the 1971 Montreux Jazz Festival and the 1973 European Radio Jazz Festival in Oslo. He premiered works by Violet Archer and Eldon Rathburn, and performed in concerts presented by the Société de musique contemporaine du Québec in Montreal. From 1958 to 1982 he was pianist for the Montreal Symphony Orchestra; Charles Dutoit valued his energetic treatment of the piano part in Stravinsky's *Petruschka.* Maiste initiated jazz improvisation classes at McGill and also taught at l'Université d'Ottawa. In 1984 he moved to Toronto, where he taught at the RCM and in the jazz program at Humber College, guiding classes of pianists making the transition from classical to jazz performance. He also continues to perform, regarding it as a challenge he feels he needs in order to keep in shape.[75] "I think that humans are very resilient. It is remarkable that one gets over things without too many scars."

HAMILTON CONSERVATORY, HAMILTON, ONTARIO

Reginald Godden was able to give postwar musical developments a significant boost by hiring several talented émigré musicians to teach at the Hamilton Conservatory. Arthur Garami had studied with Géza de Kresz at the Franz Liszt Academy in Budapest (de Kresz had returned to Europe in 1935, but came back to Toronto in 1947).[76] When Garami arrived in Canada in 1949 de Kresz, who was teaching at the RCM and heard of a position as head of the string department at the Hamilton Conservatory, recommended Garami for the job. Godden was favourably impressed, describing Garami as "a violinist of stature who brought color and vibrancy to the Hamilton scene as a faculty member, teacher, performer, and later concert master of the newly invigorated Hamilton Philharmonic ... Arthur quickly vitalized string playing in the area, and it was my pleasure to be associated with him as pianist in many of his appearances."[77] Garami remained as director of the string department until 1954 and was frequently heard on CBC broadcasts. He made his Canadian debut on 7 March 1951 with the TSO in Hamilton playing Tchaikovsky's Violin Concerto, and he subsequently appeared with major Canadian orchestras.

A meeting in 1954 with soprano Pauline Donalda and other Montreal local musicians prompted Garami's decision to move. He brought his mother and his sister with her family to Montreal from Holland. (Garami's father had died in a concentration camp and his sixteen-year old brother had been arrested and was never heard from again.) In 1968 he founded the Classical Quartet[78] which performed frequently on William Stevens's television program, *Let's Talk Music*. From 1960 to 1965 Garami was associate concertmaster of the Montreal Symphony Orchestra, and in 1965 he received a full-time teaching position at the Conservatoire de musique, but he still had hopes of a career as a solo violinist. In May 1964 he played a complete cycle of Beethoven violin and piano sonatas with pianist Charles Reiner in three recitals in New York at Carnegie Hall. He also toured the Atlantic provinces with the Jeunesses musicales.[79] During his career he performed with a number of pianists including Charles Reiner, Lise Boucher, Raoul Sosa, Dale Bartlett, and his wife Shirley Garami. His untimely death in Montreal in 1979 shocked many in the music community.

Udo Kasemets did much to expand the musical horizons of Canadian audiences. Born in Tallinn, Estonia, he studied composition, conducting, and piano at the State Conservatory, and had begun his musical career when he fled westward from the advancing Soviet forces. He was able to continue his musical training in displaced persons camps in Germany and he came to Canada in 1951. His first position was at the Hamilton Conservatory. Kasemets admired Godden's initiative in "building the Conservatory into an institution where quality things could be done."[80] Godden introduced Kasemets to members of the Canadian League of Composers, including Harry Somers and Lorne Betts, making him feel completely at home: "The fifties were very conducive to that," Kasamets commented.

The entry for Kasemets in *Bakers Biographical Dictionary of Musicians* states that his earlier works have "peaceful Romantic modalities with Estonian undertones," but that "soon he espoused serialism and the pantheatricalism of the most uninhibited avant-garde."[81] At the 1960 international composer's conference in Stratford, Ontario, Kasemets came into contact with members of ONCE,[82] a group of American composers and avant- garde artists from Ann Arbor who ran festivals that featured leading artists such as John Cage, Morton Feldman, Robert Rauschenberg, the Merce Cunningham Dance Company, and Judson Dance Theatre; several years later Kasemets went to Ann Arbor to meet ONCE members including Robert Ashley, Gordon Mumma, and Roger Reynolds. This encounter caused a major shift in his musical orientation: "My whole world-view changed in the 1960s, radically, strongly. That's when I actually withdrew most of my former music and started with completely new insights into the whole thing."

Reflecting on the "imbedded in concrete" approach to choice of repertoire, concerts, and concert-going, Kasemets constantly searches for new ways to experience and expand the limitations of the day-to-day world. "We should try to make a two-way understanding of time and space and present it in a space where it is conducive and create a particular time-frame so that there is a new excitement, a real excitement about what happens with any kind of performance. [We should not be content to merely] transport things from one time to another but create really new ways of experiencing time-space." For Kasemets, even the extended tonal system is dead: "We need new forms, new structures, and new content; we must ask new and different questions. In the twentieth century, with Einstein, Planck, and Hubble, people came to see the universe in new ways, unlike the previous concepts of Newton, Kepler, and Galileo. Suddenly there is a third dimension in the universe, a third dimension to music also."[83]

Kasemets defends his interests in varied musical fields – composition, writing, music criticism, music philosophy – by explaining that "there are so many different aspects to music-making. Composition, performance, teaching, writing about music – all these are one and the same thing really. Some people go into specialties like musicology; I try to consider myself a generalist ... When I came, I came with the understanding that I wanted to become part of this place here. This was going to be my new home. I never had any kind of other thoughts. No matter how frustrated I am here, this is still the best place to be."[84]

ACADIA UNIVERSITY, WOLFVILLE, NOVA SCOTIA

Jānis Kalejs spent about five years in German displaced persons camps, where he was able to continue his career, performing on British Army radio network broadcasts in Hamburg. In 1946 he and his wife moved to Oldenburg, Germany, then occupied by Canadian forces. He and several other Latvian musicians gave recitals for the Canadian occupation troops, for Germans, and for other displaced persons camps. On 31 May 1949 Watson Kirkconnell, president of Acadia University in Wolfville, Nova Scotia, contacted Kalejs to enquire whether he and his wife, pianist Felicita Kalejs, would be willing to move to Nova Scotia to teach violin and piano at the University. They had been recommended by Jānis Kalniņš, who had recently received a position in Fredericton. Kirkconnell pleaded that the "violin department has been particularly weak" and proposed that they begin work toward the end of September. By June, both had agreed to come bringing their son, Juris.[85] In March 1950, Kalejs conducted a performance of Brahms's Piano Concerto no. 1 in D minor with the Acadia University Orchestra and Dean Edwin Collins as soloist.[86] In 1951 the orchestra performed works by Cimarosa and Dittersdorf.[87] In 1961 Kalejs and six Acadia students traveled to Toronto to participate in the National Youth Orchestra Christmas program at Massey Hall.[88] Kalejs appeared frequently with Felicita as accompanist in the Maritime provinces and occasionally in central Canada, and the duo were also heard on national radio and television broadcasts. Felicita Kalejs also accompanied visiting artists appearing at Acadia including Jan Rubes, Teresa Stratas, Jimmy Fields, Frances Chaplin, and for seven years was the regular accompanist for CBC programs with Audrey Farnell.

Toward the end of 1954 Kalejs wrote to a friend in Ontario asking if a position in central Canada were available: "Despite the fact that days are full, I often have the feeling that this local horizon is restricted ... I do not always think that I am really fulfilling myself in what is, after all, a small country town, which is a very nice and peaceful place, but which is hardly a challenge."[89] It appears, however, that nothing came of this inquiry. Kalejs kept up a vigorous correspondence with fellow Latvian émigrés who had come to Canada. On 11 April 1962 Kalejs and Kalniņš joined forces in Saint John for a performance of Kalniņš's Violin Concerto – the work they had premiered fourteen years earlier in Germany – with the Saint John Orchestra. Kalejs served as acting dean of the School of Music in 1965, and then dean from 1966 to his death in 1973. During his tenure, the School of Music moved to new facilities in Denton Hall. Felicita Kalejs served as acting dean until 1974, and continued to teach at Acadia until 1979.

QUEEN'S UNIVERSITY, KINGSTON, ONTARIO

Istvan Anhalt replaced English-born Graham George as head of the Music Department at Queen's University in 1971 and held this position until 1981. His tenure as administrator has been characterized as "establishing a collegial, professional environment" and his teaching as "informed, imaginative, and thorough."[90] Anhalt oversaw the completion of a new music building, was instrumental in establishing an electroacoustic music studio, made academic and performance appointments that greatly strengthened the faculty, and invited leading national and international musicians to lecture at the university.

Ireneus Zuk was initially hired as a part-time instructor at Queen's in 1974 and gradually rose to become director of the School of Music, a position he held from 1997 to 2003 (the Department of Music became the School of Music in 1988, with a director as administrative head). As director, he began the PianoFest, a Queen's-sponsored piano festival, and instituted a visiting artists program.

Arnold Walter and Helmut Blume sought out, attracted, and hired a nexus of talented Canadian and émigré musicians who taught the new diploma and degree programs at the University of Toronto and McGill University. The staffing choices of these two administrators created the backbone for music education and performance in these two institutions that held strong for many decades. They created a milieu in which academic and performing arts could work together, which was not the case in the continent from which they had come. Because the émigré musicians represented widely diversified backgrounds and performing specialties they were able to broaden the repertoire of talented Canadians. Their influence was felt not only in Toronto and Montreal but in music schools in Ontario, Quebec, and the Maritimes.

"CAN MUS" – THE ÉMIGRÉS MAKE HISTORY

This account of the contributions of émigrés to music in Canadian Universities ends with two Camp Boys who never held university teaching positions but nevertheless had a significant impact on music history courses across the country. Today "Can Mus" is as firmly rooted as "Can Lit" in university and even high school curricula, but it is difficult to imagine the development of Canadian music as a serious discipline without the contributions of several émigré musicians who saw a need for Canadians to study their own musical heritage, and had the resources to carry out this research.

Helmut Kallmann's career is distinguished by his uncanny ability to uncover and methodically investigate lacunae in musical Canadiana, and to sweep scholars, librarians, and musicians into what became a growing field through the formation of organizations and the establishment of library collections devoted to Canadian music, past and present. Most institutions devoted to Canadian music are connected to him in some way or other. His passion for books and manuscripts became a search for our national musical artefacts.

> I think the best thing Canada offers to anybody who comes from Europe is that wide-open field for pioneer work. There's always something that the European will find that they haven't done yet in Canada. Certainly music history was one of those fields. And I was just lucky ... in having a career that just started at the bottom and went up in a gradual but straight line. I haven't had any reverses.[91]

After his release from the internment camp in 1943 Kallmann continued his music education at the University of Toronto, graduating in the first class of school music students in 1949, but he had set his sights on a career as music librarian. "I didn't want to become a school teacher. I thought a music library would be a wonderful place for me to work, and after waiting some time I found a position at the CBC, which was quite different from the public library or the university library. It was a wonderful opportunity to build up a library collection."[92] At the CBC Kallmann immediately became involved with Canadian musicians, and more importantly, Canadian composers. When he found there was little information available about many of these individuals and their works, he began his own research. He published his first article – "Canadian Music as a Field for Research" – and soon compiled enough material to edit a small book – *Catalogue of Canadian Composers* (1952).[93] He became devoted to learning more about the history of music of Canada, and since no one else seemed to be interested, he continued this research himself.[94] His activities and enthusiasm led to the establishment of the Canadian Music Library Association (now the Canadian Association of Music Libraries, Archives and Documentation Centres) in 1956 along with Canadian participation in the International Association of Music Libraries. In 1960 the University of Toronto Press published Kallmann's *A History of Music in Canada, 1534–1914.*

> Throughout my projects I became more and more frustrated by the lack of access to primary source material. In the mid-60s I composed a prospectus for a central repository for musical documents – manuscript compositions as well as correspondence, scrapbooks, concert programs, photos and others, in addition to printed and recorded materials. I submitted this to various institutions, among them the National Library of Canada. It happened that the National Librarian, Guy Sylvestre, having acquired the large group of manuscripts and personal memorabilia of the late Healey Willan ... decided that the time had come to establish a music division under the care of an expert in Canadian music. The dream of a national music collection that I had dreamt from the time the institution was opened in 1953 finally came true, and I was selected to be the division's chief. I assumed the position in April 1970 ... In 25 years the division has acquired the largest collection of musical Canadiana."[95]

Interest in Canadian music grew, and with the appearance of Canadian music courses in universities across Canada, a body of scholarship developed. These developments in turn made larger projects possible, including the *Encyclopedia of Music in Canada* (1981) – the first comprehensive reference tool on Canadian music.

The Canadian Musical Heritage Society was founded in 1982 with a mandate to publish historical Canadian music, making it available for study and performance. Kallman also found time to contribute articles on Canadian music and musicians to numerous Canadian, American, and European dictionaries and encyclopedias.

> I could have explained my motivation for exploring Canadian music history as a gesture of gratitude for fate having dumped me in Canada. Successful immigrants often claim to have been inspired by gratitude to do a good deed for Canada, but I distrust that assertion. I believe the fun in doing congenial work comes first; awareness of "paying back" develops only as the work comes to a close; knowledge and love of country arise through one's work. It was the chance to explore and discover that spurred me on, the fun of locating and fitting together the pieces of a jigsaw puzzle, the move from chaos to order. Through my quest I have come to admire and love Canadians, rather than the other way around.[96]

Violinist Willy Amtmann made his home in Ottawa after his release from the internment camp. In 1943 he joined the Ottawa String Quartet with Eugene Kash as first violin. A photograph from this period shows him as a dapper, optimistic, cultivated musician eager to make a way for himself. From 1945 on he occasionally stood in for Kash as concertmaster of the Ottawa Philharmonic, and held the position himself from 1957 to 1959. In 1947 he was appointed director of instrumental music for the Ottawa Board of Education Public Schools, a position he held until 1968. In the postwar years Amtmann also continued music studies that had been interrupted by a hasty departure from Vienna in 1938 followed by three years in internment camps. He received a BMus from the University of Toronto in 1950 and an MMus from Eastman in 1952 with a thesis on Bruckner's chamber music.

Willy Amtmann's older brother Bernard Amtmann remained in Europe through the war and was active with the French Resistance. He came to Canada in 1947 and established a small bookshop in Ottawa, but soon moved the business to Montreal. He became a specialist in the field of Canadiana and his advice was sought by numerous librarians and book dealers.[97] Willy Amtmann's interest in Canadian music began when he was browsing through books on his brother's shelves. The result of this new interest was "La Vie musicale en Nouvelle-France" (1956), Willy Amtmann's doctoral thesis for the University of Strasbourg. This text, published in 1975 as *Music in Canada 1600–1800* was the second book on the history of music in Canada to written by a Camp Boy.[98] He taught music history at Carleton University from 1968 to 1976 and also lectured at the University of Ottawa. Amtmann's sister Hansi Lamberger contributed to the musical life of Montreal and to CAMMAC.

7

Discovering Canada and Canadians

The previous three chapters examined the faculties of music at the University of Toronto and McGill University, created by Arnold Walter and Helmut Blume respectively, and some of the Canadian, American, and European musicians that these two administrators attracted to these schools. Now we turn to musicians who pursued careers outside the university or whose careers intersected only marginally with post-secondary institutions.[1] These musicians touched the lives of many talented Canadian musicians, an encounter that in turn presented opportunities for the émigrés to rediscover themselves in a reciprocal learning process. Even with those who spent only a short a time in Canada, this process was mutually beneficial. In Canada the personal and professional relationships among these freelance European musicians developed further in a network that also included new contacts with Canadians and with other European émigrés. Old World ties proved invaluable in alleviating the *Angst* of newcomers, and growing circles of new friends created clusters of musicians with shared interests in centres across Canada.

These émigrés settled in cities across Canada from St. John's to Victoria, congregating for the most part in centres that already had a flourishing musical life: Toronto (30), Montreal (24), Halifax (about 15), and Vancouver (about 15). The data present in figure 7.1 represents only those émigrés for whom sufficient information has been tallied. Moreover, émigrés, such as Ernesto Vinci, who were active in more than one centre have been counted in more than one column.

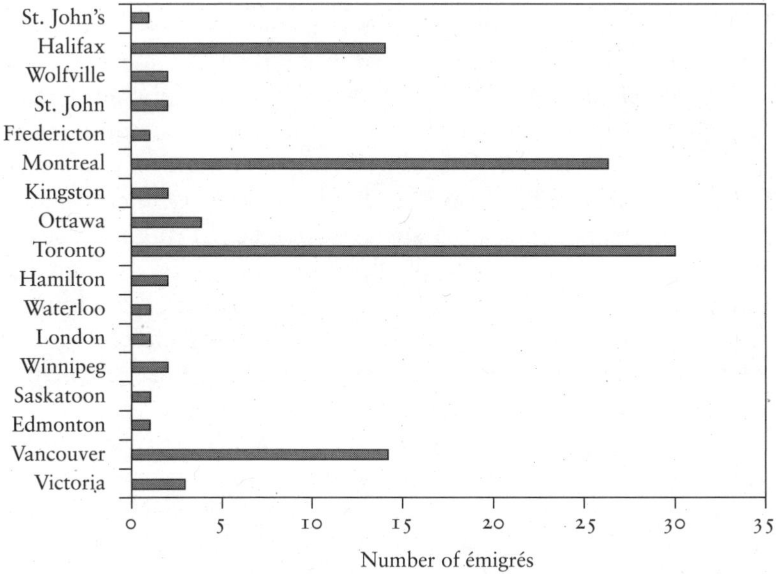

Figure 7.1 Cities in Canada: émigrés who settled in or were closely associated with specific Canadian centres.

OTTAWA

In 1940, when Frederick Charles Blair of the Immigration Branch was facilitating the immigration to Canada of a number of talented and enterprising Europeans, Ottawa was a hub of wartime activity. Arnold Walter's step-daughter Trudi Le Caine (née Gertrud Janowski)[2] was raised in Czechoslovakia and had been living in Berlin with her parents and working for the liberal opposition in Germany when Hitler first came to power. In 1933, on the evening of her twenty-second birthday, she was severely beaten up. Her life was in jeopardy not only because she was non-Aryan but also because her step-father, a social democrat, had fled the Nazis in 1933. Hearing that there was a warrant for her arrest, she made her way to Spain (then on the brink of civil war) and from there journeyed to Paris, where she earned teaching qualifications at the Sorbonne. Walter likely made the application for her to come to Canada when he was working at Upper Canada College in Toronto. The order-in-council issued for her in February 1940 implied that she had fled the impending German invasion of Paris (which took place on 14 June

1940) and found temporary refuge in the Pyrenees, in Vichy France.[3] Her escape route from Europe is unknown. She arrived in Ottawa (which she described as "a nice little village when I came here") in the summer of 1940. During the war she had a government job as a censor for prisoner-of-war mail. Later she married Canadian physicist and composer Hugh Le Caine. On her role as a prominent patron of the arts, she commented, "I'm glad I had a contribution to make, and above all, I had a debt to pay to Canada. I've had a wonderful life here. [My wish was to] foster those things I had enjoyed and always taken for granted in my childhood and teens in Europe." With the cooperation of Eugene Kash she helped to establish the Children's Concerts in Ottawa, and she promoted the Orff method, but perhaps her best-known contribution is the part she played in persuading Douglas Fullerton, chair of the National Capital Commission, to allow skating on the Rideau Canal – even though she was not a skater. Helmut Kallmann remembered meeting her in Arnold Walter's apartment at Upper Canada College in 1944: "She was a great joiner and spread the gospel of Arnold Walter – that is, public responsibility for culture."[4]

Joseph Berljawsky fled the Nazi regime in March 1938 for Switzerland; he arrived in Montreal in 1939, and soon established himself in Montreal and Ottawa as a violinist and pedagogue. It is likely that Berljawsky also arranged the emigration of his sister Betty Berljawsky (Barban), who arrived in St John's, Newfoundland, in 1947. He founded the Montreal Orchestra Society in 1954 and Musica Viva in Ottawa in 1968. In 1964 he completed a doctorate in violin pedagogy at Université de Montréal.[5] A proponent of the Viennese dodecaphonists, he brought an avant-garde perspective to his musical endeavours and corresponded with such musical luminaries as Pauline Donalda, Henri Wieniawski, Kathleen Parlow, John Beckwith, Igor Stravinsky, Georges Enesco, Nathan Milstein, Yehudi Menuhin, Leonid Kogan, Wilfred Pelletier, Claude Champagne, Pierre Monteux, Jean Papineau-Couture, and Rolf Liebermann.[6] Montreal musicians have fond memories of Berljawsky. Harvey Levitt and his daughter Roanne Levitt spoke of him as "a gentleman of the old school,"[7] and Istvan Anhalt described him with respect as "a tremendously dedicated person ... a freelance man, [who] worked very hard, taught more hours than you would care to teach a day to support his family."[8] Hansi Lamberger noted Berljawsky's close professional relations with her brother: "When Willy went on his sabbatical, Berljawsky took over his pupils."[9] Israel Libman, one of Berljawsky's first students in Montreal, later became manager of the I Medici Orchestra. He died in Ottawa in 1982.

Adam Guttmann, who adopted the stage name George Adams, was born in Radom, Poland. He was interned in the Warsaw Ghetto and then in Auschwitz. He survived the war and was reunited with his wife; the family immigrated to Canada in the late 1940s. George Adams played a season (1949–50) with the Ottawa Symphony Orchestra,[10] but found himself dreading the five days spent in the capital each week. "Not only was I separated from my family, but I didn't like it because it reminded me of the camps: you had to be on time; the strict obedience, being under command. Of course, that doesn't upset other people." He began to collect string instruments and bows, established a trade in instruments, and also became active as a violinist in the local popular music milieu. His recording *Musique de dance avec George Adams son violon et son orchestre* is an example of his superb technique and his ability to dazzle listeners with popular violin classics such as *Jalousie* and *Mon coeur est un violon*."[11] He was known in Quebec as the composer of popular tunes sung by Alys Robi, Rod Norman, Roland Montreuil, Jac Darieux, and Yvan Daniel. Aside from his music, Adams also published a number of books of poetry and the walls of his home were covered with his paintings.

TORONTO

After his release from internment camp in 1942, Gerhard Kander spent three years in Toronto studying violin with Kathleen Parlow, and then began his Canadian career. He performed extensively in Ontario with John Newmark, and occasionally with Helmut Blume. The program for a concert at the Technical School Auditorium in Ottawa on 17 November 1942, sponsored by the Ottawa Committee for Refugees, notes the patronage of the Governor-General and Princess Alice, Countess of Athlone. Blume played the Bach-Taussig Toccata and Fugue in D minor, Chopin's Sonata in B minor, Ravel's *Sonatine*, a Schumann romance, and a Delibes-Dohnanyi waltz; Kander played the first movement of Niccolò Paganini's Violin Concert no. 1 in D major, and a group of pieces by Fiocco and Wieniawski.[12] The reviewer for a second concert on 17

December at the YMCA in Toronto noted, "Toronto is fortunate in having more than 300 friendly aliens contributing to its life and work. Through the medium of the concert three of these men wish to express on behalf of their fellow refugees their deep appreciation for hospitality found in Canada."[13] Kander was also fortunate in the instruments he played. Kaspar Fraser, Kander's sponsor, purchased an Andreas Guanerius fils violin for his use, and later Eileen Larkin (one of the heirs of the Salada Tea Company) bought him a magnificent Stradivarius (The Earl of Westmoreland Strad, 1722).

Kander soon came under Columbia Artists management, and played concerts across Canada and the United States, including performances of the Brahms Violin Concerto, his favourite work, with the TSO under Sir Ernest MacMillan and with Pierre Monteux in San Fransisco.[14] At some point in the early 1950s, however, Kander decided that the career of virtuoso violinist was not for him. His friend Walter Homburger remembers him saying that he "could not be another Heifetz." He began by managing the financial affairs of his sponsor Lois Fraser, and a hobby in finance gradually became a full-time profession: "Now I'm with Wood Gundy ... first vice-president of CIBC World Markets. I've been in the chairman's club since I joined them. And that's it. C'est ca ... I play every day! Yes, I record. I have all kinds of recording machines, 'Music minus One,' I have all the concerti. I still work twelve hours a day. I start at six. I don't have to do any work in the house, I'll admit, but I get up at 6:00 with a newspaper and a pot of tea, which I make myself, then I bathe and I study and then breakfast is brought up for me."

Walter Homburger, Kander's close boyhood friend from Germany, used his post-release time in Toronto to good advantage in continuing his education. In February 1946, during one of his frequent visits to the Kiwanis Festival he heard Glenn Gould, then age thirteen, playing Beethoven's Piano Concerto no. 4. Homburger had never managed an artist, but plucking up his courage he asked Gould if he could meet his parents. Homburger was only twenty-two at the time. "Brash that I was, I said I wanted to manage Glenn. Somehow or other they didn't have any objections." Gould gave his first concert under Homburger's management on 20 October 1947,[15] and oversaw Gould's career from then until 1964. In 1955 he negotiated Gould's Columbia recording contract, and he played a significant role in obtaining permission for Gould to appear in Russia in 1957. Homburger's negotiations with Mitchell Sharp

(Department of External Affairs) resulted in a breakthrough in Canadian-Soviet relations. The United States had threatened to bar Gould from entering the US if he visited the Soviet Union. "They didn't think Glenn was important enough, but once he had made a splash, suddenly he became a great hero and they supported it completely. I got Lois Marshall in there too before an American. Byron Janis, I think, [was] the first American afterward."[16] Homburger's relationship with Gould was characterized by mutual respect. When Gould decided to abandon public performances he tried to dissuade him:

> Glenn, I have to warn you of one thing. I have noticed that when I bring an artist to town, the record sales double or quadruple, because suddenly there's interest. Then after a while, they drop off again. Nothing happens ... when you don't perform anymore, this can happen ... So he retires, and six months later he calls me up and says, "Walter, I just got my statement, would you like to guess?" The minute I heard Glenn say, "Would you like to guess?" I knew they were up. So I would guess and I was never high enough. "You see you were wrong!" And this went on for years and years. "I'm very happy I was wrong."[17]

Homburger's career as impresario had a rocky start. He was a great admirer of Lotte Lehmann, and in 1945 began to negotiate for her to sing in Toronto. When he asked Lehmann's manager in New York why Lehmann had never been to Toronto, the manager replied that no one had invited her. "Why don't you invite her?" he said, and Homburger replied, "Why not?" Lehmann was scheduled to sing a series of three Town Hall Lieder recitals in January 1947, so arrangements were made to have her repeat each recital in Toronto a week later. The piano accompanist was Paul Ulanowski (also an émigré). Homburger signed his first contract, rented Eaton Auditorium, and placed his first newspaper advertisement in the *Globe and Mail*. The Lehmann series was an artistic success with excellent reviews[18] but it was a financial disaster. Homburger learned a valuable lesson: others might not share his musical values. His next International Artists venture, a recital by Vladimir Horowitz on 18 April 1947,[19] was both an artistic and a financial success. Homburger subsequently hired Lehmann for a return engagement in Toronto on 26 January 1948. Through International

Artists Homburger brought outstanding American and European musicians to Toronto for more than thirty-five years.[20] He maintained close contacts with impresarios in New York, particularly Sol Hurok.

> [Hurok] was wonderful, great. He always had it in his contract, you have to say "Sol Hurok presents," and I said, "Sol, your name won't sell the concert, and it costs me money for that line." Occasionally I would walk into his office and I would say, "I've never heard of that pianist before. Tell me about him." He would say, "He's not for you." He probably had him for a Community Concert or for the other things, but he knew my tastes and my standards. Nobody else ever did that ... I used to go to Lincoln Centre, the big record stores and I would ask the people in charge, "Who sells these days on the classical record labels?" And on occasion, there were certain artists that sold who had never even been to New York, and I brought them here. The audience still came because they knew them from records. Daniel Barenboim made his North American debut on the Series, and Friedrich Gulda, his Canadian debut ... I brought Pavarotti here for 7,500 dollars before he was generally known. I was the first to bring Klaus Tennstedt to North America.[21]

Homburger also confessed to having made up publicity quotes for artists. "If you advertise and say, 'The greatest pianist since Horowitz,' and you put it in quotes, and you don't say where it comes from, who is to know? I never quoted my source. Some I made up myself, they were very good!"

In order to prevent artists from playing the International Artists series against the TSO concerts to obtain higher fees, Homburger suggested that they arrange for performers to appear in alternate years with the orchestra and the International Artists series; Jack Elton, then manager of the TSO agreed. When Elton was ready to retire, he recommended that the TSO Board invite Homburger as his successor. "And that's how it came about. I never applied. That was in January 1962." Homburger was manager of the TSO for twenty-five years; he helped the orchestra to grow from seventy-five musicians with a twenty-four week contract to ninety-seven musicians with a forty-eight-week season. He arranged for the TSO to play for Canadian Opera Company performances, which extended the orchestra's season by several weeks. He also promoted the careers of many Canadian musicians, including Louis Lortie, Victor Braun, and Jan Rubes.

Homburger's great personal integrity earned the respect of musicians. The "Great Gathering," held after he retired from the TSO on 9 March 1987 attracted such musical celebrities as Isaac Stern, Victor Borge, Mstislav Rostropovich, Pinchas Zukerman, Yo Yo Ma, Murray Perahia, Louis Lortie, Maureen Forrester, and Jean-Pierre Rampal, who donated their services to raise some $2.3 million for the orchestra's endowment fund.[22] In retirement he remains active by promoting the career of Canadian violinist James Ehnes.

Hans Kaufman's musical career fell victim to wartime politics. After his release from the Sherbrooke internment camp in 1942, he went to Toronto where he worked for a time at Tip Top Tailors and lived with his sponsors, the family of composer Louis Applebaum.

> One of the officers came to Tip Top Tailors [to see] if anyone was interested in the army. I had to get out of that sweatshop, so I made an application to the Army Show, had an audition, and I got in. I could choose any instrument I wanted, so I went down to Heinl's. And I got a blue set of tails and a very fine violin.
>
> I was in the Army Show for one year – *Khaki Collegians* (a revue with dancing girls...) I joined general service because I wanted to go to England. My brother was in England at that time. I had my basic training here. Then a letter came to the sergeant major (Frank Fusco) of my unit, that they did not permit me to participate in the Show because I didn't have my citizenship papers! A stupid situation. The sergeant major was so upset because the whole show broke down. I was a soloist in it. They had to re-rehearse the whole show. I was living at the Horse Palace at the Exhibition. I could only play in the army camps here, Petawawa, Camp Borden. I had to stay in Canada.[23]

At the end of the war Kaufman was given honourable discharge and free tuition to study violin for a year with Kathleen Parlow and harmony with Dr Horwood.[24] Meanwhile, he also began to explore popular music. He was hired to play for the soundtrack of the film *Canadian Pacific*,[25]followed by engagements in Toronto's hotel circuit. In 1949 the newly-formed Hans Kaufman Trio (with cellist

George Horvath and pianist Eric Schaefer) began a twelve-year stint playing dinner and dance music at the St Regis Hotel, and they also played for several years at the Franz Joseph Dining Room in Walker House on Front Street. Kaufman played dinner engagements at the King Edward Hotel and freelanced with a strolling group, first in trio format (violin, accordion, and guitar) and later as a soloist; for twelve years he appeared with Moxie Whitney's band at the Royal York Hotel. However, he did not neglect the classical repertoire completely. He taught violin at the Hambourg Conservatory for many years, and taught music for the Etobicoke School Board. He also played chamber music with Murray and Harry Adaskin, Marcus Adeney, and Boris Hambourg; his recording of the Edward Elgar's Sonata for Violin and Piano with pianist Leo Barkin is superb.[26]

In Austria bassoonist Hugo Burghauser[27] was a board member and a bassoonist with the Vienna Philharmonic Orchestra. He had been in contact with Ernest MacMillan concerning a position in the TSO. Unaware, perhaps, that his name had been included in the infamous *Judentum und Musik*[28] after the German invasion of Austria he made his way across Europe. In Paris his money ran out but he was saved from being forced into service with the French Foreign Legion in Senegal by Carla Toscanini, a close acquaintance who graciously paid his passage to New York. Burghauser arrived in Toronto in the fall of 1938,[29] knowing little about the city. "I first believed it might be Taranto in Italy. For my ignorance I got some reciprocity in Canada, when after my arrival I wanted to send a cable to Vienna. I was told there is a "Vienna" in Ontario, but they knew of no other Vienna in the world."[30] Burghauser spent three years in Toronto as principal bassoonist with the TSO and he also taught at the TCM, but after the war broke out, however, he moved south of the border.[31] He obtained a position as bassoonist in the Metropolitan Opera Orchestra in New York in 1941 and enjoyed a long performing and teaching career in the United States.

Freddy Grant,[32] the composer of the popular wartime song "You'll Get Used to It" remained in the popular music field. After his release from the Farnham internment camp in 1942, he went to Toronto where he worked as a pianist at the Prince George Hotel, the Park Plaza Hotel, the Silver Rail restaurant, and for twenty-three years at the Lichee Garden ("probably close to a world record"). He studied with Ettore Mazzoleni, Gordon Delamont, and Oscar Peterson, and led small groups in nightclubs. Grant also composed a large number of songs with an identifiable Canadian content; "They Call It Canada (But I Call It Home)," was sung in schools across Canada during the 1950s.[33]

Eli Kassner[34]was born and studied in Vienna; in 1939 he fled the Nazis, and went to Palestine where he continued his studies and began his career as guitarist. He arrived in Toronto from Israel in 1951. In Canada he held teaching positions at the RCM and the University of Toronto, but he resigned from the RCM in 1967 to found the Eli Kassner Guitar Academy. He also founded the Guitar Society of Toronto and the University of Toronto Guitar Ensemble. Carl Morey said that Kassner "virtually single-handedly created serious guitar studies in Toronto, if not in Canada."[35]

Franz Kraemer was born in Vienna and had studied composition and orchestration. He fled Vienna in 1939, made his way to England, and was sent to an internment camp in Canada. After his release in 1942 he spent the remainder of the war years in Toronto, and worked for the CBC International Service in Montreal from 1946 to 1952. From 1952 to 1970 he worked for CBC Television in Toronto. In 1971 he was appointed music director of the Toronto Arts Foundation.[36] Harvey Olnick praised his efforts: "I liked him when he started the chamber music series here at the St Lawrence Centre. He did a grand job, brought really first class people here and filled the house all the time."[37] William Littler reported that "In eight seasons he put nearly 300 musical events into the St Lawrence Centre and almost single-handedly changed the ecology of concert life in Toronto ... he is, in a sense, a taste maker. And over the past eight years he has cultivated a taste in this city for chamber music that currently borders on gluttony.[38] After his time at the St Lawrence Centre, Kraemer served as head of the music section of the Canada Council from 1979 to 1985.

Hans Gruber arrived in Toronto early in 1939 and enrolled at the University of Toronto as a philosophy student. He graduated in 1942 with a BA, but meanwhile he also studied conducting at the TCM with Ernest MacMillan.[39] During his first year at the TCM his theory teacher John Reymes King, who also conducted the Conservatory Orchestra, unexpectedly abandoned the job and Gruber was appointed conductor – the first undergraduate to hold this position. In his second year Gruber organized a 300-voice Varsity chorus in order to perform works for choir and orchestra. During the war

Gruber served for two years with the Canadian Army Intelligence Corps, translating documents and dealing with prisoner-of-war mail. One Saturday morning early in 1948 Macmillan met him in the hall at the Conservatory and barely looking up, gruffly asked "Have you got a match?" Gruber replied that he did and lit Sir Ernest's cigarette. MacMillan replied, "Oh, it's you. Thank God you've got something," then walked away. A moment later he called Gruber back, adding that he wanted to see him the following week. MacMillan had received a letter from Victoria asking him to recommend someone to take over the Victoria Symphony Orchestra. "Are you interested?" he asked Gruber.[40] This marked the beginning of a post that was to last for fifteen years.

Émigré conductor Heinz Unger had the most extensive European credentials. He led the Berlin Philharmonic when Géza de Kresz was concertmaster, and had also conducted in the Soviet Union (Moscow, Leningrad, and Kiev); as late as 2 March 1933 he conducted works by Arnold Schoenberg in Berlin.[41] He was a champion of the compositions of Vladmir Vogel, an expatriate Russian composer active in Berlin in the 1920s and early 1930s.[42] In 1933, at the pinnacle of his career, Unger was forced to leave Berlin, which he accepted with a grain of salt: "Political developments in my home country left me considerable spare time in 1933." He settled more or less permanently in England with continuing appearances in the Soviet Union, especially with the Leningrad Philharmonic, until he became disenchanted with the lethargy of the Soviet system.[43] He first appeared in Canada in November 1937 as a guest conductor with the TSO, and returned for a second engagement with the orchestra in 1938. The impact of this fiery German conductor was a mixed blessing. Toronto audiences were impressed but Ernest MacMillan was wary; there were a limited number of outlets for conductors in the city.

Unger moved to Toronto in 1948, but he continued to travel widely. His conducting activities in Toronto included frequent appearances as guest conductor of the Promenade Orchestra and the CBC Symphony Orchestra, and he also led CBC orchestras in Montreal, Winnipeg, and Vancouver. His most important contribution was with the York Concert Society, an organization founded in 1953 by his supporters as a vehicle for the maestro. Performances were held either in Eaton Auditorium or in Massey Hall. For the next twelve years, Unger led an orchestra of hand-picked musicians whipped into shape over a short rehearsal period in a series of four concerts. In the mid-1950s MacMillan still held the important music positions in Toronto, and was unwilling to relinquish anything to outsiders, no matter how talented. The rivalry continued through Walter Susskind's tenure as TSO music director with Toronto music lovers divided into two camps. Helmut Kallmann commented that Heinz Unger was in some ways a sad case: "He had suffered scarlet fever as a child and that left him partially deaf so he needed a hearing aid. In rehearsal he would often tell the players in advance how things were to go from his experience instead of letting them do it without him. When he settled in Toronto he expected Sir Ernest merely to step aside for him and when this didn't happen he asked Geoffrey Waddington for more concerts at the CBC. He lacked tact."[44] Be that as it may, Unger had the uncanny ability to inspire, or if necessary, to goad musicians to give their best; his performances were marked by an emotional intensity, rhythmic precision, and a superb sense of ensemble.[45] He excelled not only in the German masters but also in lighter fare such as Rossini and Dittersdorf. John Kraglund, the *Globe and Mail*'s abrasive music critic, championed Unger, creating a fruitful confrontation with the TSO establishment. Unger for his part introduced the symphonies of Gustav Mahler to Toronto audiences, beginning with a triumphant performance of the Symphony no. 2 ("Resurrection"), followed by Symphony no. 5 in 1959 and Symphony no. 9 in 1963.[46] Unger's death in Toronto in 1965 also spelled the end of the York Concert Society.

Walter Susskind[47] came to in Toronto in 1956 to succeed Ernest MacMillan, who had retired after twenty-five years as conductor of the TSO. During his ten-year tenure with the orchestra Susskind introduced more advanced programming and worked closely with the newly-formed Canadian Opera Company. From 1960 to 1964 he also led the Toronto Mendelssohn Choir, and frequently conducted the CBC Orchestra. Perhaps one of his most important contributions to Canadian orchestral music, however, is his role in helping to found the National Youth Orchestra of Canada in 1961; this orchestra was closely modelled on the National Youth Orchestra of Great Britain, which Susskind had founded. Highlights of his work with the TSO include the 1957 performance of Berlioz's *Damnation of Faust* and a performance of Honegger's *Joan of Arc* with actress and choreographer Vera Zorina. He also conducted the Toronto premieres of Stravinsky's *Sacre du printemps* and works by

Webern, Schoenberg, and Berio. He frequently performed piano concertos by Mozart and Ravel conducting from the piano. Susskind brought a Central European flair to the Toronto music scene and many were impressed by his keen sense of humour. After he left the TSO in 1965, he worked as a freelance conductor in Europe and the United States and in 1968 accepted an appointment with the St Louis Orchestra. He spent the remainder of his career in the United States.[48]

Karel Ančerl was born in Tucapy, Bohemia, studied composition and conducting at the Prague Conservatory, and began his career conducting for the theatre and for Prague Radio. His career was cut short by the Nazi occupation of Czechoslovakia. He was interned in several concentration camps, and was the only member of his family to survive the war years. After the war he held conducting posts at the Prague Opera, the Czech Radio Orchestra, and the Czech Philharmonic Orchestra, and he also toured widely in Europe and further abroad. He was in North America when the Soviets invaded Czechoslovakia in 1968, preventing him from continuing his regular engagements in Prague. That same year he was appointed conductor of the TSO, a position he held for the final years of his life (1968–73). Ančerl reinvigorated the orchestra and worked tirelessly to raise standards. He introduced works by a number of Czech composers (including Leoš Janácek, Bohuslav Martinu, and Joseph Suk) and conducted a Beethoven bicentennial festival of six concerts at the O'Keefe Centre in 1970.[49] He died in July 1973, shortly after his sixty-fifth birthday.

Alfred Strombergs[50] came from Liepaja, in Latvia. He studied theory and composition at the Latvian State Conservatory in Riga (1940–42) and was a conductor at the Liepaja Opera House from 1942 until 1944 when he fled the Communist regime. He spent the next four years in displaced persons camps in Germany and arrived in Halifax in 1948. In Halifax he was active as a conductor and played a major role in operatic productions. He continued his conducting studies at the Tanglewood Festival with Leonard Bernstein and Lukas Foss. Strombergs moved to Toronto in 1957 as coach with the Canadian Opera Company (a position he held until 1971). He was also a coach for the Opera School at the University of Toronto (1957–1968), and had conducting engagements with the Stratford Festival Theatre Orchestra (1957–71). He conducted premieres of two symphonies by Talivaldis Kenins. In 1971 Strombergs left Toronto for Edmonton, where he was vocal coach and opera conductor at the University of Alberta; he also worked with the opera division at the Banff School of Fine Arts (1972–73) and the Edmonton Opera (1973–74). On his retirement from the University of Alberta in 1987 he moved back to Toronto.

Emil Gartner managed to flee Vienna in 1939 and made his way to Canada by way of the United States.[51] On his arrival in Toronto he immediately took up duties as conductor of the Toronto Jewish Folk Choir. Over the next few years he increased the size of the choir to 130 voices and greatly expanded the repertoire. Guest artists included Igor Gorin, Alexander Kipnis, Lois Marshall, Jan Peerce, Regina Resnik, Paul Robeson, and Jennie Tourel. The choir retained its working-class character; most members learned their parts by ear. At one point, with Gartner's social democratic background and the choir's decided leftist leanings, the RCMP placed it under surveillance. In 1959, as revelations about Stalin's atrocities became more widely known, there was an ideological split in the choir, and some members moved away from the traditional orientation.[52] Gartner spoke tellingly of the role of the Jewish community in relation to Canadian culture:

> The culture of a people could be best described as the sum total of all its achievements ... No, we Jews need not fear of being lesser Canadians by being better Jews; on the contrary, we shall be better Canadians by being conscious Jews ... We may contribute to Canadian culture something priceless and absolutely irreplaceable: originality of creation, a beautiful colour in the rainbow of the world's cultural beauties. How could we in a better way show our love for Canada? ... As Canadians we shall be able to sing the great song of Canada that is yet to be written, and we shall have contributed to it, we may hope, a phrase or two.[53]

MONTREAL

During the winter of 1942–43 John Newmark performed concerts in Ottawa, Kingston, Toronto, Newmarket, and Hamilton with various artists including Helmut Blume and Gerhard Kander; in 1944 he appeared in a cross-Canada tour with the notable Canadian soprano Frances James.[54] He also flirted briefly with a career as teacher at the Conservatoire de musique, but abandoned the idea because of his many performing engagements.[55] Having established himself in Montreal, Newmark began partnering notable Canadian musicians including the well-known Quebec violinists Arthur LeBlanc and Noël Brunet, and cellist Roland Leduc; he also joined Alexander Brott and Roland Leduc for a series of broadcasts of the Beethoven piano trios in December 1944. In August 1945 Newmark and Noël Brunet presented a complete cycle of the Mozart sonatas for violin and piano. Rose Goldblatt, who had great care and concern for the émigrés, remembered those years:

> I got to John shortly after his arrival in Montreal in the autumn of 1943 when he lived in a small room on Crescent Street, close to the apartment we lived in ... At that time he didn't have a piano and he came to work on my piano and those pianos in the homes of other Montrealers who graciously received him ... During the early years in which John lived on Crescent Street, his apartment was the centre of the lives of many notable musicians, intellectuals, and German professionals from Montreal, Toronto, or New York. Franz Kraemer and Eric Koch shared his apartment for several years ... Very rapidly John acquired a reputation as an exceptional chamber musician. All the singers and Canadian musicians who passed through Montreal for recitals or recordings on radio or television went through Crescent Street ... He accompanied the greatest."[56]

The list of international soloists partnered by Newmark is a "who's who" of the musical world: Kathleen Ferrier, Paul Tortelier, Leopold Simoneau, Janet Baker, Arthur LeBlanc, Elizabeth Schwarzkopf, Gerard Souzay, Lily Krauss, Elisabeth Schumann, and George London. He coached and coddled Maureen Forrester throughout her brilliant career. He was a stern taskmaster but he knew the rewards of discipline and study. His sight-reading abilities astounded even hardboiled professionals. He was always dapper, urbane, courteous, under control on stage and off,[57]and known for a complete lack of nerves. He was also famous for his inability to memorize music, even the national anthem. While his crowning achievement was as a Lieder pianist, he was a superb chamber musician, and is generally considered one of the world's foremost pianists, on a par with Gerald Moore, Paul Ulanowsky, and Dalton

Baldwin. He always insisted that he was not an accompanist – he was a musician who made music with other musicians.

Newmark discovered his 1810 Clementi piano in a piano shop in Detroit but he later purchased it from a friend in Toronto.[58] He first played it publicly in a CBC broadcast of 15 September 1950, and after that recorded with it frequently. The Clementi's shallow action and clear tone was appropriate for preclassical and classical repertoire, and its five-octave range was adequate for works by Haydn, Mozart, and early Beethoven. Pierre Mercure's popular CBC television series *At Home with John Newmark*, broadcast in 1954, featured opening shots of Newmark's Crescent Street home fading to scenes of Newmark merrily playing away.[59]

> The CBC constructed a replica of John Newmark's living room in the Montreal studios for this series of chamber music performed by the German-born pianist, already well known in Canada for his CBC radio recitals. The premise of the series derived from Newmark's European background, which involved group performances in the home. The apartment set included Newmark's paintings by Canadian artists, etching by Durer, and his Steinway and Clementi pianos and, at least once, his Siamese cat. Newmark's guests included Noël Brunet, Walter and Otto Joachim, D'Arcy Shea, Lucien Robert, the Masella brothers, and Irene Salemka.[60]

Newmark also excelled in performances of contemporary music and performed works (some of which were premieres) by a number of Canadian composers, including Violet Archer, John Beckwith, Keith Bissell, Jean Coulthard, Lionel Daunais, Maurice Dela, Robert Fleming, Harry Freedman, Srul Glick, Jean-Paul Jeannotte, Kelsey Jones, Oskar Morawetz, Jean Papineau-Couture, Clermont Pépin, André Prévost, Healey Willan, Welford Russell, Otto Joachim, and John Weinzweig. His association with Otto and Walter Joachim was particularly close. Walter Joachim refused to perform with other pianists; Otto Joachim enjoyed Newmark as a brilliant musician always ready to indulge in musical repartee:

> He had a good sense of humour. I played in Maureen's debut at Town Hall in New York [12 November 1956] with John – we did the Brahms songs with viola, op. 91. Shortly afterward we did a

> recording of it which became the record of the year. We did the first Milhaud viola sonata which is based on baroque themes [by the 18th-century composer Baptiste Anet]; we had about twenty-five performances of it. So we put trills after everything, and I had to play them first; because they are canons he had to follow me. On stage during the concert I did all sorts of embellishments to see if he would repeat them and he followed me like a snake. And if you think he can't do modern music, you're mistaken. He lacked some technique, he was not totally happy sometimes, then he said very humbly, let's do it a little slower. I remember when we did Schubert's *Forelle* quintet; he had some trouble so we slowed it down a little. But he was very honest.[61]

Newmark had studied art in Dresden during the 1920s and was also a painter; he returned to art while on a concert tour in Texas in 1962. In October 1997 the Chapelle historique du Bon-Pasteur presented an exhibition of his works from 1962 to 1965; many were vibrant abstracts, created with spatula, full of vigour and life. A letter of 20 October 1983 to Gwen Koldofsky shows the grace with which Newmark was able to meet old age after a brilliant career. At the age of eighty, music had become something that was no longer important; recordings, radio, and live concerts no longer held any interest for him: "All I want from life is silence. It must be an over saturation of sounds, otherwise I can not explain it." He enjoyed being able to live "[enjoy] to the hilt something which I never knew; doing nothing. If that is what real retirement is all about, God bless it!" He spent time reading the English, French, and German classics, and commented, "I am happier than ever before."[62]

Otto Joachim thrived on the openness of the Canadian landscape. This autodidact and Renaissance man was able to teach himself whatever he felt he needed to know from painting to medieval music to electronic composition. Joachim had been active as a composer when he left Europe in 1934 (his symphonic poem *Asia*, composed between 1928 and 1939, was premiered in Montreal in 1997) but wrote little until he established himself in Montreal many years later. His first job in Canada was as a radio technician, for which he was paid seventy-five cents an hour. A month later he went to the authorities to report – in excellent English – that the visa allowing him only a brief stay in Canada on his way to Brazil, had expired.[63] The officer asked, "Is anybody bugging you?" When

Joachim replied, "No," he stamped the papers. Joachim was at last free to stay. With landed immigrant status in hand he felt he could take up composition once again, and he also branched out into other musical activities. In 1952 he accepted a position in the viola section of the Montreal Symphony Orchestra ("number five or six, all the way in the back") and gradually worked his way up to principal violist; he remained with the orchestra until 1965. He also taught at McGill University (1956–64) and at the Montreal Conservatorium (1956–76).

In 1955 Quebec composer Jean Papineau-Couture asked Joachim whether he could organize a quartet to play a concert of string quartets by seven Canadian composers. The group he formed – violinists Hyman Bress and Mildred Goodman; violist Otto Joachim, cellist Walter Joachim – became the Montreal String Quartet and remained active until 1963, tackling both new Canadian works and standard quartet repertoire including the complete Beethoven quartet cycle.[64] Joachim's involvement with early music brought him into contact with Carl Little who invited him to participate in CAMMAC at Otter Lake. Joachim formed the Montreal Consort of Ancient Instruments at McGill in 1958 and directed the group for ten years, teaching medieval, renaissance, and early baroque music and building some of the instruments they used, including two organs (one portative, one with bellows), a psaltery, a rebec, and a vielle. He also taught viol and managed to procure a set of six violas da gamba. The group made a number of recordings.[65]

Most of Joachim's Canadian compositions are based on dodecaphonic technique, which he learned while reading Krenek's *Studies in Twentieth-Century Counterpoint*; he only got about halfway through the book, however, because he "didn't want to become another Krenek." In 1967 he was commissioned to prepare an electro-acoustic work for the Canadian pavilion at Expo '67. By this time he had extensive experience in producing music by electronic means. Working in his own studio, he synthesized a monumental kaleidoscope of sounds on a four-track tape to create *Katimavik*; the title comes from the Inuktitut word meaning "gathering place."[66] Otto Joachim was closely associated with the Canadian League of Composers and worked with Quebec composers including Serge Garant, Gilles Tremblay, François Morel, and with Maryvonne Kendergi, who was active in new music organizations in Quebec including the Société de musique contemporaine du Québec. He also founded Musique de notre temps, an organization that promoted the dodecaphonic works of the Second Viennese School and works by Canadian composers. He commented that "Quebec is an open field for new music and I feel very happy here." With no one hampering his creativity, he regards the obstacles he had to overcome as just so many opportunities. *Stacheldraht* (1993), Joachim's memorial to the Holocaust, was premiered in Germany. "I do not attack Christianity," he explained. "As a matter of fact most of my music has the Christian idiom, even my last one, *Dies irae*" (a composition for organ and male choir that includes a quotation of the well-known Gregorian chant melody). His catholic interests prompted him to spend about twelve days in the Benedictine monastery of St Benoît-du-Lac, near Montreal, where he wrote the *Lord's Prayer,* a twelve-tone choral work dedicated to the monks of St Benoît.[67] Like several other émigré musicians, Joachim also took up painting, learning as he went, and creating large-scale, abstract canvases. In retirement he lives productively in Montreal, painting and composing, and he has maintained excellent relations with many Quebec composers and performers.

Walter Joachim came to Montreal in 1952 under the sponsorship of his brother Otto Joachim, who had learned of an opening in the cello section of the Montreal Symphony Orchestra and made arrangements for Walter to apply. Walter recalled that "there was a six-month waiting period before I could join the Guild and perform professionally. I became a shipper in a store on St Lawrence Boulevard at 38 cents an hour."[68] He joined the Montreal Symphony in 1953, and was soon promoted to principal cellist.[69] Around this time he also met John Newmark; the two were musical partners until Newmark retired in 1985: "Until his death, I never played with another pianist here. Never. If John was not free, I didn't play the concert." Walter Joachim frequently played works by Canadian composers, including premieres and recordings of cello sonatas by John Weinzweig, Violet Archer, and Otto Joachim.

Walter Joachim became one of the most sought-after cello teachers in Quebec and taught at a number of institutions including the Conservatoire de musique (1952–79), and McGill University (1952–63 and 1979–89). He taught "the way they did it in Cologne." At age eighty he still taught three to four students a week at his home in the NDG district of Montreal. Among his students are Denis Brott, Guy Fouquet, Hélène Gagné, Marcel St-Cyr, and Sophie Rolland.

Joachim was also active with the Orford Arts Centre, the National Youth Orchestra of Canada, the Jeunesses musicales World Youth Orchestra, and Le domaine Forget. In 1987 and 1991, he toured China as a guest teacher. He spoke impeccable German when addressed in that language and had a rich sense of humour. One of his favourite reviews came from the pen of Claude Gingras, the curmudgeonly critic for *La Presse*, who wrote: "Walter Joachim has played the cello so frequently that he can *almost* be considered a Canadian cellist!"[70] He died in December 2001 at the age of eighty-nine.[71]

Eugène Husaruk was born in Warsaw and studied in Crakow, Poland. His family fled first the Nazis and then the Communists; from 1944 to 1949 they lived in a displaced persons camp in Germany.[72] He arrived in Montreal in 1949, where he studied with Alexander Brott at the McGill Conservatory (1950–53). His continuing fascination with the violin led him to studies with Váša Přihoda and Ricardo Odnoposoff in Vienna. Husaruk particularly remembers Přihoda's astounding left-hand technique and his performances of Tartini's *Devil's Trill Sonata*. Ricardo Odnoposoff's technique was based on the Flesch system. Husaruk also studied with Ivan Galamian and Lorand Fenyves. He became one of the most sought-after violinists in Montreal, both for orchestral playing and for contemporary repertoire. He joined the Montreal Symphony Orchestra in 1957, and later served as concertmaster (1977–78 and 1979–82). He was also first violinist of the Société de musique contemporaine du Québec and premiered a number of Canadian compositions. He particularly remembers *Les États* (1973), a work by Betsy Jolas in which the violinist is surrounded by six percussionists playing a total of about 120 instruments; the performance was televised and enjoyed widespread publicity in Canada and Europe. Other demanding contemporary works include a concerto by Earle Brown that requires extensive improvisation on the part of the violinist. After his retirement from the Montreal Symphony Orchestra he became concertmaster of the orchestra for Les grands ballets canadiens and worked with orchestras at Université de Montréal and McGill. In June 2004 he visited Ukraine and returned with mixed feelings; he was elated to discover his Ukrainian roots but saddened to see recent developments in the country.

Mario Duschenes's Canadian debut as narrator in the Montreal premiere of Stravinsky's *L'histoire du soldat* in 1949 marked an auspicious beginning for a brilliant and varied musical career. Alexander Brott proposed the idea of performing the work to Les festivals de Montréal. Duschenes had performed the work in Geneva with marionettes, he knew the entire piece by heart, and could do the narration in French. "I give the Montreal Festival much credit since the people in charge of the Festival had no idea what the piece was all about; they took quite a chance. They didn't even audition me." The performance garnered rave reviews.[73] Duschenes had studied at the Geneva Conservatoire (1943–47) and toured Europe with the Ars Antiqua Ensemble before coming to Canada in 1948 with the help of his brother, Camp Boy Rolf Duschenes. After engagements as flutist with the Ottawa Philharmonic, Duschenes formed a recorder quartet, choosing "the best three" of his numerous recorder-playing friends. In 1955 he was hired to teach at McGill, and the same year co-founded the successful Baroque Trio of Montreal with Kelsey Jones (harpsichord) and Melvin Berman (oboe).[74]

Duschenes's long and fruitful musical relationship with French flutist Jean-Pierre Rampal began unassumingly when Duschenes was invited to a cocktail party in honour of the flutist. "He wasn't really well known at that time." Rampal engaged Duschenes to play a flute and recorder trio sonata with harpsichordist Robert Veyron-Lacroix and was so impressed that he continued to work with Duschenes through the years, recording and playing concerts in Paris and Montreal. "For me the wonderful thing was that when I played with him I became a much better flutist. He just sort of pulled you along. It was a tremendous inspiration to play with somebody who was so dynamic and such a total master of the flute." Duschenes also had the highest esteem for John Newmark, who he described as "The finest pianist ever. Give him a modern piece and he read it at sight." Duschenes became interested in the Orff-Schulwerk after meeting Doreen Hall, who had studied the method in Salzburg at the instigation of Arnold Walter. Duschenes is likely the first musician in Quebec to promote the method, working with Sister Marcelle Corneille and with Belgian priest Jos Wuytack.[75] With imaginative teachers Orff courses became an essential part of the CAMMAC program. Duschenes lamented the fact that "hundreds of schools have an arsenal of Orff instruments but there are so few music teachers now." During the years that the recorder was widely used as a teaching instrument, his recorder books sold by the thousands.

Duschenes had a rare ability to present orchestral concerts for children. It began when the Baroque Trio of Montreal was booked to give a series of thirty-eight school concerts in Saskatchewan; neither Berman nor Jones wanted anything to do with speaking to children from the stage, but Duschenes was accustomed to working with young people. François Magnan, a violinist and later manager of the Quebec Symphony, heard one of these concerts in 1967 and asked Duschenes to do a children's concert with the Quebec Symphony.[76] Since he was bilingual, he was eventually engaged to conduct children's concerts with orchestras from coast to coast. At first he used standard children's fare (such as Prokofiev's *Peter and the Wolf* and Benjamin Britten's *Young Person's Guide to the Orchestra*) but when he had trouble finding examples from the standard repertoire, began writing pieces himself with the required orchestration.[77] "If I wanted to highlight the woodwinds, I would start with an arrangement that I had made for flute, oboe, clarinet, and bassoon based on a French Canadian folk song. If it was something that the children knew, they would listen more carefully." He tried these piece out with his own children, and his wife (Jan Simons's sister), who was a child psychologist, also made suggestions about material that children enjoyed. Boris Brott, the National Arts Centre Orchestra, and the TSO have all made use of Duschenes's compositions.

At the time that Duschenes was hired as one of the four guest conductors for an Association of Youth Orchestras convention in Banff and was assigned to the Newfoundland Symphony Youth Orchestra, the Newfoundland Symphony had just lost their conductor (Charles Bornstein). Several young musicians recommended Duschenes to their father, who was president of the Newfoundland Symphony board. "I had a tryout with three other conductors and I won out. They asked me to become their permanent conductor in 1985. I originally was to go for two years and I stayed seven."[78]

Viennese émigré Carl Bamberger spent a short time in Montreal as the conductor of the Little Symphony during the 1947–48 season.[79] Bamberger had studied at the University of Vienna and held several conducting posts in Germany through the 1920s. In the 1930s he filled engagements in Japan and Philippines, as well as in

Eastern Europe and the Soviet Union. In 1927, with the increasing Nazi dominance of Europe, he fled to the United States where he became established as a conductor and joined the staff of Mannes College in New York (1938–75). He spent most of his career in the United States but also filled some engagements abroad, including the post of conductor for the Süddeutscher Rundfunk Orchestra (1957–72).

German émigré conductor Otto Klemperer also spent a brief period in Montreal in the early 1950s. He fled the Nazis in 1933 and spent the following years as director of the Los Angeles Philharmonic. He had been appointed music director of the Montreal Symphony for the 1951–52 season but he suffered a serious injury while disembarking from the airplane that had brought him to Montreal. He was hospitalized for several months and spent his recovery conducting from a chair; for two years he gave unofficial advice to the orchestra while he gradually resumed his international career.[80]

Lotte Brott's career is a fine example of a musical émigré who used the opportunities she found in her new homeland for the benefit of numerous Canadian musicians. The entrepreneurial spirit inherited from her father served her in good stead as she undertook the revitalization of several chamber ensembles in Montreal during the 1940s, transforming them into essential elements of Montreal's musical life. She was born Lotte Goetzel in Mannheim, where she grew up and began her cello studies. When her family fled the Nazis and emigrated to Canada in 1938 Lotte and her sister Lena were sent to Switzerland; they joined their family in Montreal a year later. Lotte met Alexander Brott at the McGill Conservatory in 1940 when she applied to join the McGill training orchestra. Brott was so impressed with her musicality that she was immediately accepted; he admired her ambitious spirit, her love of music, and her desire to pursue musical studies even against her parents' wishes. She left home for Toronto in order to study with Zara Nelsova, supporting herself with secretarial and sales jobs.

In 1941 she joined the Montreal Symphony Orchestra, and the next year she replaced Jean Belland, her former teacher, as cellist of the McGill String Quartet.[81] In 1943 she and Alexander Brott were married. Under Lotte's urging, performances began to employ larger forces – quintets, sextets, septets, and octets – as the ensemble was gradually transformed into the McGill Chamber Orchestra. The group ceased performing as a quartet in 1953 (with the exception of a single concert to commemorate the fiftieth anniversary of the McGill Conservatorium in 1954). The McGill Chamber Orchestra consists of a core of fifteen strings players supplemented by winds, brass, and percussion as occasion demands. The ensemble continues to bear the McGill name but now has virtually no connection with the university. Lotte Brott's administrative capabilities developed from her commitment to the orchestra as a performer, as she gradually assumed a managerial role, working on public relations, promotion, and fund raising. Her collection of programs and reviews also laid the foundation of the orchestra's archives. The orchestra has toured widely both in Canada and abroad. Lotte Brott was also active as manager of the Kingston Symphony while Alexander Brott was conductor from 1978 to 1981.

Helmut Blume's career in broadcasting began in the summer of 1944 when he was hired by the CBC along with Charles Wasserman and Karl Renner to prepare anti-fascist programs to be sent via the CBC International Service broadcast on shortwave to Germany. Blume worked with the German section of CBC International service from 1944 to 1946, first as a broadcaster then as head of the section. His CBC duties included a number of trips to Germany, and he brought back recordings of music broadcasts by SDR (Süddeutsche Rundfunk), RIAS (Berlin), and NDR (Norddeutsche Rundfunk). Interest in these recordings led to two radio series: *International Concert* (one-hour of music) and *Radio International* (three hours of music and spoken word), both initiated by Blume. He was a contributor to *CBC Wednesday Night*, but he is perhaps best known for *Music to See* (a series of eight lectures broadcast on CBC television in 1957 that won an Ohio State Award) and *Form in Music* (a set of six lectures broadcast in 1959 and published by the CBC the following year). Other programs included documentaries on musical, literary, and historical themes as well as fresh and well-illustrated travelogues. He even tried his hand at radio scripts and short stories.[82] Eric Koch remembered that, "in official capacities Blume was always calm and diplomatic. He had nerves of steel, and like a mole, stuck to his guns."[83] Blume later put the experience he had gained at the CBC to good use in dealing with the McGill University administration. His apprenticeship years at the CBC were important in focusing his thinking toward music and its dissemination through radio and television. He maintained contact with a number of colleagues (including Franz Kraemer, Eric Koch, Carl Little, David Dunton, and Lister Sinclair) after he left the CBC for McGill, and the contacts with professional musicians made during his broadcasting years were also valuable for his later work at the Faculty of Music.

Other émigrés who joined the CBC in the late 1940s include Franz Kraemer, who initially went to Toronto after his release from the internment camps, but came to Montreal in 1946 as a producer with the International Service. Kraemer later moved to television, and from 1952 to 1970 was an executive producer with CBC Television in Toronto. Successes of his CBC career include broadcasts of a number of operas, some of which – including *Turn of the Screw* and *Peter Grimes* by Benjamin Britten, Strauss's *Elektra*, and *Louis Riel* by Harry Somers – were Canadian or North American television premieres.

Shortly after his arrival in Montreal in 1952 Herbert Ruff[84] was hired by the CBC as a pianist and composer. By this time, Ruff was a well-travelled musician. He had studied in Vienna (1924–28) and in Berlin (1929–33). In Berlin he also worked as composer for UFA film studios. He fled to Switzerland in 1933, and then to Czechoslovakia in 1938. He lived in Hong Kong and Shanghai during the war and in Nanking from 1947 to 1952. At the CBC Ruff worked on children's radio and television programs and composed more than 2,000 chansons, some of which became extremely popular; one of the best known is "C'est dans le temps du Carnaval," with lyrics by Gilles Vigneault. He also wrote about thirty concert works. Ruff became involved in the renaissance of the Quebec chanson and collaborated on recordings by Pauline Julien and Jacques Labrecque.

Frances Heinsheimer-Wainwright was born in New York where her father, Viennese-born Hans Heinsheimer,[85] had been living since 1938. Heinsheimer was editor-in-chief of Universal Editions (a publisher of avant-garde music, particularly that of the Viennese School of Schoenberg, Berg and Webern) and had been in New York on business at the time of the *Anschluss* (13 March 1938). Knowing his position in Vienna to be very much at risk he decided to stay in the United States. He later learned that the Gestapo had come to his Viennese office to arrest him. Frances Heinsheimer-Wainwright arrived in Montreal from New York in October 1967 and joined the CBC the following year. As a senior music producer for CBC Radio Montreal she worked with a wide variety of musicians and created a number of new program concepts. Her extensive contacts with composers and musicians associated with her father were invaluable in her work. One result of her commitment to Canadian artists is the CBC/McGill Concert Series, which featured both regional performers and outstanding national and international musicians. After she left the CBC in 1997 she moved to Sechelt, British Columbia, where she holds a number of positions in music administration.[86]

George Fiala had served in the Ukrainian army, was taken prisoner by the German army, and subsequently released. In 1943 he fled the approaching Red Army from Kiev and went to Berlin with his family. In Berlin he was employed by an organization supplying musical entertainment for Russian and Ukrainian displaced persons in concerts throughout Germany. After the war he moved to Belgium and studied at the Royal Conservatory in Brussels. His immigration to Canada was sponsored by the Ukrainian Refugee Committee in Winnipeg. He was first employed in a bakery shop and then as night club musician playing Hammond organ. In 1965 his *Capriccio* was chosen as the obligatory test piece for the Montreal International Competition. Fiala also played a role in the CBC International Service:

> I found out that they had a Ukrainian section, a Russian section, and they wanted to do an interview with me because of my work for the MIC as a Russian-Ukrainian émigré who lived in Canada ... Towards the end of Expo, the Ukrainian section did an exchange program with Radio Kiev. They didn't have any professional musician to do it so they asked me to do a series of half-hour programs on Canadian music, Canadian serious music, Canadian symphonic music etc. We were talking about '67 and not that much Canadian music of any substance had as yet been composed or recorded. I did three half-hour shows in Ukrainian. They sent it to Kiev and it was such a success that they asked me for three more. Then they asked for six more and so I did twelve shows.
>
> Then the Russian section asked me to do some jazz programs for them. Russian was my mother tongue. In Russia they are very much interested in jazz, so I did six jazz programs for them and they offered me a steady job. In November 1967 I started working for the Russian section and stayed for almost twenty

> years! I ended up doing over 1,200 musical shows! These broadcasts on short wave radio were intended for Communist Russia, and covered material that they would not otherwise have had a chance to hear. It showed what was being done in Canada.[87]

Fiala had an opportunity to meet Soviet artists brought to Canada by his friend, Montreal impresario Nicolas Koudriavtzeff. Through radio interviews and after-concert receptions he had close contact with musicians such as Emil Gilels, David Oistrakh, Kiryl Kondrashin, Karen Khachaturian, and all the Soviet participants in the Montreal International Competitions. At one point he hosted Natalie Spiller, Stalin's favourite singer, and "the most beautiful person I ever met."

In Montreal violin building and restoration was dominated by three talented Czechs – Anton Wilfer and his two sons-in-law, Ewald Fuchs and Aloys Fogl – who had worked in the centuries-old violin-making school in Schönbach. They had been living in the Sudetenland when it was annexed by Germany in October 1938. Wilfer was drafted into the German army, spent the last years of the war in a British prisoner-of-war camp, and in 1946 went to Mittenwald. When all Sudeten Germans were expelled from the Czech Republic in 1946 Fuchs joined Wilfer in Mittenwald and continued to work as violin maker. After the Communist putsch in 1948 Fogl managed to escape Czechoslovakia, and spent a short time in displaced persons camps in Germany before coming to Canada. He arrived in Halifax in 1949, worked for a short time in an antique shop in Ottawa, and moved to Montreal in February 1949.

Anton Wilfer came to Montreal in 1951, worked for a short while as a cabinet maker, and then opened a violin shop above the International Music Store on St Catherine Street. Fogl joined Wilfer's shop and they soon built up a substantial clientele. In 1956 Fuchs, who had left Mittenwald in 1950 and was working as a violin maker with Mecklin in Zurich, came to Montreal to join the shop. That year the three violin makers bought a house on Mackay Street. The business, which specialized in repairs, restoration, and importation of new instruments, supplied schools with instruments and prospered until 1996, developing a reputation as master purveyors of old instruments.[88] "It was a beautiful profession," Fogl reminisced, "a beautiful life. I wouldn't have done anything differently if I would have to do it all over again. Being in touch with young people, small children, trying small violins, growing with them, today some of them are in the Montreal Symphony."[89]

Ruzena Herlinger[90] was born in Czechoslovakia and lived in Vienna from 1916 to about 1938 when she fled to England. In 1930 she commissioned and premiered Alban Berg's concert air *Der Wein*.[91] After the war she returned to Czechoslovakia where she conducted the Prague Radio Choir. She arrived in Montreal in August 1949, where she taught at first privately and then from 1957 to 1962 at the Conservatoire and at McGill. Her pupils include a number of prominent French-Canadian singers such as Josèphe Colle, Claude Corbeil, Claire Gagnier, Joseph Rouleau, Huguette Tourangeau, and André Turp. She attracted students from both Canada and the United States.

Émigré musicians also played an important role in amateur music-making circles in Quebec and made a substantial contribution to the success of CAMMAC (Canadian Amateur Musicians/ Musiciens amateurs du Canada). For Jan Simons, the society was an important part of his musical activities. In 1968, as director general, Simons spearheaded a campaign to purchase the White Forest Lodge, a building on the shores of Lake Macdonald that became the permanent home of CAMMAC.

Mario Duschenes first came to CAMMAC as a recorder teacher, hired by George Little; eventually he became director. "There was always a great atmosphere," he remembered. "People went there simply for the pleasure of doing music. The level of performance was never very high, real amateur playing, and people loved it. I loved it also and it had a big influence on my family."[92] His wife became a recorder teacher and his five children also attended CAMMAC and later became teachers. Some of Mario Duschenes's publications owe their genesis to CAMMAC; for example, *Simple Duets for Two Recorders*, and *Easy Trios for Recorders* "were probably all inspired by CAMMAC because we needed simple material for beginners." In spite of his substantial contributions, however, Duschenes considers himself and his family as beneficiaries. "I owe CAMMAC a lot. My whole family, for many years, was influenced by the camp. One of my children even married a girl he met there! It was a big item in our family."[93]

Walter and Otto Joachim were members of the CAMMAC teaching faculty for many years. Otto Joachim remembers Carl Little bringing him "to the original place, before Lake Macdonald and before Weir." For a lecture-recital he played a viola transcription of the Chaconne from J.S. Bach's Partita in D minor for solo violin, BWV 1004, using a Vega bow (a high-arched bow developed in the twentieth century)[94]

MARITIMES

Ernesto Vinci, whose sojourn in Halifax is discussed in the chapter on opera, was only one of a number of émigrés to spend time in the Maritime provinces. Dr Srul Laufer left Italy for Canada via Switzerland, applying for and obtaining an order-in-council in 1938 to allow him, his wife, and his infant son Edward (born in Switzerland in 1938) to enter the country; the family arrived in 1939. Dr Laufer went first to Toronto where he had contacts with a number of medical specialists, including Frederick Grant Banting, the co-inventor of insulin. Banting recommended that Laufer start a cardiology practice in Halifax because there was no one there with that specialty at the time. Laufer, who was well acquainted with the European musical scene, was a co-founder of the Halifax Symphonette and did much to encourage émigré musicians – including Walter Kaufmann,[95] Thomas Mayer, and Leo Müller – to come to Halifax.

Architect Rolf Duschenes (Mario Duschenes's brother) came to Canada as a Camp Boy. After his release from the internment camp he studied architecture at the University of Toronto and McGill University before establishing himself as an architect in Saint John. He became an enthusiastic supporter of music, was a co-founder of the New Brunswick Youth Orchestra, and was instrumental in helping to establish a Canadian youth orchestra festival in Banff. He was also an amateur musician and played violin and later viola with the Saint John Symphony Orchestra.[96]

Tenor Mariss Vetra became a father figure to a wave of expatriate Latvians, most of whom had known each other from professional circles in their home country. Vetra had been a director of the Latvian National Opera during the late 1930s, and in 1944 fled Riga for Sweden where he lived for three years. He arrived in Halifax in 1947 and was head of the voice department at the Halifax Conservatory from 1947 to 1953. He also brokered positions for a number of his compatriots in Halifax and other Maritime communities. In a letter of 22 April 1948, written to entice Jānis Kalniņš to come to Canada he put the best possible face on the new country.

Kalniņš, who had been a conductor at the Latvian Opera House from 1933 to 1944 was at that point living in a displaced persons camp in Germany.

> You would laugh, Janka, if you knew what I am doing at your residence. I am sitting, like Ulmanis [the president of Latvia] in the aisle, in a large chair (in a 600 seat auditorium) and everybody thinks (also myself) that I am very clever. In four days I have to listen to 535 of your future students and have to award, if I am not mistaken, ten or twelve scholarships. It is a great honour, isn't it? Only critics would have been allowed to do this in Latvia. But believe me, at least today (the first day) I am accomplishing my task with honour; even though I made one girl cry about my decision, my conscience is completely clean.
>
> Then at 10 pm Mr. Brown, a great guy, older than me, picked me up. With him was also the university's rector and your minister. Until midnight our subject here, and they don't know how to give me enough thanks for recommending you. A while ago Graudana was here giving a concert and there was much talk about your father, and the encyclopaedia in your father's honour has left such a deep impression never before seen or heard. You are a favourite of Fredericton. We discussed all the ways in which to get you here sooner. Already tomorrow there will go a telegram to Ottawa and then further to Germany. Sooner or later you will be here and since you, I think, will surely fit into the circumstances here, then I have reason to think that you will be happy. The city is not large (20,000) but much prettier and cleaner than Halifax. You, as you know, have already been arranged accommodations. Your church is very lovely, new large organ. And as I see it, interest in music is so great (though not very developed) that you will have enough bread and within a year (I think) you should here at the university open a conservatory with Latvian musicians. This would not be difficult to do. The rector was already scratching his head and did not say no. He even agreed to that. Yes, I also heard your choir today and estimated it to be 88 strong; 100 is the highest number – admitted that 88 is a little weak, but I could hear how you would have conducted it. Today it was also conducted with a bit of a heightened temperament by your future voice student. A chubby girl similar to Brilta, with sinuous round legs. I have a

feeling that you will be teaching her something else as well. Tomorrow night I will be visiting with your minister and I will hear how she sings.

It is already 1:00 am and I must crawl into bed, so that I can listen tomorrow from 10 till 10 without falling asleep. I believe that here it will be good for you, and if you will so make it yourself – very good, not worse, but probably better than for me in Halifax. Hang in there and get over one more last month! Do come please on a Saturday so that I have time to have a drink with you.

Good night ...

Your Mariss[97]

Vetra soon shifted his focus to a personal counter-intelligence campaign against the Stalinist threat. Through 1948–49 he stationed himself at the Halifax docks to meet boats bringing immigrants to Canada and warn newcomers of the long hand of communism at work in Canada. A lively article that appeared in the *Montreal Standard* in March 1948 describes these "off-stage" activities:

> A noted operatic tenor of Europe's stage and screen is today playing the greatest role of his career on the cold, windswept piers of Halifax. On this bleak icy stage, Mariss Vetra, 46, former director of the Latvian National Opera, is waging a one-man war against "Stalinism." When the ships come in bearing his compatriots from Europe's displaced persons camps, this six-foot, 200-pound Don José of the docks is there to tell them "the truth about Canada."
>
> Vetra is serious about his current role which he began almost a year ago, soon after his arrival in Canada to stake out a new life for himself, his charming wife and his two children, André, 8 and Peter, 11. Shortly after taking over his present position as director of the voice department in the Halifax Conservatory of Music, he received letters from Latvian farmers in Canada who reported the Communists were urging them to leave the farms and go to the cities. "The Communists not only sent them propaganda lies about Canada, they sent two agents from New York," Vetra said.
>
> Convinced that an organized Soviet effort was under way to stir up unrest among displaced persons in the Dominion, the

> Riga-born musician promptly launched his campaign to combat it ... Among his pupils at the conservatory is a young Halifax newspaperwoman who keeps him informed about the arrivals of ships. A few minutes before docking time, he bundles into his black beaver-collared overcoat and heads for the pier. When his schedule at the conservatory prevents him from going himself, an assistant and fellow Latvian, Teodor Brilts, takes his place ... When he is not teaching singing or at the pier awaiting the arrival of more of his compatriots, he will usually be found at his desk, penning descriptions of life in Canada for publications in Latvian newspapers in Sweden and Germany. In the former country he wrote a book on his experiences in European opera. Here, too, he managed to needle the Reds.
>
> "This country is so much like Latvia, but so peaceful," he said. "I will show you." He produces a book of Latvian photographs and pointed to a pastoral scene. "That could be Canada." "But," said Vetra with a touch of sadness, "Canada needs song. In Latvia ever [sic] there is song. In Latvia there are great musicians. Why does not Canada invite them? I do not understand." Since coming to Canada, Vetra has been instrumental in paving the way for other Latvians to come. His assistant, [Teodor] Brilts, and Juris and Irene Gotschalks, a Latvian dance team, have recently swelled a growing Latvian colony in Halifax. The Gotschalks are operating a successful ballet school.
>
> Vetra likes people and people, Stalinists excepted, like him. That the Stalinists dislike him leaves the Latvian unworried. "My enemies," he says, scornfully, "only make me strong."[98]

When Jānis Kalniņš arrived in Canada in 1948 after spending three and a half musically rewarding years in displaced persons camps in Germany he had only one suitcase (containing his white tie and tails), but he had written four operas, two ballets, and a symphony. He came to Fredericton as organist at St Paul's United Church, a position he held for forty-two years.[99] Kalniņš recalled: "My first impression was that Fredericton was the smallest city I had ever been in,"[100] but he found that the music used in churches in the area was quite similar to what he had known in Lutheran churches in Latvia. In Fredericton he also taught voice and piano at the Teacher's College and developed a music curriculum (1951–71).

Outside Fredericton Kalniņš carried on an extensive creative life as a composer and Latvian celebrity, travelling to Latvian choral festivals in New England and Ann Arbor, Michigan. He was likely much better known in the United States than he was in Canada; his works were played by major US orchestras such as the Boston Symphony Orchestra. When asked about these events on his return home, Kalniņš would pass off the comment as if nothing had happened, but it was clear that many in the international musical community were aware of his status.[101] He was also well known in Latvia. Helmut Kallmann commented that "Jānis Kalniņš in Fredericton is one of those people who have a great reputation in their home country and here no one plays a Kalniņš symphony."[102]

Most of Kalniņš's more than 300 works are written in a post-Romantic style. The Latvian community in Toronto held Kalniņš in high esteem. Describing his Piano Concerto, William Littler wrote: "Kalniņš has always been more identifiably Latvian ... by virtue of his stronger allegiance to his traditional musical roots, including the spirit of the folk song that expresses itself in the new concerto's slow movement."[103] But Kalniņš was able to reach out to his new homeland.[104] In the *New Brunswick Song Cycle* he set texts by New Brunswick poets, Fred Cogswell, Bliss Carman, Clarence Comeau, Raymond Leblanc, and Kay Smith; *New Brunswick Rhapsody,* a centennial commission from the New Brunswick Symphony, was performed throughout the Maritime provinces. His Symphony no. 2 for choir and organ was premiered in Fredericton in 1952 and ten years later was performed in Toronto. In 1975 his Symphony no. 3 was played in Cleveland, Seattle, and Toronto. A concert celebrating his 81st birthday in November 1985 at the Fredericton Playhouse was a major municipal event. He died in Fredericton in November 2000.

Like so many of his compatriots Haralds Berino[105] fled the Soviet advance into Latvia and spent the years between 1944 and 1948 in displaced persons camps in Germany. He had been active as an organist during his time in the camps, and when he came to Canada in 1950 he settled in Saint John, New Brunswick, and took the position of organist at Centenary Queen's Square United Church. In 1955 he moved to Truro, Nova Scotia, as organist and choirmaster at St James Presbyterian Church, a post he held until 1982. Berino also had a long career as a respected piano teacher. He was not widely known in the Maritimes as a composer, but many of his works were performed at Latvian song festivals and concerts in Canada and the United States and he was also known in Australia and Britain. Most of his more than 200 works are for solo voices or choir. His complete works are held in the Latvian Music Archives, Australia.

Betty and Andreas Barban left Shanghai in 1947 to establish themselves in Newfoundland; this move was likely arranged by Betty Barban's brother Joseph Berljawsky, who had come to Canada in 1939.[106] Andreas Barban[107] was conductor of the St John's Orchestra from 1963 to 1966. At Memorial University he taught music appreciation (1960–64) and piano (1978–88); he also gave master classes and a course in Lieder. Barban did much to promote the local Kiwanis music festival system by arranging repertoire, choosing materials, adjudicating, and accompanying. He was heard for many years in weekly radio recitals as soloist and as accompanist for artists including Joseph Berljawsky (his brother-in-law from Vienna), Eileen Stanbury, Jack Glatzer, Lynn Channing, and Elizabeth Benson-Guy. Maureen Volk, a professor in the Music department at Memorial University, remembers Barban as a vivacious, witty speaker who told amusing anecdotes about performers (including Josef Hoffmann) from his student days in Leipzig.[108]

Walter Kaufmann's name appears in the Halifax Conservatory syllabus for 1948–49 as a piano instructor with awe-inspiring European credentials. Even though he spent barely a year in Halifax, he made a lasting impression.[109] On 25 June 1948 he presented an illustrated talk on the Music of the Orient for the Nova Scotia Music Teacher's Association,[110] and a violinist in the Conservatory orchestra still remembers playing one of Kaufmann's works with the composer conducting.[111] During the course of the year, however, he was appointed conductor of the newly-formed Winnipeg Symphony Orchestra, and he left Halifax in November.[112]

When Thomas Mayer came to Nova Scotia to take over from Alfred Strombergs in 1955, the orchestra was reorganized as the Halifax Symphony Orchestra. Mayer achieved remarkable results during his two years in Halifax. Highlights include a Mozart festival in 1956 and a Beethoven festival in 1957. December 1955 saw the first issue of the unfortunately short-lived *Maritime Arts Review*, published by the Halifax Symphony Society to cover various arts activities, particularly those of the orchestra. On 8 February 1957 Mayer conducted the broadcast premiere of Oskar

Morawetz's *Overture to a Fairy Tale*. Mayer's final Halifax concert on 4 March 1957 included Beethoven's Symphony no. 9 with a chorus of 150 and an orchestra of about fifty musicians.[113] Mayer also served as artistic director of the Nova Scotia Opera Association and conducted productions of Verdi's *Rigoletto* (1955) and Gounod's *Faust* (1956).

In 1957 Mayer left Halifax for Ottawa where he was appointed conductor of the Ottawa Philharmonic Orchestra, a position he held until 1960 when the orchestra disbanded.[114] During Mayer's tenure the orchestra expanded the season to about sixty performances, including regular CBC broadcasts. One highlight was a performance of Beethoven's Symphony no. 9 in March 1959. During his time in Canada, Mayer also had conducting engagements at the CBC and at the Stratford Festival. In 1960 he returned to Europe where he held a number of conducting positions.[115]

The next European conductor to come to Halifax was Viennese-born Leo Müller, who had fled Europe for the United States and worked in New York until 1958. Mayer had met Müller when the two were colleagues at the Metropolitan Opera, and recommended Müller for the post in Halifax for the 1958 season.[116] Under Müller the orchestra expanded its activities to about 70 engagements over a five-month season, including an expanded subscription series, radio and television broadcasts, and performances with the Royal Winnipeg Ballet and the National Opera Association when they visited Halifax.[117] Highlights of these years included the premiere of Eldon Rathburn's *Gray City* on 13 January 1961. Plans for the 1965–66 season included eight subscription concerts, thirty school concerts, twenty radio broadcasts, and a production of Bizet's *Carmen*.[118] However, the orchestral musicians began to voice discontent and the board proved unwilling to support his more imaginative programming.[119] In spite of his impressive record Müller was seen as "unpredictable at rehearsal, a perfectionist,"[120] and the situation culminated in Müller's refusal to sign a contract for the 1965–66 season. In 1964 he left Halifax for New York; he was conductor of the Peabody Conservatory Orchestra from 1966 to 1976, and later returned to Vienna.[121]

Georg Tintner came to Halifax toward the end of a long and fruitful career. He fled the Nazis in 1938, travelled through Yugoslavia and Britain, and finally arrived in New Zealand in 1940. He had no musical employment for the remainder of the war, but between 1946 and 1954 he worked as a conductor in Auckland.

Through the 1950s, 1960s and 1970s he held both orchestral and operatic conducting positions in New Zealand, Australia, and South Africa, and was also a conductor at the Sadler's Wells Opera in London from 1967 to 1970.

Tintner's association with Canada began in 1971 when he conducted the first of many seasons with the National Youth Orchestra of Canada in 1971.[122] When he moved to Halifax in 1987 as music director and resident conductor of Symphony Nova Scotia, Halifax audiences embraced this experienced opera and orchestral conductor with international credentials.[123] Stephen Pederson, a local music reviewer, became Tintner's champion and critics across the country responded in kind. Tintner was committed to the music of his compatriot Anton Bruckner; he had recorded all of the composer's symphonic works with the Royal Scottish National Orchestra, the National Symphony Orchestra of Ireland, and the New Zealand Symphony Orchestra on the Naxos label, and in 1982 had introduced the young musicians of the National Youth Orchestra of Canada to the original version of Bruckner's magnificent Symphony no. 8. He commented that "Mahler was the prophet of *Angst* and horror, whereas Bruckner transcends this condition. Working extensively with youth orchestras, I've found that the spiritual ecstasy in Bruckner's music is what young people immediately respond to. I think they realize that we need him, desperately."[124] Tintner also spoke of the deep Catholic mysticism expressed in Bruckner's works: "Bruckner was a very religious man – we all know that. But what he created speaks even to sinners like me."[125] In addition to his work with Symphony Nova Scotia and the National Youth Orchestra, Tintner conducted the Nova Scotia Youth Orchestra and filled numerous conducting engagements in the Maritime provinces and across Canada, working with the Canadian Opera Company and with professional and youth orchestras in Ottawa, Montreal, Quebec, London, Kitchener- Waterloo, Winnipeg, Edmonton, Prince George, and Vancouver. His death in 1999 was mourned across the country.

WINNIPEG AND SASKATOON

Rudolf Lowenstein, an amateur violinist who moved to Winnipeg after his release from internment camp, established a business career as a manufacturer of headwear,[126] but he remained active in Winnipeg's musical community. "In 1942 when the time came for us to be released, I had no financial help or marketable skills, but I had worked on a farm in England. Luckily there was a German-Jewish couple, the Gumprichs, who had a farm near Winnipeg and needed someone to help out, so they were willing to sponsor me. That is how I got to Winnipeg. I participated in many amateur orchestras here and am a strong supporter of the Winnipeg Symphony and other musical organizations."[127]

Walter Kaufmann[128] came to Winnipeg in November 1948 as conductor of the newly-formed Winnipeg Symphony Orchestra. His debut on 16 December ushered in a challenging and remarkable period in the life of the orchestra. Critics praised him both as a new musical performer and a composer of new, contemporary music.[129] The first program began with Wagner's Overture to *Die Meistersinger.*[130] It is difficult to know whether anyone in the audience was aware of the irony of this choice. This glorious C major celebration is an attention-grabber in its own right, but Wagner had been highly regarded by Hitler to the point where his music, to some, represented Nazi culture. In conducting this work, Kaufmann, who had been driven from his native land by Nazi racial policies, put music once more over politics. Kaufmann also introduced a number of his own compositions and did stints as guest conductor of the CBC Orchestra in Toronto. In 1950 he married pianist Freda Trepel, who had studied with Rudolph Ganz in Chicago, and made her debut in New York in 1944. Kaufmann left Winnipeg in 1957 to accept a position as ethnomusicologist at Indiana University in Bloomington. This appointment was likely brokered by Paul Nettle, a colleague from his student days in Prague who had kept in contact with Kaufmann.[131] In Bloomington, Kaufmann wrote a number of works on Indian music, a subject that had become his passion in India during the 1930s.

Little is known about the musical career of Latvian émigré Viktor Kviesis. He was an opera conductor, fled the Communists from Riga in 1944, and for the next four years lived in displaced persons camps in Germany. Shortly after his arrival in Saskatoon in 1950 he became conductor of the Saskatoon Symphony Orchestra, a position he held until 1955. He also led the Saskatoon Oratorio Society in its early years (1952–55). In 1956 he moved to North Bay, Ontario, where, until the early 1970s he conducted the Victor Chorus. [132]

Sophie Carmen ("Sonia") Eckhardt-Gramatté[133] is not included in this study because she left Europe after 1948. Her departure from

Vienna in 1953, along with her husband Ferdinand Eckhardt, was precipitated by post-war politics. Vienna, like Berlin was partitioned and the Soviet Union had considerable authority over political developments. Ferdinand Eckhardt was being targeted by the Soviets since he was a member of the Austro-American Society that promoted close ties with the West.[134] However, their magnificent contribution must at least be noted here. They came to Winnipeg where Sonia Eckhardt-Gramatté continued to compose and Ferdinand Eckhardt became director of the Winnipeg Art Gallery. [135] Their home was for many decades a centre for visiting Austrians, and now houses the Gramatté Foundation; artefacts, archival records, recordings, paintings, and manuscripts documenting an exceptional life in music and art are held in rooms painted in the oranges and blues preferred by Sonia's first husband, the expressionist painter Walter Gramatté (1897–1929).

VANCOUVER AND VICTORIA

Imant Raminsh arrived in Canada from Latvia as a child in 1948; his family settled in Northern Ontario, where his father had secured a job with the Ontario Forestry Branch;[136] they lived first in Hearst, and in 1950 moved to Cochrane. In the late 1950s they moved to Toronto to be closer to post-secondary education for Raminsh and his sisters. He studied at the RCM (violin with Albert Pratz), and then at the University of Toronto, and graduated with a BMus in 1966. He continued his music education in Europe at the Salzburg Mozarteum Academy (1966–68), and then moved to British Columbia where, in 1968, he established a music department at the College of New Caledonia in Prince George. Since then he has had an active musical career as a teacher, violinist, and composer. Raminsh has great admiration for the Latvian musical tradition, including a repertoire of more than a million folk songs, and is aware of the influence of this heritage on his own music. Raminsh's compositions, some set to liturgical texts, have an intense, tonally-conceived lyricism well suited to the voice, and his choral works have been particularly well received in Canada, the United States, and Sweden.

Cellist Ernst Friedlander and his wife Marie Elisabeth Friedlander (nèe Werbner), a pianist, grew up and began their musical careers in Vienna. They fled the Nazis in 1937 and emigrated to the

United States where they lived for almost twenty years, and where Ernst Friedlander had a brilliant orchestral and solo career. They came to Vancouver in 1958 when Ernst joined the Vancouver Symphony Orchestra as principal cellist, and he was soon in great demand in Vancouver. The couple were also happy to be north of the border: "Canada was so much more like the Old World [than the United States] and we took to it."[137] Ernst Friedlander remained with the Vancouver Symphony Orchestra until 1966 and was also principal cellist in the CBC Vancouver Chamber Orchestra and cellist of the Vancouver String Quartet (1960–66). He was a lecturer at the UBC from 1958 to 1966 and as a composer wrote more than fifty works, mainly for cello; the best known are his Cello Concerto (1959) and *Minnelied* (1964), scored for cello and piano.

On the basis of what they could learn about Canada through materials in the Canada House in London, the Nalos family left England on 26 April 1940 (one year to the day after their departure from Prague) aboard the *Duchess of Bedford,* bound for Quebec City. On the boat they met a number of well-known individuals including Max Pirani, Lia Pirani (a violinist who later went to Vancouver), and the German actor Conrad Veit. Max Pirani recommended John Goth as a singing teacher for Erika Nalos (later Kurth). After their arrival in Montreal they drove across Canada from Toronto to Vancouver in a new Buick – an eye-opening experience for everyone. Richard Nalos – Erika's father – established Nalos Lumber in British Columbia. Soon after her arrival, the young Erika Nalos created a sensation performing Dvorák's *Gypsy Songs* in costume at the 1940 Dominion Folk Festival with an orchestra conducted by Rex Battle. In 1949 the family moved to Berkeley, California, where she continued her music studies. Kurth sang in the North American premiere of Benjamin Britten's *Ceremony of Carols* (22 December 1944) conducted by Burton Kurth (who later became her father-in-law).[138] Erika Kurth pursued an active career in British Columbia performing in both opera and oratorio and teaching at the Victoria Conservatory. She received an honorary doctorate from that institution in recognition of her television show *Arts Calendar,* which ran for twenty-five years, interviewing such celebrities such Ravi Shankar and Zara Nelsova. She continues to serve on local music committees including the Young Artists Apprenticeship Program, Pacific Opera, and the Community Arts Council.

Otto Lowy was born in Prague and studied in Czechoslovakia until 1939 when he fled the Nazis for England; he lived there until he came to Canada in the early 1950s. He is perhaps best known as the long-time host who welcomed listeners aboard *The Transcontinental,* a weekly CBC Radio broadcast that combined music with stories of Central Europe, recreating the ambience and culture of an Old World that was no more. The script was always tinged with nostalgia and, like Jan Rubes's *Songs of My People,* appealed to central Europeans who had immigrated to Canada. As host of the Vancouver Symphony Orchestra's "Tea and Trumpets," he introduced classical music to a wide audience.

When Ida Halpern arrived in Vancouver on 7 August 1939, an immigration officer asked what she intended to do in Canada. Ida coolly replied, "I want to study the music of the Indians." Apparently, the immigration officer replied, "You'll have to do better than that!"[139] Perhaps Halpern had learned of the riches of the music-cultural traditions of the North West Coast Indians from her Viennese mentor, Robert Lach, who must have been aware of the pioneering work of Franz Boas among those peoples. Halpern soon established herself in the academic musical life at the University of British Columbia and later at Simon Fraser University, and began her research and collecting activities. Her investigations focussed on the traditional musics of the First Nations peoples of the Pacific Northwest. First, however, she set about gaining the confidence of informants who knew and could perform traditional songs, an arduous process that took about six years.[140] "A song traditionally belongs to a person or family; the chief might inherit a song, acquire it by marriage, or commission it for some important occasion in order to give himself and his ... clan added prestige." These songs were an integral part of a hereditary legacy and could not be passed from one family to another. The law banning the potlatch in 1884 – combined with pressure from missionaries and from representatives of the Department of Indian Affairs, and the confiscation of ceremonial masks and other objects – suppressed the First People's cultural traditions to such an extent that the songs associated with the potlatch and other traditional ceremonies had almost disappeared. Young people had no interest in the old songs, nor any desire to memorize the ceremonial chants. Halpern's breakthrough came in 1947 when she was speaking with the Kwakiutl Chief Billy Assu. She commented that when he died his songs would die with him, but that he might help to ensure their survival if he would record them. When he understood this, he said "You come: I give you hundred songs;" Assu was then in his seventies.[141] At first Halpern was able to record eight songs. Mungo Martin, a carver of totems, knew about 124 songs, and allowed them to be recorded. With this interest and activity came a renewed sense of pride and consciousness of their heritage that in time led to a revival of potlatch, and in 1951, the repeal of the potlatch law.

Halpern went on to collect several hundred songs, and she catalogued and analysed a total of some 340 hereditary songs, each prefaced with commentary provided by the singer or the informant.[142] A group of 114 songs were released on a series of eight recordings on the Folkways Ethnic Library label. Selections from these recordings have been used in radio and television broadcasts, museum galleries, theatrical productions, academic theses, and also by contemporary composers.[143] Some scholars have criticized Halpern's inability to work within existing analytical criteria. Her idiosyncratic method of analysis was unlike that used by other scholars in the field.[144] Halpern solved the complex problem of rhythm by representing melody and rhythm in two independent parallel courses.[145] For the most part however, Halpern's writings and recordings have largely been ignored by the scholarly community. More recently Kenneth Chen has argued that Halpern's work on North West Coast musics has been unjustly neglected.[146] While acknowledging that her work is dissonant with North American ethnomusicological, anthropological, and folklore practices as well as the claim to "primary authority" espoused by First Nations Peoples, he nevertheless lauds Halpern for her work under extremely difficult circumstances and for her ability to break free from the constraints of her "Berlin (comparative) school" training to place this music within its unique cultural and social context. Halpern gained the trust of her native informants at a time when such practices were illegal and recorded and studied a vast resource of our First Nations heritage

In Vancouver Ida Halpern was also active in founding the Friends of Chamber Music, an organization that took its name from the nineteenth-century Viennese "Verein der Musikfreunde." The program of the first concert presented by the Friends, on 13 May 1948 in the Mayfair Room of the Hotel Vancouver, included John Weinzweig's *Divertimento no. 1* (1946) – certainly not conventional Viennese fare, but a choice that revealed the society's keen interest in contemporary Canadian music.[147] Halpern was also able to overcome local resistance to the new organization from individuals who feared that it might not be in the best interests of the Vancouver Symphony Orchestra, and a four-concert series was planned for the 1948–49 season. When Halpern heard that friends from Vienna – harpsichordist Alice Ehlers and viola da gambist Eva Heinitz, both political refugees – were to receive honorary degrees in Portland, Oregon, she persuaded the board to engage them, with their instruments. A recital presented on 14 November 1949 featured music of Carl Friedrich Abel, J.S. Bach, and Marin Marais. Audience members filed past the 18th-century harpsichord resplendent in red, green, and gold, and string players contemplated the viola da gamba, a fine instrument of an even earlier date. Fundraising events (a North American necessity) reached the society pages of the local newspapers, and suddenly, chamber music was "in." Halpern began lobbying to have a smaller auditorium for chamber music included in the plans for the new Queen Elizabeth Theatre, and finally persuaded civic alderman George Cunningham that a civic auditorium, "like parks, libraries, and museums, must be made available to responsible users even if the city lost money." The struggle continued for several years before Dorothy Hauschka (another Viennese expatriate) finally reached an agreement with the city that allowed the Friends of Chamber Music the right to present their season in the newly-named Playhouse on 19 August 1964; this hall is now known as the Vancouver Playhouse.

The Leon and Thea Koerner Foundation was established in Vancouver in 1955 a philanthropic organization dedicated to support of the arts and music.[148] Motivated by a sense of gratitude towards their adopted homeland the founders and subsequently the Trustees of the Foundation made substantial donations to numerous individuals and artistic groups across the country. Other members of the family also participated in recognizing the viability of Canada's musical life and encouraged it in many ways.[149]

Paul and Edwina Heller were also strong supporters of music in Vancouver. They were well acquainted with Ida Halpern, Irwin Hoffman (conductor of the Vancouver Symphony for twelve years), Hoffman's wife violinist Esther Glazer, and cellist Malcolm Tait. As a pianist, Edwina Heller was one of the first local artists to play for the Friends of Chamber Music; Ernst Friedländer, another émigré, also played in the series.

The Bentley (Bloch-Bauer) and the Prentice (Pick) families also used their knowledge and appreciation of the arts to benefit the province of British Columbia. Viennese immigrants Leopold Bloch-Bauer and Otto Pick had established the Pacific Veneer and Plywood Company, which began production in 1939. John Prentice (Hans Pick), a prominent supporter of the arts in British Columbia, financed the Playhouse for many years,[150] and served as chair of the Canada Council from 1969 to 1974. Peter Bentley feels that industry has an obligation to promote the arts and encourages employees to serve on local arts committees and boards.[151] Bentley's aunt Rita Georg, a Viennese operetta singer, made a number of public performances after her arrival in Vancouver, including a production of the *Merry Widow* in Stanley Park, and occasional charity events.

Eva and Herbert Schaefer were prominent music and arts patrons in Victoria and received honorary doctorates from the University of Victoria in 1996 for their contributions to Victoria's musical life. The citation for Eva Schaefer describes her as a patron of the arts, active in the Victoria arts community for more than twenty years as a member of the board of the Victoria Symphony, Greater Victoria Music Festival, the Arts Council, the Conservatory of Music, and the Commonwealth Games. Herbert Schaefer is described as a patron of the arts, who had been a recording engineer with the BBC in London for more than 30 years; when the Schaefers moved to Victoria, he began a second career as a volunteer with the Victoria Symphony and for twenty-one years recorded almost every concert or opera held in Victoria, providing a valuable musical archive of the city.[152] The couple had fled the Nazis and settled in London, England. They arrived in Victoria in 1975.

Hans Gruber was witness to one of the most moving encounters of local musicians with a great émigré, Bruno Walter. Walter's brief Canadian sojourn came about through the efforts of Nicholas Goldschmidt, who invited him to open the Vancouver International Festival in 1958. Walter conducted in both the 1958 and 1959 festivals, and his sincere and conscientious manner made a lasting impression on Goldschmidt and the orchestral musicians.[153] Hans Gruber remembered Walter's first rehearsal with the Vancouver Symphony Orchestra:

> To watch that old man, he was in his eighties, get to work with an orchestra that was, let's face it, not the New York Philharmonic

> ... was really an extraordinary experience. The very first time he came in front of them in the morning, they were shaking in their boots ... They began with Brahms's Second Symphony. He gave the down beat, no score, he looked and there were fluffs, all nervousness. So after five or six minutes he said to them – I will never forget – "Gentlemen, there is only one important name here this morning, and this name is Brahms; not me, not you, only Brahms. Now we are going to play Brahms in the best way we know how and forget everything else." And you know it, there was in an instant an almost miraculous transformation. He found a way to make them relax. Then he went on ... rolling up his sleeves. "And now we shall get to work." ... He stopped and almost literally taught them how to play their instruments, fingerings in the cellos, bowings there. This went on but always, always, he justified to them why he asked them; never the attitude you do it because I say so.[154]

Hans Gruber had come to Victoria as conductor of the Victoria Symphony Orchestra, and his time there was fruitful for both orchestra and audience.[155] "There was a lot of unevenness in the orchestra at the beginning. There were some really very good winds, there were some pretty good brass, very respectable horns, but the strings, they were a problem for a while."[156] Gruber was modest about his accomplishments, claiming that the only positive attribute of himself and the orchestra at the time was the courage to tackle "anything from the Bach Suites to the Bartók Concerto for Orchestra." He also performed Morawetz's *Carnival Overture*.[157] Everything he did in Victoria was "for the first time," and he conscientiously memorized the scores so as not to have a barrier between himself and the musicians. During his tenure with the Victoria Symphony Gruber also appeared as a guest conductor with orchestras in Calgary and Edmonton, and in 1954 with the CBC Orchestra in Toronto. Later, he turned down offers of permanent positions with the St Louis Philharmonic and the Calgary Philharmonic.

In spite of his success, however, Gruber began to reconsider his qualifications for the "voodoo" craft of conducting, as he called it, and to question his right to stand in front of an orchestra and take charge of the musical lives of a hundred accomplished artists. In 1963, he gave up conducting as a profession and returned to

Toronto to take over the family textile business from his ailing father. After that, he commented, "I began to enjoy music again. There was no pressure to perform."[158] He returned to Victoria in 1995 to conduct for the Victoria Symphony's 50th anniversary. The response to the concert was positive and manager Steven Smith invited the 75-year-old Gruber back for a subscription pair in January 2000. Gruber claims that he never suffered from the political situation in Europe: "I was born with a silver spoon in my mouth, and I lived my life with a silver spoon." He spoke clearly and crisply with an unmistakably polite central-European bearing. In March 2001 Gruber arrived for an interview with me dressed in a snowmobile suit and riding a motorcycle. He passed away soon after.

NICHOLAS GOLDSCHMIDT

Nicholas Goldschmidt's career provides a perfect conclusion to this cross-country examination of émigrés in Canada. Who but an émigré looking at Canada with the eyes of an outsider could realize the potential for a music festival – the Algoma Fall Festival – amid the resplendent fall colours of northern Lake Superior? Who could be so brazen as to stage a music competition in 1985 in honour of Glenn Gould, who considered music competitions the most unmusical event imaginable? The Glenn Gould International Piano Competition, subsequently renamed The 1985 International Bach Competition, became the launching pad for Canadian pianist Angela Hewitt, and raised $139,000 for the support of the Glenn Gould Foundation.[159] In 1968 Goldschmidt initiated the Guelph Spring Festival, featuring a chamber opera and a Canadian commission in honour of tenor and Metropolitan Opera administrator Edward Johnson, who was born in Guelph.[160] Who but an émigré could conceive of an international choral festival that involved 4,000 performers in seventy-one concerts presented in thirty-five locales, and attract an audience of 65,000 to indulge in the "joy of singing?"[161] The 1989 Toronto extravaganza was repeated in 1993 and 2002. Goldschmidt's international connections also ensured that the Vancouver International Festival, launched in 1959, could attract the world's finest – Joan Sutherland, Bruno Walter, and Herbert von Karajan, an old schoolmate from Vienna; with a twinkle in his eye Goldschmidt confided that "it was front-page news in Toronto!"[162] Who but Niki could paint on a musical canvas stretching 8,000 km across the continent for the glorious trans-Canada music festivals in the centennial and millennial years? Music Canada Musique 2000, which ran from December 1999 to February 2001, showcased Canadian musicians and composers as never before as commissions for new works showered from Goldschmidt's twentieth-storey office to eager and talented Canadians. The last opportunity I had to see Goldschmidt in action was at Pollack Hall in Montreal when he gave a master class on the Lieder of Hugo Wolf in February 2003. At age ninety-four – perhaps physically frail but exuding immense energy – he summoned up moving images of the texts, chided accompanists when necessary for not entering into the spirit of the music, and encouraged young singers not to overdo the romanticism.

This chapter has portrayed the second half of the twentieth century as the period of émigrés in Canadian music. The influence of these many musicians in numerous disciplines across Canada was so pervasive that it is virtually impossible to think of this time span without their presence. They not only carved out careers for themselves but coached talented Canadians to do likewise. As outsiders they were often better able to see what needed to be done than we who had grown up within the system. We can only pay tribute to their accomplishments by continuing to welcome musicians who come to Canada from around the world to contribute to our unique musical tapestry.

Epilogue: Looking Forward, Looking Back

Canada's musical émigrés made certain not to let a good opportunity slip through their fingers as they began to interact with Canadian society and the Canadian musical scene. Their collective experience and knowledge proved an invaluable asset in their new Canadian environment. They had been closely acquainted with some of the finest European musicians in educational and performing institutions on the Continent. They were keenly aware of the importance of the state in the promotion of music and the crucial role of local and national government funding. They had been educated in the vast network of European music academies and conservatories and they had worked in the apprenticeship system of municipal, provincial, and national opera houses for which there was no Canadian equivalent. They knew first hand that high performing standards were possible and they had heard some of the finest European musicians in superb concert halls. They were intimately acquainted with the intellectual and academic side of the music; many had studied with leading scholars at major universities. They were also well versed with developments in contemporary music, including the dodecaphonic schools in Berlin and Vienna, and recent works by leading composers such as Bartók, Stravinsky, and Hindemith.

One important element in their reactions to their new surroundings is a sense of gratitude to a country that may not always have welcomed émigrés with open arms but nevertheless provided an environment in which they could develop and flourish. Istvan Anhalt commented:

> I came to Canada in search of a fair opportunity to be and to do. I didn't know what Canada was like. What I found here was a very complex land, demographically, and a huge land physically that gave me enough elbow room to be, to evolve. One learned fast that our cities are not built with gold, and one had to stretch hard and do this and that and work hard, and if one does that eventually one will survive. And I am very grateful that I pitched my tent in Canada. I feel that I'm part of it. Canada spoke to me, I spoke in response, and I'm still in dialogue with Canada, if you wish, and that was a good way of spending my life. The greatest gift Canada gave me was my landing card, to admit me, and that was the greatest gift that I ever received and I don't need any pats on the back in addition to that. That was an unearned credit given by this country to me. All the rest that I did could be regarded as a partial payback for that landing card.[1]

For Helmut Kallmann the joy of doing something creative was perhaps thanks enough:

> I could have explained my motivation for exploring Canadian music history as a gesture of gratitude for fate having dumped me in Canada. Successful immigrants often claim to have been inspired by gratitude to do a good deed for Canada, but I distrust that assertion. I believe the fun in doing congenial work comes first; awareness of "paying back" develops only as the work comes to a close; knowledge and love of country arise through one's work ... Through my quest I have come to admire and love Canadians, rather than the other way around.[2]

For Udo Kasemets the country seemed to represent the limitless possibilities of a new beginning:

> Politically it was hopeless [in Europe]. You were not going to go back. Therefore my mind right away that day when I approached the shores of Canada was "This is a new land and I am going to live here and make the most of it. I have no credentials of any kind so I have to start a new life here and build whatever needs to be built and if I can, be part of it."[3]

Over the years a number of émigrés returned to the countries from which they had fled. Their reactions vary from violent revulsion to a desire and willingness to reach out in a spirit of reconciliation. Some returned to visit colleagues. For example, Helmut Blume visited his native Berlin a number of times, seeking out old friends including Detlev Kraus. Several returned to Europe for their retirement years. Conductors Thomas Mayer and Leo Müller went back to Vienna. Bernard Diamant retired in 1985 after a long and fruitful career as vocal pedagogue in Montreal and Toronto, and returned to Amsterdam where he lived in an elegant canal house on the Leidsegracht. He died in 1999.[4]

GERMANY AND AUSTRIA

In Germany Otto Joachim achieved not only reconciliation but also recognition. He was honoured by his native city of Düsseldorf in 1985 on his 75th birthday, and in 2000 on his 90th birthday: "I was touched with gloves by the Düsseldorf celebration. They were very careful with me ... It was a big affair, sponsored by many groups. It was absolutely superb! I also composed a piece especially for this occasion." An exhibition of Joachim's works was on display at the City Library and the Jewish Museum, and a concert was given in his honour at the Tonhalle.[5] A German film crew made a documentary entitled *Weltreise Wider Willen,* about Joachim in Montreal.[6] Joachim summed up his feelings toward Germany in the following statement:

> Through my works, through my ideas, through whatever, I am a citizen of this world. When I go back, I go back to *my* country which *they*, my neighbours, my friends, took away from me without any right. They took it away from me; therefore the burden is on their shoulders. Because if they are proud of Beethoven, Goethe, or Schiller, the same shoulders should bear Hitler and what he has done to them and to us ... When I go back it means they have stepped on my property. I have said this very often. The property is Germany, *my* Germany, *my* language, *my* education, *my* parents, *my* grandparents, *my* great grandparents. They are all from Germany. Besides I'm an atheist, so if they say, "Are you Jewish?" I say my parents were, yes, but I do not believe in any doctrine – philosophy, yes, doctrine, no.

> When I came to Düsseldorf, I had a very small speech and they had to try very hard to understand me, the so-called *haut volé,* because I spoke to them in their own dialect! Physically it's possible to take me away; culturally, it's not possible. Whatever I do in my painting, in my music making, in my music creating, has its foundation in my country, which is Germany. I might have Canadian influence by observing, by being here I keep my eyes and ears open. I know I have Asiatic influence because I was there sixteen years. But the fundamental root is Germany, my country ... Wherever they let me stay, I stayed. In Germany they didn't let me stay, in Singapore they didn't let me, in Shanghai they didn't let me. The first place where they let me stay was Canada, where I was allowed to stay for the first time after twenty-three years of being a DP. I'm a fighter. Some gave up hope, but they were cowards.[7]

Walter Homburger's return to Germany was also positive. He took his children because he wanted them to know where their roots were. The family bank building had survived the war and now bears a plaque stating that it had been the premises of the Veit L. Homburger Bank. On his first return trip, Homburger had asked his father if there was anyone at the bank that he ought to be remembered to, and his father had given him two names. Homburger asked for one of the gentlemen, and when he identified himself, the man "practically dropped dead, but was very cordial." Homburger also showed his children where the family had lived and his wife rang the bell. They introduced themselves to the woman who answered the door; she knew the name, and invited them in to see the house.[8]

Gerhard Kander's return to Germany was more painful. He made his first visit with his benefactress Lois Fraser, a few years after the death of her husband Kaspar. Kander told her that he wanted to lay a few ghosts to rest in Baden-Baden, Mannheim, Karlsruhe, and Heidelberg. In Baden-Baden they stayed in the Brenner's Park Hotel – "where we didn't stay when we lived there in the '30s," he later commented – and he drove around to places he had been at the time, and where the violin pedagogue Carl Flesch had lived. In Mannheim, Karlsruhe, and Munich, however, he couldn't even get out of the car, and became ill. In Heidelberg (the only time he got out of the car) they asked if the asparagus season was still on in

Schwetzingen. He returned for a second visit with his wife Claire Bombardier, once again indulging his penchant for white asparagus![9]

Ulrich Leupold found it impossible to look back, and refused to talk about his past, even with his wife. After the war he made two trips to Germany, where he held services in Berlin and gave lectures at Oxford, Munich, and Hannover. His father's church, then in East Berlin, had been badly damaged by bombs during the war and was closed. Fred Otto, an American friend with whom he was traveling, said, "That hit Rick very hard – not being able to get in and knowing the church would be demolished."[10]

Jan Simons returned from visits to Germany feeling happier to be living in Canada. His birthplace Düsseldorf had become architecturally much like an American city and was rather unfriendly, but he enjoyed talking with the younger generation of Germans who were eager to learn what had taken place before and during the war. "Many had feelings of guilt, mostly because of what they felt their parents and grandparents had not done to prevent Hitler and the ensuing war. I do not feel they should feel guilty."[11]

Peter Bentley has made a number of visits to his native Vienna and admires the beauty and excellent cuisine he can enjoy there, but returning to Canada, he counts his blessings that his parents left when they did. "I am grateful and proud to be a Canadian. This country has given our family so much."[12]

Hans Kaufman returned to Vienna in 1967, but his attempt to re-establish himself in his native city was unsuccessful. He stayed only six months. At first he looked for work as a strolling musician in one of the larger hotels. He finally found a job at Der feuchte Stock, a popular *Heuriger* close to St Stephen's Cathedral. One evening, when he was tired and had sat down behind the piano for a few minutes rest, the manager told him, "Mr Kaufmann, we have a business here and you can't take a rest. Twenty minutes dinner and then you should be playing again." Kaufmann finished the week and left, ruefully remarking that his wages were less than the cost of transportation.[13]

Greta Kraus made her first postwar visit to Vienna with her husband Erwin Dentay in 1947. Most of her friends and relatives who had stayed behind had died in the gas chambers, but her immediate family, with great difficulty, had survived. "What struck me most was that no one was interested in what had happened in my life.

They had lived through such incredible things that they couldn't stop talking."[14]

CZECHOSLOVAKIA AND THE BALTIC STATES

Aloys Fogl described his return visit to the Czech Republic: "I was at a reunion of my 1925 classmates – as a seventy-eight-year-old! I do not feel any animosity towards them. The children are so well dressed, so polite. The standard of living in the Czech Republic is very high; education and health are well taken care of. I consider myself an exile, yes. I would like to have returned. I didn't leave because I had made enemies or because I was fleeing debts or a wife. Where you grow up, it becomes a part of you."

Armas Maiste returned to Estonia in 1995 at the invitation of the Music Academy in Tallinn, and again in 1999 for a choral festival during which he played several recitals. He found Estonians interested in his work, but he had mixed feelings about visiting places where he had lived in the 1930s. "I had a strange feeling in my stomach. It was rather sad, but my later visit was more positive." The young people he met in 1999 seemed to represent better times for the future. "It will take a long time for all the scars to heal. Some resented the fact that we had escaped, but certainly they had the same chance to leave that we did. But Canada has become my home."

Alfred Strombergs regards the current political situation in his native Latvia as an opportunity for that country to "come clean" with its past. "During the fifty years of Communist rule in Latvia, they never told the truth about the Latvian republic of 1919–1940; they said it was [the Communists] who brought culture to Latvia. This myth was propagated for two generations and they managed to indoctrinate everyone with it. Hopefully the truth will come out now and that the new generation in Latvians will come to a more balanced view of their own history."[15]

Talivaldis Kenins had refused an earlier invitation from the Soviet Latvians but in 1989 he finally visited Latvia. In 1990 Latvia gained independence, and in 1991 there were five concerts of Kenins's music in honour of his seventieth birthday.

Imant Raminsh has established contacts in Latvia: "I think I look forward to going back, it just has not been possible until now.

Friends in Latvia wanted to organize a performance of some of my works but it hasn't worked out yet."[16]

Jānis Kalniņš declined an invitation to visit Latvia to celebrate his 85th birthday. "I had not been back for forty-two years, and it would not be the same. I have seen people go back and come home with long faces because everything is so changed. No, I would not like to go back. Fredericton is home now."[17] Nevertheless, Kalniņš's final resting place is in Riga. In July 2001, six months after his death, his remains were brought back to Riga and placed beside those of his father Alfreds Kalniņš (1879–1951), a revered Latvian composer. That evening there was an exhibition and memorial concert at the Latvian National Opera where he had been a conductor.[18] Reconciliation had finally been achieved.

UKRAINE

George Fiala found the return to his former homeland distressing:

> By 1990 the whole Communist thing collapsed. Because I was quite well known through radio and television, through the competitions, through the Ukrainian organizations, I received an invitation from the first free Ukrainian Music Festival in Kiev to come as a guest and bring what in my opinion was my best orchestral work to be performed during the festival. This was a difficult decision for me to make. I left Kiev in1943 and now this was almost half a century later during which, to the best of my ability, I had resisted the Communist ideas, hating the blasted thing as much as I could. My father died in 1982, just before the political change in Ukraine. I received the invitation from the same people who had imposed the Communist traditions on Ukraine for almost half a century! The same people who yesterday were dedicated Communists were today Ukrainian nationalists!
>
> My first decision was not to accept the invitation. However my wife suggested that I sit down and cool off. Ukraine was announcing its independence. She told me that whoever the people are, this was still the place where I was born .... This was an experience that is hard to explain, returning to the place where I was born. They received me very nicely, I met quite a few friends I had studied with at the Conservatory. One in particular

received me a little bit on the cautious side, but quite friendly. I wanted them to play my *Eulogy in Memory of President J.F. Kennedy* (1965, rev. 1980). Unfortunately it was a poor performance because the Kiev Philharmonic was quite weak, no comparison to our [Montreal Symphony Orchestra].

It's a funny feeling – you cannot go back. It's impossible. You cannot return to something you knew as a child. Things are completely different now, people and situations have changed. It's not the same world anymore. I felt myself a stranger. Yes I spoke the language, I was walking the same streets, the spot where my house once stood, the place where I was born, I met some old friends, but you can't go back emotionally to what it was before. By the way, in 1992 when I celebrated my seventieth anniversary, they organized a concert of my symphonic music and invited me to come a second time. They played my Fourth Symphony, the *Kurelek Suite*, and the Violin Concerto, the one that Steven Staryk premiered. But general conditions were appalling. All you heard were people asking, "Please help us to get out." Everything was destroyed, nothing was organized, the Soviet system had collapsed, the new system wasn't yet up and running, they didn't have much to eat, there was no work. The old Conservatory had been destroyed during the bombardment of the German occupation, everything was demolished, Conservatory, Music School, and Concert Hall so they built a new Conservatory on the main street. It was so tough, mentally, so hard for me, so I decided to never to go back again. Seeing those people in the conditions they were after over seventy years of the Soviet regime, what happened to their way of thinking and living.

Yes, it was rather tough for me here in Canada for the first fifteen or twenty years, but I found my place. This is where I belong now. I have my home, my family. This is my country, I belong here!

Ireneus and Luba Zuk made several visits to Ukraine and returned with positive impressions. In 1968 they came with letters of introduction from Helmut Blume to directors of music schools in Khazkiv, Odessa, and Lviv, and Luba told everyone that she was from Canada. "That was the magic word, absolutely." In 1982, the Zuks toured several countries playing a program of Canadian works.[19] During the tour, the Canadian Embassy in Warsaw offered them a car to take them to their birthplace Lubaczow, a four-hour drive. They found their house still standing, but did not go inside; it had been given to Polish citizens relocated from the West. Luba Zuk asserts that the standard of music performance in Ukraine is high with much young talent and excellent educational facilities. "The general attitude is rather conservative but they organize festivals of new music in which we perform a lot of new things; they promote and are interested in new music. They also treat us like royalty but with very limited means. "They do not send their best students to Moscow any more; they cannot afford it. They cannot afford to go to Vienna either. They have excellent faculty, the training is rigorous, the standard is overwhelming."

CONCLUSION

The stories of the musicians who came to Canada provide uniquely personal views of European history through the 1930s, the Second World War, and the immediate postwar years. Their experiences illustrate the many ways in which political systems gone awry can affect individual lives, forcing people to question their personal values and beliefs. First-person accounts from interviews and other sources describe the tragic implications of ideologies that promised so much and yet produced the worst forms of human degradation. To the person in the street, rightwing and leftwing totalitarianism were much the same. Both types of regimes supported the arts only to the extent to which art could be used to serve the political agenda. In such circumstances liberty and art cannot be conjoined; if freedom was to be preserved, it was necessary to leave everything behind. The émigré experience as recounted through this study is essentially a story of liberation.

We have seen that Soviet Communism was quite willing to snuff out legitimate national social democratic movements that stood in the way of a Moscow-guided ideology. We have also seen that the Nazis had no qualms about losing the finest representatives of German culture as the most talented, disciplined, and creative minds of Europe were driven from the Continent. The democracies became the true beneficiaries of this fascist folly.

Discussions of the process of immigration and adjustment to a new country are usually characterized by terms such as assimilation, integration, Europeanization, deprovincialization, deradicalization, sea change, interculturality, or cultural transfer. While radical change is undoubtedly possible in such areas of human endeavour as the social sciences and nuclear physics, with music the process was much more gradual. The musicians who came to Canada reacted in a myriad of ways, depending on their own individual experience and expectations; their interface with their adopted homeland was an ongoing process. They took whatever opportunities became available and worked within the existing framework. We have observed a dialogical process between individuals that resulted in the creation and transformation of institutions. As Istvan Anhalt said, "I wanted to respond to what I found in this country. I was exhilarated by the openness and freedom. It was not perfect. No environment is totally open, totally free and receiving, but there was enough openness, enough freedom, enough welcoming, I felt I could find my niche. I could find my path, but it would be up to me to recognize what needed to be done and what I could possibly do."[20]

Many of the musicians who came to Canada came from families that played a leading role in artistic, scientific, and business circles. They had enjoyed close contact with Europe's foremost musicians and scholars at a time when central Europe can be said to have dominated in the world. Some – including Emmy Heim, Heinz Unger, Thomas Mayer, Leo Müller, Irene Jessner, and Ruzena Herlinger – had established significant careers in Europe before they came, but the majority were young people, students, or even children. Most of the émigrés remained in Canada for a major part of their careers. Émigrés also participated in Canada's war effort, and a few were employed in postwar Canadian intelligence work; in both, their first hand experience of the threats posed by totalitarian regimes and their fluency in European languages and dialects were invaluable assets. Other musicians boosted the morale of Allied troops by giving concerts and composing songs.

This study has examined how central Europeans cracked British bastions in cities across Canada, transforming them into internationally acclaimed musical centres. The path was not smooth. There was resistance to newcomers and the new ideas they brought; in some cases self-interest permeated the interplay of cultural forces. Musical émigrés had to "play their cards" carefully so as not to offend. While some met substantial resistance from existing musical establishments, a large number gradually found their rightful places within those structures. In steering through these troubled waters, expatriates founded or refashioned many of the institutions we now consider integral to our musical life: faculties of music at the University of Toronto and McGill University; the Royal Conservatory of Music and the Opera School, the Canadian Opera Company, the Music Division of the National Library of Canada, the Canadian Association of University Schools of Music, the Guelph Spring Festival, the Algoma Fall Festival, the Vancouver International Festival, the Festival of the Sound, and the magnificent festivals during the centennial year in 1967, and Music Canada Musique in 2000.

Émigré musicians provided backbone faculty and administrative direction in post-secondary music schools across Canada. In their ranks were Canada's first musicologists and ethnomusicologists who studied the wealth of First Nations music. They pioneered Baroque performance practice in Toronto in the 1940s and built period instruments for the performance of Renaissance music in Montreal in the 1950s. They nurtured Canadian musical talent by working to build educational institutions equivalent to the finest in the world. They encouraged the musical development of their students, coaching, encouraging, and promoting careers on national and international stages. Canadians who studied with musicians associated with the Second Viennese School broadened our knowledge of the dodecaphonists. Musicians with new ideas and live imaginations extended our horizons to include electronically-generated sounds and pushed the definition of music into realms of aleatoric, chance, and multi-media presentations. Business people with musical backgrounds provided much-needed financial support to music and arts organizations across Canada. Émigré conductors enhanced the repertoire of Canadian orchestras and encouraged greater community participation and support. Instrumentalists introduced children to the joys of music in amateur settings and schools. Twenty-one of these émigré musicians have been inducted into the Order of Canada.[21]

As performers, teachers, managers, adjudicators, and festival organizers, émigrés with the keen eye of an outsider saw the potential of talented students and promoted Canadian musicians both here and abroad. They helped to place opera on a permanent footing in Toronto. They took the first steps in researching Canadian music history, and they developed imaginative radio and television music programming at the CBC. They served on committees established to chart the course of music in Canada and to publicize our accomplishments in international forums. Émigré musicians helped us to move beyond a colonial mentality by opening our musical consciousness and giving us a new appreciation of the rich tapestry that constitutes the Canadian mosaic. Their efforts brought about a Canadianization of our musical life: Canadian opera sung by Canadian singers; Canadian musicians educated in Canada; a repertoire of Canadian musical heritage available for performance, study, and enjoyment; Canadian talent well-taught and well-promoted. Their contributions have made it possible for today's Canadian musicians to take responsibility for Canada's musical life.

Émigré musicians played an important role in forging our national musical identity by precipitating a new amalgam of central European and British music traditions. From the beginning there was a common bond – the shared musical repertoire drawn mainly from the rich central European tradition. This repertoire was broadened and intensified as émigré creators and performers interacted with Canadian musicians in a myriad of personal and professional relationships. Yes, there were inevitable clashes, but these were mitigated by the fact that our central Europeans worked and played with Canadian musicians in an enterprise that had no ethnic or national limitations.

The present study has examined the contributions of musical émigrés to Canada's musical life – but what can it contribute to other areas of human endeavour? It seems this question can be adequately answered only with the establishment of a new academic discipline: Canadian exile studies. The study of exile from a Canadian perspective would provide us with a much fuller understanding our own history, and by extension, an understanding of ourselves.

What could such a discipline have to offer European readers? Canadian exile studies has the potential to offer a more comprehensive vision of European history. Outsiders may well be amazed by the extent to which European studies pay allegiance to municipal, provincial, and national boundaries, but fail to consider the broader perspectives of interrelationships between countries. In such a perspective, through the first half of the twentieth century Nazism and Communism appear as Europe's yin and yang, with each side desperately needing the other; when these two totalitarian regimes were locked in a fatal embrace at Stalingrad, it was probably only Allied lend-lease and the Russian winter that tipped the balance.

Canadian exile studies could also function as a corrective to the more restrictive boundaries of European exile studies, where the only category of refugees is those who fled from the Nazi sphere. Such a view robs accounts of the complex reality that was Europe. A number of individuals in this present study confronted tyranny from both Nazi and Communist regimes and were forced to go with one or the other. In addition, the tyranny of wartime carried over into postwar Europe at a new level. Present European exile studies do not address these issues. Nor do they seek to integrate the two aspects of the life of a refugee: the "loss" from one side balanced by the "gain" on the other. Exile studies from this new Canadian perspective could allow this process to take place. Yet another unsettling aspect of European exile studies, at least to date, is the view of human nature as a pawn of blind fate. This present study demonstrates that even if constrained by a multitude of external forces, human freedom always has a place.

How can Canadian exile studies address our understanding of Canadians and Canadian history? Although much research is yet to be undertaken about immigration procedures and practices during the years between 1933 and 1948, this study has established a number of basic facts. Canadian immigration policy was pro-British and reflected the makeup of Canadian society. British Jews were free to come and go to Canada as they pleased. As storm clouds gathered over Europe, Canadian immigration offices throughout continental Europe and as far east as Gydnia slipped into high gear, processing applications from an increasing number of prospective immigrants. As the Nazi grip on the Continent became tighter, however, these offices were forced to close. The normal channel for immigration to Canada from Continental Europe was by means of an order-in-council; these documents were prepared from the applications received from the Continent, sent to the Immigration Branch in Ottawa, vetted by the Privy Council, and returned to Europe, usually within a matter of weeks. The orders-in-council gave Canada a means of integrating citizens of "countries under enemy domination," even though it was, technically speaking, illegal to do so. This process continued throughout the war years although at a diminished level.

Aside from a number of temporary anomalies, the category designated as "Continental European Jewish," was one of the most highly favoured – and in some years the most highly favoured – group compared with the distribution of the Jewish community in the Canadian population as a whole. It remains to be determined how "Jewish" was defined in the period under question. The orders-in-council gave Frederick Charles Blair the opportunity to bring a large number of Jews and other persons at risk from central Europe to Canada without public scrutiny at a time when it was politically unpopular to do so. Blair has been a target of vilification by the Jewish community. One musician in the present study (the only musician interviewed for *None is Too Many*) followed this practice, but I have been able to determine that this émigré had unresolved personal issues that were transferred to Blair. As a general rule academic rigour requires that no statement of the émigrés can be accepted unless corroborated by external evidence.

For too long Canadians have proudly believed that one of the main characteristics that sets us apart from our neighbours to the south is an abiding loyalty to the British crown and its associated institutions. This present study has demonstrated that, in order to achieve maturity, we too had to cast off the tutelage of the Mother Country and assert our own independence. According to this view, the real birth of the Faculty of Music at McGill University came about on 30 May 1957, when the entire department put their own jobs on the line to fend off authoritarian British arrogance. In Toronto the struggle was more like a war of attrition that lasted from September 1944 to July 1952; the last person left standing was the one without personal ambition. The émigrés were better democrats than the Anglo-Saxons. Those who had risked everything to free themselves from tyranny treasured much more profoundly the gift that gives an equal opportunity to all.

In their personal struggles to come to terms with totalitarian regimes the émigrés endured a heart-wrenching process as homes and possessions, and even families were lost, but this process led to self-liberation as they freed themselves from tyranny and set their lives in a completely different direction. Such a decision is one that we can only applaud. The dark side of the human spirit does not always have the last word: Lamentations may well end in Te Deums.

Appendices

APPENDIX A

Bio-Bibliographies of Émigré Musicians

The following list presents brief biographical details and bibliographical and archival sources of information about the 121 émigré musicians included in this study. For some individuals a great deal of information is available; for others, little is known. A number of musicians had local significance only; others were known nationally and internationally.

ADAMS, GEORGE (né Adam Gutman) b. Radom, Poland, 20 March 1916; d. Montreal, 10 August 2003; violinist, violin dealer, violin teacher, poet, painter.
Studied at Warsaw Cons; interned in Auschwitz-Birkenau ca. 1943–45; arr. Canada late 1940s; performances and recording in popular music milieu; violin teacher and violin dealer.
Interview: 31 August 2000.
Resources: "Artist's Alter-egos Create Music, Poetry, Paintings," *Canadian Jewish News*, 15 February 1996: 7; Canadian Jewish Congress Archives and Resource Centre, Montreal, P0195.
Discography: *Au coin du feu,* [1955?], Aladin Records ALA-701.

AMTMANN, WILLY b. Vienna, 10 August 1910; d. Ottawa, 22 July 1996; violinist, violin teacher, chamber musician, musicologist; brother of Hansi Lamberger.
Studied at Vienna Academy of Music 1924–30; performed in dance bands, toured Far East; fled Nazis for England, 1938; interned in England, sent to Canada 1940; released 1942, moved to Ottawa; BMus U of Toronto 1950; MMus Eastman 1952; DLitt. Strasbourg 1956; concertmaster Ottawa Philharmonic Orchestra 1957–59;

director of music, Ottawa Board of Education Public Schools; specialist in history of music in Canada, particularly *ancien régime*; taught at Carleton U 1968–76, lecturer U of Ottawa.
Interviews: Hansi Lamberger, 4 December 2000; David Gardner, 28 February 2001.
Resources: "Willy Amtmann," EMC 23a; Pass, Scheit, and Svoboda, *Orpheus im Exil*, 230; Koch, *Deemed Suspect*, 93, 155, 264; Kreyszig, "Interkulturalität aus musikwissenschaftlicher Perspektive am Beispiel Kanada/Österreich," 202; Engelmann, Prokop, and Szabo, *History of the Austrian Migration to Canada*, 193.

ANČERL, KAREL: b. Tucapy, Bohemia, 1908; d. Toronto 3 July 1973; conductor.
Studied at Prague Cons 1926–30; promoter of avant-garde music at IGNM festivals 1932–37; persecuted under Nazis 1939–45, interned at Theresienstadt 1942 and Auschwitz to 1945; most of his family perished in the camps; conductor for Czech Radio Orchestra 1947–50; conductor Czech Philharmonic 1950–68; tours to North America, Europe, Far East; in North America when Communists invaded Czechoslovakia 1968; conductor TSO 1968–73.
Resources: "Toronto Symphony," EMC, 1302c–3a; LAC, vertical file, "Ančerl"; *MGG1* 15: 191; *Baker's* 1: 73–74; *New Grove* 2 1: 603–4; *MGG2* 1: 627–8.

ANHALT, ISTVAN b. Budapest, 12 April 1919; composer, teacher, pianist.
Studied at Franz Liszt Academy with Zoltán Kodály 1937–41; Hungarian forced labour brigade under Nazis 1942–44; spent remainder of war in hiding; fled Communists from Budapest 1946; studied Paris Conservatoire with Louis Fourestier (conducting), Nadia Boulanger (composition), and Soulima Stravinsky (piano) 1946–49; arr. Montreal 1949; taught at McGill U 1949–71, chair theory department 1963–69; concert of electronic music 1959; founder Electronic Music Studio at McGill U 1964; to Kingston, Ontario 1970; head of music department at Queen's U 1971–81; OC, 2003.
Interviews: 31 October 2000; 27 November 2001.
Resources: "Istvan Anhalt," EMC 26c–8a; LAC, Istvan Anhalt fonds (MUS 164) ACM 22; *Baker's* 1: 90; *New Grove* 2 1: 680–82;

MGG2 1: 729–31; *Contemporary Canadian Composers*, 8–11 (Udo Kasemets); Hollfelder, *Geschichte der Klaviermusik*, 1133–4; Robin Elliot and Gordon Smith eds, *Istvan Anhalt: Pathways and Memory.*

Discography: *Canadian Composer Portraits*, Canadian Music Centre, CMC-CD 10204 (2004), 2-CD set.

BAMBERGER, CARL b. Vienna, 21 February 1902; d. New York, 18 July 1987; conductor.

Studied at University of Vienna 1918–20; conductor in Danzig Theatre 1924–27; Darmstadt 1927–31 Kapellmeister of the State Theatre; conducting engagements in Japan and Philippines 1931–35, Soviet Union (Moscow and Leningrad Philharmonic Orchestras), Austria, Egypt, Finland, Czech Republic, Yugoslavia; fled Austria for United States 1937; conductor New York Philharmonic, NBC Opera Orchestra, New York City Opera, Marlboro Festival; faculty member at Mannes College, New York, 1938–75; conductor Little Symphony of Montreal 1947–48; chamber concerts in New York 1950–22; conductor Süddeutscher Rundfunk Orchestra 1957–72.

Writing: *The Conductor's Art* (first published New York, 1965).

Resources: "Little Symphony of Montreal," EMC 767a; *Biographisches Handbuch der deutschsprachigen Emigration nach 1933*, 2: 51 [incorrect Montreal date 1952–] and 3: 194; Pass, Scheit, and Svoboda, *Orpheus im Exil*, 234–5; Stompor, *Künstler im Exil*, 67, 161 (Vienna), 508 (USA), 573 (USA), 607 (Cuba).

BARBAN, ANDREAS b. Leipzig, 5 February 1914; d. St John's, Newfoundland, 23 May 1993; pianist, teacher, conductor; husband of Betty Berljawsky.

In Leipzig, sang in Thomanerchor, studied at Leipzig Cons 1934–36; fled Nazis from Vienna 1939; taught piano in Shanghai 1939–47; fled Communists from Shanghai 1947; arr. St John's 1947; taught music appreciation (1960–64) and piano (1978–88) at Memorial U; also taught piano privately; conductor St John's Symphony Orchestra 1963–66.

Interview: Betty Barban, 7 May 2001.

Resources: "Andreas Barban," EMC 87a; papers in the possession of Betty Barban.

BARBINI, ERNESTO b. Venice, 15 July 1907; d. Toronto, 17 November 1985; conductor, pianist.
Studied piano, organ, and composition at Benedetto Marcello Cons (Venice) and Cesare Pollini Cons (Padua); conducting debut at La Fenice, 1934; pianist in Barbini-Ferro-Pais piano trio; concerts for the Istituto fascista di Cultura in Portogruaro, 1934–35; concerts in Venice and Padua 1929–33; returned a contract (unsigned) to La Scala, Milan 1938; presumably fled Nazis from Italy in 1938; Chicago Opera School from 1938, Civic Opera 1946; assistant conductor New York Metropolitan Opera 1946–53; coach, conductor Opera School 1953–75.
Resources: "Ernesto Barbini" EMC 88 a–b; LAC, vertical file "Barbini"; LAC, Ernesto Barbini fonds (MUS 200).

BENTLEY, PETER (né Bloch-Bauer) b. Vienna, 1930; industrialist, music patron
Family fled Nazis from Vienna March 1938; arr. Vancouver August 1938; father Leopold (1905–86) and brother-in-law John Prentice (Hans Pick) cofounded Pacific Veneer and Plywood Company (now Canfor) 1938; music patron in Vancouver; OC 1983.
Interviews: Peter Bentley, 26 January 2005; Edwina Heller, 30 May 2001.
Resources: Engelmann, Prokop, and Szabo, *History of the Austrian Migration to Canada*, 180–2.

BERINO, HARALDS b. Riga, 12 March 1906; d. Truro, Nova Scotia, 18 August 1982; composer, pianist, organist, teacher.
Studied composition and piano at Latvian Cons; repetiteur at Latvian Cons and Latvian National Opera; fled Communists from Riga 1944; displaced persons camps in Germany 1944–48; arr. Saint John, 1950; organist Centenary Queen's Square United Church 1950–55; organist-choirmaster St James Presbyterian Church, Truro, Nova Scotia, 1955–82; taught piano in Truro.
Resources: "Haralds Berino," EMC 112a–b.

BERLJAWSKY, JOSEPH b. Przemysl, Austria-Hungary (later Poland), 1911; d. Ottawa, 17 February 1982; violinist, teacher.
Studied at Vienna Academy of Music; fled Nazis for Switzerland 1938; arr. Montreal 1939; founder Montreal Orchestra Society 1954, Ottawa Musica Viva 1968; taught violin in Montreal.

Interviews: Harvey Levitt, 20 January 2004; Betty Barban, 7 May 2001.

Resources: EMC references (38b, 59a, 87a, 1374b); LAC, Joseph Berljawsky fonds (MUS 171); Kreysig, 202; Pass, Scheit, and Svoboda, *Orpheus im Exil*, 394.

Writings: *Violin Technique, Its Evolution and Pedagogy* (1964).

BLUME, HELMUT b. Berlin, 12 April 1914; d. Montreal, 16 October 1998; pianist, music broadcaster, writer, music administrator, music educator.

Studied at Berlin Hochschule für Musik 1932–38; fled Nazis to England 1939; interned in England, sent to Canada 1940; concerts in internment camps 1940–42; released 1942; studied in Toronto; taught piano at Hambourg Cons; propaganda broadcasts for CBC International Service 1944–46; contributor to CBC *Wednesday Night* series; initiator of CBC *International Concerts;* CBC television series *Form in Music* 1959; piano instructor McGill U from 1946, dean McGill U Faculty of Music 1963–75; adjudicator, jury member for numerous festivals; cofounder Canadian Association of University Schools of Music 1964.

Interviews: Helmut Blume, 10 December 1997; Ljerka Blume, 15 February 2001; Maria Jerabek, 16 February 2001.

Resources: "Helmut Blume," EMC 135a–b; "McGill University," EMC 830b; LAC, Helmut Blume fonds (MUS 302); Koch, *Deemed Suspect*, 21, 39, 138, 155–6, 205, 231–2, 246, 264; Stompor, *Künstler im Exil*, 589.

Writings: piano accompaniments for Edith Fowke and Alan Mills, eds., *Canada's Story in Song* (1960); *A National Music School for Canada* (Canada Council study, 1978).

BÖSZÖRMENYI-NAGY, BÉLA b. Budapest 1912; d. Boston, 1990; pianist, teacher.

Studied at Franz Liszt Academy [1920s]–1937, and taught piano there 1937–48; fled Communists from Budapest; arr. Toronto 1948; taught at RCM 1948–53; moved to United States 1953, taught at Indiana University 1953–62, Boston University 1962–78, and Catholic University 1978–90.

Interview: Linda Jiorle-Nagy, communication 18 May 2004.

Resources: LAC, Music Section vertical file "Boszormenyi-Nagy" includes: Mairi MacLean, "Pianist a link to Hungary's musical past," *Edmonton Journal*, 13 May 1988 (from Calgary Philharmonic program, 27 February 1961); CBC *Times*, (16–22 March, 1952): "BBN gives 3 Canadian piano music recitals." 25 January 1949; announcement for Massey Hall, Beethoven's Piano Concerto no. 4 with TSO and Ernest Macmillan; announcement for Eaton Auditorium debut on 17 October [1948]; transcript of speech to RCM faculty in 1948.

BRENTANO, FELIX b. Vienna ca. 1910; d. New York ca. 1970; operatic stage director.
Associate of Max Reinhardt in Vienna ca. 1920s–37; fled Nazis from Vienna; Broadway productions in New York from 1937; Columbia Opera Workshop, New York 1940s; Toronto Opera School 1946–47.
Resources: *EMC* references (211a, 1155b, 1347c); Setterfield, 59–60, 61, 64; www.ibdb.com (for Broadway productions 1940–45); Stompor, *Künstler im Exil*, 476–77 (New York), 499, 525, 538, 569.

BRILTS, TEODORE b. Latvia, 1907; d. Halifax, 1976; singer, teacher.
Fled Communists from Riga[?] 1944; displaced persons camps, Germany 1944–47; taught at Halifax Cons from 1947, assistant to Mariss Vetra; appeared in Halifax opera productions; director of Nova Scotia Opera Association 1954–55.
Resources: *EMC* references (34b, 569b, 722c, 954b, 1222c).

BROTT, LOTTE (née Goetzel) b. Mannheim, 8 February 1922; d. Montreal, 6 January 1998; cellist, music administrator; wife of Alexander Brott.
Studied in Mannheim to 1938; family fled Nazis from Mannheim 1938, arr. Montreal; Lotte and sister Lena in Neuchâtel, Switzerland 1938–39, arr. Montreal 1939; studied in Toronto with Zara Nelsova; cellist, McGill String Quartet 1942–54; cellist and manager McGill Chamber Orchestra 1940s–1998; cellist Montreal Symphony Orchestra 1941–87; manager, Kingston Symphony. Orchestra 1978–81; taught at McGill U; CM, 1990.
Interviews: Alexander Brott, 25 February 2000, 17 November 2000.
Resources: "Lotte Brott," *EMC* 170b.

BURGHAUSER, HUGO b. Vienna, 1896; d. New York 10 December 1982; bassoonist, music administrator, teacher.
Bassoonist, board member Vienna Philharmonic Orchestra 1919–38; fled Nazis from Vienna 1938; arr. Toronto 1938; bassoonist TSO 1938–41; bassoonist Metropolitan Opera Orchestra 1941–[1970?].
Resources: Daniel N. Leeson, "A Righteous Person," *Double Reed* 22, no. 4 (1999) (available at http://www.idrs.org/Publications/DR/dr22.4); Pass, Scheit, and Svoboda, *Orpheus im Exil*, 247; Claudia Maurer-Zenck, *Ernst Krenek,* 89; Newman and Kortly, *Alma Rosé,* 30, 94, 322, 326, 331; Brückner, *Judentum und Musik,* 3rd edition 48; Flotzinger, *Oesterreichisches Musiklexikon*, 1: 239; *Biographisches Handbuch der deutschsprachigen Emigration nach 1933*, 2: 51 and 3: 194; Stompor, *Künstler im Exil*, 588.
Writings: "Philharmonic Adventures with Bassoon," *Journal of the Double Reed Society,* 1 November 1973 (available at available at http://www. idrs.org/Publications/Journal); *Philharmonische Begegnungen. Erinnerungen eines Wiener Philharmonikers.* Zurich: Atlantis, 1979.

CIRULIS, JĀNIS b. Riga 1897; d. Toronto 1962; conductor, composer, teacher.
Taught at Riga Music School to 1944; fled Communists from Riga 1944; displaced persons camps, Germany 1944–8; arr. Toronto ca. 1948; conductor Hamilton Latvian Society Choir; conductor Latvian song festivals.
Resources: "Latvia," *EMC* 722c.

DAMBERGS, MIRDZA (née Grikes) b Riga, ca. 1925; dancer, teacher
Studied in Riga and Paris; prima ballerina Riga Opera; fled Communists from Riga 1944; displaced persons camps, Germany 1944–48; France 1948–53; Dambergs School of Ballet, Halifax 1957–82; taught at Halifax Cons from 1954; numerous ballet performances in Maritimes.
Interviews: Mirdza Dambergs, 25 April 2001; Robert Dambergs, 30 May 2003.
Resources: "Latvia," *EMC* 722c.

DIAMANT, BERNARD b. Rotterdam, 11 October 1912; d. Amsterdam, August 1999; singer, teacher.
Studied at Royal Cons, Den Hague, and Berlin Hochschule für Musik, 1930s; studied with Charles Panzéra; fled Communists from Czechoslovakia 1945; France 1945–50; arr. Montreal 1950; taught at McGill U and École Vincent d'Indy; taught at U of Toronto 1972–91; returned to Holland 1991.
Resources: "Bernard Diamant," *EMC* 364a–b.

DUSCHENES, MARIO b. Hamburg/Altona, 27 October 1923; d. Montreal, 31 January 2009; flutist, recorder player, teacher, conductor, arranger, narrator, animateur; brother of Rolf Duschenes.
In Prague 1937–38; family fled Nazis for Switzerland 1938; studied at Geneva Conservatoire 1938–48; appearances with Ars Antiqua in France and Belgium; arr. Montreal 1948; taught at McGill U from 1955; cofounder Baroque Trio 1957–73; animateur for children's concerts; teacher at CAMMAC from 1953; concerts and recordings with Jean-Pierre Rampal; Orff Schulwerk (Music for Children); conductor Newfoundland SO 1985–92; CM, 1985.
Interview: 27 January 2003.
Resources: "Mario Duschenes," *EMC* 393c–4b; "Baroque Trio of Montreal," *EMC* 90b–c, "CAMMAC," *EMC* 189a.
Writings: methods and studies for recorder published by Berandol.

DUSCHENES, ROLF b. Hamburg/Altona, 6 January 1918; architect, music patron, violinist, violist; brother of Mario Duschenes.
In Prague 1937–38; family fled Nazis for Switzerland 1938–39; England 1939–40; interned in England, sent to Canada 1940; studied at U of Toronto 1942–43 and at McGill U from 1943; architect in Saint John; organized youth orchestras on provincial and national levels; CM, 1987.
Interview: 28 January 2003.
Resources: *EMC* 1432b; Koch, *Deemed Suspect*, 265.

ECKHARDT-GRAMATTÉ, SOPHIE-CARMEN b. Moscow 6 Jan 1899; d. Stuttgart 2 Dec 1974.
[Eckhardt-Gramatté is not included in this study because she did not flee Europe for political reasons between 1933 and 1948. She spent the war years in Berlin and Vienna with her husband, Ferdinand Eckhardt. See appendix D for a description of her confronta-

tions with Nazi authorities and a full list of references. Ferdinand Eckhardt fell afoul of the Russian authorities in postwar Vienna, which may have precipitated their departure from Vienna. They came to Winnipeg in 1953.]

FABIJANCIC, MIJO b. Yugoslavia, 1899; [death date unknown]; music teacher.
Entered Canada by order-in-council, October 1938.

FENYVES, LORAND b. Budapest, 20 February 1918; d. Switzerland, 23 March 2004; violinist, teacher.
In Budapest 1918–36; studied at Franz Liszt Academy; concertmaster Palestine SO 1936–57; concertmaster Orchestre de la Suisse romande, Geneva 1957–65; taught at U of Toronto 1965–2004.
Interview: 8 March 2001.
Resources: "Lorand Fenyves," EMC 444b–c.

FIALA, GEORGE b. Kiev, 31 March 1922; pianist, organist, composer, broadcaster, philatelist.
Studied piano and composition Kiev Cons; in Ukrainian army, prisoner of German army; after release fled Red Army from Kiev 1943 for Berlin; concerts for displaced persons in camps throughout Germany; to Belgium 1946, studied at Royal Cons in Brussels; arr. Canada January 1949; Ukrainian and Russian section of CBC International Service from 1967; wrote ca. 250 compositions.
Interview: 10 June 2007.
Resources: "George Fiala," EMC 453c–54b; University of Calgary Special Collections, George Fiala fonds 1935–2002: radio scripts, compositions, essays, sound recordings (www.ucalgary.ca/lib-old/SpecColl/fiala.htm); Arthur Kaptainis, "Musical Memories of Wartime Germany," *Globe and Mail,* 27 November 1982, E5; ACM 27, interview with Edward Farrant.

FOGL, ALOYS b. Mistroveice, 20 May 1925; violin maker and restorer, social democrat.
Studied violin making in Schönbach to 1948; fled Communists 1948; displaced persons camps Germany 1948; arr. Montreal 1949; joined string instrument repair and sales shop with Anton Wilfer and Ewald Fuchs; recipient of Masaryk Award.
Interview: 30 September 2003.
Resources: "Anton Wilfer," EMC 1404a.

FREIMANE-PLAMPE, ERIKE b. [Riga?] ca. 1910?; d. [Toronto?] 1960; composer, teacher, conductor.
Taught music in Talsi, Riga; conducted Varavítsne Choir, Riga; fled Communists from Riga 1944; displaced persons camps, Germany 1944–48; arr. Toronto ca. 1948; conductor Daina choir.

FRIEDLANDER, ERNST (Friedländer) b. Vienna, 6 October 1906; d, Vancouver, 28 October 1966; cellist, teacher, composer; husband of Maria Friedlander.
Vienna 1906–37; studied at Vienna Cons 1928–29 with F. Buxbaum, H. Schenker; studied at Hochschule 1929–30; principal cellist Vienna Konzerthaus O 1935–37; fled Nazis 1937 with wife; principal cellist Pittsburgh O 1937–38; Indianapolis 1939–42; U of Wisconsin 1943–55; U of Wyoming 1952–54; Chicago Symphony O 1955; taught at U of Oklahoma 1956–8; principal cellist Vancouver SO 1958–66; Vancouver String Quartet; lecturer U of British Columbia.
Resources: "Ernst Friedlander," EMC 501C; LAC vertical file "Friedländer"; Pass, Scheit, and Svoboda, *Orpheus im Exil*, 397; Engelmann, Prokop, and Szabo, *History of the Austrian Migration to Canada*, 159–60.

FRIEDLANDER, MARIA (née Werbner) b. Vienna, 6 September 1917; pianist, teacher; wife of Ernst Friedlander.
Studied Vienna Academy 1930s; fled Nazis for United States 1937; in 1937–58; Vancouver from 1958; pianist for husband.
Resources: "Ernst Friedlander," EMC 501C.

FUCHS EWALD b. Schönbach (Luby), 9 September 1932; d. Montreal, 17 April 1991; violin maker and repairer.
In Schönbach 1932–47; Mittenwald violin making school 1947–50; Zurich violin making school with Mecklin 1950–55; arr. Montreal 1955; worked in string instrument shop with Aloys Fogl and Anton Wilfer 1956–91.
Resources: "Anton Wilfer," EMC 1404a.

GARAMI, ARTHUR (Gutman) b. Derecske, 20 November 1921, d. Montreal, 12 January 1979; violinist, teacher.
Studied with Géza de Kresz at Franz Liszt Academy 1935–42; Hungarian forced labour brigades under Nazis 1943–44; fled Commu-

nists from Budapest 1946; freelance musician Paris 1946–49; prize winner Jacques Thibaud Competition 1946, Geneva International Competition 1947; arr. Hamilton 1949; taught at Hamilton Cons 1949–54; concertmaster McGill Chamber Orchestra 1956–59; assistant concertmaster Montreal Symphony Orchestra 1960–65; taught at McGill U 1955–64, École Vincent-d'Indy 1958–64, and Conservatoire de musique de Montréal 1962–79; cofounder and first violin Classical Quartet of Montreal 1968–76; radio and television appearances with Dale Bartlett and Charles Reiner.
Interviews: Shirley Garami, 26 November 2001; Charles Reiner, 26 November 2001.
Resources: "Arthur Garami," EMC 512c.

GARTNER, EMIL (Gaertner) b. Vienna, 1913; d. Toronto, 31 May 1960 (car accident); conductor, social democrat.
Studied in Vienna 1930s; fled Nazis for United States 1938; conductor Toronto Jewish Folk Choir 1939–60.
Resources: "Toronto Jewish Folk Choir," EMC 1297c–8a; LAC, vertical file, "Gartner" and Toronto Jewish Folk Choir fonds (MUS 43); Pass, Scheit, and Svoboda, *Orpheus im Exil*, 397; Kreyszig, "Interkulturalität aus musikwissenschaftlicher Perspektive am Beispiel Kanada/Österreich," 202; Engelmann, Prokop, and Szabo, *History of the Austrian Migration to Canada*, 194.

GEIGER-TOREL, HERMANN (né Geiger) b. Frankfurt am Main, 13 July 1907; d. Toronto, 6 October 1976; opera stage director, teacher, administrator.
Studied at the Hoch Cons, Goethe U, Frankfurt; asst director Frankfurt Opera, Aussig, Czechoslovakia 1930–31, Bremerhaven, Germany, 1931–32, Troppau, Czechoslovakia, 1934–37; productions Teatro Colón, Buenos Aires 1934–37; fled Nazis to South America 1937; Buenos Aires 1938–43; stage director for SODRE national opera Montevideo, Uruguay 1943–47, Teatro Municipal, Rio de Janeiro; arr. Toronto 1947; stage director Opera School 1947–67; cofounded CBC Opera Company and COC; OC, 1969.
Resources: "Canadian Opera Company," EMC 211a, "Hermann Geiger-Torel," 520a–c; LAC Hermann Geiger-Torel fonds (MUS 70); Joachim Martini, "Vom "Oberregisseur in Frankfurt zum "Mr. Opera' in Toronto," in Heister, Zenck, and Petersen, *Musik im Exil,* 80–101; *Biographisches Handbuch der deutschsprachi-*

gen Emigration nach 1933, 2: 363 and 3: 194; Stompor, *Künstler im Exil*, 140 (Troppau), 587–88 (Canada), 608 (Cuba), 612 (Guatemala), 639, 646, 654–55, 657 (Teatro Colón, Buenos Aires, Argentina), 665 (Brasil), 675 (Uruguay), 697 (Venezuela). Geiger-Torel, Arnold Walter, Nicholas Goldschmidt, and Ernesto Vinci appear in the National Film Board documentary, *Opera School,* 1952.

GEORG, RITA b. Vienna 1900; d. Vancouver, ca. 1980; singer; aunt of Peter Bentley (Bloch-Bauer).
Viennese operetta productions with Richard Tauber; appeared in Berlin and Paris; fled Nazis from Vienna 1938; performed in Folies Bergères, Paris 1938; arr. Vancouver 1941.
Resources: Engelmann, Prokop, and Szabo, *History of the Austrian Migration to Canada*, 162; www.foliesbergere.com/histoire-7.htm.

GOLDSCHMIDT, NICHOLAS b. Tavikovice, Moravia, 6 December 1908; d. Toronto, 8 February 2004; enterpreneur, singer, pianist, conductor, music administrator.
Tavikovice, Vienna 1927–33; conductor Troppau 1933–37; fled Nazis 1937 for United States; San Francisco Cons; conductor/coach New Orleans Opera; New York, opera coach Columbia U; cofounder Opera School 1946; cofounded CBC Opera Company and COC; Centennial Commission; artistic director Guelph Spring Festival, The 1985 International Bach Competition, International Choral Festivals, Algoma Fall Festival, Vancouver International Festival, Music Canada Musique; OC, 1978, CC, 1989.
Interview: 1–2 November 2000.
Resources: "Nicholas Goldschmidt," EMC 535c–36b, EMC references (17b, 211a, 949c, 1347c, 1359a); LAC Nicholas Goldschmidt fonds (MUS 223); Gwenlyn Setterfield, *Niki Goldschmidt;* Pass, Scheit, and Svoboda, *Orpheus im Exil*, 398; Engelmann, Prokop, and Szabo, *History of the Austrian Migration to Canada*, 163–4: Stompor, *Künstler im Exil*, 140 (Troppau).

GOTSCHALKS, IRENE (née Apinée) b. Riga, ca, 1920s; dancer.
Fled Communists from Riga 1944; displaced persons camps, Germany 1944–47; Halifax Cons 1947–51; principal dancer National Ballet, Toronto 1951–55.

GOTSCHALKS, JURY (Juris) b. Riga[?], ca. 1920s; dancer.
Fled Communists from Riga, 1944; displaced persons camps, Germany 1944–47; Halifax Cons 1947–51; principal dancer National Ballet, Toronto 1951–52, 1953–55.

GRANT, FREDDY (né Grundland) b. Berlin, 17 October 1913; d. Toronto, 10 April 1996; composer, pianist.
Studied in Berlin to 1934; England 1934–40; interned in England, sent to Canada 1940; released 1942; composed "You'll Get Used to It"; in Toronto from 1942; composer numerous popular songs; performer in popular music milieu, hotels.
Resources: "Freddy or Freddie Grant," EMC 551a–b; LAC Vertical file "Grant"; Koch, *Deemed Suspect*, 5–6, 94–5, 154, 195, 266.

GRUBER, HANS b. Vienna, 11 July 1925; d. Toronto, 2001; conductor, industrialist.
Studied in Brno to 1937; family fled Nazis from Brno 1938; student Chambéry-sur-Montreux, Switzerland 1937–39; studied U of Toronto 1939–48; conductor TCM Orchestra from 1939; conductor Victoria SO 1948–63; guest conductor; business pursuits in Toronto 1963–2001.
Interviews: Hans Gruber, 9 March 2001; Edith Howard, 3 November 2003.
Resources: EMC references (59a, 1129b, 1347a, 1370c); Kreyszig, "Interkulturalität aus musikwissenschaftlicher Perspektive am Beispiel Kanada/Österreich," 202; Robert Dale Macintosh, *Documentary History of Music in Victoria,* 2: 382; 15 letters to Oskar Morawetz in LAC, Oskar Morawetz fonds (MUS 76), Acc. 92/93, vol. 1, no. 100, 1954–85.

HAENDEL, IDA b. Chelm, Poland, 15 December 1928; violinist.
[Haendel was not included in this study because she did not consider herself an émigrée; she left Central Europe for England in 1935 because her teacher Flesch had emigrated there before the war, and studied in Paris and London with Flesch and Enesco. She came to Montreal in 1952 and her international career included occasional appearances there and elsewhere in Canada.]
Interview: 29 March 2001.
Resources: "Ida Haendel," EMC 565–6; Kater, *Twisted Muse,* 101; Adrienne Clarkson, Summer Festival *Our Unknown Super-*

star/La voie de la musique, 1988 (original title: Ida Haendel: Voyage of Music); *Baker's* 3: 1411; *New Grove* 2 10: 653–4; MGG2 8: 384–5.

Writings: *Woman with Violin* (references to Canada, 216, 219, 224, 226, 247, 269, 275–6).

Discography: available at http://www.jose-sanchez-penzo.net/ihaendel.html; early recordings reissued on *Ida Haendel: The Decca Years* 1940–47 CD 460 6582 75.10.

HALPERN, IDA (née Ruhdörfer) b. Vienna, 17 July 1910; d. Vancouver, 7 February 1987; ethnomusicologist, music patron, music critic.

Vienna 1910–38, studied at U of Vienna; Shanghai 1938–39; Vancouver 1939–87, instructor U of British Columbia; Simon Fraser U; music reviewer; cofounder of Friends of Chamber Music; recordings and transcriptions traditional musics of Northwest Coast First Nations Peoples; CM 1978.

Interview: David Duke, 7 May 2001.

Resources: "Ida Halpern," *EMC* 571a–b; Kenneth Chen, "Ida Halpern: A Post-Colonial Portrait of a Canadian Pioneer Ethnomusicologist," *Canadian University Music Review,"* 16/1 (1995): 41–59; Pass, Scheit, and Svoboda, *Orpheus im Exil*, 275; Kreyszig, "Interkulturalität aus musikwissenschaftlicher Perspektive am Beispiel Kanada/Österreich," 199, 203; Engelmann, Prokop, and Szabo, *History of the Austrian Migration to Canada*, 164; Flotzinger, *Oesterreichisches Musiklexikon*, 2: 274; *New Grove* 2 10: 710; Simon Fraser University, fonds F582, 3; (www.SFU.ca/archives, Halpern fonds); British Columbia Archives, Halpern fonds, MS-2768; Stompor, *Künstler im Exil*, 588 as "Rohdörfer-Halpern."

Writings: "Music of the Kwakiutl Indians," *Journal of the International Folk Music Council* 14 (1962): 159–60; "Music of the BC Northwest Coast Indians," *Proceedings of the Centennial Workshop on Ethnomusicology,* ed Peter Crossley-Holland (Victoria: Queen's Printer, 1968): 23–42; "On the Interpretation of 'Meaningless-Nonsensical Syllables' in the Music of the Pacific Northwest Indians," *Ethnomusicology,* 20 (May 1976): 253–71.

Discography (Folkways Ethnic Library, New York): *Indian Music of the Pacific Northwest*, FE4523 (1967); *Nootka Indian Music of the Pacific Northwest*, FE4524 (1974); *Kwakiutl Indian Music* of the Pacific Northwest, FE 4122 (1981); *Haida Indian Music of the Pacific Northwest*, FE 4119 (1986).

HEIM, EMMY b. Vienna, 10 September 1885; d. Toronto, 13 October 1954; singer, teacher.
Vienna 1885–1930; acquainted many Viennese artists, musicians, poets and painters; premiered works by Schoenberg; appeared in Toronto from 1934 with Ernest MacMillan; taught at Salzburg summer festivals 1930–38; fled Nazis for England 1938; England 1938–46; numerous wartime concerts in England; Toronto RCM 1946–54.
Resources: "Emmy Heim," *EMC* 594c–5a; Pass, Scheit, and Svoboda, *Orpheus im Exil*, 278–79; Raab Hansen, *NS-verfolgte Musiker in England*, 419; Engelmann, Prokop, and Szabo, *History of the Austrian Migration to Canada*, 162; Stompor, *Künstler im Exil*, 327 (England); U of Toronto Archives, A75–004/109.

HELLER, EDWINA b. Warsaw, ca. 1920; pianist, music patron.
Warsaw ca. 1920–39; fled Nazis from Warsaw September 1939; Budapest 1939; London 1940; arr. Montreal 1940; in Montreal 1940–41; in Vancouver from 1941.
Interview: 30 May 2001.

HELLER, PAUL b. Warsaw, ca. 1920; industrialist, music patron.
Warsaw ca. 1920–39; fled Nazis from Warsaw September 1939; Budapest 1939; London 1940; arr. Montreal 1940; in Montreal 1940–41; in Vancouver from 1941.
Interview: 30 May 2001.

HERLINGER, RUZENA (née Ruzena Schwartz) b. Tabor, Czechoslovakia, 8 February 1890; d. Montreal, 19 February 1978; soprano, teacher.
In Vienna 1916–ca.1938; commissioned and sang premiere Alban Berg's *Der Wein*; England ca. 1938–46; Prague 1946–49; Montreal 1949–78; taught at Montreal Conservatoire 1957–62, McGill U 1963–70.
Resources: "Ruzena Herlinger," *EMC* 599a–b; Pass, Scheit, and Svoboda, *Orpheus im Exil*, 399; LAC, Ruzena Herlinger fonds (MUS 76).

HOMBURGER, WALTER b. Karlsruhe, 22 January 1924; music impresario.
Karlsruhe 1924–39; Kindertransport to England 1939–40; studied at Eastbourne College; interned in England, sent to Canada 1940; released 1942; in Toronto from 1942; manager International Artists; manager TSO 1962–87; manager of Glenn Gould and James Ehnes; CM, 1984.
Interviews: 27 May and 6 October 2002.
Resources: "Walter Homburger," EMC 609c–10b; LAC, Walter Homburger fonds (MUS 259); Koch, *Deemed Suspect*, 267; Esther Ramon, *The Homburger Family from Karlsruhe 1674–1990*, 81–2; *Biographisches Handbuch der deutschsprachigen Emigration nach 1933*, 2: 536 and 3: 195.

HUSARUK, EUGÈNE b. Warsaw, 2 March 1932; violinist, teacher.
Studied in Cracow; displaced persons camp in Holzminden, Germany, 1944–49; arr. Montreal 1949; studied at McGill U with Alexander Brott; Vienna Academy with Přihoda, Odnoposoff, also Ivan Galamian, Lorand Fenyves; violinist Montreal SO 1957–99, concertmaster 1979–82; first violinist Société de musique contemporaine du Québec; numerous premieres; concertmaster Grands ballets canadiens.
Interview: 9 February 2001.
Resources: "Eugène Husaruk," EMC 618a.

JESSNER, IRENE b. Vienna, 29 August 1901; d. Toronto, 9 January 1994; singer, teacher.
Studied at Vienna Cons; opera career in Germany, Austria, Czechoslovakia 1930–36; New York Metropolitan Opera 1936–52; taught at U of Toronto 1952–86.
Resources: "Irene Jessner," EMC 653b–c; F.C. Engelmann, *History of Austrian Migration to Canada*, 162; Stompor, *Künstler im Exil*, 142, 456–60 [Metropolitan, New York.]

JOACHIM, OTTO b. Düsseldorf, 13 October 1910; composer, violist, violinist, teacher, painter, entrepreneur and manager, instrument builder (historical and electronic).
Studied at Buths-Neitzel Cons, Düsseldorf and Rheinische Musikschule, Cologne; freelance musician in Düsseldorf 1929–34; fled Nazis 1934; in Singapore 1934–40; in Shanghai 1940–49; fled

Communists from Shanghai 1949; arr. Montreal 1949; CAMMAC; violist Montreal Symphony Orchestra 1952–65; Montreal String Quartet (1955–61); McGill Chamber Orchestra (1959–66); taught at McGill Cons (1956–64) and Conservatoire de musique de Montréal (1956–77); founded and directed Montreal Consort of Ancient Instruments 1958–66; composed electro-acoustic and dodecaphonic music.
Interview: 11 March 2003.
Resources: "Otto Joachim" EMC 656c–7c, "CAMMAC," EMC 189c; LAC Otto Joachim fonds (MUS 270), fonds catalogue at www.LAC.bac.gc.ca/pubs/fonds/joachim/joachime.pdf; Centre Directory of Associate Composers www.musiccentre.ca/CMC/dac_rca/eng /f_/Joachim_Otto.html; ACM 14, interview with Hugh Davidson; *Contemporary Canadian Composers*, 103–6; *Survivors of the Shoah* (video): Visual History Foundation; *Baker's* 3: 1740–1; *New Grove* 2 13: 127; MGG2 9: 1067–8; *Biographisches Handbuch der deutschsprachigen Emigration nach 1933*, 2: 570–1 and 3: 195; Hollfelder, *Geschichte der Klaviermusik*, 1129; Kreyszig, "Interkulturalität aus musikwissenschaftlicher Perspektive am Beispiel Kanada/Österreich," 202; Stompor, *Künstler im Exil*, 724 (Shanghai); Compositions; ACM 14.

JOACHIM, WALTER b. Düsseldorf, 5 May 1912; d. Montreal, 19 December 2001; cellist, teacher.
Studied at Buths-Neitzel Cons, Düsseldorf, and Rheinische Musikschule, Cologne 1929–31; musician in Calcutta; fled Nazis 1934; Prague 1934–38; Kuala Lumpur 1938–40; Shanghai 1940–51; fled Communists from Shanghai; Düsseldorf 1951; arr. Montreal 1951; CAMMAC; cellist Montreal Symphony Orchestra 1953–79; Montreal String Quartet; taught at McGill U and Conservatoire de musique de Montréal; numerous broadcasts, concerts; CM, 1992.
Interview: by Rachel Anderson, 26 April 2000.
Resources: "Walter Joachim," EMC 657c–8a; "CAMMAC," EMC 189c.

KALEJS FELICITA b. Riga, 20 October 1911; d. 2000, Wolfville, NS; pianist, teacher, music administrator.
Studied at Latvian State Cons to 1940, taught there 1940–42; coach for Latvian National Opera 1940–44; fled Communists from Riga

1944; displaced persons camps in Germany 1944–49; arr. in Canada 1949; taught piano at Acadia U, 1949–79, acting dean 1973–74; numerous concerts and broadcasts.

Resources: "Felicita Kalejs," *EMC* 672b; LAC Jānis and Felicita Kalejs fonds (MUS 55); Acadia University Archives, Kalejs Family fonds Acc. no. 1999.001.

KALEJS, JĀNIS b. Riga, 7 January 1912; d. Wolfville, Nova Scotia, 7 November 1973; violinist, teacher, music administrator; husband of Felicita Kalejs.

Studied at Berlin Hochschule für Musik, 1920s; graduated from State Cons, Riga, 1934; violinist Latvian National Radio Orchestra and National Opera Orchestra; taught at State Cons, Riga; fled Communists from Riga 1944; displaced persons camps in Germany 1944–49; arr. in Canada 1949; taught at Acadia U from 1949, dean 1966–73; numerous concerts and broadcasts.

Resources: "Janis Kalejs," *EMC* 672b; LAC Jānis and Felicita Kalejs fonds (MUS 55); Acadia University Archives, Kalejs Family fonds Acc. no. 1999.001

KALLMANN, HELMUT b. Berlin, 7 August 1922; music librarian, lexicographer.

Studied in Berlin; sent on Kindertransport to England 1939; England 1939–40; interned in England, sent to Canada 1940; released 1943; in Toronto from 1943; BMus U of Toronto 1949; CBC music librarian; cofounder Canadian Music Library Association, 1956; proposed and founded Music Division, LAC, 1970; cofounded Canadian Musical Heritage Society 1982; CM, 1986.

Interviews: 28 February 2001; 15 March 2004.

Resources: "Helmut Kallmann," *EMC* 672b–673a; *MGGI* 16: 898–899; *Baker's* 3: 1810; Dawn L. Keer, "Helmut Kallmann: An Account of his Contributions to Music Librarianship and Scholarship in Canada"; *Biographisches Handbuch der deutschsprachigen Emigration nach 1933*, 2: 588 and 3: 196; Stompor, *Künstler im Exil*, 589.

Writings: *Encyclopedia of Music in Canada*, 1981, 2nd ed., 1992; *A History of Music in Canada 1534–1914*, (1960, rev. ed. 1987); "Mapping Canada's Music"; "Music in the Internment Camps and after World War II: John Newmark's Start on a Brilliant

Canadian Career"; contributions to *Dictionary of Canadian Biography, Encyclopedia Canadiana, Canadian Music Journal, New Grove* 1st ed., *Riemman Lexikon,* 12th ed., MGG (1958, 1995), *Fontes Artis Musicae, Répertoire des Sources Musicales, Répertoire international de la Presse musicale,* and *Répertoire international d'iconographie musicale.*

KALNIŅŠ, JĀNIS b. Pärnu, Estonia, 3 November 1904; d. Fredericton, 30 November 2000 (final burial Riga July 2001); composer, conductor, organist, pianist, music teacher; son of Latvian composer Alfred Kalniņš.

Studied at Latvian State Cons; conductor, Latvian National Theatre 1923–33; Latvian National Opera 1933–44; fled Communists from Riga 1944; displaced persons camps in Germany 1944–48; Fredericton 1948–2000; organist St Paul's United Church 1948–90; taught at Teacher's College; conductor Fredericton Civic Orchestra 1951–62, conductor New Brunswick Symphony 1962–8; numerous performances for Latvian Festivals in Toronto and United States.

Interviews: Janet Toole, 21–22 May 2001; Nan Gregg 21 May 2001; Sadie Turner-Miller, 22 May 2001; Helen Craig 22 May 2001; Arvid Landva, 22 May 2001.

Resources: "Jānis Kalniņš," *EMC* 673a–b; New Brunswick Archives, MC 2037; *Baker's* 3: 1811; *New Grove* 2 13: 336; *MGG1* 16: 900; *MGG2* 9: 1419; *Contemporary Canadian Composers,* 109–110; *International Cyclopedia of Music and Musicians,* 10th ed. (1975), 1139.

KANDER, GERHARD b. Mannheim, 1921; d. Toronto, 1 January 2008; violinist, investment banker.

Studied in Mannheim with Carl Flesch, and in Baden-Baden, 1932–34; tours with Jüdischer Kulturbund 1934–38; fled Nazis for England 1938; interned in England, sent to Canada 1940; concerts in internment camps 1940–42; released 1942; in Toronto from 1942; numerous appearances as soloist in Canada and United States to 1953; executive CIBC World Markets.

Interviews: 7 March 2001; 6 October 2002.

Resources: *EMC* references (524b, 1019b); Koch, *Deemed Suspect,* 155, 246, 268; Stompor, *Künstler im Exil,* 589.

KARLSONE, LÍNA b. Riga, ca. 1910; d. [Toronto?], ca. 1960; singer.
Studied at Latvian Cons; soloist at National Theatre in Riga; studied in Berlin with Hussler; fled Communists from Riga 1944; displaced persons camps in Germany 1944–48; arr. Montreal 1948; appearances in Montreal, Toronto, Ottawa, and Hamilton.

KASEMETS, UDO b. Tallinn, 16 November 1919; composer, pianist, organist, writer, music reviewer.
Studied in Tallinn; family fled Communists from Tallinn 1944; displaced persons camp, Geislinger-an-der-Steige, Germany 1944–51; studied at Stuttgart Hochschule für Musik and Kranichstein Institute; studied with Ernst Krenek and Hermann Scherchen; arr. Hamilton 1951; taught piano, theory, and composition at Hamilton Cons 1951–57; music reviewer for *Toronto Daily Star* 1959–63; taught at Brodie School of Music and Modern Dance 1963–67; lecturer on music and mixed media Ontario College of Art 1970–87.
Interview: 6 March 2001.
Resources: "Udo Kasemets," EMC 674b–6a; *Baker's* 3: 1827–8; *New Grove* 2, 13: 391–2; *MGG2* 9: 1523–6; Hollfelder, *Geschichte der Klaviermusik*, 1134; Kreyszig, "Interkulturalität aus musikwissenschaftlicher Perspektive am Beispiel Kanada/Österreich," 202.

KASSNER, ELI b. Vienna, 27 May 1924; guitarist, teacher.
Studied in Vienna to 1939; fled Nazis for Palestine 1939; in Palestine 1939–51; arr. Toronto 1951; studied with Andre Segovia; cofounder (1956) and president (1960–66) of Guitar Society of Toronto; taught guitar at RCM and U of Toronto; founded Eli Kassner Guitar Academy, 1967; founded U of Toronto Guitar Ensemble, 1978.
Resources: "Eli Kassner," *EMC* 676b-c; Pass, Scheit, and Svoboda, *Orpheus im Exil*, 400; Engelmann, Prokop, and Szabo, *History of the Austrian Migration to Canada*, 161.

KAUFMAN, HANS b. Vienna, 1912; violinist, teacher of popular and classical music, tailor.
Studied violin in Vienna; assistant concertmaster of Jewish Symphony Orchestra; freelance musician in Vienna 1928–38; fled Nazis for England 1938; interned in England, sent to Canada 1940; con-

certs in internment camps 1940–42; released 1942; in Toronto from 1942; hotel musician; taught music for the Etobicoke School Board; frequent performances of dance music and popular music; brief return to Vienna 1976.

Interview: 8 March 2001.

Resources: Koch, *Deemed Suspect*, 155, 268; Stengel, *Lexikon der Juden in der Musik*, 132; Brückner, *Judentum und Musik* 2nd edition 123, 3rd edition 144.

Writings: "Behind Barbed Wire" (unpublished collection of chronicles from the Sherbrooke Internment Camp, 1940–42).

KAUFMANN, WALTER b. Carlsbad, Bohemia (now Karlovy-Vary, Czechoslovakia), 1 April 1907; d. Bloomington, Indiana, 9 September 1984; composer, conductor, ethnomusicologist, teacher.

Studied at Hochschule für Musik, Berlin, with Franz Schreker and Curt Sachs ca. 1927–30; studied at German U, Prague, with Franz Becking and Paul Nettl 1930–34; graduated with dissertation on Gustav Mahler (refused degree as protest against Nazism); music director Carlsbad Theatre; corresponded with Albert Einstein, Hans Busch, Franz Werfel, Max Brod, Otto Pick, Heinz Politzer (poet), and the family of Franz Kafka; married Kafka's niece, Gerty Herrmann; fled Nazis in 1934 for India; director of music All India Radio Bombay 1937–46; founded Bombay Chamber Music Society; film composer for J. Arthur Rank Films, England 1947–48; arr. Halifax 1948; taught at Halifax Cons of Music 1948; conductor Winnipeg Symphony Orchestra 1948–56; professor of ethnomusicology U of Indiana 1957–84.

Interview: Allan Andrews (son-in-law of Walter Kaufmann), 7 December 2003.

Resources: "Walter Kaufmann," EMC 677a–b; MGG1 7: 759–60; *Baker's* 3: 1835; *New Grove* 2 13: 423; MGG2 9: 1558–60; Agate Schindler, "Walter Kaufmann," in *Jewish Exile in India: 1933–1945*, ed. Anil Bhatti, 87–112 (1999); Stompor, *Künstler im Exil*, 264 (Holland), 727 (India); www.music.indiana.edu/collections/kaufmann/biograph.html.

Writings: *The Ragas of North India* (1968); *The Ragas of South India* (1976); *Altindien* (1981).

KENINS, TALIVALDIS b. Liepaja, 23 April 1919; d. Toronto, 20 January 2008; composer, organist, teacher.

Studied in Grenoble 1933–40; studied at Latvian State Cons in Riga, 1940–44; fled Communists 1944 for Germany; studied at Paris Cons 1945–51; arr. Toronto 1951; taught at U of Toronto 1952–84
Interview: 26 February 2001.
Resources: "Talivaldis Kenins," EMC 679c–81a; Hollfelder, *Geschichte der Klaviermusik*, 1134–5; *Contemporary Canadian Composers*, 117–20.
Compositions: ACM 33.

KLAMKA, SZALAM ZALMA b. Poland, 1893; [death date unknown]; cantor.
Entered Canada by order-in-council 9 April 1938.

KLEIN, LOTHAR b. Hannover, 27 January 1932; d. Toronto, 3 January 2004; composer, teacher.
Family fled Nazis 1940; immigration to United States; BMus (1954), MA (1956), and PhD in musicology and composition (1961) U of Minnesota; composition studies with Paul Fetler (Minnesota), Goffredo Petrassi (Tanglewood), with Josef Rufer and Boris Blacher at Berlin Hochschule für Musik (1956–58), and with Luigi Nono in Darmstadt; assistant to Blacher, Berlin 1958–60; taught at U of Minnesota 1962–64, U of Texas 1964–68, and U of Toronto 1968–2004.
Interview: Eric Klein (son of Lothar Klein), 6 January 2004.
Resources: "Lothar Klein," EMC 689a–b; *Baker's* 3: 1899.
Compositions: U of Toronto Music Library, Klein fonds.

KLEMPERER, OTTO b. Breslau, 14 May 1885; d. Zurich, 6 July 1973; conductor.
Conductor Berlin Kroll opera to 1931 and Berlin Staatsoper 1933; *Tannhäuser* production vilified by Nazis; fled Nazis 1933 to United States; conductor Los Angeles Philharmonic Orchestra; conductor, Montreal Symphony Orchestra 1951–52.
Resources: EMC references (307a, 872c, 880b); *Baker's* 3: 1901; *Biographisches Handbuch der deutschsprachigen Emigration nach 1933*, 2: 631; Stengel, *Lexikon der Juden in der Musik*, 136–7; Brückner, *Judentum und Musik*, 2nd edition, 126.

KOERNER, IBY b. Troppau, 28 July 1899; d. Vancouver, 27 December 1983; arts and music patron.

Prague 1926–38; fled Nazis for London 1938–39; arr. Vancouver 1939; cofounder Vancouver International Festival 1949; initiator, international instrumental exhibition, "The Look of Music," 1980–81 Vancouver; CM 1971.
Resources: *EMC* references (1359a; *EMC* 432c); Iby Koerner fonds, Vancouver Public Library.

KOERNER LEON b. Moravia, 24 May 1892; d. Vancouver, 25 September 1972; industrialist, arts patron; husband of Thea Koerner.
Studied in Troppau; in Prague and Vienna 1926–38; fled Nazis for London 1938–39; arr. Vancouver 1939; in Vancouver 1939–72; founder Leon and Thea Koerner Foundation 1955; music and arts patron British Columbia; numerous benefactions to U of British Columbia; Koerner Recital Hall.
Resources: "Koerner Foundation," *EMC* 691a; British Columbia Archives, NW 361.763 L579; U of British Columbia Archives "Koerner Foundation"; www.koernerfoundation.ca, link; "Founders."

KOERNER, THEA (née Thea Rosenquist) b. Vienna 8 May 1896; d. Vancouver 26 July 1959; actress, arts and music patron; wife of Leon Koerner.
Classical actress in Vienna to 1938; fled Nazis for London 1938–39; arr. Vancouver 1939; author of text for "Song of an Immigrant" (1955).
Resources: British Columbia Archives, NWP 821 K78s, "Song of an Immigrant"; British Columbia Archives, NW 361.763 L579; U of British Columbia Archives, "Koerner Foundation"; www.koernerfoundation.ca, link, "Founders."

KOLESSA, LUBKA b. Lvov, Galicia (now Ukraine), 19 May 1902; d. Toronto, 15 August 1997; pianist, teacher.
Studied at Vienna Academy 1914–21 with Emil Sauer; toured Russia and South America 1937–39; fled Nazis 1937[?]; in England 1937–40; arr. Ottawa 1940; taught at TCM and Senior School 1942–48; numerous radio and public appearances; New York Philharmonic Orchestra 1949; commuted to Montreal to teach at McGill U (1952–730, École Vincent d'Indy (1955–66), and Conservatoire de musique de Montréal (1952–73).
Interviews: Luba Zuk, 6 May 2002; 25 September 2003.

Resources: "Lubka Kolessa," *EMC* 692c–693a; *MGG1* 11: 1431; LAC, vertical file "Kolessa"; Engelmann, Prokop, and Szabo, *History of the Austrian Migration to Canada*, 161.

Discography: *Lubka Kolessa (1929–49)* DHR 7743–5, Doremi, 1999 (re-mastered by Jacob Harnoy).

KOLINSKI, MIECZYSLAW b. Warsaw, 5 September 1901; d. Toronto, 7 May 1981; ethnomusicologist, composer, teacher.

Studied at U of Berlin with Sachs and Hornbostel; fled Nazis from Berlin 1933; in Prague 1933–38; fled Nazis from Prague 1938; in Belgium from 1938 through war years, in hiding 1942–44; New York 1951–66, music therapist at several hospitals; taught ethnomusicology at U of Toronto 1966–76.

Resources: "Mieczyslaw Kolinski," *EMC* 693a–b; "Canadian Reflections on Palindromes, Inversions, and Other Challenges to Ethnomusicology's Coherence," *Ethnomusicology*, 50/2 (Spring/Summer 2006): 325; *Contemporary Canadian Composers*, 124–6; Raymond Kennedy, "Bibliography of the Writings of Mieczyslaw Kolinski"; Michael Schulman, "Kolinski's Music Affected by International Travelling"; John Beckwith, "Kolinski: An Appreciation and List of Works"; LAC, vertical file "Kolinski"; *Baker's* 3: 1925; *New Grove* 2 13: 754–5; Hollfelder, *Geschichte der Klaviermusik*, 1126–7; *Biographisches Handbuch der deutschsprachigen Emigration nach 1933*, 2: 645–6 and 3: 195, 196; Stompor, *Künstler im Exil*, 273 (Belgium).

Writings: PhD diss., "Die Musik der Primitivstämme auf Malaka und ihre Beziehungen zur samoanischen Musik" (Humboldt U, Berlin, 1930; *Anthropos*, xxv [1930], 585–648); numerous articles in: *Ethnomusicology*, *Journal of the* IFMC, *Yearbook of the* IFMC, *Musical Quarterly*; transcription and analysis of 117 French-Canadian Folksongs and Versions, (1972, unpublished); "A Study of Melodic Analysis, as Applied to a Collection of Medieval Tunes" (1974, unpublished); "The Universe of Chords: Complete Chord Classification, Based on the Cycle of Fifths" (1978, unpublished); transcription of 152 Kwakiutl Indian Songs (unpublished); transcriptions of 309 Haitian folksongs (unpublished). The present location of Kolinski's papers are not known.

KOZARUK, JACOB b. Poland, ca. 1903, [death date unknown]; cantor, music director.
Entered Canada on order-in-council, 29 November 1938.

KRAEMER, FRANZ. b. Vienna, 1 June 1914; d. Toronto, 27 August 1999; composer, music broadcaster, music administrator.
Studied in Vienna with Alban Berg 1932–35; orchestration with H. Scherchen; fled Nazis for England 1939–40; interned in England, sent to Canada 1940; released 1942; in Toronto 1942–46; Montreal CBC International Service 1946–52; CBC TV Toronto 1952–70; music director Toronto Arts Foundation (St Lawrence Centre) from 1971; documentary films on Igor Stravinsky, Glenn Gould, Mstislav Rostropovich; director of televised opera productions; head music section Canada Council 1979–85; CM, 1981, OC, 1987.
Resources: "Franz Kraemer," EMC 696a–b; LAC, Franz Kraemer fonds (MUS 290); Pass, Scheit, and Svoboda, *Orpheus im Exil*, 305, 400; Koch, *Deemed Suspect*, 39, 155, 169–70, 228–9, 268; Engelmann, Prokop, and Szabo, *History of the Austrian Migration to Canada*, 163; Stompor, *Künstler im Exil*, 589.

KRAUS, GRETA b. Vienna, 3 August 1907; d. Toronto, 30 March 1998; harpsichordist, teacher.
Studied in Vienna with Hans Weisse 1924–30 and Heinrich Schenker 1931–33; concert appearances in Vienna 1933–38; appearances in England 1937; fled Nazis from Vienna 1938; arrived in Hawkesbury, Ontario, 1938; taught at Havergal College, Toronto, 1939–43; numerous concerts, radio, chamber music; specialist Baroque repertoire Toronto; taught at RCM 1943–69; taught harpsichord and Lieder at U of Toronto 1951–76; led Collegium Musicum, U of Toronto 1963–76; founder Toronto Baroque Ensemble 1958–63; formed Aitken-Kraus Duo 1965–86; partner of Lois Marshall in lieder recitals; Order of Ontario 1991.
Resources: "Greta Kraus," EMC 697a–c; LAC, vertical file "Kraus"; LAC, Greta Kraus fonds (MUS 230); Harvey Sachs, "She Shall Have Music"; Pass, Scheit, and Svoboda, *Orpheus im Exil*, 400; Engelmann, Prokop, and Szabo, *History of the Austrian Migration to Canada*, 161.

KUERTI, ANTON b. Vienna, 21 July 1938; pianist, composer, teacher, piano technician, social democrat.
Family fled Nazis for Ankara, Turkey, 1938; emigrated to United States, 1939; BMus from Cleveland Institute, 1955; studied at Curtis Institute with Rudolf Serkin and Mieczyslaw Horszowski 1955–57; Leventritt Award 1957; numerous appearances in United States, Canada, Far East, Latin America; to Toronto in 1966; pianist-in-residence U of Toronto 1965–68, associate professor 1968–72, and artist-in-residence to 1989; founder and director Festival of the Sound 1980–85; intégrales of Beethoven, Schubert, Carl Czerny piano sonatas; OC, 1998.
Interview: 6 March 2001.
Resources: "Anton Kuerti" *EMC* 698c–9c; *Baker's* 3: 1979; *New Grove* 2, 13: 950; Kreyszig, "Interkulturalität aus musikwissenschaftlicher Perspektive am Beispiel Kanada/Österreich," 202; Engelmann, Prokop, and Szabo, *History of the Austrian Migration to Canada*, 161.

KURTH, ERIKA (née Nalos) b. Prague, 1935[?] singer, teacher, music broadcaster.
Family fled Nazis from Prague, April 1939 for Italy, then England 1939; arr. Vancouver 1940; studied in Berkeley, California; taught Victoria Cons; singer in British Columbia; television show *Arts Calendar*; promoter of community talent.
Interview: 4 February 2004.

KVIESIS, VICTOR b. Riga, ca. 1920; d. ca. 1980; conductor, lawyer, judge.
Fled Communists from Riga 1944; displaced persons camps in Germany 1944–48; arr. Saskatoon 1950; conductor Saskatoon Symphony Orchestra 1950–55, Saskatoon Oratorio Society 1952–55; conductor North Bay "Victor Chorus" 1956–ca. 1970.
Resources: *EMC* references (952b, 1181b, 1182a); http://www.usask.ca/communications/ocn/Jan23/archives.html.

LAMBERGER, HANSI (née Johanna Amtmann) b. Vienna, ca. 1910; d. Montreal, 2004; music patron, violist; sister of Willy and Bernard Amtmann.
Studied in Vienna to 1938; fled Nazis for London, 1938; domestic service England 1939–40; New York 1940–50s; arr. Montreal

1950s; learned viola, amateur chamber musician, patron of CAMMAC.
Interview: 4 December 2000.

LANGRIDGE, HILDA b. Austria, 1901; [death date unknown]; music teacher.
Entered Canada by order-in-council, 21 June 1938.

LAUFER, EDWARD b. Zurich, 25 November 1938; theorist, composer, teacher.
Family fled Nazis 1938 for Switzerland; in Halifax 1939–54; BMus 1957 and MMus 1960 U of Toronto; MFA Princeton 1964; studied with Vincent Persichetti, Milton Babbitt, Roger Sessions, Eduard Steuermann, Ernst Oster; taught at Smith College 1969–71, State U of New York at Purchase 1972–74, Mannes College of Music, New York 1973–74; taught at U of Toronto from 1974; Schenkerian specialist.
Personal communications: 8 December 2003, 28 November 2007.
Resources: "Edward Laufer," *EMC* 724b; Kreyszig, "Interkulturalität aus musikwissenschaftlicher Perspektive am Beispiel Kanada/Österreich," 202.
Writings: contributor to *Perspectives of New Music*, *Journal of Music Theory*, *Music Theory Spectrum*, and *Intégral*.

LAUFER, SRUL b. Romania 1903; d. Halifax 2002; physician, music patron; father of Edward Laufer.
Medical training Italy; fled Nazis for Switzerland, Italy, Switzerland 1938–39; arr. Toronto 1939; cardiology practice in Halifax from 1939; promoter of arts and music in Halifax; friend of Walter Kaufmann; cofounder Halifax Symphonette, 1951; supporter Halifax Symphony.
Resources: Nova Scotia Archives, MG20 vol. 188, 3: Phyllis R. Blakeley, "Halifax Symphony Orchestra"; Albrecht Gaub, "From Swastika to Maple Leaf: Refugee Musicians from Nazi Germany and Austria in Canada."

LE CAINE, TRUDI (née Gertrud Janowski) b. Passau, 1911; d. Ottawa, 5 September 1999; arts patron; step-daughter of Arnold Walter, wife of Hugh Le Caine.
In Brno and Berlin to 1933; in Spain 1933–ca. 1938; studied at Sorbonne, Paris ca. 1938–40; fled Nazis from Paris; in Ottawa

from 1940; promoter Orff Schulwerk (Music for Children), National Arts Centre Orchestra; cofounder Opera Lyra Ottawa; initiator of skating on the Rideau Canal; CM, 1991.

Resources: EMC references (62b, 736b, 991b, 992a, 1382c); LAC, vertical file "Le Caine"; LAC, Trudi Le Caine fonds (MUS 215).

LEUPOLD, ULRICH b. Berlin, 15 January 1909; d. Waterloo, Ontario, 9 June 1970; musicologist, organist, theologian, pastor.

Musicological studies at Friedrich Wilhelms University 1927–34; theological studies at University of Zürich; theological education Confessing Church 1936–ca. 37[?]; England 1939; Toledo, Ohio 1939; arr. Waterloo 1939; pastor St Matthew's Lutheran Church, Kitchener, from 1939; dean, director to 1970 of Waterloo Lutheran Seminary (later Waterloo Lutheran University, then Sir Wilfrid Laurier University).

Interview: Gertrude Leupold, 5 October 2002.

Resources: "Ulrich Leupold," EMC 748b; Stengel, *Lexikon der Juden in der Musik*, 156; *Vita Laudanda: Essays in Memory of Ulrich S. Leupold*, ed. Erich R.W. Schultz (Waterloo, 1976), includes bibliography of Leupold's writings, 173–92.

Writings: PhD thesis, *Die liturgischen Gesänge der evangelischen Kirche im Zeitalter der Aufklärung und der Romantik* (Kassel: Bärenreiter, 1933); *Canada Lutheran*, "Musical Echoes," numerous articles 1941–68; *Liturgy and Hymns*, vol. 53 of Luther's works (Philadelphia, 1965); ed. *Laudamus: Hymnal for the Lutheran World Federation*, 4th ed. (Geneva, 1970).

LOWENSTEIN, RUDOLF b. Düsseldorf, 1921; violinist, manufacturer.

Studied in Düsseldorf to 1939; sent with Kindertransport to England 1939–40; interned in England, sent to Canada 1940; released 1942; businessman in Winnipeg from 1942.

Interview: 29 November 2003.

Resources: Koch, *Deemed Suspect*, 269; Stompor, *Künstler im Exil*, 588.

LOWY, OTTO b. Prague, 1921; d. Vancouver, 28 May 2002; actor, writer, music broadcaster.

Studied in Czechoslovakia to 1939; fled Nazis for England 1939–1950s: in Vancouver 1950s–2002; host of CBC Radio *Trans-*

continental; director Theatre Under the Stars, Vancouver, 1970s; host of Vancouver Symphony Orchestra Tea and Trumpets; Masaryk Award 1999; Czech Republic President's Award.
Resources: "Theatre under the Stars," EMC 1281b; *Journey to Prague* (http://fcit.coedu.usf.edu/holocaust/resource/videogl. htm).

MAISTE, ARMAS b. Tallinn, Estonia, 9 March 1929; pianist, teacher jazz and classical repertoire.
Studied at State Academy of Music, Tallinn; fled Communists from Tallinn in 1944; studied at State Academy, Stockholm 1944–50; arr. Montreal 1950; BMus McGill U 1972; taught at McGill U 1974–83; proficient in jazz and classical music; taught at Humber College, Toronto from 1984.
Interview: 3 December 2002.
Resource: "Armas Maiste," EMC 795b–c.

MARCUS, ERWIN b. Vienna, 1902; d. Montreal, April 1956; pianist, conductor, composer.
Studied at U of Vienna; coach for Vienna Philharmonic Choir 1920–24; accompanist for Leo Slezak and Vera Schwarz 1930–34; fled Nazis to Shanghai 1938–49; taught at the National Cons Shanghai; conductor at the Grand Opera and International Choral Society Shanghai; fled Communists from Shanghai; arr. Montreal 1949; conductor Workmen's Circle Choir; taught at McGill Cons 1955–56.
Resources: "Erwin Marcus," EMC 803c; Pass, Scheit, and Svoboda, *Orpheus im Exil*, 319 [birth date 1904]; LAC, vertical file "Marcus"; Julius Schloss Collection, file 47, Special Collections, Marvin Duchow Music Library, McGill U; *North China Daily News*, 10 August 1948; Stompor, *Künstler im Exil*, 722 (Shanghai).

MAYER, THOMAS b. Nowawes (near Potsdam), 1907; d. Vienna, 2002; conductor.
Studied at Academy of Music, Berlin; assistant conductor, Upper Silesia Landestheater Beuthen 1929–31; asst. conductor Munich Opera 1931–33; fled Nazis for Czechoslovakia 1933; conductor Teplitz-Schönau 1933–38, then Aussig; fled Nazis for South America 1938; Buenos Aires, assistant to Erich Kleiber and Fritz Busch Teatro Colón 1938–45; Santiago, Chile; State Radio Orchestra in

Montevideo, Uruguay 1945–47; assoc. conductor Metropolitan Opera, New York 1947; Cincinnati 1948–49; conductor Buffalo, Chicago, Bogota 1950–54; conductor Halifax Symphony 1955–57; Nova Scotia Opera Association 1955–7; Ottawa Philharmonic Orchestra 1957–60; Civic Orchestra, Essen, 1960–63; engagements in Hamburg, Cologne, Stuttgart, England 1961–62; Australia 1965–73; Vienna 1983–2002.

Resources: EMC references (168a, 307a, 566c, 568b, 570b, 954b, 1005a, 1006b); LAC, vertical file "Meyer"; *Biographisches Handbuch der deutschsprachigen Emigration nach 1933*, 2: 793 and 3: 195; Stompor, *Künstler im Exil*, 143 (Czechoslovakia), 145–47, 492–93 (Metropolitan Opera, New York), 605 (Mexico), 608 (Cuba), 648–49 (Teatro Colón, Buenos Aires, Argentina), 652–53, 674 (Uruguay), 680–81 (Chile), 695 (Colombia), 697 (Venezuela).

MORAWETZ, OSKAR b. Svetlá nad Sázavou, east Bohemia, 17 January 1917; d. Toronto, 13 June 2007; composer, teacher.

Studied piano in Vienna 1937–38; fled Nazis via Paris, Néris-les-Bains, Trieste, Canary Islands, Santo Domingo, New York, 1938–40; arr. Toronto 1940; BMus 1944 and DMus 1953 U of Toronto; taught theory and composition RCM 1946–51 and U of Toronto 1951–82; CM, 1988.

Interviews: Oskar Morawetz, 4 November 2000; Herbert Morawetz and Claudia Morawetz, 9 May 2003

Resources: "Oskar Morawetz," EMC 883b–5b; Engelmann, Prokop, and Szabo, *History of the Austrian Migration to Canada*, 196; LAC, Oskar Morawetz fonds (MUS 76); *MGG1* 16: 1290–1; *Baker's* 4: 2503–4; J.P. Gonder, "Style and Form in selected Piano Works of Oskar Morawetz" (Masters thesis, U of Western Ontario, 1979); *New Grove* 2 17: 100–1; *Canadian Contemporary Composers*, 156–60; Pass, Scheit, and Svoboda, *Orpheus im Exil*, 323–4, 401; Hollfelder, *Geschichte der Klaviermusik*, 1133; Abella, *None Is Too Many*, 289 (interview 19 September 1979); Stompor, *Künstler im Exil*, 588; http:// www.oskarmorawetz.com.

MOSCHETTI, GUISEPPE b. Italy, 1909; [death date unknown]; organist.

Entered Canada by order-in-council, 3 February 1939, for Toronto.

MÜLLER, LEO b. Vienna 19 September 1906; d. Vienna 2002; conductor.

Studied in Vienna to 1927; conductor Leningrad and Prague 1927–37; fled Nazis for New York 1937–58; Halifax Symphony 1958–64; conductor in Baltimore from 1964, and Vienna to 2002

Resources: Pass, Scheit, and Svoboda, *Orpheus im Exil*, 102–7: interview 16 November 1992, 324–5; correspondence with Morawetz in LAC, Oskar Morawaetz fonds (MUS 76).

NEWMARK, JOHN (né Hans Neumark) b. Bremen, Germany, 12 June 1904; d. Montreal, 14 October 1991; pianist, radio broadcaster, painter.

In Berlin 1904–23; art studies in Dresden 1923–27; accompanied violinists and singers in Germany and Spain 1925–38; Neue Kammermusik Bremen 1929–33; director of music programs for Bremen radio 1930–33; Berlin 1933–39; fled Nazis from Berlin to England 1939; concerts in London 1939–40; interned in Britain, sent to Canada, 1940; concerts in internment camps 1940–42; released 1942; in Toronto 1942–44, then Montreal 1944–91; official pianist for Expo 67; pianist and coach for Maureen Forrester, Kathleen Ferrier, Noël Brunet, Arthur LeBlanc, Paul Tortelier, Leopold Simoneau, Janet Baker, Arthur LeBlanc, Elizabeth Schwarzkopf, Gerard Souzay, Lily Krauss, Elisabeth Schumann, George London; Clementi piano broadcasts from 1950; CBC television series, *At Home with John Newmark*; premiered works by Canadian composers Violet Archer, John Beckwith, Keith Bissell, Jean Coulthard, Lionel Daunais, Maurice Dela, Robert Fleming, Harry Freedman, Srul Glick, Jean-Paul Jeannotte, Kelsey Jones, Oskar Morawetz, Jean Papineau-Couture, Clermont Pépin, André Prévost, Healey Willan, Welford Russell, Otto Joachim, John Weinzweig; OC., 1973.

Resources: "John Newmark," EMC 942c–3b; LAC, John Newmark fonds (MUS 175); Koch, *Deemed Suspect*, 5, 121, 154–6, 231–2, 246, 269; *Baker's* 4: 2596–7; Raab Hansen, *NS-verfolgte Musiker in England*, 445; Stengel, *Lexikon der Juden in der Musik*, 204; Renée Maheu, *Un piano sur la mer,* 1997; Helmut Kallmann "Music in the Internment Camps and after World War II: John Newmark's Start on a Brilliant Canadian Career," *German-Canadian Yearbook,* 14 (1995): 181–91.

NIEDRA, JĀNIS b. Riga, 1887; d. London, Ontario, 1956; opera singer, teacher.
Studied at Imperial Music School; soloist in opera ensembles from 1912; Riga National Opera 1918–44; appearances France, Spain, Italy; 86 roles including operas by Wagner and Tchaikovsky; fled Communists from Riga 1944; displaced persons camps, Rostock, Germany, 1944 and Flensburg, from 1945; arr. Toronto ca. 1948.

NORVILIS, JĀNIS, b. Riga[?] 1906; d. Toronto[?] 1994; conductor, composer.
Fled Communists [from Riga?] 1944; displaced persons camps, Germany, 1944–ca. 1948; in Toronto[?] 1948–94.
Resources: *EMC* reference (722c).

PRENTICE, JOHN (né Hans Pick) b. Vienna, 1907; d. 1986; industrialist, arts patron.
Family fled Nazis from Vienna 1938; arr. Vancouver August 1938; cofounder (with Leopold Bloch-Bauer) of Pacific Veneer and Plywood Company (now Canfor) 1938; music and arts patron in Vancouver; president of Canada Council 1969–74; OC 1977.
Resources: Engelmann, Prokop, and Szabo, *History of the Austrian Migration to Canada*, 181–2.

RAMINSH, IMANT b. Ventspils, Latvia, 18 September 1943; composer, teacher, violinist.
Family fled Communists from Riga 1944; displaced persons camps in Germany 1944–48; arr. in Hearst, Ontario, 1948; Cochrane, Ontario, 1950; studied at RCM 1958–64; BMus U of Toronto 1966; studied at Mozarteum in Salzburg 1966–68; founded music department at College of New Caledonia, Prince George, BC, 1968; choral director of Okanagan Symphony Choir 1978–82; founder 1979 and director of Aura Chamber Choir; founder 1989 and music director Youth Symphony of the Okanagan; taught at Vernon Music School from 1977.
Interviews: 9 and 17 January 2003.
Resources: "Imant Raminsh," *EMC* 1105c–6a.

REINER, CHARLES b. Budapest, 7 April 1924; d. Montreal, 19 August 2006; pianist, teacher.

Hungarian forced labour brigades under Nazis 1943–44; internment in concentration camp at Mauthausen 1944–45; studied at Franz Liszt Academy, Budapest, with Arnold Szekely and Béla Böszörmenyi-Nagy; Budapest 1945–47; fled Communists from Budapest 1948; studied at Geneva Cons with Dinu Lipati and Louis Hiltbrand 1948–49; Geneva International Concours 1948; premier prix Geneva Cons 1949; arr. Montreal 1951; debut Montreal 1952; taught at McGill U from 1955; cofounder Canadian Piano Quartet, Musica Camerata; concerts with singers and instrumentalists including Henry Szeryng, Colette Boky, Hyman Bress, Maureen Forrester, Antonio Janigro, Arthur Leblanc, Igor Oistrakh, Louis Quilico, Jean-Pierre Rampal, Ruggiero Ricci, Joseph Rouleau; appearances throughout Canada and United States.

Interviews: 19 April 2000 (by Katharine Neufeld); 26 November 2001.

Resources: "Charles Reiner," EMC 1122a.

ROSÉ, ALFRED b. Vienna, 11 December 1902; d. London, Ontario, 7 May 1975; conductor, pianist, composer, teacher, music therapist.

Conductor at Vienna State Opera 1922–27; toured United States with Rosé Quartet 1928; conductor Komische Oper, Berlin, 1929–32; Vienna 1932–38; fled Nazis from Vienna 1938; Cincinnati 1939–48; Western Ontario Cons of Music Opera Workshop 1946, 1947; U of Western Ontario 1948–75; music therapist, Westminster Hospital, London.

Resources: "Alfred Rosé," EMC 1146c–7a; Raab Hansen, *NS-verfolgte Musiker in England*, 453; Pass, Scheit, and Svoboda, *Orpheus im Exil*, 341; Kreyszig, "Interkulturalität aus musikwissenschaftlicher Perspektive am Beispiel Kanada/ Österreich," 197–8; Engelmann, Prokop, and Szabo, *History of the Austrian Migration to Canada*, 159; Stengel, *Lexikon der Juden in der Musik*, 226; Gustav Mahler–Alfred Rosé Collection, Music Library, U of Western Ontario (www.lib.uwo.ca/music/gmar.html); Stephen McClatchie, *The Gustav Mahler-Alfred Rosé Collection: An Inventory* (1996); LAC, vertical file "Rosé"; Newman, *Alma Rosé*.

ROSSINGER, ANDRÉ b. Budapest, 1898; d. Montreal, 1987; ethnomusicologist, writer on music, engineer.

In Budapest 1889–ca. 1939; arr. Montreal ca. 1939–87; CBC scripts and journal articles on various musical topics.

Resources: LAC, André Rossinger fonds (MUS 222); "Andre Rossinger, Musical Anthropologist Extraordinaire and His Legacy at the National Library of Canada," CAML *Newsletter* 22/1, 15–16.

RUBES, JAN b. Volyne, southern Bohemia, 6 June 1920; singer, opera director, film actor, teacher, tennis player.

Studied at the Prague Cons., graduated 1945; engagements Pilsen Opera House 1945–48; fled Communists from Czechoslovakia 1948; Geneva International Competition 1948; arr. Toronto 1948; CBC Opera 1949–58; COC appearances from 1950; numerous operatic roles in Canada, United States, Latin America, Europe; touring director COC 1974–76; CBC radio *Songs of My People* with Ivan Romanoff orchestra, 1954–64; taught at Wilfrid Laurier U and U of Windsor; numerous film roles; CM, 1996.

Interview: 9 December 2002.

Resources: "Jan Rubes," *EMC* 1159b–60a; LAC, vertical file "Rubes."

RUFF, HERBERT b. Idaweich (now Wroclaw, Poland), near Breslau, 16 September 1918; d. Montreal, 19 May 1985; pianist, composer.

Studied in Vienna 1924–28, Berlin 1929–33 with Walter Gieseking at Stern Cons; composer for UFA film studios, Berlin; fled to Switzerland 1933, then Czechoslovakia 1938; in Hong Kong 1939–41, Shanghai 1941–49; fled Communists from Shanghai; in Nanking 1947–52; arr. Montreal 1952; pianist and composer for children's radio and television; composed numerous chansons.

Resources: "Herbert Ruff," *EMC* 1160b–c; LAC, Herbert Ruff fonds (MUS 241).

SCHAEFFER, ERIC b. Germany, 1920s; d. Toronto, ca. 1970; organist, pianist.

Arrived in Canada 1938; organist at Holy Blossom Synagogue Toronto from 1938; Toronto trio with Hans Kaufman.

SCHAEFER, EVA b. [Germany or Austria?], ca 1920; d. ca. 2000; music and art patron.

Fled Nazis for England 1938–39; in London to 1975; arr. Victoria 1975.
Personal communication: Veronica Platts, 16 August 2002.

SCHAEFER, HERBERT b. [Germany or Austria?] ca. 1920; d. ca. 2000; music and art patron.
Fled Nazis for England 1938–39; recording engineer for BBC in London 1945–75; arr. Victoria 1975.
Resources: http://ring.uvic.ca/96jun05/Hon-degrees.html.

SCHULTZE, ANNA KATHERINA b. Germany, 1915; [death date unknown]; music teacher.
Entered Canada by order-in-council, 12 January 1938.

SIMONS, JAN b. Düsseldorf, Germany, 11 November 1925; d. Montreal, 7 May 2006; singer, teacher, music administrator.
Family fled Nazis for Holland 1933; studied Den Haag 1933–39; arr. Montreal 1939; vocal studies with Emilio de Gogorza in New York 1950–3, Emmy Heim and Ernesto Vinci RCM 1953–58, Yvonne Rodd-Marling; teacher, CAMMAC from 1957, Marianopolis College 1963–67, Vanier College 1973–77; McGill U from 1961; general director CAMMAC 1969–90; recitals in Canada, Europe, Japan; 2005 Prix hommage from Conseil quebecois de la musique.
Interview: 2 December 2002.
Resources: "Jan Simons," *EMC* 1221b–c, "CAMMAC," *EMC* 189b, c.

SREBRNIK, ZELMAN-GUDEK b. Poland, 1911, [death date unknown]; cantor.
Entered Canada by order-in-council, 9 April 1938.

STEIN, FRANTISEK b. Czechoslovakia, 1897; [death date unknown]; musician.
Entered Canada by order-in-council, 23 March 1939.

STEINER, KARL b. Vienna, 12 March 1912; d. Belleville, Ontario, 20 June 2001; pianist, teacher.
Studied at U of Vienna to 1938; interned concentration camp Dachau 1938; fled Nazis via France to Shanghai 1939–49; fled Communists from Shanghai; arr. Montreal 1949; taught at McGill Cons 1964–89; advocate of Second Viennese School.

Interview: 4 October 1999.

Resources: Pass, Scheit, and Svoboda, *Orpheus im Exil*, 362; Engelmann, Prokop, and Szabo, *History of the Austrian Migration to Canada*, *164; Österreichische Musikzeitschrift* 43 (1988): 678; 50: 10 (1995): 721; 52: 9 (1997): 48–50; 55: 8/9 (2000): 80; 56: 8/9 (2001) 78; Arthur Kaptainis, "Generation EX German and Austrian Expatriates of the War Years"; Albrecht Gaub, "Karl Steiner, Canadian Apostle of the Second Viennese School" (available at http://www.utoronto.ca/icm/0102a.html); Claude Gingras, "Une belle collection, une musique difficile," *La Presse,* 14 Oct 1995, D6; James H. North, *Fanfare* 19, no. 2 (Nov–Dec 1995): 486–7; Mike Silverton, *Fanfare* 19, no. 3 (Jan– Feb 1996): 460–1; Arthur Kaptainis, *Gazette,* "Music of the Second Generation of the Second Viennese School," 13 July 1996, C7; Arved Ashby, "Second Generation Second Vienna School," *American Record Guide* 59 no. 2 (March–April 1996): 226.

Discography: *Music of the Second Generation of the Second Viennese School* (works by Julius Schloss, Schoenberg, Eduard Steuermann, Hans Erich Apostel, Alban Berg, William Keith Rogers, Anton Webern, and Hanns Jelinek; Centaur CRC 2241/42).

STROMBERGS, ALFRED b. Liepaja, Latvia, 19 February 1922; d. Toronto, 22 February 2006; conductor, opera coach, pianist, teacher.

Studied theory and composition at Latvian State Cons Riga 1940–42; conductor Liepaja Opera House 1942–44; fled Communists from Liepaja 1944; displaced persons camps, Germany 1944–48; arr. Halifax 1948; opera productions, Halifax, 1949–55; conductor Halifax Symphonette 1949–55; conducting studies with Leonard Bernstein, Lukas Foss at Tanglewood Festival 1953; coach, COC 1957–71, Opera School 1960–71; conductor Stratford Festival Theatre Orchestra 1957–68; vocal coach and opera conductor U of Alberta, Edmonton, 1971–87; opera division Banff School of Fine Arts 1972–73; Edmonton Opera 1973–74; in Toronto from 1987.

Interview: 28 November 2003.

Resources: "Alfred Strombergs," EMC 1260b.

SUSSKIND, WALTER (Süsskind) b. Prague, 1 May 1913; d. Berkeley, California, 25 March 1980; conductor, pianist.

Studied at Prague Academy for Musical Arts with Karel Hoffmeister, George Szell, Josef Zuk, Alois Hába; assistant to Szell at German Opera, Prague 1934–38; fled Nazis for London 1938; conductor for Carl Rosa Opera (1943–45), Sadler's Wells (1946–54), Scottish National Orchestra (1946–52), Victoria SO of Melbourne, and Philharmonia Orchestra, London; founded National Youth Orchestra of Great Britain; conductor TSO 1956–65; Toronto Mendelssohn Choir; CBC Symphony Orchestra; numerous opera appearances with COC, CBC television; Toronto premieres of Stravinsky's *Sacre du printemps* and works by Webern, Schoenberg, and Berio; United States 1965–80; music director of St Louis Symphony Orchestra 1968–75; taught at U of Southern Illinois; Cincinnati Symphony Orchestra 1978–80.
Resources: "Walter Susskind," *EMC* 1266b; "Toronto Symphony Orchestra, *EMC* 1302b–c; LAC, vertical file "Susskind"; Raab Hansen, *NS-verfolgte Musiker in England*, 466; Pass, Scheit, and Svoboda, *Orpheus im Exil*, 368–9; Stompor, *Künstler im Exil*, 139 (Reichenberg, Czechoslovakia), 310 (Scotland).

TIMERMANE-OZALA, EDÍTE b. Riga[?], ca. 1910; d. Toronto, ca. 1960; pianist, organist.
Studied at Riga Cons; fled Communists from Riga 1944; displaced persons camps, Germany 1944–48; arr. Toronto ca. 1948; organist St John's Latvian School.

TINTNER, GEORG b. Vienna, 22 May 1917; d. Halifax, 2 October 1999; conductor.
Studied at Vienna Academy 1930s–37 with Joseph Marx, Felix Weingartner; conductor Vienna Volksoper; fled Nazis from Vienna 1938; Yugoslavia, England, arr. in New Zealand 1940; non-musical work during war; conductor Auckland Choral Society 1946–54; conductor Auckland String Players 1947–54; conductor Elizabethan Trust Opera Company (Australian Opera) 1956–63, 1965–67; director New Zealand Opera 1964; music director Capetown Symphony Orchestra 1966–1967; Sadler's Wells Opera in London 1967–70; Australian Opera 1973–76; music director Queensland Theatre Orchestra 1976–87; numerous conducting appearances throughout Canada; National Youth Orchestra of Canada from 1971; music director and resident conductor Symphony Nova Scotia 1987–99; Nova Scotia Youth Orchestra from 1988; CM, 1998.

Resources: "Georg Tintner," EMC 1291a–b; LAC, vertical file "Tintner"; *Baker's* 6: 3645; *New Grove* 2 25: 503; Pass, Scheit, and Svoboda, *Orpheus im Exil*, 372–3; *Biographisches Handbuch der deutschsprachigen Emigration nach 1933*, 2: 1165–6 and 3: 195; Kreyszig, "Interkulturalität aus musikwissenschaftlicher Perspektive am Beispiel Kanada/Österreich," 202; Mark McGinnes, "Uncompromising conductor dedicated to art," *The Australian*, 14 October 1999; Stompor, *Künstler im Exil*, 394 (Yugoslavia), 705 (New Zealand).

TOMASZEWSKI, IWAN b. Poland, 1905; [death date unknown]; singer.
Entered Canada by order-in-council, 31 October 1938.

UNGER, HEINZ b. Berlin, 14 December 1895; d. Toronto, 25 February 1965; conductor.
Law studies, D Juris, 1917; conductor in Berlin 1919–33, conductor Berlin Philharmonic; director, Gesellschaft für Musikfreunde 1924–33; founder (1921) and conductor Caecilienchor, Berlin; conducted in Vienna, Oslo, Moscow, Leningrad, and Kiev; fled Nazis from Berlin for Soviet Union 1933, later to London; conducted TSO 1937, 1938; appearances in Spain, Russia; conductor of Northern Philharmonic, (Leeds) Orchestra, BBC Symphony Orchestra, Hallé Orchestra, London Philharmonic, orchestras in Liverpool, Birmingham 1942–45; moved to Toronto 1948; conductor CBC Symphony Orchestra 1952–64; York Concert Society series 1953–65; appearances throughout Canada, Latin America, Europe; Mahler specialist, Canadian premieres of Symphonies nos. 2, 5, 9.
Resources: "Heinz Unger," EMC 1328b–9a; LAC, Heinz Unger fonds (MUS 56); *MGG1* 7: 505; Raab Hansen, *NS-verfolgte Musiker in England*, 469–70; *Biographisches Handbuch der deutschsprachigen Emigration nach 1933*, 2: 1184 and 3: 195; Stengel, *Lexikon der Juden in der Musik*, 276; Brückner, *Judentum und Musik*, 2nd edition 225, 3rd edition 283 (as Heinrich Unger); Schabas, *MacMillan*, 122–3, 147, 196, 240; Stompor, *Künstler im Exil*, 608 (Cuba).
Writings: *Hammer, Sickle and Baton* (London, 1939).

VETRA, MARISS b. Riga 1902; d. Toronto 1965; singer, teacher, opera producer, political activist.

Director Latvian National Opera; tours Soviet Union 1937–8; fled Communists from Riga 1944; Sweden 1944–7; head voice department, Halifax Cons 1947–53; anti-Stalinist campaign Halifax; 1949 production of *Don Giovanni;* NS Opera Association 1950–3; Toronto 1953–65

Interviews: Walter Kemp, Valda Kemp, 24 May 2001.

Resources: *EMC* references (340c, 458c, 568b, 722c, 805c, 954b 1222c); Nova Scotia Archives, "Mariss Vetra," MG9 nos. 43, 24.

VINCI, ERNESTO (né Wreszynski) b. Gnesen, Prussia (now Gniezno, Poland), 20 April 1898; d. Moncton, 7 November 1983; medical doctor, singer, teacher.

Studied law and medicine at Friedrich Wilhelms University; medical officer (*Sanitätsdienst*) Lorraine, Palestine; singer in Max Reinhardt's German Theatre Berlin from 1915; concerts, opera, radio; vocal studies at Hochschule für Musik Berlin with Ernst Grenzebach, Louis Bachner; fled Nazis for Milan, 1933; MD Milan 1933; vocal studies and performances in Italy, Switzerland 1933–38; fled Nazis for New York, 1938; head voice department Halifax Cons 1938–45; numerous wartime concerts in aid of Victory Bond appeal; vocal recitals Canada; taught at RCM 1945–79, and U of Toronto 1952–72; Banff School of Fine Art 1949–69.

Interview: Tom Vinci (son of Ernesto Vinci), 3 October 2003

Resources: "Ernesto Vinci," *EMC* 1372c–3a; York University Archives, "Ernesto Vinci fonds," http://archivesfa.library.yorku.ca/fonds/ON00370-F0000439.htm (pdf); LAC, vertical file "Vinci."

WAINWRIGHT, FRANCES (née Heinsheimer) b. New York 1942; radio music producer; daughter of Hans Heinsheimer (who was in New York at the time of Nazi *Anschluss*)

Arr. Montreal 1967; senior music producer CBC Radio 1967–97; initiated CBC/McGill Concert Series, CBC Montreal Christmas Sing-In; in Vancouver from 1997, music consultant provincial and national cultural organizations, artistic coordinator DEBUT/BC Series for Young Performers and Coast Recital Society.

Interview: 8 February 2001; communication 9 April 2004.

Resources: *EMC* references (228c, 1225a).

WALTER, ARNOLD b. Hannsdorf, Moravia, 30 August 1902; d. Toronto, 6 October 1973; musicologist, composer, music administrator, music educator, social democrat.

Studied law, U of Prague 1926; musicology, U of Berlin 1923–24; medicine, Masaryk U, Brno 1927–29; Berlin 1930–33, contributor to *Die Weltbühne, Vorwärts,* and *Anbruch*; fled Nazis February 1933; Mallorca, 1933–36; London 1936–37; arr. Toronto 1937; music master Upper Canada College 1937–44; director of Senior School, TCM, from 1944; director of Faculty of Music, U of Toronto, 1952–68; transformed faculty programs; introduced Orff teaching methods at RCM 1955; president Canadian Music Council 1965–66; president, Canadian Music Centre 1959 and 1970; president Canadian Association of University Schools of Music 1965–67; chair, editorial board, *Canadian Music Journal* 1956–62; president, ISME 1953–55; president Inter-American Music Council (CIDEM) 1969–72; OC, 1972.

Interviews: Harvey Olnick, 21 May 2000; Ezra Schabas, 4 November 2000.

Resources: "Arnold Walter," *EMC* 1382a–83a, *EMC* references (1346a, b, 1347c); LAC, Arnold Walter fonds (MUS 71) (uncatalogued); Seiffert, "Arnold M. Walter," 81–6; Pass, Scheit, and Svoboda, *Orpheus im Exil*, 378; Engelmann, Prokop, and Szabo, *History of the Austrian Migration to Canada*, 163; *MGG1* 7: 505; 16, 1916–1917; *Baker's* 6: 3840; *New Grove* 2 27: 52; Opera School materials in the Joan Baillie Archives (uncatalogued); *Biographisches Handbuch der deutschsprachigen Emigration nach 1933*, 2: 1205 and 3: 195, 196; Raab Hansen, *NS-verfolgte Musiker in England*, 472; Hollfelder, *Geschichte der Klaviermusik*, 1127; Stompor, *Künstler im Exil*, 254 (Spain), 588.

Writings: "Was heißt und zu welchem Ende studiert man Musiksoziologie?" *Melos* 11(1932): 191–95; "Musikorganisation und Staat" *Melos* 12 (1933): 61–64; "Introduction," in *Aspects of Music in Canada*, Toronto: University of Toronto Press, 1969, 3–25.

WALTER, BRUNO (Schlesinger) b. Berlin, 1876; d. Beverley Hills, California, 1962; conductor, writer.

Music director Städtische Oper, Berlin 1929–33; fled Nazis 1933 for Austria, France, United States; conductor Metropolitan Opera

and New York Philharmonic; return engagements in Europe from 1956; conductor Vancouver International Festival 1957–58.
Resources: *MGG1* 14: 186–9 [1933 ging er nach Österreich]); EMC 485c; *Biographisches Handbuch der deutschsprachigen Emigration nach 1933*, 2: 1205; Stengel, *Lexikon der Juden in der Musik*, 283; Brückner, *Judentum und Musik*, 2nd edition 202.

WEISS, AARON b. Germany 1884; d. [Ottawa?], [death date unknown]; cantor.
Entered Canada by order-in-council, 28 February 1939; cantor, Congregation of United Brethren, Ottawa.

WILFER, ANTON b. Schönbach, 30 April 1901; d. Montreal, 31 August 1976; violin maker and restorer.
Schönbach 1901–43; fled Czechoslovakia 1946; Mittenwald violin-making school 1946–51; string instrument shop in Montreal with Aloys Fogl and Ewald Fuchs 1951–76.
Resources: "Anton Wilfer," *EMC* 1404a.

WONSOW, MARIE b. Poland 1893; [death date unknown]; choir director.
Entered Canada by order-in-council, 13 December 1938.

ZUK, IRENEUS b. Lubaczów, German Protectorate, 5 August 1943; pianist, teacher, music administrator.
Family fled Communists from Lubaczów 1944; Austria 1944–50; arr. Montreal 1950; piano studies with Lubka Kolessa, Friedrich Wuehrer, Boris Roubakine, Kendall Taylor, Sol Gorodnitzki, Leon Fleischer; Peabody Cons DMA, 1985; McGill U; piano duo with sister Luba Zuk from 1977, toured Canada, United States, and Europe (1982, 1984, 1986, 1987); premieres of Canadian works; taught at Queen's U, Kingston, from 1974, director, School of Music, Queen's 1997–2003.
Resources: "Luba and Ireneus Zuk," EMC 1438b–c.

ZUK, LUBA b. Lubaczów, Western Ukraine, 5 April 1930; pianist, teacher.
Family fled Communists from Lubaczów 1944; Austria 1944–50; arr. Montreal 1950; piano studies with Helmut Blume, Lubka

Kolessa, Boris Roubakine; taught at McGill U from 1955; piano duo with brother Ireneus from 1977, toured Canada, United States, and Europe (1982, 1984, 1986, 1987); premieres of Canadian works.
Interviews: 6 May 2002, 25 September 2003, 3 May 2007.
Resources: "Luba and Ireneus Zuk," EMC 1438b–c.

APPENDIX B

List of Interviews

Transcripts and recordings of the interviews are in the possession of the author. Personal communications are designated as "[C]."

George Adams (Adam Gutman), 31 August 2000
Allan Andrews (son-in-law of Walter Kaufmann), 7 December 2003 [C]
Istvan Anhalt, 31 October 2000; 27 November 2001
Betty Barban, 7 May 2001 [C]
Helmut Blume, 10 December 1997
Ljerka Blume, 15 February 2001
George Brandak, UBC Library, 19 September 2006 [C]
Alexander Brott, 25 February 2000; 17 November 2000
Peter Bentley, 26 January 2005 [C]
Charles Cahn, 17 August 2001
Helen Craig, 22 May 2001
Mirdza Dambergs, 25 April 2001
Robert Dambergs, 30 May 2003
Edith Della Pergola, 14 June 2007 [C]
Beverley Diamond, 7 November 2006 [C]
David Duke, 7 May 2001
Mario Duschenes, 27 January 2003, 7 February 2009
Rolf Duschenes, 28 January 2003
Lorand Fenyves, 8 March 2001
George Fiala, 10 June 2007
Aloys Fogl, 30 September 2003
Shirley Garami, 26 November 2001 [C]
David Gardner, 28 February 2001

Alan Gillmor, 11 January 2002; 7 and 9 November 2006 [C]
Nicholas Goldschmidt, 1–2 November 2000
Hans Gruber, 9 March 2001
Ida Haendel, 29 March 2001 [C]
Edwina Heller, 30 May 2001
Paul Heller, 30 May 2001
Walter Homburger, 27 May 2002, 6 October 2002
Edith Howard, 3 November 2003 [C]
Eugène Husaruk, 9 February 2001 [C]
Linda Jiorle-Nagy, 18 May 2004
Maria Jerabek, 16 February 2001
Otto Joachim, 11 March 2003
Walter Joachim, 26 April 2000 (interview by Rachel Anderson, used by permission), 16 September 2000 [C]
Helmut Kallmann, 28 February 2001, 15 March 2004 [C]
Gerhard Kander, 7 March 2001, 6 October 2002
Udo Kasemets, 6 March 2001
Hans Kaufman, 8 March 2001
Valda Kemp, 24 May 2001
Walter Kemp, 24 May 2001
Talivaldis Kenins, 26 February 2001 [C]
Eric Klein, 6 January 2004 [C]
Eric Koch, 8 March 2001, 7 November 2006 [C]
Michael Koerner, 10 February 2006 [C], 23 June 2006
Anton Kuerti, 6 March 2001
Erika Kurth, 4 February 2004 [C]
Hansi Lamberger, 4 December 2000
Edward Laufer, 8 December 2003 [C] 28 November 2007 [C]
Gertrude Leupold, 5 October 2002
Dr Harvey Levitt, 20 January 2004 [C]
Rudolf Lowenstein, 29 November 2003 [C]
Gill MacKenzie, 22 May 2001
Armas Maiste, 3 December 2002 [C], 24 February 2003 [C C
Claudia Morawetz, 9 May 2003 [C]
Herbert Morawetz, 9 May 2003 [C]
Oskar Morawetz, 4 November 2000, 6 March 2001
Harvey Olnick, 21 May 2000
Sister Mary O'Neill, 25 May 2003
Imant Raminsh, 9, 17 January 2003 [C]

Charles Reiner, 19 April 2000 (interview by Katharine Neufeld), 26 November 2001
Jan Rubes, 9 December 2002 [C]
Ezra Schabas, 4 November 2000
Jan Simons, 2 December 2002
Karl Steiner, 4 October 1999
Alfred Strombergs, 28 November 2003 [C]
Sadie Turner-Miller, 22 May 2001
Tom Vinci, 3 October 2003 [C]
Lorne Watson, 9 May 2001
Frances Wainwright (Heinsheimer), 8 February 2001 [C], 9 April 2004 [C]
Paul von Wichert, 8 May 2001
Luba Zuk, 6 May 2002, 25 September 2003, 3 May 2007

APPENDIX C

Arnold Walter, "Music in the University"

This lecture was prepared for the dedication of the Edward Johnson Building at the University of Toronto, 1962. The original is held at LAC, Arnold Walter fonds (MUS 71), vol. 18 (uncatalogued). It is reprinted here through the kind permission of Margot Sunter, Community Foundation of Ottawa.

Music study in our days is very different from what it once was. It is more demanding, it has reached higher levels, it certainly has ceased to be that amiable mixture of professionalism and dilettantism which characterized so many music schools in the past. Such schools failed to distinguish between cultural aspirations and professional training, between education "for music" and education "in music." Both are desirable goals, of course. We need the enlightened music lover as much as we need the competent professional. They complement each other, there is no argument about it; but they can't be herded together and treated alike, they must be segregated and taught differently. Perhaps it didn't matter too much if that was not done in the past. Until a few decades ago our professionals were educated abroad in any case. But it is of great concern to us now since we have undertaken to train Canadian talent in Canada. And not without success. It is no accident that Canadian performers are suddenly in demand all over the world; it has a great deal to do with the re-organization of our music education since the end of the last war. We don't ship raw material to foreign ports any more. We offer a finished product, with gratifying results: even ten years ago it would have been unthinkable for young Canadians to sing in Covent Garden or in Glyndebourne, in Vienna, in Bayreuth, in the Met, but that is what they do; and we are almost inclined to take it for granted.

Having made the distinction between education "for" and "in" music, we still must decide where such training should take place – in the Conservatory? In the University? In Europe, professional musicians are always taught in Conservatories. But these "Conservatories" are in fact State Academies without staff or scholarship problems; fees are negligible or non-existent, the whole apparatus is traditionally maintained by government, whether in Paris, Vienna or Moscow.

However, such "Conservatories" never existed anywhere in North America. What the Americans referred to by that name were music schools on various levels all struggling to make ends meet. They were money-making enterprises with an appalling teacher-to-student ratio, they were clearing houses for private studios rather than schools – they had to be, since there were no subsidies available. During the twenties of this century the Americans set out to remedy the situation. They could not do what the Europeans had done, for lack of subsidies from public funds. They had to find an American solution to the problem; and they found it in the university school of music which might best be defined as a mixture of a conservatory (in the European sense of the term) and a University department retaining the best features of both.

The conservatories so-called, were soon put out of business since University schools of music proved quickly superior. They profited by the prestige of the Universities to which they were attached; being subsidized they could afford good teachers, could offer attractive curricula, scholarships – and an all-round education. It's true, of course, that it is rather a difficult assignment to combine a general education with the rigorous training program necessary for virtuoso performers; yet that was the best solution to be found on this continent. There was only one alternative: to establish State Academies of Music. It's just possible that the new Juilliard School to be constituted in Lincoln Centre will become an Academy on that level – in essence if not in name, and privately endowed. But in the past the alternative was totally disregarded – with one exception: The Conservatoire de Musique in Montreal, which is a faithful replica of the Paris Conservatoire and liberally financed by the

Province of Quebec. So that Montreal has the only real "Conservatory" on the whole continent, while Toronto (without direct grants from the Province) had to organize itself on American lines ...

As presently constituted, the Faculty of Music of the University corresponds to an American School of Music; it also corresponds to an Academic Music Department. The vital distinction between education "for" music and "in" music is clearly kept in mind. On one hand, the Faculty functions like an European Academy, supervising the training of future musicians: on the other, it offers courses and electives to students from other divisions of the University, presenting music as an integral part of a cultural pattern in its relation to history and to society ... Modern conditions are such that well-trained technicians have much less of a chance to survive than well-educated musicians. Whether composers, performers or teachers, they need a cultural background, a historical awareness, a flexibility of mind which one can give then only by offering university training in music academies (as the Russians do, for instance) or by bringing the music academy into the University.

Toronto, we said, is organized on American lines. Basically it is, but even in the States there are few Universities which offer as wide a spectrum of music studies as Toronto does. Some specialize in performance, others in music education, still others in musicology. We provide for all three on an equal footing. Research in electronic music is found in Columbia and Princeton only; our opera school (a department of the Royal Conservatory and affiliated with the Faculty) is the envy of many.

In our days, music is back where it once started many centuries ago: as one of the *Artes Liberales*, as great as mathematics, as enlightening as astronomy, and an indispensable part of education.

APPENDIX D

The German Reich vs. Sophie-Carmen Eckhardt-Gramatté

The experiences of Sophie-Carmen (Sonia) Eckhardt-Gramatté[1] in Nazi Germany shed light on the toxic brew resulting from the combination of German bureaucracy and National Socialist ideology. During the Third Reich, certification from the Reichsmusikkammer (RMK), the sole authorized composers' and musicians' union, was indispensable for anyone pursuing a public music career. Sophie-Carmen suffered ongoing harassment from the RMK from 1936 to 1940. Had her struggle not ended successfully, her life would have been in jeopardy.

Sophie-Carmen spent the major part of her career in Berlin (1914–39), with the exception of two years in Spain (1924–26), and her early studies in both piano and violin at the Paris Conservatoire, 1904–14; as a student she also composed a number of instrumental works, some of which were published. In Berlin a scholarship from the banker Franz von Mendelssohn enabled her to study violin with Bronislav Hubermann, and she appeared occasionally in the dual role of pianist and violinist. Forced by straightened circumstances to practice after hours in piano studios that had closed for the day, she sometimes worked until midnight. Her marriage to expressionist painter Walter Gramatté (1897–1929) in December 1920 brought a lifelong interest in art; Gramatté made numerous portraits of Sonia and the couple became close friends with some of the major representatives of that period, including Karl Schmidt-Rottluff and Erich Heckel.[2] During a sojourn in Barcelona (1924–26) she became friends with Pablo Casals. She also played her own works for both piano and violin with the Philadelphia Orchestra during the 1929–30 season, at the invitation of

Leopold Stokowski, and with the Chicago Symphony under Frederick Stock. In spite of her developing career as a performer, she was increasingly drawn to composition during the 1930s. Throughout this period she was supported by Chicago businessman Max Adler. In 1926, on the advice of Stokowski, she joined the composition class of Max von Trapp,[3] who led master classes in composition at the Prussian Academy of Sciences (a position that Arnold Schoenberg had been forced to vacate in 1933); Trapp, a composer in the post-Romantic vein, drilled Sonia in counterpoint and harmonic structure, and he likely also played a role in arranging performances of her works during the war.[4]

Sophie-Carmen's confrontation with Nazi authorities began in July 1936 when she applied for membership in the RMK. In July 1936 she received a letter[5] containing copious quotations from the Nuremberg Citizenship Laws of November 1935, including the odious fractioning of racial qualifications (full, partial, and mixed blood Jewish), ostensibly to clarify the proof required to establish Aryan descent. Her reply of 10 September 1936 criticizes the RMK for incorrectly citing her name (she insisted on Sophie-Carmen, not Sophie); she also states that she is of Aryan descent and that her second husband, Ferdinand Eckhardt (whom she had married in Berlin-Schöneberg on 24 February 1934), was also Aryan. A reply from the RMK of 3 December 1936 states that her Aryan parentage is not sufficiently clear and asks for documents proving her assertion to be sent by 31 January 1937; a reminder was sent on 13 February 1937. On 15 March 1937 Sophie-Carmen submitted five documents, including a notarized translation of a decision of the *Appelationsgerichtshof* (Paris Appellate Court) from 8 June 1911; this document, she states "clearly proves that my father was of hereditary nobility and my grandfather from my mother's side was a lieutenant (later general). In Czarist Russia, both hereditary nobility and higher officers' positions ranks were restricted to non-Jewish persons."[6] She also states that her brother was an officer in the Czarist army.

In a letter of 13 July 1937 the RMK requests additional documents including photographs of Sophie-Carmen, her parents, certificates of her change of confession and that of her mother, baptismal or birth and marriage certificate of her parents, and a death certificate of her father. They also offered the name of a *Sippenforscher* (genealogist) who could advise her in matters of heredity. On 15

September 1937 Gramatté wrote to ask for additional time to procure the requested documents, but the authorities were gradually losing patience. Deadlines were given for 22 January and 24 March 1938; a final deadline of 25 April 1938 included the threat that she stood to lose the right to practice her profession ("Verlust der Berechtigung zur Berufsausübung") if the documents were not forthcoming. Two days before this final deadline Sophie-Carmen sent a portfolio of photographs of herself and various members of her family, copies of the certificates concerning the investiture of her brother Nicolas in the book of nobility as son of Charles de Fridman (a photocopy of the Russian original and a translation by her brother), a notarized letter from her brother establishing the authenticity of the photographs, and a notarized copy of her change of confession from the Greek Orthodox church to the Lutheran State Church of Prussia on the occasion of her wedding to Ferdinand Eckhardt in 1934. She added that there was no document attesting the change of confession for her mother because her mother had remained Greek Orthodox, explained that she did not possess any other documents, and pointed out that her mother had been estranged from her father for a considerable period. She also disputed the RMK information regarding her father's birth and death dates. (According to the RMK records her father, Nikolaus Friedmann, was born in Graudenz in 1865 and died in Moscow before 1934.)

On 4 May 1938 the RMK requested an *Abstammungsurkunde* (hereditary certificate) for Ferdinand Eckhardt and on 5 October 1938 she was asked to fill out an application form – presumably an official request for RMK membership.[7] On 31 October 1938 the RMK via the Reichsstelle für Sippenforschung (bureau of geneology) requested the exact birth and death dates of her father. Her reply of 3 December 1938 contains additional biographical details that she had obtained from her brother, who was now living in France, according to which, her father had been born in 1855 and had died in 1918 in Moscow.[8]

This final submission seems to have been successful: Sophie-Carmen was granted membership in the RMK[9] but her troubles with the authorities were by no means over. During 1938 or 1939 Hans Joachim Moser, a well-known German musicologist who was researching Sophie-Carmen's compositions for an article in the magazine *Silberspiegel*, asked Gramatté whether she was Jewish, and told her that her name was listed in the *Jewish ABC*, the book used by all party functionaries in which non-Aryan artists are listed.[10] This perhaps explained why several recent performances of her works had been cancelled at the last moment "for technical reasons." Ferdinand Eckhardt immediately contacted Hans Brückner to ask how Sophie-Carmen's name had come to be included. Brückner replied that her maiden name made it obvious. He stated that the first edition of the work had appeared in 1932; if there was no challenge to the citation, it was assumed to be correct and was carried through to later editions. Ferdinand Eckhardt subsequently discovered that the "first edition" was a purely fictional construction that gave Brückner license to carry forward anything he wished. The second edition appeared in 1937, and the third, with corrections, in 1938.[11] On 12 January 1939 Sophie-Carmen wrote to Moser to ask whether he had misgivings about publishing his forthcoming article on her work, stating that "my Aryan descent is completely genuine – otherwise I could not be a member of the RMK." Much of January 1939 was spent trying to undo the damage caused by Brückner's book. On 14 January 1939 she wrote complaining vehemently against her inclusion in the *Juden-ABC*, demanding that a retraction – in the form she dictated[12] – be published immediately, and threatening further action. On 16 January 1939 she wrote Dr Theophil Stengel[13] of the RMK confirming the protest made by Ferdinand Eckhardt regarding the inclusion of her name in the *ABC*, demanding that Stengel inform all relevant RMK functionaries about the oversight, and requesting that her performance opportunities be not adversely affected in any way, particularly in light of the forthcoming Reichsmusiktag in Düsseldorf. In a letter of 20 January 1939 Brückner attempts to excuse himself by claiming that the entry in the November 1935 edition (the ficticious first edition) was so inexact that it did not occur to him that the entry referred to Sophie-Carmen, even though he knew her work, and that he merely reproduced the entry "in good faith" in subsequent editions.[14] By 10 February 1939 *Das Deutsche Podium, Kampfblatt für Deutsche Musik* had published a retraction and sent ten copies in confirmation.[15]

On 26 April 1939 Ferdinand Eckhardt wrote to the Carl Lindstrom company (a record company in Berlin that had distributed recordings of Gramatté's compositions) confronting them with the fact that they had withdrawn Sophie-Carmen's works from circulation, demanding an explanation, and asking how the company intended to rectify the situation. Their reply of 4 May 1939 states that they believed the composer was non-Aryan and points to the *ABC* entry; they agreed to request information from the RMK and asked for her membership number. At this point Brückner was in hospital and was unable to answer correspondence, but on 20 May 1939 he forwarded a certificate "to whom it may concern" attesting Sophie-Carmen's full Aryan heredity; Ferdinand Eckhardt was authorized to use this document as he saw fit. The document merely states that the "Gramatté, Sonja," cited in the first three editions of the *ABC* was not identical with "Frau S.C. Eckhardt-Gramatté" and that the entry was based on an erroneous source. In a letter to Ferdinand Eckhardt of 23 May 1939 Lindstrom acknowledged receipt of this correction and agreed to include Gramatté's recordings in all new catalogues and distribution arrangements. The apology expresses deep regrets for the inconvenience and promises to bring the highly regarded recordings of his wife into circulation as soon as possible.

Toward the end of 1939, after war was declared and the couple had moved to Vienna, the Berlin concert agency Adler wrote to the Breslau String Quartet – who had frequently performed Sophie-Carmen's works, quoting a message from Radio Hamburg and asking if they knew the composer's name was in the *Juden-ABC*. On 14 December 1939, writing to Hamburg from Vienna, Sophie-Carmen pointed out that the *Juden-ABC* entry was false and asked that it be corrected; on the same date she also sent a letter to Adler in Berlin also correcting the error. On 10 January 1940 the Hamburg agency acknowledged the correction.

How did Sophie-Carmen respond to the sound and fury around her? Her letters tell us little beyond a feeling that she was not properly accepted but that she knew her time would eventually come. On 7 February 1939, regarding a concert in Berlin of contemporary choral music, she writes, "Du, mein ewiges Memeland" [sic]; "That is what the people want, superficial stuff, a sign of good political will, but it has less to do with music as such."[16] Through these years Ferdinand Eckhardt held a position in the publicity and promotions department of Bayer (ZEPRO) and was able to commission a series of stained glass windows designed by Karl Schmidt-Rottluff (an expressionist painter and print maker whose work the Nazis condemned as "degenerate art"), a surprising breach of artistic protocol for the period. When this position was terminated because of the outbreak of war, the couple moved to Vienna. After the war Sonia was one of the cofounders of the re-formed Austrian branch of the International Society for Contemporary Music (Internationale Gesellschaft für neue Musik), whose goal was to renew links with advances in music and to shake up Viennese audiences accustomed to resting on their glorious past.[17]

Notes

INTRODUCTION

1 The voluminous literature concerning the Reichstag fire centres on the question of whether the act was a Nazi conspiracy or the work of an individual psychotic. For a selective bibliography, see Eckhard Jesse, "Der Reichstagsbrand: 70 Jahre danach," 32–3.

2 Hans-Albert Walter describes the arrest of many German artists, writers, journalists, and publicists during the night of 27–28 February and gives details of how individual writers managed to escape from Germany either legally or illegally during the following week and later (*Bedrohung und Verfolgung bis 1933*, 154–65). See also E. Bethge, *Dietrich Bonhoeffer: Theologe, Christ, Zeitgenosse*, 327: "Berlin erlitt seinen größten Aderlass an wissenschaftlichen Kapazitäten in seiner Universitätsgeschichte" [Berlin University suffered the most severe bloodletting of scientific personnel in its entire history].

3 C.D. Krohn (*Intellectuals in Exile*, 20) estimates academic losses through 1933–35 in Berlin (32.4%), Frankfurt (home of the "Frankfurter Schule," 32.3%), and Heidelberg (24.3%).

4 Lewis A. Coser, *Refugee Scholars in America*, 10. There are a number of important works on this topic. In *Illustrious Immigrants* Laura Fermi investigates scholars in the social sciences and atomic sciences (for musicians, see 225–31); her father, Enrico Fermi, was a noted nuclear physicist recruited for the Manhattan Project. Other significant studies include: Tom Ambrose and Peter Owen, *Hitler's Loss: What Britain and American Gained from Europe's Cultural Exiles*; Stephanie Barron and Sabine Eckmann, *Exil: Flucht und Emigration Europäischer Künstler 1933–1945*; Günter Berghaus, ed., *Theatre and Film in Exile: German*

Artists in Britain, 1933–45; Lewis A. Coser, *Refugee Scholars in America: Their Impact and Their Experience;* Maurice R. Davie, et al. *Refugees in America: Report of the Committee for the Study of Recent Immigration from Europe*; Alisa Douer, *Vertriebene der Vernunft: Emigration und Exil österreichische Wissenschaftler*; Donald Fleming and Bernard Bailyn, *The Intellectual Migration: Europe and America, 1930–1960*; Anthony Heilbut, *Exiled in Paradise: German Refugees, Artists, and Intellectuals in America from the 1930s to the Present*; H. Stuart Hughes, *The Sea Change: The Migration of Social Thought, 1930–1965*; Jarrell C. Jackman and Carla M. Borden, eds, *The Muses Flee Hitler: Cultural Transfer and Adaptation, 1930–1945*; Martin Jay, *Permanent Exiles: Essays on the Intellectual Migration from Germany to America*; Donald Peterson Kent, *The Refugee Intellectual: The Americanization of the Immigrants of 1933–1941*; Hermann Kesten, ed. *Deutsche Literatur im Exil: Briefe europ. Autoren 1933–1949;* Wulf Koepke and Michael Winkler, eds., *Exilliteratur, 1933–1945: Studien zu ihrer Bestimmung im Kontext der Epoche 1930 bis 1960*; Claus-Dieter Krohn, *Intellectuals in Exile: Refugee Scholars and the New School for Social Research*; Peter M. Lindt, ed., *Schriftsteller im Exil: zwei Jahre deutsche literarische Sendung am Rundfunk in New York*; Jean Medawar and David Pyke, *Hitler's Gift: The True Story of the Scientists Expelled by the Nazi Regime*; Jean-Michel Palmier, *Weimar en exil: le destin de l'émigration intellectuelle allemande antinazie en Europe et aux États-Unis*; Helge Pross, *Die deutsche akademische Emigration nach den Vereinigten Staaten, 1933–1941*; Alfred Schutz and Aron Gurwitsch, *Philosophers in Exile: The Correspondence of Alfred Schutz and Aron Gurwitsch, 1939–1959;* Ilja Struber, ed., *Exil, Wissenschaft, Identität: Die Emigration deutscher Sozialwissenschaftler, 1933–45;* Hans-Albert Walter, *Deutsche Exilliteratur 1933-1945;* Matthias Wegner, *Exil und Literatur: deutsche Schriftsteller im Ausland.*

5 Brigitte Hamman, *Winifred Wagner oder Hitlers Bayreuth*, 525.

6 Quoted in *Das Nibelungenlied und seine Welt*: "Und aus all diesen gigantischen Kämpfen ragt nun gleich einem gewaltigen, monumentalen Bau Stalingrad, der Kampf um Stalingrad heraus. Es wird dies einmal der größte Heroenkampf gewesen sein, der sich jemals in unserer Geschichte abgespielt hat ... Wir kennen ein gewaltiges, heroisches Lied von einem Kampf ohnegleichen, das hieß 'Der Kampf der Nibelungen.' Auch sie standen in einer Halle von Feuer und Brand und löschten den Durst mit eigenem Blut – aber kämpften und kämpften bis zum letzten. Ein solcher Kampf tobt heute dort, und jeder Deutsche noch in tausend Jahren muss

mit heiligen Schauern das Wort Stalingrad aussprechen und sich erinnern, dass dort Deutschland letzten Endes doch den Stempel zum Endsieg gesetzt hat" (175).

7 "Practically speaking, it will make little difference whether totalitarian movements adopt the pattern of Nazism or Bolshevism, organize the masses in the name of race or class, pretend to follow the laws of life and nature or of dialectics and economics" (Hannah Arendt, *Origins of Totalitarianism,* 313). There is some evidence that the Vatican considered fascism and communism equally reprehensible from a Roman Catholic perspective. Peter Godman (141–54) points out that the pastoral letter "Mit brennender Sorge" (With Burning Anxiety) of March 1937 fell far short of the condemnation of the Nazi regime that the Holy Office had originally intended, and that atheistic communism was thoroughly denounced in the encyclical "Divini Redemptoris" of 19 March 1937.

8 Charles Reiner, interview, 19 April 2000.

9 Eugene Husaruk, interview, 9 February 2001.

10 Quoted in *The Illustrated History of Canada,* ed. Craig Brown (Toronto: Lester & Orpen Dennys, 1987), 19.

11 Claudia Morawetz, interview with Oskar Morawetz, July 1995, available at http://www.oskarmorawetz.com/Tabs/TabPerson/index.php?page=LifeBio (accessed March 2009).

12 Peter Newman, *Maclean's* 22 July 1996, 56.

13 *An Accompanist's ABC*, 99, in LAC, John Newmark fonds, MUS 175/1, 1. Acc. May 1996.

14 Paul Heller, interview, 29 May 2001.

15 Series A-1-d, DPM, "Orders in Council," vol. 86 (1937, 1938) and Series A-2-b, vol. 87 (1939–48) in LAC, RG 26. There were 3,976 permits issued between 1938 and 1940. The entries by orders-in-council were only a fraction of total immigration for this period. There is one case in which an individual was given permission via an order but did not come to Canada: Austrian industrialist Ferdinand Bloch-Bauer (1865–1945, a great-uncle of Peter Bentley), who possessed an important private art collection in Austria (now the subject of an international Nazi art-theft court case) spent the war years in Zurich and died there in 1945 (P.C.408, 31 Jan, 1940, no. 20). Bloch-Bauer's wife Adele was the subject of several well-known paintings by Gustav Klimt.

16 Frederick Charles Blair, *Report of the Department of Mines and Resources ... for the Fiscal Year Ended March 31, 1941*, 193. The annual reports are a gold mine of information for anyone wanting to trace the rich immigration history of Canada.

17 Abella and Troper, "'The Line Must Be Drawn Somewhere': Canada and Jewish Refugees, 1933–9," 181.
18 *International Biographical Dictionary of Central European Émigrés 1933–1945*, I: xxiii.
19 Abella and Troper, "Canada and the Refugee Intellectual," 259.
20 Donald Kerr and Deryck Holdsworth, eds., *Historical Atlas of Canada*, 3: 100; Paula Jean Draper, "Fragmented Loyalties: Canadian Jewry, The King Government and the Refugee Dilemma," 163.
21 Harold Troper, "Canada," in *Encyclopedia of the Holocaust*, ed. Israel Gutman, I: 275.
22 "nahm ab 1933 etwa 60000 Emigranten auf, von denen 80 Prozent Juden waren; bis Juli 1935 folgten weitere 200 000 Einwanderer" (Stephan Stompor, *Künstler im Exil*, 587, my translation).
23 Of the twenty-four questions put to every prospective landed immigrant, one referred to "Nationality, Country of which a Citizen or Subject" and one to "Race or People." A printout relating to the arrival of the S.S. *Dresden* in Halifax on 18 April 1929 indicates that persons designated as Romanian or Swiss nationals were categorized as German. None of the questions referred to religion. We have no way of knowing how many Jewish persons were also classified as German. If "Continental European Jewish" was narrowly defined by immigration authorities, the figure of 23,160 is decidedly on the low side.
24 Frederick Charles Blair, in Canada, *Report of the Department of Mines and Resources ... for the Fiscal Year ended March 31, 1941*, 194.
25 Series A-2-b, DPM: "Orders in Council," vol. 87, P.C. 2653, 14 September 1939, LAC, RG 26: "The Gov. General ... is pleased to make the following regulation: From and after the date hereof and until otherwise ordered, the entry to or landing in Canada shall be and the same is hereby prohibited, of enemy aliens and nationals of any territory now occupied by an enemy country." Blair had however left himself two exceptions: prisoners of war and persons who were not Nazis ("provided that this regulation shall not be held to exclude persons coming within the above-mentioned classes who may be arrested and detained as enemy aliens under the Defense of Canada Regulations or who satisfy the Minister of Mines and Resources that they are opposed to an enemy Government"). It is clear that these provisions were initiated by Blair himself, allowing him a free hand for the duration of the war to bring in valuable Europeans.
26 Organizations include the Gesellschaft für Exilforschung (http://www.exilforschung.de, accessed March 2009), which publishes works almost exclusively devoted to the Nazi era; the Österreichische Gesellschaft für

Exilforschung; the Orpheus Trust, a privately-funded organization ("Verein zur Erforschung und Veröffentlichung vertriebener und vergessener Kunst") that sponsors concerts, lectures, and publications. The "Arbeitsgruppe Exilmusik" of the Musikwissenschaftliches Institut of the University of Hamburg and the Zentrum für musikalische Exilforschung at the Folkwang Hochschule are devoted exclusively to the topic. The Hamburg institute maintains a website devoted to exiles who fled German fascism and to music in European displaced persons camps (http://www1.uni-hamburg.de/musik//exil/home.html, accessed March 2009); and www.exilmusik.de (accessed March 2009) has links to research on exile musicians in other countries. The North American Society for Exile Studies is devoted to exile research; note the number of titles in the list of references that include the word "exile."

27 The proceedings of the Essen conference are published in *Musik in der Emigration, 1933–45: Verfolgung, Vertreibung, Rückwirkung*, ed. Horst Weber. The proceedings of "The Musical Migration: Austria and Germany to the United States, ca. 1930–1950," held at Harvard, 5–8 May 1994, are published as *Driven into Paradise: The Musical Migration from Nazi Germany to the United States*, ed. Reinhold Brinkmann and Christoph Wolff.

28 Roger Daniels, "American Refugee Policy in Historical Perspective." The only year that this quota was filled was 1939. Daniels also points to a restrictive US policy concerning the emigration of Jewish scholars to the United States.

29 Laura Fermi, *Illustrious Immigrants: The Intellectual Migration from Europe, 1930–1941*, 74.

30 Milton Babbit, "My Viennese Triangle at Washington Square, Revised and Dilated," in Brinkman and Wolff, eds. *Driven into Paradise,* 51.

31 The Austro-centric research of Tyranauer, Pichler, and the Orpheus Trust are cases in point. Their orientation is even more untenable since for the period in question (1938–45) Austria did not technically exist; it had been transformed into "Ostmark" and was administered from Berlin.

32 George Adams (Adam Gutman), interview, 31 August 2000.

33 The three-volume *International Biographical Dictionary of Central European Émigrés 1933–1945* contains individual biographies and an index of institutions and professions; the Leo Baeck Institute in New York (http://www.lbi.org, accessed March 2009) holds records of many émigrés; a branch of the archives opened in September 2001 in the Jewish Museum, Berlin; Stephen Spielberg's monumental project *Shoah* has recorded interviews of Holocaust survivors.

34 *Canadian Oxford Dictionary*, 2nd edition (Toronto: Oxford University Press, 2004), s.v. “exile.”

35 Hans-Albert Walter, *Bedrohung und Verfolgung bis* 1933, 1: 199 (my translation).

36 Istvan Anhalt, interview, 31 October 2000.

37 Morawetz’s claim that Blair’s actions “almost cost [him] his life” (http://www.oskarmorawetz.com/Tabs/TabPerson/Escape.html; accessed July 2009) cannot be substantiated. By March 1940 – twenty-four months after the Nazis occupied Austria, twelve months after they occupied Bohemia and Moravia, and seven months after they occupied Poland, forcing the Allies into declaring war with Germany – Morawetz was in Triest, Italy. His parents, his sister Sonia, and his brother Herbert were safely in Canada. Why did he not initiate immigration procedures to Canada at a consular office in Paris, Rotterdam, Antwerp, or London? It would have been easy to complete arrangements when he was in Paris in September 1939, but instead he left for Néris-les-Bains in free France (where he met up with Peter Newman’s family who were also Czech refugees) and then travelled to fascist Italy, which was by then closely allied to Nazi Germany. The Morawetz family were in direct contact with Blair through their lawyer, H.E. Dansereau, and it is clear from Blair’s letter of 30 November (see link from above website) that his hands were tied until Morawetz made contact with Canadian authorities. His brother Herbert Morawetz said that “at first, Oskar didn’t want to come with us to Canada because he thought his musical career would be finished, since he assumed that there were no musicians in Canada,” and asserted that Blair “knew that Oskar was in Genoa at the time and could not get to a Canadian consular office in Paris to proceed with his emigration to Canada” (personal communication, 9 May 2003); the second part of this last statement, however, is unlikely. Granted after September 1939 it became increasingly difficult for Jews to travel within continental Europe, but equipped with an Aryan certificate (now in the Morawetz *fonds*) provided by his cousin Walter Stein, he would have been able to reach Paris or London as late as March 1940. Indeed, Paul and Edwina Heller, along with Paul’s brother Samuel, wife Sarah, and son Horace Michael, similarly equipped, managed to make their way safely from Budapest via Italy to London, albeit just in time for the Blitz. The difficulties that Oskar Morawetz encountered were of his own making. As for the assertion that Blair’s “refusal to admit no more than 5000 Jews during the war ... cost many Jewish refugees their lives,” it can only be said that, given the present knowledge of the topic, no one can make such a claim.

38 Antony Beaumont and Alfreds Clayton, "Alexander Zemlinskys amerikanische Jahre," in *Alexander Zemlinsky Ästhetik, Stil und Umfeld*, ed. Hartmut Kronos, 247–58.

39 See "Flucht ins Ungewisse," *Frankfurter Rundschau*, 19 June 1999; Mark Jonathan Harris and Deborah Oppenheimer, *Into the Arms of Strangers;* Rebekka Göpfert, *Der jüdische Kindertransport* (excellent bibliography, 206–17).

CHAPTER ONE

1 This figure is necessarily approximate; the inclusion of a number of names is based on circumstantial evidence.

2 The figure of 13 million dollars is based on an inflation factor of thirteen (http://www.bankofcanada.ca/en/rates/inflation_calc.html).

3 The signing of the capitulation treaties between the Allies and the Third Reich occurred on 4 May 1945 in Lüneburg, on 7 May 1945 in Reims with the Western allies, and on 8 May 1945 in Berlin with the Russian military authorities.

4 Gerald Dirks (*Canada's Refugee Policy*, 100) estimates 21 million by the end of 1943, and 30 million at the end of the war; DTV-*Atlas zur Weltgeschichte*, vol. 2, 498–9.

5 Dirks, *Canada's Refugee Policy*, 105.

6 Roger Daniels, "American Refugee Policy in Historical Perspective," 71.

7 Hansi Lamberger, interview, 4 December 2000.

8 Nicholas Goldschmidt, interview, 1–2 November 2000. German contralto Maria Olszewska (1892–1969) was renowned for roles such as Herodias in *Salome*. She appeared at the Metropolitan Opera in 1933–35.

9 *MGG* 11: 906 states that Rosé "ging 1938 nach England"[sic].

10 'See Richard Newman and Karen Kortley, *Alma Rosé: Vienna to Auschwitz.*

11 Richard Newman, "The Canadian Connection," 5.

12 Karl Kraus (1874–1936), a guiding light of the social democratic circle in Vienna, astonished most of his friends in July 1934 with a 315-page diatribe, "Warum *Die Fackel* nicht erscheint" (Why *The Torch* no longer appears). Having initially remained silent in the face of increasing persecution of social democrats in Germany and elsewhere, Kraus refused to accept responsibility for carrying on the struggle against the National Socialists, considering the Dollfuss regime a possible bulwark against them.

13 Anton Kuerti, interview, 6 March 2001.

14 LAC MUS 290 2000–6, vol. 8/83. Kraemer describes his *Five Pieces for Piano Written in the System of Arnold Schoenberg* (1934) as "die ersten Studien in der Zwölftontechnik" [the first studies using the twelve-tone technique]. This student work – an aspect of early European forays into dodecaphonic writing – written after he studied with Alban Berg in Vienna, includes a brief analysis, and the various forms of the row are carefully notated in red, blue, and green pencil.

15 SFU F28–203, Biographical Info 1986–89, 11, Simon Fraser University Archives. The identity of the author of this biography is unknown; David Duke (Ida Halpern's colleague and executor) believes that it may have been written by Doug Cole.

16 SFU F28–203, Biographical Information. 14, Simon Fraser University Archives.

17 Ukrainian ethnomusicologist Filaret Kolessa (1871–1947) and his son, the composer Mykola Kolessa (b. 1903–2006).

18 M. Schulman, "Kolinski's Music"; for additional details, see the LAC vertical file, "Kolinski."

19 Hindemith retained the favour of his political masters until 1935; having lost it he emigrated first to Ankara, Turkey, then to Yale University in New Haven, Connecticut.

20 The Hochschule is now a department within the Universität der Künste, Berlin.

21 In June 1933 opera conductor Kurt Singer proposed to Hans Hinkel that the NSDAP organize a Kulturbund deutscher Juden; among others involved in this venture were Leo Baeck (Berlin's chief rabbi), theatre critic Julius Bab, and conductor Joseph Rosenstock. From 1934 until September 1941 when political pressures led to its demise, the Kulturbund – affectionately called KuBu – was the only authorized public cultural outlet for Jewish artists in Germany; see Martin Goldsmith, *The Inextinguishable Symphony: A True Story of Music and Love in Nazi Germany*. In early 1935 the name was changed to Jüdischer Kulturbund because Jews were considered a priori not German. Performances of Gotthold Ephraim Lessing's *Nathan der Weise* (a play with a theme of religious tolerance among the three Abrahamistic religions) were forbidden. Successful branch groups all over Germany provided work for unemployed Jewish actors and musicians and entertainment for the remaining Jewish population (Goldsmith, 51–67). Only Jews were allowed to attend. As late as 27 February 1941, the Berlin KuBu orchestra performed Mahler's Symphony no. 2, "Resurrection" (Goldsmith, 268–72).

22 Arnold Walter, "A Composer's Story," 8; Elaine B. Seiffert, "Arnold M. Walter: His Contribution to Music Education in Canada, 1946–1968," 8. *Vorwärts* was the newspaper of the Social Democratic Party, published in Berlin; *Die Weltbühne* was a weekly magazine covering, politics, art, and business that published writing by leftist or socialist intellectuals.
23 Walter, "A Composer's Story," 8.
24 Otto Joachim, interview, 11 March 2003.
25 Letter to Ted Jones, 9 May 1981, LAC, MUS 175, John Newmark fonds, vol. 2, no. 45.
26 MGG 16: 497. Szymon Goldberg (1909–1993) was concertmaster of the Dresden Philharmonic from 1925 to 1929 and concertmaster of the Berlin Philharmonic from 1929 to 1934. In Berlin he formed a string trio with Paul Hindemith and Emmanuel Feuermann (who left Europe in 1938 for the Curtis Institute in Philadelphia) and a duo with Lily Kraus (who left for the United States around 1938).
27 Renée Maheu, *Un piano sur la mer: John Newmark et son temps*, 70.
28 Since Leupold was not of "Aryan" descent he could not be ordained in the Reichskirche, which had accepted the civil service law of 7 April 1933; Hubert G. Locke, ed., *Exile in the Fatherland: Martin Niemöller's Letters from Prison*, 7.
29 Hans Gruber, interview, 9 March 2001; The order-in-council is dated December 1938; "Orders in Council," vol. 86: P.C. 3176, 13 December 1938, no. 17, LAC RG 26, DPM.
30 Mario Duschenes, interview, 27 January 2003.
31 Alexander Brott, interview, 25 Feb 2000.
32 Helmut Kallmann was one of about 2,000 surviving Kindertransport children to attend a London reunion in June 1999; see "Flucht ins Ungewisse," *Frankfurter Rundschau*, 19 June 1999.
33 Paul Hymans (1865–1941) had represented Belgium at the Paris Peace Conference in 1919. In 1920 he was appointed Belgian representative to the League of Nations and in the same year became president of the first assembly at Geneva. He was the Belgian minister for foreign affairs from 1927 to 1935; see *Encyclopaedia Britannica*, 11: 984a–b, s.v "Hymans."
34 Harvey Sachs, "She Shall Have Music," 26.
35 Sachs, "She Shall Have Music," 27; "Orders in Council," vol. 86: P.C. 2114, LAC RG 26, DPM. The application for the order-in-council to regularize Greta Krauss's immigration status, made from Hawkesbury, Ontario, on 2 August 1939, stated that she would be a music teacher in a private school in Toronto.

36 Albrecht Gaub, "Karl Steiner, Canadian Apostle of the Second Viennese School," 3; Gaub states that Steiner travelled through France to Shanghai, presumably via Marseilles.

37 The following account and quotations are summarized from Michael Schulman, "Kolinski's Music Affected by International Travelling."

38 Schulman, "Kolinski's Music Affected by International Travelling," 8. John Beckwith ("Kolinski: An Appreciation," xviii) states that Kolinski lived for two-and-a-half years at the home of "well-known Belgian painter, Fritz van der Berghe, who made a closed-off room in the house for him. Later he and Edith van der Berghe, the painter's daughter, were married."

39 Lorand Fenyves, interview, 8 March 2001.

40 Jānis Kalejs, "Gives a Vivid Picture of Life under Red Domination," account of a speech given to the Wolfville Rotary Club in Wolfville *Acadian*, 29 June 1950, 3; Acadia University Archives, Kalejs fonds, Acc. no. 1999.001, file "1949–52."

41 Mirdza Dambergs, interview, 25 April 2001.

42 *Encyclopaedia Britannica*, 1969, 13: 803–4.

43 Mirdza Dambergs, interview, 25 April 2001.

44 "Mit Genehmigung der Britischen Militärregierung."

45 "Résumé," Acadia University Archives, Kalejs Family fonds, Acc. No. 1999.001/1/3/9.

46 Acadia University Archives, 1999.001/1/3/1.

47 Alfred Strombergs, interview, 28 November 2003.

48 Imant Raminsh, interview, 9 January 2003.

49 Today this building is occupied by WMF, a German manufacturer of household products.

50 Siegfried Mauser, "Emigranten bei den Internationalen Ferienkursen für Neue Musik in Darmstadt (1946–1951)," 241–248, in Horst Weber, ed. *Musik in der Emigration.*

51 Udo Kasemets, interview, 6 March 2001.

52 Udo Kasemets, interview, 6 March 2001.

53 Robert Dambergs, interview, 30 May 2003.

54 Talivaldis Kenins, interview, 26 February 2001.

55 By the terms of the Munich Agreement of 29 September, the Western powers acquiesced in the annexation.

56 After the war Jan Masaryk became foreign minister of the democratic Czechoslovakia that was crushed in the Soviet-fomented putsch of February 1948. Masaryk's death under suspicious circumstances shortly after the putsch was presumed to be a Communist assassination.

57 Stompor, *Künstler im Exil,* 131.

58 Fogl's account gains credence with recent revelations about the Spanish Civil War. Many left-leaning democrats were at greater risk from Moscow-guided "comrades" than they were from Franco; see Marko Martin, "Schatten der Vergangenheit."

59 Aloys Fogl, interview, 30 September 2003. The border town of Asch is the same place that Robert Schuman encrypted in *Carnaval*, op. 9, as "quatre notes mignonnes," representing the birthplace of his beloved Ernestine von Fricken, the illegitimate daughter of Baron von Fricken of Asch (*MGG* 12, 278).

60 Robin Elliott and Gordon Smith, eds., *Istvan Anhalt: Pathways and Memory*, 13–16.

61 Shirley Garami, interview, 26 November 2001.

62 Shirley Garami, interview, 26 November 2001.

63 "Charles Reiner," *EMC* 1122a; Charles Reiner, interview by Katharine Neufeld, 19 April 2000.

64 Lorand Fenyves, interview, 8 March 2001.

65 Strauss had made his peace with the Nazi authorities and continued to live in Germany, albeit under close observation after he resigned as president of the Reichsmusikkammer in 1936. In Fenyves's opinion Heifetz had likely brought the encounter upon himself. A number of people had tried to persuade Heifetz to reconsider, but the violinist refused.

66 The MGG entry for Walter Kaufmann (*MGG* 2, 9: 1558–60) was written by Paul Nettl; he and his son Bruno were also refugees from Czechoslovakia, and immigrated to Bloomington, Indiana. Walter Kaufmann's son-in-law Alan Andrews pointed out that Kaufmann had taken a grilling from Becking at his doctoral defence and the dissertation title was never entered in the official records (personal communication, 7 December 2003). See also Richard Schaal, *Verzeichnis deutschsprachiger musikwissenschaftlicher Dissertationen 1861–1960* and *Verzeichnis deutschsprachiger musikwissenschaftlicher Dissertationen 1961–1970*.

67 Joachim Oesterhold, "British Policy towards German-speaking Emigrants in India 1933–1945," 31.

68 According to Kaufmann, the producer Mohan Bhavani was "not particularly successful with the Indian public because he had too much taste" (quoted in Agate Schindler, "Walter Kaufmann: A Forgotten Genius," 98).

69 Schindler, "Forgotten Genius, "100.

70 *The Ragas of North India* (1968), *The Ragas of South India* (1976), *Altindien: Musikgeschichte in Bildern*, Bd. 2, Lfg. 8 (Leipzig, 1981).

71 "Dann, es sieht so aus als ob meine Berufung an die Prager Universitaet wahr werden wuerde"; there is a facsimile of this letter in Schindler, "Forgotten Genius," opposite p. 109.

72 Otto Joachim's landing certificate in Singapore is dated 28 January 1934. The information in the following paragraphs is from an interview with Otto Joachim, 11 March 2003.

73 Renata Berg-Pan, "Shanghai Chronicle: Nazi Refugees in China," 283–9. The substance of the following description is taken from this article.

74 Berg-Pan, "Shanghai Chronicle, 289.

75 Ulrike Ottinger's documentary film *Exil Shanghai* traces the lives of six German, Austrian, and Russian Jews through interviews and historical photographs. The book *Exil Shanghai: Jüdisches Leben in der Emigration 1938–1947*, edited by Georg Armbrüster, Michael Kohlstruck, and Sonja Mühlberger, is based on material from the Japanese occupation authorities and contains names of 14,700 exiles. The Rickshaw group maintains a website (www.rickshaw.org). The documentary *Fleeing to Shanghai*, produced by Shanghai Television in 2000, portrays a 1980 reunion in Los Angeles attended by some 1,000 exiles.

76 Simon Fraser University Archives F28-1-1-1 vol. 1 and F58-4; Fanny Halpern remained in Shanghai until 1951, when she moved to Vancouver. She died a year later.

77 These plans may explain why George and Ida Halpern obtained baptismal and wedding certificates from the Roman Catholic Church of the Sacred Heart in Shanghai in May and July 1939.

78 Otto Joachim, interview, 11 March 2000.

79 For an excellent summary of the press campaigns for and against internment, see Hans-Albert Walter, *Deutsche Exilliteratur 1933–1950*, 3: 203–7. John Anderson worried that in wartime people are easily worked up and that spy scares could be instigated at any time as "stunts."

80 Sources on this issue include: Yves Bernard and Caroline Bergeron, *Trop loin de Berlin*; Paula Jean Draper, "Fragmented Loyalties," "'The Camp Boys,'" and "Muses behind Barbed Wire"; Frederick C. Engelmann, et al., eds., *A History of the Austrian Migration to Canada*; Peter Gillman and Leni Gillman, *Collar the Lot!*; Ted Jones, *Both Sides of the Wire*, 1–25; Eric Koch, *Deemed Suspect*; Ronald Stent, *A Bespattered Page*; Hans-Albert Walter, *Deutsche Exilliteratur 1933–1950*, vol. 3. In his excellent summary of the Canadian and Australian internees H.A. Walter draws on both Gillman and Stent and on material from *Aufbau*, the New York-based exile newspaper.

81 Frederick C. Engelmann and Manfred Prokop, "Achievements and Contributions of Austrian-Canadians," 180–1.

82 "Orders in Council," vol. 86: P.C. 2098, 31 August 1938, no. 1, LAC RG 26, DPM. Subsequent orders were issued for the remaining members of

the family: Robert and family (P.C. 2583, 18 October 1938, no. 8); Ferdinand Bloch-Bauer (P.C. 408, 31 January 1940, no. 20 "coming forward to reside with nephew"). Ferdinand Bloch-Bauer never came to Canada; he died in Zürich. Orders for Edvard Pick and family: (P. C. 1187, 12 May 1939, no. 30); Josef Pick and family (P.C. 2427, 11 August 1939, no. 45); Karl Bloch-Bauer and Rita Georg (P.C., 1941 date not ascertained).

CHAPTER TWO

1 Mario Duschenes, interview, 27 January 2003.
2 Istvan Anhalt, interview, 31 October 2000.
3 George Fiala, interview, 10 June 2007.
4 The following account of the British internment of Austrians and Germans who had fled to Britain is substantially extracted from Peter and Lena Gillman, *Collar the Lot!: How Britain Interned and Expelled Its Wartime Refugees*, 30–170.
5 Gillman and Gillman (*Collar the* Lot, xii) state that as late as 1980 the relevant documents were still not open to public scrutiny. Hans-Albert Walter (*Deutsche Exilliteratur 1933–1950, 3*: 115n283) concludes that "even though a number of important documents are at present and for the foreseeable future unavailable, nevertheless the currently available sources allow a fairly accurate assessment of British practice during the period in question."
6 For a detailed description of the sinking of the *Arandora Star* from the perspective of Günter Prien, the German submarine officer in charge, see Gillman and Gillman, *Collar the Lot,* 185–201.
7 University of Toronto Archives, "Heim, Emmy," A75-0014, vol. 109. This account was written in 1946 at the time she assumed her duties at the TCM. She continues, "Twice in a lifetime this had to happen for I was in Vienna during 1914–18 and sang in nine languages to [the] wounded and [the] prisoners from many lands. To see it all again – the terrible wounds of war upon men who yet could be lifted out of their pain by the songs of Schubert!"
8 The information in table 2.1 has been assembled from details given in Yves Bernard and Caroline Bergeron, *Trop loin de Berlin: des prisonniers allemands en Canada (1939–1946)*, 17–19; this book also contains maps of the camps (20–21), obviously drawn by a German prisoner of war. David J. Carter, *Behind Canadian Barbed Wire*, identifies the camps and presents a somewhat different account of numbers and categories of

inmates; his list includes Camp V at Valcartier, Quebec, and Camp 45 in Sorel, Quebec (309–12). Carter estimates that there were 3,450 inmates in the Quebec camps, 9,925 in Ontario, 900 in New Brunswick, and 24,150 in Alberta. Many internees were moved from one camp to another. I have corrected a number of errors in the dates given by Bernard and Bergeron and by Carter according to the account given by Helmut Kallmann in "Music in the Internment Camps after World War II." (For example, according to Carter's list, all internees were given amnesty and released on Dominion Day, 1941!) There was also a camp for prisoners of war near Hailebury, Ontario, close to Highway no. 11 that is not included in table 2.1; as children we passed this camp frequently. Of the twenty-four camps for prisoners of war and internees, about six were set aside for those identified by the British tribunals as low security risks (Class B and C refugees).

9 All reports and archival documents related to the camps are contained in LAC RG 24, Department of National Defence; pictures from the camps are in PA files.

10 Titles of these newspapers include: *Camp Chronicle* (Camp L at Cove Fields, Quebec); *Stackeldraht* [sic] (Camp A, at Farnham, Quebec); *Die andere Seite* (Camp B, at Ripples, New Brunswick); *Lewoker tageblatt* (Camp I, at Île-aux-Noix, Québec); *Das Nebengleis* (Camp N, at Newington, Quebec).

11 Bernard and Bergeron, *Trop loin de Berlin*, 125–6.

12 John Newmark, quoted in Ted Jones, *Both Sides of the Wire*, 313.

13 Hans Kaufmann, "Behind Barbed Wire," following p. Iva; Kaufmann's work is a unpublished compilation of camp chronicles, letters, and other items pertaining to camp life.

14 Ronald Stent, *A Bespattered Page?*, 227. The Allan Bill stipulated that the United States border was closed to anyone who had relatives in Germany or in German-occupied Europe, and any alien who been released from internment for less than a year. In June 1940 US immigration services were transferred from the Department of Labor to the Department of State. Breckenridge Long, the assistant secretary, was a "virulent foe of foreigners" who saw Jewish refugees and internees as a risk to the country: Cynthia Jaffee McCabe, "Wanted by the Gestapo – Saved by America: Varian Fry and the Emergency Rescue Committee," 80; Hans-Albert Walter, *Deutsche Exilliteratur 1933–1950*, 3: 250; Draper, "Fragmented Loyalities," 160. The American Legion, supported by the restrictive policies of the US State Department, would ensure America's security.

15 Kaufmann, "Behind Barbed Wire," 57 a, b.
16 Melady, *Escape from Canada*, 33.
17 Melady, *Escape from Canada*, 52–3.
18 Kaufmann, "Behind Barbed Wire," 76–81.
19 Jones, *Both Sides of the Wire*, 153.
20 Keith MacMillan, "Ernest MacMillan: The Ruhleben Years," 164–82.
21 John Newmark, "An Accompanist's ABC," 95. MacMillan earned his DMus from Oxford during this period with a setting of Swinburne's ode *England;* see K. MacMillan, "Ernest MacMillan: The Ruhleben Years," 178–80; "Ernest MacMillan," EMC 788c.
22 Jones, *Both Sides of the Wire*, 143.
23 Quoted in Jones, *Both Sides of the Wire,* 143.
24 Eric Koch, interview, 9 March 2001.
25 Walter Homburger, interview, 28 April 2002.
26 LAC MUS 71, vol. 18 (uncatalogued). These performances were sponsored by Oxford University Press; the first program was broadcast on 12 January 1942.
27 Kaufmann, "Behind Barbed Wire," 71–2.
28 Kallmann, "Music in the Internment Camps," 185.
29 Kallmann, "Music in the Internment Camps," 182. Kallmann lists the works on each program; pages 181–8 of this article are quoted in Renée Maheu, *Un piano sur la mer,* without citation.
30 Maheu, *Piano sur la mer,* 152–3; Walter Homburger, interview, 27 May 2002.
31 This concert received mixed reviews. The *Musical America* (quoted in Maheu, *Piano sur la mer*, 153) noted that "neither Mr Kander nor Mr Newmark disclosed a real conception of the Franck Sonata which they delivered without any of its dramatic sweep or sensuousness and on altogether too miniature a scale." The *New York Times* (12 February 1947, 34) was more sanguine: "R.P." writes that "Both the Mozart [Sonata no. 5 in A major] and the Bach [Sonata in G minor for solo violin] were marked by a good style. They were seriously and correctly played, having a forward impetus that kept them alive ... The tone [in the Franck sonata] was more pleasant, there was a greater variety of inflection, and in general the playing was more supple and expressive."
32 Gerhard Kander, interview, 7 March 2001. Jones, *Both Sides of the Wire*, presents an excellent summary of life in Camp B (Ripples) and the men who were interned there. He includes a complete list of the 711 internees as well as reminiscences of a number of old "Camp Boys." According to Helmut Kallmann, about half of the internees in Fredericton were

between sixteen and twenty years of age ("Music in the Internment Camps," 182).

33 Clarkson visited the Ripples museum on 11 October 2000. Homburger's account of the reception is from the interview, 27 May 2002. For more information on the museum see http://www.village.minto.nb.ca/internment.htm.

34 Kallmann, "Music in the Internment Camps," 186.

35 "You'll Get Used to It," EMC 1429a.

36 Kaufmann, "Behind Barbed Wire," 75.

37 "Victor Gordon" is a pseudonym for the publisher. John Bird wrote the text at the request of a local Kiwanis Club (personal communication from Mrs. John C. Bird, 5 April 2006).

38 This description of camp songs is found in an appendix to Hans Kaufmann, "Behind Barbed Wire."

39 Vernon Brooks, "Brigadoon." Brooks was a professor of psychology at McGill University from 1950 to 1956, and later taught at the University of Western Ontario.

40 Kaufmann, "Behind Barbed Wire," 38.

41 Newmark's sponsor was Lady Hamilton, a patron of the arts who had studied music in Leipzig in 1888 and had known Brahms and Clara Schumann. Lady Hamilton also sponsored Helmut Blume.

42 Maheu, *Piano sur la mer*, "Temoinages Helmut Kallmann," [n.p.].

43 Kaspar Fraser was a leading corporation lawyer; Lois Fraser's father, Dr Maurice McPhedran had been dean of medicine at the University of Toronto and was known internationally.

44 Gerhard Kander, interview, 7 March 2001. At an interview with immigration authorities, the commander of Kander's camp, having been appraised of the situation by the Frasers, said, "Well, I know Kaspar."

45 A portrait of Simons's father painted by Otto Dix at present hangs in the Montreal Museum of Fine Arts; for the intriguing story behind this portrait, see Darlene Caroline Cousins, "Otto Dix's Portrait of the Lawyer Hugo Simons."

46 Exhibitions in honour of Max Stern include "A Dealer for 'Living Art': Selected Works from the Max and Iris Stern Donation to Montreal," 1 September 2004 to 2 January 2005 at the Montreal Museum of Fine Art and "Max Stern: The Taste of a Dealer," 1 September to 9 October 2004, at the Leonard and Bina Ellen Art Gallery, Concordia University.

47 Maheu, *Piano sur la mer*, "Temoinages Rose Goldblatt," [n.p.], my translation.

48 John Newmark to Ted Jones, 9 May 1981, LAC, MUS 175, John Newmarks fonds, vol. 2, no. 45.
49 Charles Cahn, personal communication, 17 August 2001.
50 Helmut Kallmann, personal communication, 15 March, 2004.
51 Until 1937 the Cahn family were the proprietors of a magnificent neo-Gothic castle in Bad Godesberg overlooking the Rhein. The castle was recently restored by German businessman Wolfgang Brönna; see *Die Villa Cahn: ein Deutsches Haus am Rhein*, Beiträge zu den Bau- und Kuntstdenkmälern im Rheinland (Cologne: J.P. Backem, 1991).
52 These broadcasts were intended both to reinforce resistance movements and to lower morale among supporters of fascist or Communist regimes. In 1940 the BBC were already engaging émigrés who were proficient in Berlin and Viennese dialects to satirize the Nazi mentality in popular series such as *Alois mit'n grünen Hut* and *Frau Werniche*, while *Hier spricht London* made reports on the course of the war available in central Europe. See Jutta Raab Hansen, *NS-verfolgte Musiker in England*, 156–9.
53 Eric Koch, personal communication, 7 November 2000.
54 A photograph of a dapper-looking Blume, cigarette in hand, interviewing an internee for the CBC is reproduced in Bernard and Bergeron, *Trop loin de Berlin*, 171; the original is held in LAC, RG 24, vol. 6584, no. 237.
55 Karl D. Renner went on to pursue a career with the CBC; he died in Ottawa in 2005. See Eric Koch, *Deemed Suspect*, 270. Renner was the grandson of Karl Renner (1870–1950), a prominent social democrat who was chancellor of Austria from 1918 to 1920 and president from 1945 to 1950.
56 Wasserman also pursued a career with the CBC; see Koch, *Deemed Suspect*, 272.
57 Eric Koch, interview, 8 March 2001.
58 Bernard and Bergeron, *Trop loin de Berlin*, 171.
59 Mario Duschenes, interview, 27 January 2003.
60 Bernard and Bergeron, *Trop loin de Berlin*, 340–1.

CHAPTER THREE

1 For an overview of the British influence on Canadian music, see "England," *EMC* 416b–18c; for a discussion of the French influence in Canada, see "France," *EMC* 495a–97a.
2 For additional biographical information on Ernest MacMillan, see Ezra Schabas, *Ernest MacMillan*; "Ernest MacMillan," *EMC* 788c–91c.
3 "Toronto Symphony," *EMC* 1300c–305b.
4 "Wilfrid Pelletier," *EMC* 1030b–31c.

5 "The Montreal Festivals / Les Festivals de Montreal," EMC 875a–c; the Montreal Symphony Orchestra presented summer concerts as the Festival de musique de Montréal (1936–38); in 1939 this concert series became the Montreal Festivals, founded by Louis-Athanase David and his wife, Mme. Athanase David. The Festivals presented many Montreal and Canadian premières. In EMC Cécile Huot names Pelletier as a co-founder of the Montreal Festivals (347a). Sir Thomas Beecham was briefly associated with the Festival during the 1940s.

6 For details on Canadian piano and organ manufacturing, see "Piano Building," EMC 1053–5.

7 Elaine Keillor, "Musical Activity in Canada's New Capital City in the 1870s," 130.

8 Ezra Schabas, *There's Music in These Walls,* 30–4.

9 Schabas, *There's Music*, 84; the broadcasts, sponsored by a facial tissue company, began on 19 September 1943 and continued for seven years.

10 I have a vivid memory of a six-year old ball of yellow organza who gave a superb rendition of the "Yellow Butterfly," fluttering away lightly to the astonished oohs and aahs of parents. The artist was Claire Woodall, winner of the piano solo under eight years (class 324B), Kiwanis Music Festival, "Stars of the Festival," Massey Hall, Toronto, 10 March 1949.

11 Harvey Olnick, interview, 21 May 2000.

12 John Beckwith, *Music at Toronto*, 19; Beckwith later became dean at the Faculty of Music in Toronto.

13 Stanley Bryce Frost, "A Short Account of the History of the Faculty of Music," presented to the James McGill Society, 7 December 1978, McGill University Archives, Reference Files, "Stanley Frost," 13.

14 See the following sources in the McGill University Archives, RG 39, C 1: File 42, "Sub-Committee on Music: Minutes, 27 January–26 April;" File 43, "Sub-Committee on Music: Correspondence, Agendas and Reports, 19 February–8 May, 1937."

15 "Prix d'Europe," EMC 1079b–80a.

16 "Quebec City," EMC 1095b.

17 Anonymous personal communication, 3 December 2003.

18 Schabas, *Ernest MacMillan*, 105; there were two all-Wagner concerts in 1931.

19 Schabas, *Ernest MacMillan*, 105, 156–60. In 1939, MacMillan wrote: "I was very distressed that a cry against German music as such should have been raised at this early stage. Nazism has attacked the cultural and intellectual life of its own, as of other lands; for that reason, amongst others we are fighting it. If it is going to be considered unpatriotic to perform

German music during the war it seems to me that we are surrendering to the thing we are fighting. To perform music by living composers like Richard Strauss and others who are more or less in accord with the Nazi regime might be debatable, but it will be quite impossible for any orchestra or any other musical organization to go on without the German classics. I can see no earthly reason why they should. Should such a question become acute here I would certainly change my mind about continuing as Conductor for the present season. Germany was jingoistic enough, Heaven knows, during the last war, but, having read the Berlin papers almost throughout that period, I can testify that there was very rarely a time when some theatre in Berlin was not performing Shakespeare. This matter may require a little propaganda to clarify the public mind, but I think the sooner it is done the better. Any attempt to omit the standard classics would, in the long run, diminish the popular appeal of the orchestra" (quoted in Schabas, *Ernest MacMillan*, 156).

20 See "Opera Guild of Montreal, Inc," EMC 972a–b. Donalda's studies in Paris were funded by Donald Alexander Smith (Lord Strathcona), a one-man Canada Council of his day, and her stage name was adopted from that of her patron; see "Strathcona Scholarship," EMC 1256b. Other recipients of scholarships funded by Strathcona include Kathleen Parlow, Béatrice La Palme, Sara Fischer, Rose Goldblatt, and Alexander Brott.

21 For a summary of the many attempts to establish opera on a permanent basis, see "Opera Performance," EMC 973a–5c.

22 Gladstone Murray, Canadian Club address, Ottawa, 14 January 1942, as quoted in Schabas, *Ernest MacMillan*, 172. If Murray's comment did not come from personal experience it perhaps came from eighteenth-century English writers who defined Britain's attitude towards serious opera. Jonathan Swift excoriated Italian opera: "This comedy [John Gay's 1728 *Beggar's Opera*] exposes, with good justice, that unnatural taste for Italian music among us which is wholly unsuitable to our northern climate, and the genius of the people, whereby we are over-run with Italian effeminacy, and Italian nonsense." The biting satire of Joseph Addison in *The Spectator* also ridicules the genre. Ironically much of this literary effort was directed against England's claim to fame in the person of the German-born George Frideric Handel; see Swift as quoted in Paul Henry Lang, *George Frideric Handel*, (Norton, 1977), 196–7. Handel realized to his dismay that his most valiant efforts to establish Italian opera seria in London were fruitless and in desperation turned to oratorio. Foreign opera certainly had snob appeal for England's aristocracy but it never gained the broad support that it enjoyed in central Europe.

23 "CPR Festivals," EMC 326c–7c; "John Murray Gibbon," EMC 526b. A trio consisting of Murray Adaskin, Louis Crerar, and Cornelius Ysselstyn alternated between the Banff Springs Hotel in summer and Toronto's Royal York Hotel during the rest of the year; see Lazarevich, *Musical World of Frances James and Murray Adaskin*, 36–42.

24 "Bands," EMC 76c–85a.

25 "Salvation Army / Armée du Salut," EMC 1175a–76a.

26 In francophone Canada they were known as Sociétés des concerts; see "Community Concert Associations, EMC 288a–c.

27 "Women's Musical Clubs," EMC 1420a–b. For example, in 1895 the Ladies' Morning Musical Club in Montreal sponsored the Canadian debut of EugèneYsaÿe, probably the greatest violinist of his day, because no other arts institution had done so; see "Ladies' Morning Musical Club," EMC 707c–708a.

28 An overview of the field in EMC (422b–431a) notes two German publications on indigenous musics of Canada that were among the first scholarly studies in the budding discipline of comparative musicology: Theodore Baker's *Musik der nordamerikanischen Wilden* (Leipzig, 1882) and Carl Stumpf's article on the music of the Bella Coola Indians in the 1886 *Vierteljahresschrift für Musikwissenschaft*.

29 See MGG 16: 1870.

30 "Marius Barbeau," EMC 87b–88b. Several essays in *Around and About Marius Barbeau*, ed. Lynda Jessup, Andrew Nurse, and Gordon E Smith, discuss aspects of the relationship between Boas and Barbeau; see especially pp. 71–3 and 121–2.

31 "Helen Creighton," EMC 329b.

32 "John Weinzweig," EMC 1392a.

33 The list of Boulanger's Canadian pupils includes John Beckwith, Maurice Blackburn, Richard Boulanger, Walter Buczynski, Gabriel Charpentier, Kenneth Gilbert, Kelsey Jones, Jeanne Landry, Claude Lavoie, Roger Matton, Boyd McDonald, Pierre Mercure, Arthur Ozolins, Jean Papineau-Couture, John Ronan, Reginald Stewart, Kenneth Winters, and Robin Wood; see "France,"EMC 496b. Some years earlier, several Canadians studied with Boulanger in Madison, Wisconsin, or Lake Arrowhead, California, where Boulanger spent the war years.

34 "Broadcasting," EMC 162c–67a.

35 "Harry Adaskin," "John Adaskin," and "Murray Adaskin," see EMC, 6a–7b.

36 Eric Koch, *The Brothers Hambourg*; "Hambourg," EMC 572a–3a.

37 "Massey," EMC 814a–b.

38 "Hart House String Quartet," EMC 588a–90a.

39 The Massey Commission report, which was completed in 1951, laid the groundwork for the creation of the Canada Council and an increased role for government in support of the arts

40 "Masella," EMC 811b–12b.

41 Walter Joachim, interview by Rachel Anderson, 26 April 2000. Michel Hirvy (ca. 1900–66, né Hirschowitz) was born in Warsaw, studied piano in Berlin, and lived in Austria and Paris before coming to Montreal in 1941; EMC 605c. He might have been included in this study but I could not find an order-in-council for him.

42 Names of newly arrived musicians were often announced in the *New York Times*; see David Josephson, "Exile of European Music."

43 Schabas, *Ernest MacMillan*, 37–51.

44 Wilfred Pelletier was also involved in obtaining Vinci's appointment at the Halifax Conservatory (Tom Vinci, personal communication, 3 October 2003).

45 Schabas, *Ernest MacMillan*, 139–40. MacMillan accompanied Heim in her first Toronto recital in 1934 and was captivated by her charm and musicianship. He also visited her in Salzburg in 1935.

46 Schabas, *Ernest MacMillan*, 122–3. The rave reviews for Unger's performance probably led to some professional jealousy between the two conductors; for other incidents of rivalry between the two men, see Schabas, *Ernest MacMillan*, 156, 196.

CHAPTER FOUR

1 For a photograph of the Toronto Conservatory of Music building at 135 College Street, see Ezra Schabas, *There's Music in These Walls*, 29.

2 Donald MacKay, *The Square Mile*, 104.

3 Perhaps the most persuasive brief account of musicology as a humanistic discipline is Walter Wiora, "Musikwissenschaft," MGG 9, 1192–220.

4 Or "performing practise" (*Aufführungspraxis*). I do not intend to imply that a historical awareness of performance practice began only in the 1920s. For example, late nineteenth-century editions of Palestrina reveal that the editors were aware of sixteenth-century treatises written by professional singers in leading ecclesiastical institutions on the embellishment of motets by Palestrina and other composers, but for aesthetic reasons – their desire for a romantic, pure, unadulterated sixteenth-century polyphonic, a cappella vocal style they rejected such documents as the productions of unknowledgeable singers. The organ movement of the early

part of the twentieth century led to increased awareness of the role of historical studies in illuminating performance, but a more academic approach to performance practice came about only after the First World War in the universities of Vienna and Berlin.

5 "Arnold Walter," *EMC* 1382c.

6 The date of the initial memorandum, although not written on official TCM stationery, implies that Walter's appointment began in September 1944. The information and quotations in the following paragraph are from Walter's more complete proposal (1 December 1944) for the Senior School, "Senior School, Est," University of Toronto Archives, A75–0014, file 100. This typescript proposal has handwritten comments (not in Walter's hand) in the margin. The second paragraph states that an original proposal had been submitted to the Board in a "Memorandum" of 1 October 1944.

7 *The Globe and Mail*, 18 July 1945, 6; Peaker's article acknowledges the Quebec Conservatoire as a model.

8 *The Globe and Mail*, 25 June 1946, 8.

9 Mazzoleni and MacMillan also had a personal bond, in that Mazzoleni had married Macmillan's sister, Winifred MacMillan.

10 "Report on the Senior School", typescript with handwritten revisions in Walter's hand, 13 pp., LAC, Arnold Walter fonds (MUS 71), (uncatalogued) vol. 18. The report does not have a specific addressee and its somewhat rough state suggest that it was an internal document not meant for public distribution. At the time of writing the Walter fonds at LAC had not been catalogued and the individual volumes were not subdivided into separate files. This document is also referred to in Elaine B. Seiffert, "Arnold M. Walter: His Contribution to Music Education in Canada, 1946–1968"; I consulted a copy of this document held at the University of Toronto Archives, A75, vol. 15. A reference to the establishment of the school music program "two years ago" suggests that the letter was written in 1948.

11 "Report," 6, ibid.

12 "Report,"7–10, ibid.; the remaining quotations in this paragraph are also from this "Report." Ezra Schabas (*Ernest MacMillan*, 200) implies that Walter merely "urged" MacMillan to undertake the school music program within the faculty, and does not point out the fact that this program was not conceived as a Faculty program;.

13 Harvey Olnick, interview, 21 May 2000.

14 "Director's files 1937–52," University of Toronto Archives, Acc. A1975/0015, vol. 1. This document is also quoted in Seiffert, "Arnold M. Walter," 23–4.

15 "Kathleen Parlow," EMC 1018c–19c.
16 "Memorandum Respecting the Establishment of a School of Music of the University of Toronto," LAC, Arnold Walter fonds (MUS 71), (uncatalogued) vol. 18. The document is not dated but refers to the Hutcheson report [1937] prepared "about twelve years ago." Seiffert, "Arnold M. Walter," 27–8 also refers to this document.
17 "Memorandum," 2, ibid.
18 "First Meeting of the Committee to Study the System of Music Education within the Conservatory in Relation to the University of Toronto," 5 pp, University of Toronto Archives, A75–0014, vol. 100, File "RCM, Conservatory Reorganization." All quotations in this paragraph are from this document. See also Seiffert, "Arnold M. Walter," 9.
19 File "Statement Approved Unanimously by the Board of Directors of the Royal Conservatory of Music of Toronto," [February 1950], 7 pp., University of Toronto Archives, A75–0014, vol. 99.
20 The interpersonal rivalry between Walter and MacMillan is described in Schabas, *Ernest MacMillan*, 213–24; see also John Beckwith, *Music at Toronto*, 22–5. Schabas documents the thrust and parry of the reorganization (*Ernest MacMillan*, 213–24); for MacMillan's reaction to Mazzoleni's capitulation, see Schabas, *Ernest MacMillan*, 222.
21 John Beckwith, personal communication, 28 January 2009.
22 For details of Neel's career, see "Boyd Neel," EMC 937a–c.
23 "Was it spontaneous" asks Schabas? (*Ernest MacMillan*, 221).
24 Oskar Morawetz, interview, 4 Nov 2000; Schabas (*Ernest MacMillan*, 221) describes the event from the Conservatory perspective.
25 Sidney Smith, quoted in Schabas, *Ernest MacMillan*, 214.
26 "Keith Bissell," EMC 125a–26a.
27 Harvey Olnick, interview, 21 May 2000: "Arnold Walter was *persona non grata* to Claude Bissell. For example, much as I tried to keep him there as active dean of the Faculty, for a few years after he (Walter) was supposed to resign. Claude Bissell wouldn't hear of it." In his biography of Ernest Macmillan Schabas comments, "Teachers referred to [Walter] as 'The Prussian,' yet if truth be known, few disliked Prussianism more than Walter. Then, too, diplomacy plays an important role in the Anglo-Saxon world, and Walter didn't know the fundamental rules" (Schabas, *Ernest Macmillan*, 216).
28 Harvey Olnick, interview, 21 May 2000.
29 Boyd Neel, *My Orchestras and Other Adventures*, ed J. David Finch, quoted in Beckwith, *Music at Toronto*, 41.
30 At a meeting with Mazzoleni in 1956 to discuss my future studies, he said that my wish to continue my studies in the Artist Diploma program

at the Senior School was not a betrayal of the Conservatory but was "the natural thing to do." Reconciliation had been achieved.

31 Arnold Walter, *Music and the Common Understanding*, 13.

32 Olnick commented that, "[Walter's] letter made a point of telling me that the position in question was the first chair of musicology to be created in all of Canada" (interview, 21 May 2000). Ulrich Leupold and Ida Halpern, who both arrived in 1939, were the first European-trained musicologists to arrive in Canada, but at that time no Canadian music school or university had established musicology as a discipline.

33 Harvey Olnick, interview, 21 May 2000.

34 "Music in the University," lecture delivered on the occasion of the dedication of the Edward Johnson Building at the University of Toronto [1962], 5 pp., LAC, Arnold Walter fonds (MUS 71), vol. 18 (uncatalogued). The main text of this lecture is given in appendix C. The date 1962 is inferred from the statement in his opening comments that "[i]n a few months from now, the Faculty of Music building will rise on Queen's Park Crescent." Seiffert ("Arnold M. Walter," 85) states that the lecture was an address to the Guild of Community Music Schools, Toronto, 1967.

35 "University of Toronto," *EMC* 1346b.

36 "Arnold Walter," *EMC* 1382a.

37 "Canadian University Music Society," *EMC* 214b;

38 Istvan Anhalt, interview, 31 October 2000.

39 Arnold Walter,"The Growth of Music Education," 257, 279–80, 282–3.

40 In a lecture delivered in Brussels to the First International Conference on Music Education Walter described the achievements in music education in North America; his audience "could not believe it! ... Now we are doing great things musically." Walter refers to his Belgian experience in *Music and the Common Understanding*, 4.

41 Walter Kemp, personal communications, 23 and 25 May 2001.

42 Edward Laufer, personal communication, 28 Nov 2007.

43 Alan Gillmor, personal communication, 9 Nov 2006; Renato Poggioli, *Teoria dell'arte d'avanguardia*; Walter used Gerald Fitzgerald's English translation, *The Theory of the Avant-Garde* (Cambridge, 1968). A shortened version of Gillmor's thesis appears in Alan Gillmor, "Erik Satie and the Concept of the Avant-Garde," *Musical Quarterly*, 69/1 (1983): 104–19.

44 Helmut Kallmann, interview, 28 February 2001.

45 Harvey Olnick, interview, 21 May 2000.

46 Hindemith taught composition at the Hochschule from 1927 to 1937 when he left Germany because of political pressures: his *Mathis der Maler* became a cause célèbre. His works were proscribed in Germany in

October 1936. He arrived in the United States in 1940. See Michael Kater, *The Twisted Muse*, 21 and 179–82.

47 Helmut Blume, interview, 10 December 1997; the personal account given here is taken from this interview.

48 Blume later joked that "according to the racial policies of the time, I was *besudelt* (polluted)."

49 A letter of 2 March 1959 from Blume's father, Dr. med. G. Blume, Nervenarzt, LAC, MUS 302 (2002–1) Box 6, states "Damals warst Du Militärsoldat und ich fuhr eines Sonntags nach Küstrin, um Dich los zu eisen."

50 Yves Bernard and Bergeron, Caroline. *Trop loin de Berlin*, 26: Helmut Blüme [sic] It was necessary for Helmut to fulfill the requirement otherwise the charge of desertion would have stayed. The penalty for "Kriegsdienstverweigerung" was death.

51 Helmut Blume, interview, 10 December, 1997.

52 Renée Maheu (*Un piano sur la mer*, 130) notes that Lady Hamilton was also John Newmark's sponsor.

53 Ljerka Blume, interview, 15 February 2001.

54 Eric Koch, interview, 8 March 2001.

55 "Sub-Committee on Music: Minutes, 27 January–26 April," Ref. 4/3, " Consultative Subcommittee on Music, Correspondence, Agendas and Reports, 19 February–8 May, 1937," McGill University Archives, RG 39, C 1, File 42. A consultative sub-committee struck in April 1937 had a mandate to examine the faculty offerings, and discussions included possible residency requirements for the bachelor degree.

56 "Annual Announcements of the Faculty and Conservatorium, 1904–56," "Calendar 1955–56," 2213, McGill University Archives, RG 39, C 1, Acc. 102.

57 The Lady Davis Fellowships provided stateless European scholars with teaching positions at Canadian universities. Lady Isabelle Henriette Davis was the widow of Sir Mortimer Barnett Davis (1864–1928) of Imperial Tobacco. MacKay (*The Square Mile*, 164) states that "in 1917 [Davis] became the first Canadian Jew to be knighted. He married Henrietta Myers of San Francisco and had one son, who was killed in an auto crash." Anhalt, who met Lady Davis in 1949, described her as "very aristocratic in bearing. She had a beautiful town house on Simpson Street in Montreal, and she invited me several times."

58 Istvan Anhalt, interview, 31 October 2000.

59 Istvan Anhalt, interview, 31 October 2000. See "Douglas Clarke," *EMC* 274b–c. The records for these concerts can be found in RG 39, C 1, file nos. 79–89: "Fiftieth Anniversary Festival" (1953–54). Financial records

indicate that Clarke had estimated seat sales of $8,170 and costs of $7,490; the final deficit was $7,858.12.

60 According to Blume's biography in the LAC vertical file "Blume," he was appointed associate professor in 1955.

61 "Reports on Proposals for Reorganizing the Faculty and Conservatorium, by the Principal's Committee, 1955–1955," Ref. 4/5, "Report by the Principal's Committee on Plans," McGill University Archives, RG 39, C 1, File 44.

62 "Office of the Principal and Vice-Chancellor," "F. Cyril James, 1939–62," McGill University Archives, RG 2 (http://www.archives.mcgill.ca/resources/guide/vol1/rg2.htm). The quotation is from the archivist's description of the papers.

63 Bizony had taught music history (1949–54) and directed a *Schola cantorum* (1949–50) at McGill. She had hoped for a full-time appointment within the faculty, and when it was not granted, returned to England in 1956. Materials related to Musica Antica e Nuova in the Otto Joachim fonds LAC (MUS 270), E, 4, include programs and a letter from Bizony in England to Joachim regretting that Montreal couldn't offer her a position. In Joachim's opinion Bizony's programs were "under-rehearsed but clever" (Otto Joachim, interview, 1 May 2003). Mario Duschenes commented that the concerts were "not a terribly happy memory for me" (Mario Duschenes, interview, 27 January 2003).

64 "Faculty meeting: Draft Minutes and Notes 1949–1961," Ref. 17/5, MUA, RG 39, C 5, File 123.

65 "Reports on Proposals for Reorganizing the faculty and Conservatorium, by the Principal's Committee," Ref. 4/5, "Implementation of Recommendations," Dec 1955, 7 pp., McGill University Archives, RG 39, C 1, File 44.

66 The musicians hired at this time constitute a who's who of Montreal artists, including a significant number of émigrés: Hyman Bress, Louis Charbonneau, Neil Chotem, Natalie Clair, Bernard Diamant, Mario Duschesnes, Myron Galloway, Arthur Garami, Edna-Marie Hawkin, Walter Joachim, Kelsey Jones, Stephen Kondaks, Jacques LeComte, Carl Little, George Little, Erwin Marcus, Joseph Masella, Ralph Masella, Rudolf Masella, Donald McGill, Gilles Potvin, Charles Reiner, Arthur Romano, Dorothy Weldon, Lubomyra Zuk, and Joseph Zuskin.

67 "Minutes 1904–63," Ref. 17/5, "Meeting of the Faculty of Music, 6 July, 1955," McGill University Archives, RG 39, C 5, File 123.

68 Istvan Anhalt, interview, 31 October 2000.

69 Istvan Anhalt, interview, 31 October 2000.

70 Helmut Blume, personal communication; Blume did not specify whether this exchange occurred during the 1955 year of crisis or later.

71 The first performance degree was established at Acadia Universty in 1911; see "Acadia University," EMC, 2c.

72 Luba Zuk, interview, 6 May 2002.

73 "McGill String Quartet," EMC, 829b–c; "McGill Chamber Orchestra," EMC, 828b–9a.

74 *MGG* 12, 1288; see also *New Grove* 2, 24: 373–5.

75 Stanley Frost, *McGill University*, 2: 292.

76 "Correspondence re Denis Stevens 1957–1958," McGill University Archives, RG 39, C 44, File 2363. Note that the EMC articles on Marvin Duchow (EMC, 386b) and McGill University (EMC, 830b), and the "Chronology" in Eleanor Stubley, ed., *Compositional Crossroads*, 337–8 are in error in their assertion that Duchow was appointed dean in 1957. His letter of resignation to the principal, 24 May 1963, is signed "Acting-Dean" ("Duchow, Marvin – Correspondence with the Principal 1963–1963," McGill University Archives, RG 39, C 44, File 2361).

77 Ellen Ballon (1898–1969) was then living at a prestigious address in New York. For more information on her career, see EMC 72c–73b.

78 "Correspondence re Dean Stevens 1957–1958," McGill University Archives, RG 39, C 44, File 2364.

79 Other members of the faculty, including Alexander Brott and Kenneth Meek, who were not in attendance that day were informed of the decision and concurred in it.

80 "Correspondence re Denis Stevens 1957–1958," McGill University Archives, RG 39, C 44, File 2363.

81 First non-British deans of music at other Canadian universities include Howard Brown at Mount Allison University (1953), Jānis Kalejs at Acadia University (1966), and Istvan Anhalt at Queen's University in 1971. The University of Manitoba continued to hire English music-administrative heads until the 1974 appointment of Leonard Isaacs. I had an opportunity to see another side of Denis Stevens during my musicological studies with him at Columbia University 1966–71. His knowledge of medieval liturgy was outstanding and his series of recordings on sixteenth-century ornamentation were pioneer achievements in performance practice. On the basis of my studies I initiated performance practice seminars at McGill in 1973, and sent him a recording of the *Missa Sancti Iacobi*, a product of McGill students. He congratulated me on the excellent singing and although he was almost blind did his best to write his

thanks; on one level at least, reconciliation between Stevens and McGill had been achieved.

82 Ljerka Blume, interview, 10 December 1997.

83 "Annual Reports of the Dean 1958–1962," "An Appraisal," McGill University Archives, RG 39, C 44, File 2377. All references in the following synopsis refer to the wording in this document.

84 Walter, "Growth of Music Education," 256.

85 Frost, *McGill University for the Advancement of Learning*, 2: 292.

86 Istvan Anhalt, interview, 27 November 2001.

87 Sister O'Neill, interview, 25 May 2003.

88 "McGill University," *EMC* 830b.

89 Blume, "A National Music School for Canada / Une école nationale de musique pour le Canada: An Inquiry by Helmut Blume," written for the Canada Council, March 1978: LAC Helmut Blume fonds (MUS 302); see also Franz Kraemer fonds LAC (MUS 290), vol. 3, file 22.

90 For a list of musicologists who came to the United States see Reinhold Brinkmann and Christoph Wolff, eds., *Driven into Paradise*, 341–4. The majority of essays in this collection were presented at the conference, "The Musical Migration: Austria and Germany to the United States, ca. 1930–1950" (Harvard University Music Department, 5–8 May 1994). For details of a conference held two years earlier at the Folkwang Hochschule in Essen, see Horst Weber, ed. *Musik in der Emigration, 1933–45*.

91 Flora Roy, *Sir Wilfrid Laurier Faculty of Music Newsletter* (Summer, 1999): 6. In 1959, the Seminary became Waterloo Lutheran University; in 1973, the Lutheran church relinquished control of the University which was renamed Sir Wilfrid Laurier Laurier University, but retained control of the Seminary which federated with the new university.

92 "Walter Kemp," *EMC* 679a–b. Kemp ("Lutherans," *EMC* 781b) later acknowledged Leupold as the "foremost church musician in Canadian Lutheranism."

93 Gertrude Leupold, interview, 5 October 2002.

94 *Laudamus: Hymnal for the Lutheran World Federation*, 4th edition, ed. Ulrich Leupold (Geneva: Lutheran World Federation, 1970).

95 *Liturgy and Hymns*, vol. 53 of Luther's Works, Philadelphia: Fortress Press, 1965; *Evangelisches Gesangbuch: Ausgabe für die Evangelische Landeskirche Anhalts Die Evangelische Kirche in Berlin-Brandenburg … Stuttgart*: Biblia, 1994, no. 116. Each province of Germany published its own version of the hymn book, but all include this text, translated by Leupold from the Swahili song "Mfurahini, Haleluya."

96 Trueman was director of the Canada Council from 1957 to 1965.

97 UNB *Alumni News* 3, no. 4 (April 1949).

98 "Music Director Appointed by Dr. Trueman," *Brunswickan*, 21 March 1949.

99 New Brunswick Archives, PUNB Presidential Papers, Senate Minutes, 1949. I am indebted to Mary Flagg, University Archivist for this information.

100 I held that position from 1962 to 1964. The University subsequently hired Arlene Nimmons and Joe Pach who formed the Brunswick String Quartet.

101 "Musical Appreciation Class to Commence Tuesday," *UBYSSEY*, 7 January 1941: "Musical appreciation classes under Dr Ida Halpern, graduate of the University of Vienna, will begin in Brock Hall at noon Tuesday, January 14. ... L.S.E. President Bob Bonner feels that these ... classes will meet a need common to many U.B.C. students. 'Since there is a keen desire on the part of many students to learn more about music, there is a real need for someone to discuss and explain the Carnegie records [a local collection]." "Viennese Refugee Lectures on Music to U.B.C. students," *Vancouver Daily Province*, 8 February 1941: "A month ago the literary and scientific executive of the U.B.C.'s Alma Mater Society engaged Dr Halpern to give three lectures on music appreciation, one each week, to students who cared to attend during lunch hour. About 100 turned out for the first lecture [on polyphonic and homophonic music.] Since then, two dozen more chairs have been required, and in many cases, students are 'doubling up' to increase accommodation."

CHAPTER FIVE

1 The desert image was used by from Herman Geiger-Torel; see Ezra Schabas and Carl Morey, *Opera Viva*, 124; and is also used by Lindsay Moore in "Herman Geiger-Torel, Nicholas Goldschmidt and Arnold Walter: Prophets in the Desert."

2 "Alfred Rosé," *EMC* 1146c–47a.

3 This list of operas comes from programs for workshop concerts and productions in "Opera Workshop File" (uncatalogued), Gustav Mahler-Alfred Rosé Collection, University of Western Ontario.

4 Four letters (dated 26 August, 5 September, 9 September, and 18 September 1946) pertaining to Walter's negotiations with Rosé are held in the Gustav Mahler-Alfred Rosé Collection, University of Western Ontario. Mary Portis, executor of the estate of Maria Rose Rosé, kindly gave per-

mission to quote from these letters, which were brought to my attention by Lisa Philpott in October 2002. On 26 August 1946 Walter writes to Rosé care of the Western Ontario Conservatory of Music, introducing himself as a fellow Austrian and proposing a discussion on the proposed opera school. On 5 September 1946 Walter writes to Rosé's home address in Cincinnati offering a salary of $4,200 to $4,500 to take charge of the Opera School's musical activities. He also mentions the possibility of hiring Felix Brentano as stage director, notes that the School would be mainly a pedagogical venture but professional performances would be possible at a later date, and adds that Edward Johnson, general manager of the Metropolitan Opera and chair of the TCM board, was "very much interested in plans of this kind." On 9 September 1946 Rosé replies that the offer looked "very interesting and is worth while considering." However he mentions his large class in Cincinnati that he had built up over a period of six years. He offers to come for $7,000 per annum for a three-year contract. On 18 September 1946 Walter replies that he could not guarantee a three-year contract, although "I am pretty certain that in the course of time things would most probably turn out the way you want them to." The deal was off.

5 Nicholas Goldschmidt, interview, 1–2 November 2000. The version given by Goldschmidt in this interview differs slightly from that in Gwenlyn Setterfield, *Niki Goldschmidt*, 55.

6 Setterfield, *Niki Goldschmidt*, 59.

7 Brander Matthews Hall, on 117th Street, was opened in 1940 and seated about three hundred; see Setterfield, *Niki Goldschmidt*, 51.

8 Setterfield, *Niki Goldschmidt*, 44.

9 Nicholas Goldschmidt, interview, 1–2 November 2000.

10 Nicholas Goldschmidt, interview, 1–2 November 2000.

11 Hermann Geiger-Torel, quoted in Kenneth Peglar, "Opera and the University of Toronto," 7–8.

12 The Geiger family history has been traced back several centuries in Frankfurt by his mother, pianist and composer Rosy Geiger-Kullmann (1886–1964); Rosy Geiger-Kullmann, "Lebenserinnerungen" 1961, ms. Stadtarchiv, Frankfurt am Main (as quoted in Martini, 101), LAC MUS 77 (unfortunately on Gestetner negatives that must be read backwards). Herman Geiger-Torel was born Hermann Geiger; he added "Torel" to his surname during a season with the Société du Cinéma du Panthéon in Paris (1937–38); *EMC* 520a.

13 LAC, MUS 70 Box II, 1.

14 For an excellent treatment of German opera productions in Latin America during the war years, see Stephan Stompor, *Künstler im Exil*, 590–698.
15 Program notes, Nova Scotia Opera Association production of *Countess Maritza*, Halifax, 1951 (unpaginated), Nova Scotia Archives, MG20, vol. 482, 1b.
16 Nicholas Goldschmidt, interview, 1–2 November 2000.
17 LAC, Arnold Walter fonds (MUS 71), vol. 18 (uncatalogued).
18 At an anniversary meeting of the Canadian Opera Women's Committee, 22 June 1972, Jean Chalmers paid tribute to Walter: "Dr Walter recognized the need for an alert, hard-working committee to help build audiences ... He had a secondary purpose in mind as well ... He wanted to show them off to the music lovers of Toronto. So he established the 'Five O'Clocks' – a series of informal concerts ... held in the Recital Hall of the old Conservatory Building." (This reference is from a box labelled "Guarantors, History, Insurance....," files related to Opera and Concert Committees (one of eight unnumbered boxes) housed in the Joan Baillie Archives. For a list of the major productions of the Opera Division beginning in 1946, see http://www.music.utoronto.ca/programs/Opera/Major_Prodns.htm (accessed April 2009)
19 Helmut Kallman, interview, 28 February 2001. In 1942 CBC general manager Gladstone Murray described the typical British attitude to opera: "The Anglo-Saxon temperament does not on the whole take to the themes and declamatory style of grand opera. The Briton, on the whole, prefers musical comedy or light opera with its simple emotions, catchy tunes and words that can be appreciated." G. Murray, "Broadcasting," Address to the Canadian Club, Ottawa, 14 January 1942, quoted in E. Schabas, *Ernest MacMillan*, 172.
20 Oskar Morawetz, interview, 4 November 2000.
21 Nicholas Goldschmidt, interview, 1–2 November 2000.
22 "Alfred Strombergs," *EMC* 1260b.
23 Gordana Lazarevich, *The Musical World of Frances James and Murray Adaskin*, 109–12.
24 CBC Music brochure, "Outstanding Programs to be Broadcast on CBC Wednesday Nights during the Fall and Winter Season 1948–1949," 3, LAC, Nicholas Goldschmidt fonds (MUS 223), file 53.
25 "CBC Opera Company," *EMC* 229a–b.
26 "The Present Stage of Opera in Canada," 8 pp., LAC, Arnold Walter fonds (MUS 71), vol. 18.

27 Although the title "Canadian Opera Company" was not officially adopted until 1977 the designation was used with some frequency from 1958 on. For details on the administrative history of the COC, see "Canadian Opera Company," *EMC* 211b.

28 The Joan Baillie Archives – the repository for materials relating to the Canadian Opera Company – holds eight uncatalogued and unnumbered boxes relating to the Opera School of the Conservatory (G 1000, vol. no. 2: Royal Conservatory Opera School 1946–71; 1972–96; vol. no. 3: Opera School and Productions 1946–69: Reviews, programs, articles). The Conservatory Archives, or more correctly, parts of what once were the Conservatory Archives, are now housed in the Robarts Library as University of Toronto Archives deposits but the materials related to the Opera School as well as additional materials from the former Conservatory Archives were removed from that collection and placed in the Baillie Archives.

29 Nicholas Goldschmidt, interview, 1–2 November 2000; see also Setterfield, *Nicholas Goldschmidt*, 71; Schabas and Morey, *Opera Viva*, 31–3.

30 For a discussion of some of the problematic productions staged by Torel, see Schabas and Morey, *Opera Viva*, 123–4.

31 Thomas Hathaway, "I Shudder – An Opera Is About to Descend on Me," *Queen's Quarterly* 85 (Fall 1978), 425, quoted in Lindsay Moore, "Herman Geiger-Torel, Nicholas Goldschmidt and Arnold Walter."

32 Schabas and Morey, *Opera Viva*, 124.

33 Hermann Geiger-Torel, "The Coming of Age," in *Remembered Moments of the Canadian Opera Company 1950–1975*, quoted in Lindsay Moore, "Herman Geiger-Torel, Nicholas Goldschmidt and Arnold Walter."

34 This information comes from the brief biography that accompanies the Ernest Vinci fonds at York University. Vinci was raised as a Reform Jew by his father Adolf Wreszynski and his mother Anna Kalinski. It is doubtful that he used the names Vinci or Wygram to disguise his Jewish background, since all early correspondence and documents, including immigration records, bear his given name. However, his son Tom Vinci was unaware of his Jewish heritage until 1999.

35 Tom Vinci, "A Remembrance…" 3 October 2003, York University Archives 1999-074/001, File 02. It appears that Vinci returned to Italy to pick up his wife so that they could land together on 23 June 1939, just two months before the outbreak of the war.

36 White had a brilliant but brief career in the 1940s in Canada and the United States, making her Toronto debut in 1941 and her New York debut in 1944. She resumed her career in the late 1950s after studies with

Irene Jessner in Toronto; see "Portia White," EMC 1400b; Elaine Keillor, *Music in Canada*, 213, 398n5.

37 This information comes from a Halifax newspaper account of Vinci's application for Canadian citizenship; he told County Judge R.H. Murray that "politics in Nazi Germany and in Italy had often interfered with the free expression of art." Vinci also stated that he had given more than 256 voluntary performances for Allied servicemen during the war. The clippping is in the Vinci fonds, York University Archives, S00154, biographical material 1898–1999-074/001, file 02.

38 Curriculum vitae, LAC, vertical file "Vinci."

39 Nicholas Goldschmidt, interview, 1–2 November 2000.

40 *Globe and Mail*, 20 October 1952, 13.

41 "Scholarly Songs please in recital with harpsichord," *Globe and Mail*, 13 October 1948, 12.

42 "Brief Courtship," 9, *Toronto Star*, 11 April 1959.

43 Jan Rubes, interview, 9 December 2002.

44 "COC names Rubes touring director," *Globe and Mail*, 25 January 1974, 10.

45 Nicholas Goldschmidt, interview, 1–2 November 2000; Florence Schill, "Soprano finds teaching as exciting as singing," *Globe and Mail*, 27 October 1955, 18.

46 Some writers claim that it was Luciano Della Pergola and his wife Edith who "founded" or "established" the Opera Studio in 1956; see "McGill University," EMC 831a; "McGill Opera Studio / Atelier d'opéra de McGill," EMC 829a–b; Arthur Kaptainis "The voice is with her," *The Gazette*, 8 December 2002, E 20; Eleanor Stubley, Heather White, and Bruce Minorgan, "Chronology," in *Compositional Crossroads: Music, McGill, Montreal*, ed. Eleanor Stubley, 338. While the Pergolas put the operatic experience from their European careers to good use in the Studio, Blume must be given credit for conceiving the idea in 1955, for gaining approval and funding from the university administration, for working out the material details of the program, and for hiring the Pergolas in 1956.

47 "Reports on Proposals for Reorganizing the Faculty and Conservatorium, by the Principal's Committee, 1955–1955," Ref. 4/5, "Report by the Principal's Committee on Plans," 18, McGill University Archives, RG 39, C 1, File 44.

48 Luciano Della Pergola, *Opera at McGill*, 6.

49 Della Pergola, *Opera at McGill*, 7.

50 *Don Giovanni*, program notes, 1949, Nova Scotia Archives, MG20, vol. 487, no. 1d.

51 *Tales of Hoffmann*, program notes, 1950, Nova Scotia Archives, MG20 vol. 482, nos. 1b.
52 *Countess Maritza* and *Madama Butterfly*, program notes, Nova Scotia Archives, MG20 vol. 482, nos. 1b and 1c.
53 Setterfield, *Niki Goldschmidt*, 79.
54 Irving Guttman (b. 1928) was the founding artistic director of the Vancouver Opera (*EMC*, 563a–b). The April 1960 performance of *Carmen* starred Nan Merriman, Richard Cassily, and Louis Quilico ("Vancouver Opera," *EMC* 1360a).
55 Paul and Edwina Heller, interview, 30 May 2001.

CHAPTER SIX

1 Harvey Olnick, interview, 21 May 2000.
2 *Lubka Kolessa* (1929–49) DHR 7743–5, Doremi, 1999; re-mastered Jacob Harnoy.
3 Eric Koch, interview, 8 March 2001.
4 "Lubka Kolessa," *EMC* 692c–3a; pamphlet in the possession of Luba Zuk.
5 A review in the *Globe and Mail*, 17 July 1949, 12, describes her "arresting presence and attractive style." When Kolessa appeared with Ernest MacMillan and the Mendelssohn Choir, 24–25 February 1948, the guest list for the gala reception following the concert was published in the society column of the *Globe and Mail*; those named include the Heintzmanns, the Eatons, the Gilmours, the Oslers, and the Morawetzes (*Globe and Mail*, 25 February 1948, 12).
6 Luba Zuk, interview, 6 May 2002.
7 Ezra Schabas, *There's Music in These Walls*, 107.
8 Harvey Olnick recalled, "I often used to take him wherever he wanted to go. Only once in a while did he ... at five or five-thirty, something like that, when he would go to his house on Roselawn..asked me to let him off at Roxborough and he was going to Lubka ... I didn't know her personally ... I don't know all the [details,] that was before my time, she used to be there and teach, but in my time was only teaching privately. There was some scandal, I don't know exactly what. She was his woman. No question. Lubka Kolessa was at his funeral, and you know who was there too, his foster daughter, Trudi who married Hugh LeCaine. She died just a year ago in Ottawa.
9 John Beckwith, *Music at Toronto*, 25.
10 LAC, vertical file "Böszörmenyi-Nagy."

11 Court Stone, *The Globe and Mail,* 26 January 1949, 11: "refined and sensitive piano tone, delicately balanced ... a delicate colouring, with subtle inflections and spiritual implications"; Hugh Thomson, *Toronto Daily Star,* 26 January 1949, 30: "every possible ounce of dynamic shading in the second movement ... subtle in the extreme."
12 I studied with Dr B from 1948 to 1953; this quotation is from my notes taken at the Banff School of Fine Arts, 11 July 1952.
13 Ibid., notes of 12 August 1952.
14 Kraus had come to Hawkesbury from Vienna in 1938, having managed to obtain a position as secretary to a Viennese chemist who had been sent to Canada as an employee of the International Paper Company.
15 Harvey Sachs, "She Shall Have Music," 27.
16 "Six Monday Evening Broadcasts beginning 12 January 1942, on the national Network CBC," LAC, MUS 71, vol. 18, uncatalogued handbill. The concerts were sponsored by Oxford University Press. John Newmark heard the broadcasts in the Sherbrooke internment camp (Camp N, Newington).
17 Sachs, "She Shall Have Music," 27.
18 Harvey Olnick, interview, 21 May 2000.
19 Oskar Morawetz, interview, 4 November 2000: "Dr Walter gave me the job on the recommendation of Greta Kraus. Greta Kraus and myself were extremely good friends from the very beginning."
20 Sachs, "She Shall Have Music," 60.
21 P.C. 1757, 4 May 1940, no. 13: "Oscar [sic] Morawetz, aged 22 years old, citizen of Czechoslovakia, coming forward to reside with parents and continue studies."
22 Oskar Morawetz, interview, 4 November 2000.
23 See Norma Beecroft's interview with Oskar Morawetz, *Anthology of Canadian Music,* vol. 16.
24 The photograph of Arnold Walter and Greta Kraus rehearsing on double-manual harpsichords is reproduced in Schabas, *There's Music,* 84. In 1931 the T. Eaton Company purchased a two-manual seven-pedal Pleyel harpsichord for Eaton Auditorium. This instrument was later sold to Frances Duncan Barwick (see "Harpsichord playing and teaching" *EMC,* 585b). This may be one of the two instruments shown in this photograph; the second instrument may have been supplied by Lady Eaton, who maintained a valuable collection of older instruments. The brochure for the concerts is contained in LAC MUS 71, vol. 18 (uncatalogued).
25 Renée Maheu, *Piano sur la mer*, 121. Newmark asserted that the bond paid by his sponsors was $1,400. Most former internees who were inter-

viewed said the amount was $500 – the money was a type of cautionary bond, required to ensure that former internees would not become public charges.

26 Maheu, *Piano sur la mer*, 150.

27 "Talivaldis Kenins," EMC 679c–81a; Talivaldis Kenins, interview, 26 February 2001; Talivaldis Kenins, interview with Eric McLean, *Anthology of Canadian Music*, 33.

28 Liner notes for *Concertante for flute and piano* on the CD *Music of Talivaldis Kenins*, Centrediscs, 1997.

29 Talivaldis Kenins, interview with Eric McLean, *Anthology of Canadian Music*, 33.

30 Edgers Kariks, "Talivaldis Kenins: *Beatae Voces Tenebrae* 'Beautiful Voices of the Past': Issues and Sources for a Biographical and Aesthetic Study of Talivaldis Kenins," PhD. dissertation, University of Adelaide, 1989. For studies on Kenins's works for cello, organ, orchestra, and choir see the bibliography in "Talivaldis Kenins," EMC 681a.

31 Sonata no. 3 for Piano, 19, liner notes, *Anthology of Canadian Music*, 33.

32 "Kenins," in Keith MacMillan and John Beckwith, eds., *Contemporary Canadian Composers*, 119.

33 See William Littler, "Latvian artists rally round the flag," *Toronto Daily Star*, 7 July 1986, D3 for a review of Kenins's *Eighth Symphony*.

34 "Kenins," in MacMillan and Beckwith, *Contemporary Canadian Composers*, 120.

35 Jan Simons, interview, 2 December 2002.

36 Paul McIntyre, "The Empire Replanted," 118.

37 Nicholas Goldschmidt, interview, 1–2 November 2000; *Emmy Heim, A Self-Portrait*, Hallmark, LAC, item number 304684, accession number 1977–0014, audio. The private recording includes the three folk songs with MacMillan accompanying. In the EMC article on Heim this disc is identified as "*Emmy Heim – A Self-Portrait*. E. MacMillan, piano, 1949–54, Hallmark SS-2."

38 Ernest MacMillan, *Toronto Conservatory Bulletin* (November 1954): 2.

39 Quoted in Gordana Lazarevich, *The Musical World of Frances James and Murray Adaskin.*, 89.

40 Hindemith's praise so flustered James that when Dr Walter offered her a ride back to the Conservatory with Hindemith she accepted, completely forgetting her husband, who was also in the room: "When we got to College and University Avenue, I was let out of the car, and as I was on my

way home I continued walking east on College. With my head still in the clouds, I barely noticed the car that pulled up to the curb, and a head that poked through the window saying, 'Do you remember me? I'm your husband!'" Lazarevich, *Musical World of Frances James,* 100.

41 Lazarevich, *Musical World of Frances James,* 100.

42 Anton Kuerti, interview, 6 March 2001.

43 Lorand Fenyves, interview, 8 March 2001.

44 Michael Schulmann, "Kolinski's Music Affected by International Travelling," 8.

45 Beverley Diamond, personal communication, 27 Nov 2006.

46 Beverley Diamond, "Canadian Reflections," *Ethnomusicology* 50/2 (2006): 325.

47 John Beckwith suggested that Kolinski's papers were in the possession of his widow.

48 Kolinski, as quoted in Schulmann, "Kolinski's Music."

49 "Lothar Klein," EMC 689a–b.

50 Eric Klein, interview, 6 January 2004.

51 Luba Zuk, interview, 6 May 2002. Zuk also remembered an occasion in the 1950s when she was still a student. "Blume was scheduled to play a concert in Moyse Hall ... He was terribly nervous. He said he hadn't played for a long time. 'I want to play my program for somebody. Would you just come and make me nervous?' It takes courage to say this to a student. I think it's a very human trait.

52 See Robin Elliott and Gordon Smith, eds., *Istvan Anhalt,* especially Robin Elliott, "Life in Montreal" (33–64) and Gordon Smith, "The Kingston Years," (65–92). Helmut Kallmann describes the Anhalt fonds at Library and Archives Canada as "one of the largest and most detail-intensive units among the over 300 fonds and collections housed in the manuscript section." See also "Istvan Anhalt," EMC 26c–8a.

53 Istvan Anhalt, interview, 31 October 2000.

54 Eric Mclean, "Unusual Program at Moyse Hall," *Montreal Daily Star,* 21 January 1950: 21; Gilles Potvin, "McGill Stages Unusual Concert," *The Gazette,* 23 January 1950: 11; Brian Macdonald, *Montreal Herald,* 21 January 1950.

55 Essay by Anhalt on *Comments,* in Elliott and Smith, *Istvan Anhalt,* 434–8.

56 "Istvan Anhalt," EMC 26c; Eric Mclean, *Montreal Daily Star,* 1 December 1959, 28.

57 For a personal view of Anhalt's compositional development, see "In Anhalt's Voice," in Elliott and Smith, *Istvan Anhalt,* 369–464.

58 The dodecaphonic phase includes *Fantasia*, *Sonata* (violin and piano), *Symphony* (1958), and *Symphony of Modules* (1967). The final phase includes vocal commentaries and dramatizations: for example, *Cento, Foci, La Tourangelle, Winthrop, Traces, Millenial Mall, Simulacrum, SparkscrapS* and *Sonance-Resonance*. This division is based on Walter Benjamin's discussion in Elliott and Smith, *Istvan Anhalt*, 165–9. Benjamin also refers to a slightly different distribution given by Udo Kasemets and Louis Applebaum on the Canadian Music Centre Directory of Associate Composers website (302).

59 Smith, "The Kingston Years," in Elliott and Smith, *Istvan Anhalt*, 65.

60 *Celebrating Music Together*, 50th anniversary program of the Kingston Symphony, 29. The work has now been recorded (Canadian Composers Portraits / Portraits de compositeurs canadiens, *Istvan Anhalt*, Centrediscs, 2004, CMCCD 10204).

61 "Charles Reiner," *EMC* 1122a.

62 Charles Reiner, interview by Katharine Neufeld, 19 April 2000.

63 "The Last Composition of the late Erwin Marcus played by Rose Goldblatt," CBC *Times* (December 1957), 1–7.

64 Albrecht Gaub, "Karl Steiner, Canadian Apostle of the Second Viennese School"; Gaub states that an uncle of Steiner "bailed him out" of Dachau.

65 *Music of the Second Generation of the Second Viennese School*, contains works by Julius Schloss, Schoenberg, Eduard Steuermann, Hans Erich Apostel, Alban Berg, William Keith Rogers, Anton Webern and Hanns Jelinek; Centaur CRC 2241/42. 2 CD set.

66 Otto Joachim, interview, 11 March 2003.

67 Only about twenty people attended his final Montreal lecture, "The Interpretation of the Piano Music of the Second Viennese School," given on 18 October 1999.

68 *Österreichische Musikzeitschrift* 43 (1988): 678; 50: 10 (1995): 721; 52: 9 (1997): 48–50; 55: 8/9 (2000): 80; 56: 8/9 (2001): 78.

69 Steiner had about twelve letters from Jelinek addressed to himself; after Steiner's death the letters were donated to the Gesellschaft der Musikfreunde in Vienna (Gaub, "Karl Steiner, 7).

70 The collection of scores, letters, and publications includes a score of Berg's *Lyric Suite* set to Baudelaire's poem, *de Profundis Clamavi* (in Stefan George's translation) linking the work to Berg's beloved Hanna Fuchs; Marvin Duchow Music Library, Special Collections, Schloss Collection, file 1. Berg's dedication to Schloss reads "Herbst 1927, Meinem lieben Schloss, der in den Tagen der Korrekturen an dieser Quartett

wahrhaft bewiesen hat, daß er auch den Schlüssel zu meiner Musik hat" (Autumn, 1927. To my dear Schloss, who in the days devoted to correcting this quartet has truly proven that he has the key to my music." George Perle refers to the annotated scores in his study of the Lyric Suite (*Style and Idea in the Lyric Suite of Alban Berg* [Hillsdale: Pendragon, 2001], 29–31). The collection also contains letters from Arnold Schoenberg, Alban Berg, Leopold Stokowski, Egon Wellesz, and Willi Reich, among others. Berg's death mask from the collection is on display in the foyer of Pollack Hall.

71 Jan Simons, interview, 2 December 2002. Simons admired not only Newmark's musicianship but also his sense of humour, which rivalled his own. On one occasion when Newmark sensed that Simons was nervous before a concert he started to pour Simons a glass of water, knowing that the glasses were upside down. The water went all over the place and both musicians had a good laugh.

72 "Bernard Diamant," EMC 364a–b.

73 Maheu, *Piano sur la mer*, 195.

74 Armas Maiste, personal communication, 3 December 2002 and 24 February 2003; see also "Armas Maiste," EMC 795b–c.

75 A recital in the fall of 2002 at Remenyi Piano House included Bartók's Piano Sonata (1926), Prokofiev's Piano Sonata no. 3, Brahms's *Fantasien*, op. 116, and works by Debussy and Scriabin.

76 "Géza de Kresz," EMC 353a–b. The political situation in Hungary, which by 1947 had become precarious with Moscow-style show trials, may well have prompted his decision to return to Toronto in 1947 after an absence of twelve years.

77 Reginald Godden and Austin Clarkson, *Reginald Godden Plays,* 37.

78 The Classical Quartet players were Garami, first violin; Adolfo Bornstein and later Luis Grinhauz, second violin; Robert Verebes, viola; William Valleau, and later Ifan Williams, cello; the quartet disbanded in 1976.

79 Shirley Garami, interview, 26 November 2001; Charles Reiner, interview, 26 November 2001.

80 Now the Royal Hamilton College of Music (EMC 1157a–b). Godden was principal from 1948 to 1953.

81 *Bakers* 3: 1827.

82 John Rockwell, "ONCE," *New Grove* 2, 18: 408.

83 Udo Kasemets, interview, 6 March 2001.

84 Udo Kasemets, interview, 6 March 2001.

85 Transportation was organized by the International Refugee Organization, and by 15 July, immigration permission had been received "under the

provisions of a special arrangement dealing specifically with displaced persons"; Acadia University Archives, Jānis Kalejs and Felicita Kalejs sous-fonds: 1999–001/1/3/4. There are three letters in the file regarding this appointment: 31 May, 16 June, and 15 July 1949. Permission for Mr and Mrs Jānis Maizite (the parents of Felicita) to immigrate to Canada was also given at this time. The University undertook the arrangements.

86 *Acadia Bulletin,* vol. 36 (March 1950): 23, Acadia University Archives.
87 *Acadia Bulletin,* vol. 37 (May 1951): 20, Acadia University Archives.
88 *Acadia Bulletin,* vol. 47 (Jan 1961): 8–9, Acadia University Archives.
89 Letter of 6 December 1954, Acadia University Archives, 1/3/1.
90 Gordon E. Smith, "The Kingston Years" in Elliott and Smith, *Istvan Anhalt,* 69–73.
91 Dawn L. Keer, "Helmut Kallmann," 15.
92 Helmut Kallmann, interview, 28 February 2001.
93 Helmut Kallmann, "Canadian Music as a Field for Research"; Helmut Kallmann, ed., *Catalogue of Canadian Composers.*
94 Helmut Kallmann, "Mapping Canada's Music."
95 Kallmann, "Mapping Canada's Music," 24.
96 Kallmann, "Mapping Canada's Music," 31.
97 See John Mappin and John Archer, *Bernard Amtmann, 1907–1979,* 20.
98 Willy Amtmann, *Music in Canada 1600–1800* and *La musique au Quebec, 1600–1875.* The French edition is 100 pages longer, with a section on music in nineteenth-century Quebec and extensive illustrations.

CHAPTER SEVEN

1 This chapter is devoted mainly to those émigrés for whom we have personal accounts from interviews or archival sources; further information can be found in the bio-bibliographies in appendix A.
2 See passing references to Trudi Le Caine in EMC (62b, 736b, 991b, 992a, 1382c). See also interview with Ezra Schabas, 12 February 2001, LAC, vertical file "Trudi le Caine." Additional details about her career are from Hattie Klotz, "Ottawa's 'mother of the arts,' dies," *Ottawa Citizen,* 7 September 1999, C1; Janice Kennedy, *Ottawa Citizen,* 15 Mar 1997: F1; Jerry Gray, text of audiotape accompanying the exhibition "Rare Spirits: A Personal Tribute to Vintage Elders," Ottawa Art Gallery, 7 December 2000 to 4 February 2001, in LAC, vertical file, "Trudi Le Caine."
3 LAC RG 26, vol. 87: P.C. 676, 20 February 1940, no. 26: "citizen of Czechoslovakia, aged 27 years, presently residing at Chateau de

Beaudeans, Htes. Pry., France, coming forward to reside with mother and stepfather."

4 Helmut Kallmann, interview, 28 February 2001.

5 Joseph Berljawsky, "Violin technique, Its Evolution and Pedagogy: A Historical and Comparative Study," PhD diss, Université de Montreal, 1964.

6 These letters are held in LAC, Joseph Berljawsky fonds (MUS 171).

7 Roanne Levitt, interview, 20 January 2004.

8 Istvan Anhalt, interview, 31 October 2000.

9 Hansi Lamberger, interview, 4 December 2000.

10 "Artist's alter-egos create music, poetry, paintings," *The Canadian Jewish News*, 15 February 1996, 7, in Canadian Jewish Congress National Archives and Reference Centre, "Gutman, Adam."

11 The recording *Au Coin du Feu* ([1955?] Aladin Records, ALA-701) contains: *Golden Earrings*; *Jalousie*, *Hello, le soleil brille*, *Rose Marie Polka*, *Ma prière*, *Beer Barrel Polka*, *Danube bleu*, *Les feuilles mortes*, *Le canarie* [sic], and *Mon coeur est un violin.*

12 LAC, John Newmark fonds (MUS 175), vol. 3, file no. 93.

13 Ibid.

14 In San Francisco, between the rehearsal and the performance, concertmaster Naoum Blinder (who had also taught Isaac Stern) advised him, "Don't ever play softly. Play as loudly as you can at all times." Kander returned to San Francisco during several summers to study with Blinder.

15 Walter Homburger, interview, 27 May 2002.

16 Walter Homburger, interview, 27 May 2002. The US Pianist Byron Janis made a successful tour of the USSR in 1960, three years after Gould.

17 Walter Homburger, interview, 28 April 2002.

18 Colin Sabiston wrote, "Of Mme. Lehmann it can only be said that she has the power and the glory, as well as the details of sensitive musicianship, which makes of her singing a great art. In its near-approach to perfection it just about fills the prescription for 'absolute song' (*Globe and Mail,* 23 January 1947, 10). The concerts were held on Wednesday 15 January, Wednesday 22 January, and Monday 27 January 1947; Lehmann performed the same programs in New York on the previous Sundays. The first recital included songs by Schubert and Beethoven's *An die ferne Geliebte;* the second, Schumann's *Dichterliebe,* and two groups of four songs by Brahms; the third, songs by Hugo Wolf and Richard Strauss.

19 Horowitz played Beethoven's *Moonlight Sonata* and works by Scarlatti, Liszt, and Rachmaninoff.

20 LAC, Walter Homburger fonds (MUS 259,) vol. 16 contains the International Artists series programs and correspondence 1946–82 (1946–47 and 1967–68 missing).
21 Walter Homburger, interview, 27 May 2002.
22 Arnold Edinborough, "Majestic orchestral send-off for Homburger," *Financial Post*, 23 February 1987: 39. See also William Littler, "Musical notes from Symphony boss," *Toronto Daily Star*, 21 February 1987: J1; Richard Warren, *It Begins with the Oboe*, 168–9.
23 Hans Kaufman, interview, 8 March 2001. A photograph shows the girls enrobed in tulle and holding golden violins. Kaufman explained that the bows were soaped so that the girls could move them in time to the music without producing a sound. He remembered playing *Intermezzo*, Jack Benny's favourite number. Upon his release from the internment camp, Kaufman dropped the second 'n' from his name.
24 Hans Kaufman, interview, 8 March 2001.
25 The plot of the film, concerning the building of the Canadian Pacific Railway, is historically inaccurate. It was made in 1949 and stars Randolph Scott, Jane Wyatt, and Nancy Olson. Kaufman recalled, "We were shooting out of the train compartment windows at the Indians running around."
26 This performance was broadcast on CBC *Sunday Morning Recital*, 7 August 1949.
27 Hugo Burghauser, "Philharmonic Adventures with Bassoon," *Journal of the Double Reed Society* 1 (November 1973), available at http://www.idrs.org/Publications/Journal; Daniel N. Leeson, "A Righteous Person," *Double Reed* 22, no. 4 (1999), available at http://www.idrs.org/Publications/DR/dr22.4.
28 A vulgarly anti-Semitic "handbook" listing Jewish musicians.
29 Burghauser's order-in-council was approved in February 1939.
30 Burghauser, "Philharmonic Adventures."
31 Since Burghauser had come to Canada under an order-in-council, and was therefore a landed immigrant, he was in no danger of internment. His decision to move to the United States was likely made for professional reasons.
32 "Freddy or Freddie Grant," *EMC* 551a–b.
33 LAC, vertical file "Grant." An American version, "They Call it America" became popular in the United States.
34 "Eli Kassner," *EMC* 676b–c.
35 *Guitar Canada* (Spring 1989), quoted in "Eli Kassner," *EMC* 676c.
36 *Toronto Daily Star*, 31 August 1971, 50.

37 Harvey Olnick, interview, 21 May 2000.
38 William Littler, *Toronto Daily Star*, 31 March 1979, D3.
39 Robert Dale Macintosh (*A Documentary History of Music in Victoria,* 2: 382) notes that Gruber studied conducting with Wildemuth in Lausanne before coming to Toronto. A reference to Gruber in the EMC article on the Victoria Symphony notes that between 1943 and 1947 Gruber took summer courses with Fritz Mahler, Leonard Bernstein, and Pierre Monteux ("Victoria Symphony," EMC 1370c; other references to Gruber in EMC are found on pp. 59a, 1129b, and 1347a).
40 Hans Gruber, interview, 9 March 2001.
41 Michael Kater, *The Twisted Muse,* 86.
42 MGG 13: 1887–8; Albrecht Gaub, "Nördlich der Unbegrenzten Möglichkeiten: Von den Nationalsozialisten vertriebene Musiker im kanadischen Exil," 3. A number of Vogel's compositions are contained in the Unger fonds, LAC MUS 56.
43 Heinz Unger, *Hammer, Sickle, and Baton*, 18.
44 Helmut Kallmann, interview, 28 February 2001.
45 This is my observation from working with Unger at close quarters for a performance of Mozart's Piano Concerto in D minor, K 466, in 1963.
46 "Heinz Unger," EMC 1328–9.
47 LAC, vertical file "Susskind."
48 At his death Toronto critics were somewhat tight-lipped with their praises; William Littler described him as a "rare gentleman" (*Toronto Daily Star*, 28 Mar 1980, D2); John Kraglund grudgingly acknowledged him as "an outstanding musician" (*Globe and Mail*, 27 March 1980, 16).
49 "Toronto Symphony," EMC 1302c–1303a.
50 "Alfred Strombergs," EMC 1260b.
51 "Toronto Jewish Folk Choir," EMC 1297c–8a; LAC RG 26, vol. 86: P.C. 1588, 23 June 1939, no. 14.
52 Wolters-Fredlund, Benita. "Music, Culture, Ethnicity and Nationalism: The Toronto Jewish Folk Choir and Conceptions of Canadian Multiculturalism."
53 LAC, Toronto Jewish Folk Choir fonds (MUS 43), vol. 2, concert program, "Our Life, Our Art," 25 March 1947, quoted in Wolters-Fredlund, "Music, Culture, Ethnicity and Nationalism."
54 Gordana Lazarevich, *The Musical World of Frances James and Murray Adaskin,* 120: "Not yet full-time, Newmark would spend hours in the library copying out music for her, and the two of them would rehearse five hours at a stretch, indulging in the pleasures of making music and

learning new repertoire." The concerts took place in April–May 1944; the EMC article on Newmark (EMC 943a) states that James engaged him for the tour in 1943.

55 Renée Maheu, *Piano sur la mer*, 153; Newmark's memoirs point to a definitive moment when he encountered a pianist who had no idea of the meaning of *andante* or even the language the term was from (252).

56 Maheu, *Piano sur la mer*, "Témoignages Rose Goldblatt" (unpaginated).

57 I was witness to a rare outburst. The occasion was a concert at Leaside High School Auditorium during the 1957–58 season in which Maureen Forrester and John Newmark played the first half and I played the second. Coming offstage after a performance of Schumann's *Frauenliebe und -leben*, furious at the poor reception from the audience, Newmark threw his music on the floor muttering something like "They just don't get it."

58 Maheu, *Piano sur la mer*, 183–6.

59 Maheu, *Piano sur la mer*, 220.

60 Blaine Allan, CBC Television Series, 1952 to 1982, http://www.film.queensu.ca/CBC/A.html (accessed April 2009).

61 Otto Joachim, interview, 11 March 2003.

62 Maheu, *Piano sur la mer*, "Témoignages."

63 "Citizenship and Refugee Status" – "Extension of temporary stay in Canada authorized, 3 Aug 1950," LAC, Otto Joachim fonds (MUS 270), series A, 3.

64 "Hyman was flamboyant but capable; Mildred was a local girl, she fitted in; my brother could play, he had a good foundation." Otto Joachim, interview, 11 March 2003.

65 Recordings of the Montreal Consort of Ancient Instruments, distributed by Vox and Turnabout, include music of Guillaume Dufay (with the Bach choir), music of the Spanish Renaissance, music from the time of Henry VIII, and an anthology of music from Charlemagne to Elizabeth I. The consort instruments and two of Otto's paintings (large abstract works reminiscent of Soulages) are now held at the Museum of Civilization in Gatineau, Quebec.

66 Radio Canada International, *Anthology of Canadian Music* 14, Otto Joachim, vol. 5.

67 Otto Joachim, interview, 11 March 2003.

68 Walter Joachim, interview by Rachel Anderson, 26 April 2000.

69 "Walter Joachim," EMC 657c–8a.

70 Walter Joachim, personal communication, 16 September 2000.

71 Arthur Kaptainis, "Walter Joachim was MSO cellist," *The Gazette,* 22 December 2001, D11.
72 "Eugène Husaruk," *EMC* 618a.
73 "The Montreal Festivals / Les Festivals de Montréal," *EMC* 875a–c.
74 "Baroque Trio of Montreal," *EMC* 90b–c.
75 See "Orff-Schulwerk," *EMC* 991c–2b; and "Marcelle Corneille," *EMC* 318b.
76 See "François Magnan," *EMC* 794a; "Quebec Symphony Orchestra, *EMC* 1096c–8a, especially 1097c.
77 Duschenes's published compositions and arrangements are listed in the Berandol Rental Catalogue, 1–6.
78 Mario Duschenes, interview, 27 January 2003.
79 The Little Symphony of Montreal was formed in 1942 and survived for ten years; "Little Symphony of Montreal," *EMC* 767a.
80 See references in *EMC* (307a, 872c, and 880b).
81 "Jean Belland," *EMC* 107c–8a.
82 The Helmut Blume fonds at LAC (MUS 302) consists of radio scripts and reports. Materials relating to *CBC* Wednesday Night include: "The Trial of Modern Music," "Music and the Church," Joseph Haydn" Life and Work," Berlioz: Portrait of a Romantic," Gustav Mahler," "A Passion for Freedom (Friedrich Schiller)," "The Devil's General," a dramatic adaptation of Zuckmayer's play. Materials relating to CBC Radio include: "The Story of Music," "Opera Stars and Stories," "History of Music Instruments," "Music and the Dance," "European Music festivals," Radio International," "International Concert," "Footloose in Europe," "The Musical Mind." Materials relating to television include "Music to See," "The Magic of Music," "The Tower of Babel" (drama). Materials relating to Blume's activities at McGill are held at the McGill University Archives, RG 39: Music.
83 Eric Koch, interview, 8 March 2001.
84 See "Herbert Ruff," *EMC* 1160b–c. The Herbert Ruff fonds (MUS 241) at LAC contains compositions, recordings from radio programs, printed programs from the 1950s and 1960s and a recording of his sonata for violin and piano with violinist Eugene Kash.
85 MGG I 16: 634; *Baker's* 3: 1515; *New Grove* 2 11: 330; Hans Heinsheimer was second cousin once removed to Walter Homburger.
86 Frances Wainwright, personal communication, 9 April 2004: music consultant to provincial and national cultural organizations; artistic coordinator of Debut BC Series for Young Performers; artistic director of Coast Recital Society.

87 George Fiala, interview, 10 June 2007.

88 On one occasion Fogl worked on Arthur LeBlanc's Stradivarius (now owned by Angèle Dubeau); see "Arthur LeBlanc," EMC 735b.

89 Aloys Fogl, interview, 30 September 2003.

90 "Ruzena Herlinger," EMC 599a–b.

91 Jacob Siskind, "A Lady from Another World," *The Gazette,* 17 May 1969, 29: "Have you ever had a student you could teach ["Der Wein"] to?" "I tried, maybe Huguette [Tourangeau]."

92 Mario Duschenes, interview, 27 Jan 2003.

93 Mario Duschenes, interview, 27 Jan 2003.

94 The Vega (or Bach) bow, has a high arch. "Promoted in the 1950s by Emil Telmányi and Albert Schweitzer to address the misconception that Bach's polyphonic violin music should be sustained precisely as written, it enabled all four strings to be sounded individually or in combination, its hair tension being controlled by a mechanical lever operated by the thumb. It had no precedent in the Baroque and made little impression." See "Violin 1, 5(i)(b) – (d) The Bow," *New Grove* 2 26: 725. Joachim commented that this bow made the polyphony more difficult to play "because you only have four fingers to work with. It's successful if you use the right intonation."

95 Alan Andrews (son-in-law of Walter Kaufmann) commented that Dr Laufer was his father-in-law's "closest friend in Halifax" (personal communication, 7 December 2003).

96 Rolf Duschenes, interview, 28 January 2003.

97 New Brunswick Archives, MC2037: MS5: 11/4/48; trans. Valda Kemp, 2 July 2001.

98 *Montreal Standard*, 20 March 1948, 3.

99 New Brunswick Archives, MC 2037: MS2–12. The New Brunswick Archives holds correspondence from the period when Kalniņš was in displaced persons camps in Germany (1944–48). I am indebted to Janet Toole for putting this material at my disposal and for arranging interviews with three church members who were close to Kalniņš: Rev. Gill MacKenzie, Sadie Turner-Miller, and Helen Craig.

100 Connie Shanks, *Daily Gleaner,* 20 April 1990, 3rd section.

101 Gill MacKenzie, interview, 22 May 2001.

102 Helmut Kallmann, interview, 28 February 2001.

103 William Littler, "Latvian artists rally round the flag," *Toronto Daily Star,* 7 July 1986, D3.

104 The New Brunswick Archives holds a five-page typewritten biography with an appended list of works list compiled by Arvis Landva, a friend of Kalniņš (MC 2037: MS2–12).

105 "Haralds Berino," EMC 112.
106 Betty Barban, interview, 7 May 2001.
107 "Andreas Barban," EMC 87a.
108 Maureen Volk, personal communication, "Musical Intersections Conference," Toronto, November 2000.
109 Files of the Alumni Association of the Maritime Conservatory for the Performing Arts.
110 Nova Scotia Archives, MG20, 193, no. 1.
111 Anonymous personal communication, 3 December 2003.
112 Curriculum vitae, LAC, vertical file "Kaufmann, Walter"; personal communication from Albrecht Gaub.
113 Adrian Hoffmann, "Artists Find Refuge in WWII Halifax," CBC Radio Two, 13 November 2001.
114 The Ottawa Philharmonic Orchestra was suspended in 1960 when the board could not meet the musicians' salary payments; plans for reorganization were abandoned because of the formation of a resident orchestra at the National Arts Centre; see "Ottawa Philharmonic Orchestra," EMC 1006b.
115 Albrecht Gaub interviewed Thomas Mayer in Vienna shortly before Mayer's death in 2002 at age 95.
116 Albrecht Gaub, "From Swastika to Maple Leaf," 11 and following.
117 J. Stirling Dorrance, "The Halifax Symphony," *Atlantic Advocate* 51, no. 5 (January 1961): 25–32, quoted in Phyllis R. Blakeley, "Halifax Symphony Orchestra," 4, typescript, 1967, Nova Scotia Archives, MG 20, vol. 188. It is not known whether this report was published.
118 *Halifax Mail-Star,* 26 October 1965, 33, as quoted in Blakeley, "Halifax Symphony Orchestra," 4.
119 "Halifax Symphony Orchestra," Nova Scotia Archives MG20 vol. 641: "Mr Mueller who has long advocated enlarging the symphony expressed disappointment over the situation ... Mueller wanted cooperation between the symphony and the theatre, possibly in the production of a small opera" (Donna Logan, "Symphony Faces Money Problems" [Halifax] *Mail Star*, 28 September 1963); "Some Musicians' Attitudes seen Symphony Threat ... The unfortunate attitude of certain locally resident musicians ... until this attitude changes, or is changed, the security of the HSO will be at stake" ([Halifax] *Mail Star,* 5 June 1963).
120 Helen Golding, *Atlantic Advocate* 54, no. 5 (January 1964): 44.
121 Albrecht Gaub visited Leo Müller and his wife, Tomiko, in Vienna in September 2000. Surprisingly, in his interview with Walter Pass Müller did not mention the Halifax engagement although he spoke of his years in the United States at great length: Walter Pass, *Orpheus im Exil,* 102–7, interview, 16 November 1992, Vienna.

122 Tinter led the National Youth Orchestra of Canada in 1971, 1974, 1975, 1977, 1979, 1982, and 1986; see "NYOC" *EMC* 922b and "Georg Tintner," *EMC* 1291a–b.

123 One report describes Tintner as "quite frankly a far better conductor than Halifax could ever normally hope to attract ... Symphony Nova Scotia, which was launched in 1983 after the debt-ridden Atlantic Symphony went into bankruptcy, has enjoyed a dramatic improvement in its fortunes since Tintner took over from Boris Brott in 1987. Concert attendance has nearly doubled ... At the same time, audiences and orchestra members agree that the orchestra had never sounded better" (*Maclean's*, 22 April 1991, 59).

124 Richard Osborne, "Bruckner Meister," *Gramophone*, January 1999, 12; the cover of this issue has a picture of Tintner.

125 Arthur Kaptainis, "Requiem for a heavyweight: Unconventional maestro was among foremost interpreters of Bruckner." *The Gazette,* 16 October 1999, E10.

126 Eric Koch, *Deemed Suspect,* 269.

127 Rudolf Lowenstein, interview, 29 November 2003.

128 "Walter Kaufmann." *EMC* 677a–b.

129 Frank Morriss, "Winnipeg's New Conductor means New Music Era," *Saturday Night,* 11 December 1948. The *CBC News,* 13 February 1949, proclaimed a "new era in the city's musical history ... triumphant ... vastly enthusiastic."

130 I am indebted to Albrecht Gaub for this information.

131 Bruno Nettl reveals his own and his father's émigré experiences in the United States in "Displaced Musics and Immigrant Musicologists, Ethnomusicological and Biographical Perspectives," in *Driven into Paradise*, ed. Reinhold Brinkmann and Christoph Wolff, 54–65.

132 See references to Kviesis in *EMC* (952b, 1181b, 1182a).

133 An account of Eckhardt-Gramatté's confrontation with Nazi bureaucracy is given in appendix D.

134 I am indebted to Paula Kelly for this information.

135 See Lorne Watson's interview with Sonia Eckhardt-Gramatté, Radio Canada International, *Anthology of Canadian Music* 21.

136 Imant Raminsh, interview, 9 January 2003.

137 Terry French, *Province,* 25 November 1966.

138 "Burton Kurth," *EMC* 701b.

139 Immigration identification card, Simon Fraser University Archives, F28: 1-1-4; P.C. 3246, no. 533, 21 October 1939, no. 6; SFU, F28–203. For details on materials relating to Ida Halpern held by the Simon Fraser Uni-

versity Archives, see http://www.sfu.ca/archives2/F-58/F-58.html (accessed June 2009).

140 This description of Halpern's collecting and analysis of West Coast First People's music is taken from an anonymous account given in SFU, F28–203, pp. 3–20; the author may have been Douglas Cole, a professor at Simon Fraser University who died in 1997.

141 "Biographical Information," SFU, F28:2–1–0–3.

142 Halpern's recordings are housed in British Columbia Archives, MS–2768. Most of this material has never been transcribed or discussed in the scholarly literature. The collection comprises musico-anthropological materials from the Kwakwaka'wakw (Kwakiutl), Nuuchahnulth (Nootka), Haida, Nuxalk (Bella Coola), and the Coast Salish. The terminology for these First Nations peoples is from Kenneth Chen, "Ida Halpern: A Post-Colonial Portrait of a Canadian Pioneer Ethnomusicologist," *Canadian University Music Review* 16, no. 1 (1995): 44.

143 Halpern also pioneered the electronic analysis of this music through collaboration with the University of Vienna and the University of Washington; see "Sound recordings," Introduction, 2, British Columbia Archives MS–2768: Donation A.

144 For example, Bruno Nettl, Edward Curtis, Franz Boas, and George Hunt on Kwakiutl songs; Edward Sapir and Philip Drucker on Nootka songs.

145 Halpern used a medieval modal notation for stressed and unstressed beats – iambus, dactyl, trochee, and anapest – in which singing never began at the same time as the accompanying beat. Pitch concepts were based on a fundamental note with microtonal shadings, the third playing a prominent role. By 1981 she had isolated twenty-nine "style characteristics" and had analysed same-genre songs sung by several generations of singers. Her concepts of form were determined by variety, unity, and lawful complexity. The songs thus revealed a full awareness of compositional principles and techniques refined over generations and restated with creativity and regularity by generations of song makers.

146 Kenneth Chen, "Halpern," 41–59.

147 "Friends of Chamber Music 1940– Programs," Simon Fraser University Archives, BI vol. 6. Correspondence and programs for all concerts up to 1987 are in vols. 7 and 8; vol. 23, files 1 and 2 contain newspaper clippings from 1939–86. For an excellent summary of the work of the society, see Rachel Giese, *Friends of Chamber Music,* particularly 5, 7, and 19.

148 "Koerner Foundation," *EMC* 691a; for a short history of the Koerner family see the link for "founders" on the Leon and Thea Koerner Foundation website (www.koernerfoundation.ca; accessed June 2009).

149 In 1949 Iby [Mrs Otto] Koerner helped to found the Vancouver International Festival in 1949 and was also one of the sponsors for "The Look of Music," an international instrumental exhibition (1980–81) in Vancouver that included extensive loans from European instrument collections; see Philip Young, *The Look of Music: Rare Musical Instruments* (Vancouver: Vancouver Museums and Planetarium Association, 1980) and "Exhibitions," EMC 432c. Other Koerner family donations include the Koerner Recital Hall in the Vancouver Academy of Music, Vanier Park.

150 Peter Bentley, interview, 26 January 2005.

151 Edwina Heller, interview, 29 May 2001; Bentley sponsored Cecilia Bartoli's first concert for the Recital Society, and brought her back to Vancouver on two other occasions. He also sponsored a Vancouver recital of Kiri Te Kanawa.

152 Veronica Platts, personal communication, 16 August 2002; see also http://ring.uvic.ca/96jun05/Hon-degrees.html (accessed June 2009).

153 See Gwenlyn Setterfield, *Niki Goldschmidt*, 86–9, 102–4.

154 Hans Gruber, interview, 9 March 2001.

155 Macintosh, *Documentary History of Music in Victoria* 2: 382.

156 Hans Gruber, interview, 9 March 2001.

157 Gruber always had the highest regard for Morawetz, who had been one of his teachers in Toronto. In his interview Gruber claimed that he had premiered the work with the Victoria Symphony, but according to EMC (884c) that credit goes to the Winnipeg Symphony. Perhaps a study of the correspondence between Gruber and Morawetz (LAC, MUS 76, vol. 1, letters 100–16, 1954–85) will shed light on the topic.

158 Macintosh (*Documentary History of Music in Victoria* 2: 382) notes that "after 1963 Gruber appears to have disappeared from the musical world."

159 "The 1985 International Bach Competition," EMC 949c. Setterfield (*Niki Goldschmidt*, 163–6) puts the figure at $148,000.

160 "Guelph Spring Festival," EMC 558b–59a; see also Setterfield, *Niki Goldschmidt*, 127–45.

161 "International Bach Competition," EMC 949c; see also Setterfield, *Niki Goldschmidt*, 167–70.

162 Nicholas Goldschmidt, interview, 1–2 November 2000.

EPILOGUE

1 Istvan Anhalt, interview, 31 October 2000.

2 Helmut Kallmann, "Mapping Canada's Music," 31.

3 Udo Kasemets, interview, 6 March 2001.
4 See http://www.cursa-ur.com/cv/profdiamant.htm (accessed June 2009).
5 The exhibition was coordinated by Jeannine Barriault of the Music Division, Library and Archives Canada. Joachim's new composition was *Petite oeuvre*, scored for flute, viola, and cello.
6 *Weltreise Wider Willen, Der Komponist Otto Joachim,* WDR 2001, by Gabriele Faust; the documentary was broadcast in Germany on the West German Rundfunk 27 January 2001; the concert took place in Düsseldorf on 28 January.
7 Otto Joachim, interview, 11 March 2003.
8 Walter Homburger, interview, 27 March 2002. More recently Homburger met a woman in Berkeley, California who had lived across the street from his family in Karlsruhe. She was twelve at the time, and he hadn't seen her since. "Then I remembered she had brothers; one is dead, one is still alive. Amazing."
9 Gerhard Kander, interview, 7 March 2001.
10 Gertrude Leupold, interview, 5 October 2002.
11 Jan Simons, interview, 2 December 2002.
12 Peter Bentley, interview, 26 January 2005.
13 Hans Kaufman, interview, 8 March 2001.
14 Harvey Sachs, "She Shall Have Music," 27, 60.
15 Alfreds Strombergs, interview, 28 November 2003.
16 Imant Ramnish, interview, 9 Jan 2003.
17 Connie Shanks, *The Daily Gleaner,* 20 April 1990, 3rd section.
18 The repatriation of Kalniņš's remains came about through the efforts of Paul Horncastle, a close friend. The reinternment ceremonies in Riga on 26 July 2001 consisted of a funeral service in the cathedral and a premiere of Kalniņš's *Requiem* sung by one of Latvia's leading choirs. Some of these details come from a letter of 13 July 2001 from Jānis Lusis, the Latvian ambassador to Canada, to Mark Leonard, which Mark Leonard kindly shared with me.
19 This tour was sponsored by the Department of External Affairs.
20 Istvan Anhalt, interview, 31 October 2000.
21 The following émigré musicians have received the Order of Canada: Istvan Anhalt, OC, 2003; Peter Bentley, OC 1983; Lotte Brott, CM, 1990; Rolf Duschenes, CM, 1987: Mario Duschenes, CM, 1985 Hermann Geiger-Torel, OC, 1969; Nicholas Goldschmidt, OC, 1978, CC, 1989; Ida Halpern, CM 1978; Walter Homburger, CM, 1984; Walter Joachim, CM, 1992; Helmut Kallmann, CM, 1986; Iby Koerner, CM 1971; Franz Kraemer, CM, 1981, OC, 1987; Anton Kuerti, OC, 1998; Trudi Le Caine,

CM, 1991; Oskar Morawetz, CM, 1988; John Newmark, OC, 1973; John Prentice, OC, 1977; Jan Rubes, CM, 1996; Georg Tintner, CM, 1998; Arnold Walter, OC, 1972.

APPENDICES

The Eckhardt-Gramatté Foundation in Winnipeg is the major repository for materials relating to Sophie-Carmen Eckardt Gramatté; the collection has been catalogued until recently by Paul von Wichert. This brief account of the composer's career in Europe is based on a number of sources including the lengthy article in EMC (399a–400c) and material held by LAC (MUS 33), Ferdinand Eckhardt's "Das Leben der Komponisten S.C. Eckhardt-Gramatté" (Winnipeg, 1977), a 500-page unpublished typescript, is a well-documented study of the composer's European period. Other sources include Ferdinand Eckhardt, *Music from Within: A Biography of the Composer SC Eckhardt-Gramatté*, ed. Gerald Bower; Walter Kreysig, *A History of Austrian Migration,* 202; Glen B. Carruthers, "The career and compositions of S.C. Eckhardt-Gramatté," MA thesis, Carleton University, 1981; Peter Hollfelder, *Geschichte der Klaviermusik*, 1123–24; an interview and documentation by Lorne Watson in the *Anthology of Canadian Music*, 21; and the entry on Eckhardt-Gramatté in *Contemporary Canadian Composers*, 62–3. The feature-length documentary *Appassionata: The Extraordinary Life and Music of Sonia Eckhardt-Gramatté*, written by Paula Kelly, includes this part of Eckhardt-Gramatté's career. There are also articles on the composer in a number of music reference works including *Baker's* 2: 983; *New Grove* 2 7: 867–8; MGG2 6: 66–73; and Peter Hollfelder's *Geschichte der Klaviermusik*, 1123–4.

1 Sophie-Carmen (Sonia) Eckhardt-Gramatté changed her professional name a number of times throughout her life. Until around 1920 she was known professionally as Sonia Fridman. She married Walter Gramatté in December 1920, and from 1922 until 1929 she used Sonia Fridman-Gramatté; after her husband's death she changed this to Sonia Gramatté. In 1934 she married Ferdinand Eckhardt. In 1939, when the couple moved to Vienna, she adopted the professional name S.C. Eckhardt-Gramatté. She is referred to through these paragraphs as Sophie-Carmen.

2 See photographs of both artists with Eckhardt-Gramatté in *Eckhardt-Gramatté Gedenkschrift für das Familiengrab in Berlin-Wilhelmshagen,* 62.

3 MGG 13: 624–6; Michael Kater, *Composers in the Third Reich*, 26, 152.

4 Her Symphony in C major was premiered on 2 and 3 March 1942 in Breslau, during a prestigious concert series that featured, among others, Carl Schuricht, Friedrich Wührer, Wilhelm Backhaus, and Walter Gieseking. Around this time, her string quartets were performed by members of the Silesian Symphony Orchestra.

5 Copies of Sophie-Carmen Eckhardt-Gramatté's correspondence with the RMK is held by the Eckhardt-Gramatté Foundation (EGA) in Winnipeg: letters from the RMK are original; Eckhardt-Gramatté's replies are either handwritten diplomatic copies or carbon copies. The translations are mine.

6 "Wie daraus aber einwandfrei hervorgeht ist mein Vater vom erblichem Adel und mein Grossvater mütterlicherseits Oberstleutnant (später General) gewesen. Sowohl für den erblichen Adel, wie die höhere Offizierslaufbahn war aber im alten Russland nichtjüdische Abkunft die Voraussetzung"; letter of 15 March 1937 to the RMK, EGA. There has been some discussion about Eckhardt-Gramatté's birth date and the identity of her father. The article in *EMC* states that "Fridman was definitely not the father" (*EMC* 399a). If she was born in 1899 (the year given in *EMC*) she would have been nine years old when she entered the Paris Conservatoire; if the correct birth date is 1902 she would have been the even more precocious age of six. For purposes of her acceptance into the RMK and the subsequent permission to continue her career as a composer in the Third Reich, the documents that she was able to provide convinced the authorities that she was born in 1902 and that she was the daughter of Nicolas Fridman, who was a member of the hereditary Russian nobility with Georgian-Caucasian blood, and hence of Aryan descent.

7 The copy of this application at EGA is undated; since she mentions a performance of her *Passacaglia and Fugue* at the Prussian Academy of Arts and Sciences in 1937, it was likely drafted in 1938.

8 According to her brother, their father was born in 1855 and died in 1918 in Moscow (overcome by the fact that Russia had fallen into the hands of the *jüdisch-kommunistischem Bande* ("Jewish-Communist alliance"). She learned of her father's death by a telegram sent a year later from Princess Troubetzkoy, who was employed at the old Russian embassy in Paris. Sophie-Carmen's paternal grandfather was named Charles; his wife was Emma Lapré. Her family was originally French and had immigrated to Russia with the Huguenots at the time of the revocation of the Edict of Nantes in 1685, and had intermarried with Caucasians. From the Lapré side they had Georgian blood. Emma Lapré died in Moscow around 1912; her grandfather Charles died in St Petersburg, probably some time before his grand-daughter's birth in 1889.

9 In her letter of 12 January 1939 to Prof. Hans Joachim Moser, she asserts that she is now a member of the RMK.

10 Hans Brückner's *Judentum und Musik*; for a full description of the conversation with Moser, see Ferdinand Eckhardt, "Das Leben," 353–4.

11 Eckhardt states that "the tragedy of Sonia's mention in the *Juden-ABC* was that all radio stations, concert agencies, music publishers etc. felt that they had to respect the source. We later found out that many of our friends knew about it but no one had the courage to tell us so that we could have done something about it" (Ferdinand Eckhardt, "Das Leben," 353–4).

12 His retraction reads: "Die Komponistin, Geigerin und Pianistin Sophie-Carmen Eckhardt-Gramatté geborene von Fridman-Kochevskaia in Moskau 1902, die fälschlicherweise in den ersten drei [sic] Auflagen vom 'Judentum und Musik' unter dem Namen Sonja Gramatté, geb. Fridmann 1892 zu Moskau als nichtarisch bezeichnet wurde, legt Wert darauf festzustellen, dass sie Vollarierin ist." [The composer, violinist and pianist Sophie-Carmen Eckhardt-Gramatté, born von Fridman-Kochevskaia in Moscow 1902, who incorrectly was cited in the first three edition of "Judaism and Music" under the name Sonja Gramatté, née Fridmann 1892 in Moscow as non-Aryan, wishes to assert that she is full Aryan.]

13 Stengel edited three editions of an even more odious sequel to Brückner's efforts, the *Lexikon der Juden in der Musik* (Berlin, 1940). Eva Weissweiler (*Ausgemertzt! Das Lexikon der Juden in der Musik und seine mörderischen Folgen*) compares Stengel's books with lists of those sent to the death camps and describes his black list as "an open invitation to extermination."

14 "So dass ich im guten Glauben den Eintrag in die nächste Auflage [übernahm.] Der Eintrag ist jedoch derart ungenau, dass ich, obwohl ich Sie und Ihr Wirken kenne, gar nicht auf den Gedanken kam, dass Sie gemeint sein könnten."

15 *Das Deutsche Podium: Fachblatt für Unterhaltungs-Musik und Musik-Gaststätten. Kampfblatt für deutsche Musik* 7, no. 5 (1939). Hugo Burghauser's name was also removed, but by this time he was safely in Toronto; other names, interestingly include Sergei Prokofieff! The letterhead for Brückner's publishing house included such slogans as "Überwinde den Musikjuden! Er nagt an der Seele der Menschen und entartet sie" ["Defeat the Jewish musician, he gnaws on the soul of mankind and makes it degenerate]. He was oblivious, it seems, to the fact that such sentiments had already cost Germany – and was to cost Austria and Czechoslovakia – its finest musicians.

16 "Gestern war ich im Bachsaal, hoerte ich mir Choere Zeitgenoessischen Musicker Gau Musick. "Du, mein ewiges Memeland" [sic] etc. Das ist was die Leute haben wollen. Substanzloses Zeug, Zeugnis von gutem politischen Willen, hat aber mit Musick an sich weniger zu tun" (*Das Leben,* 358).

17 "Gerade in einem mit so großer Tradition erfüllten Lande wie Österreich wird die Erreichung solcher Ziele [den Anschluss an die inzwischen nicht stehengebliebene Musikkultur des Auslandes] da es gilt, den besonders in musikalischen Fragen sehr am Althergebrachten hängenden Geist des Wiener Publikums ein wenig wachzurütteln und ihn zur Aufnahmswilligkeit und zu verantwortlichem, sachlichem Denken und Urteil der neueren Musik gegenüber hinzuführen."

References

This list does not include the numerous archival sources and newspaper articles cited through the text. For a list of libraries and archives, see p. 373.

Abella, Irving M. and Harold Martin Troper. *None Is Too Many: Canada and the Jews of Europe 1933–48*. Toronto: Lester & Orpen Dennys Limited, 1982; reprint with new preface, 1983, 2000.

– "'The line must be drawn somewhere': Canada and Jewish Refugees, 1933–9," *The Canadian Historical Review* 60 no. 2 (1979): 178–209.

– "Canada and the Refugee Intellectual." In *The Muses Flee Hitler: Cultural Transfer and Adaption, 1930–1945*, edited by Jarrell C. Jackman and Carla M. Borden, 257–70.

Adorno, Theodor, et al. *The Authoritarian Personality*. New York: Harper & Brothers, 1950.

Ambrose, Tom, and Peter Owen. *Hitler's loss: What Britain and America Gained from Europe's Cultural Exiles*. London: Peter Owen, 2001.

Amtmann, Willy. *Music in Canada 1600–1800*. Montréal: Habitex, 1975.

– *La musique au Québec, 1600–1875*. Montréal: les éditions de l'homme, 1976.

Anthology of Canadian Music / Anthologie de la musique canadienne. Radio Canada International 1978–91.

Appignanesi, Lisa. *Losing the Dead*. London: Chatto & Windus, 1999.

Arendt, Hannah. *The Origins of Totalitarianism*. Rev. ed. New York: Harcourt, 1966.

Armbrüster, Georg, Michael Kohlstruck, and Sonja Mühlberger, eds. *Exil Shanghai: Jüdisches Leben in der Emigration 1938–1947*.

Schriftenreihe des Aktiven Museums Berlin. Teetz : Hentrich & Hentrich, 2000.

Babbitt, Milton. "My Viennese Triangle at Washington Square, Revised and Dilated." In *Driven into Paradise*, edited by Reinhold Brinkman and Christoph Wolff.

Baker's Biographical Dictionary of Musicians. Centennial Edition. 6 vols. New York: Schirmer, 2001.

Barron, Stephanie, and Sabine Eckmann. *Exil: Flucht und Emigration Europäischer Künstler 1933–1945*. Catalogue on the occasion of the exhibition "Exil: Flucht und Emigration Europäischer Künstler 1933–1945," Neue Nationalgalerie, Staatliche Museen zu Berlin, 10 October 1997 to 4 January 1998. Munich: Prestel, 1997. The exhibition also travelled to Los Angeles and Montreal.

Beaumont, Antony, and Alfred Clayton. "Alexander Zemlinskys amerikanische Jahre." In *Alexander Zemlinsky Ästhetik, Stil und Umfeld: Wiener Schriften zur Stilkunde und Aufführungspraxis, Sonderband I*, ed. Hartmut Kronos. Vienna: Böhlau Verlag, 1995, 247–58.

Beckwith, John. "Kolinski: An Appreciation and List of Works." In *Cross-Cultural Perspectives on Music*, edited by Robert Falck and Timothy Rice. Toronto: University of Toronto Press, 1982.

– *Music at Toronto: A Personal Account*. Toronto: University of Toronto Press, 1995.

Beckwith, John, and Frederick A. Hall, eds. *Musical Canada: Words and Music Honouring Helmut Kallmann*. Toronto: University of Toronto Press, 1988.

Belkin, Simon. *Through Narrow Gates: A Review of Jewish Immigration, Colonization and Immigrant Aid Work in Canada (1840–1940)*. Montréal: Canadian Jewish Congress and the Jewish Colonization Association, 1966.

Berghaus, Günter, ed. *Theatre and Film in Exile: German Artists in Britain, 1933–45*. Oxford, New York, Munich: Wolff, 1989.

Berglund, Gisela. "Deutsche Opposition gegen Hitler in Presse und Roman des Exils." Dissertation, Stockholm, 1972.

Bernard, Yves, and Caroline Bergeron. *Trop loin de Berlin: Des prisonniers allemands en Canada (1939–1946)*. Sillery: Éditions du Septentrion, 1995.

Bethge, Eberhard. *Dietrich Bonhoeffer: Theologe, Christ, Zeitgenosse*. Munich: Kaiser, 1967.

Bhatti, Anil, and Johannes H. Voight, eds. *Jewish Exile in India: 1933–1945*. New Delhi: Manohar, 1999.

Bio-Bibliographical Finding List of Canadian Musicians and Those Who Have Contributed to Music in Canada, A. Compiled by a Committee of the Canadian Music Library Association. Ottawa: Canadian Library Association 1961.

Bonhoeffer, Dietrich. *Illegale Theologenausbildung: Finkenwalde 1935–1937*, ed. Otto Dudzus. Bd 14 of *Dietrich Bonhoeffer Werke*. Edited by Eberhard Bethge. 17 vols. Munich: Kaiser, 1996.

Bonhoeffer, Dietrich. *Illegale Theologenausbildung: Sammelvikariat 1937–1940*, ed. Dirk Schulz. Bd. 15 of *Dietrich Bonhoeffer Werke*. Edited by Eberhard Bethge. 17 vols. Munich: Kaiser, 1998.

Brinkmann, Reinhold, and, Christoph Wolff, eds. *Driven into Paradise: The Musical Migration from Nazi Germany to the United States*. Berkeley: University of California Press, 1999.

Brooks, Vernon. "Brigadoon," *McGill News* (Winter 2001–02): 34–7.

Boyers, Robert, ed. *The Legacy of the German Refugee Intellectuals*. 2nd ed. New York: Schocken, 1972.

Brusten, William. *The Logic of Evil: The Social Origins of the Nazi Party 1925–1933*. New Haven, Conneticut: Yale University Press, 1996.

Brückner, Hans. *Judentum und Musik: mit dem ABC jüdischer und nichtarischer Musikbeflissener*. Gegründet von Hans Brückner und Christa Maria Rock. Munich; Brückner, 2nd ed. 1936; 3rd ed. 1938 [There was no 1st edition].

Burghauser, Hugo. *Philharmonische Begegnungen. Erinnerungen eines Wiener Philharmonikers*. Zurich: Atlantis, 1979.

Canada. *Report of the Department of Mines and Resources, including the Report of Soldier Settlement of Canada for the Fiscal year ended March 31, 1939*. Ottawa: King's Printer, 1940, pp. 268–347.

– *Report of the Department of Mines and Resources including Report of Soldier Settlement of Canada for the Fiscal year ended March 31, 1940*. Ottawa: King's Printer, 1941, pp. 211–54.

– *Report of the Department of Mines and Resources including Report of Soldier Settlement of Canada for the Fiscal year ended March 31, 1941*. Ottawa: King's Printer, 1941.

– *Report of the Department of Mines and Resources including Report of Soldier Settlement of Canada for the Fiscal year ended March 31, 1942*. Ottawa: King's Printer, 1942, pp. 156–82.

Canada Year Book, The: The Official Statistical Annual of the Resources, History, Institutions, and Social and Economic Conditions of the Dominion. Ottawa: Census and Statistics Office, 1945.

Carter, David J. *Behind Canadian Barbed Wire: Alien, Refugee and Prisoner of War Camps in Canada, 1914–1946*. Calgary: Tumbleweed Press, 1980.

Chamberlain, Houston Stewart. *The Foundations of the Nineteenth Century*. Translated by John Lees. 2 vols. London: John Lane, 1913.

Conway, Martin, and José Gotovitch, eds. *Europe in Exile: European Exile Communities in Britain 1940–1945*. New York: Berghahn, 2001.

Corbett, David C. *Canada's Immigration Policy: A Critique*. Toronto: University of Toronto Press, 1957.

Coser, Lewis A. *Refugee Scholars in America: Their Impact and Their Experience*. New Haven, Connecticut: Yale University Press, 1984.

Cousins, Darlene Caroline. "Otto Dix's Portrait of the Lawyer Hugo Simons: German Art for a Canadian Museum." M.A. thesis, Concordia University, Montreal, 2002.

Daniels, Roger, "American Refugee Policy in Historical Perspective." In *The Muses Flee Hitler: Cultural Transfer and Adaption, 1930–1945*, edited by Jarrell C. Jackman and Carla M. Borden, 61–78.

Davie, Maurice R., and Samuel Koenig. *The Refugees Are Now Americans*. Public Affairs Pamphlets 111. New York: New York Public Affairs Committee, 1945.

Della Pergola, Luciano. *Opera at McGill: The Della Pergola Years 1956–1989 with Edith and Luciano Della Pergola*. Edited by John Rea. Montreal: McGill University, 1991.

Dirks, Gerald. *Canada's Refugee Policy: Indifference or Opportunism?* Montreal: McGill-Queen's University Press, 1977.

Douer, Alisa. *Vertriebene der Vernunft: Emigration und Exil österreichischer Wissenschaftler*. 2 vols. Vienna: Jugend und Volk, 1999.

Draper, Paula Jean. "The Accidental Immigrants: Canada and the Interned Refugees." PhD dissertation, University of Toronto, 1983.

– "The 'Camp Boys': Interned Refugees from Nazism." In *Enemies Within: Italian and other Internees in Canada and Abroad*, edited by Franca Iacovetta, Robert Perin, and Angelo Principe, 171–93.

– "Fragmented Loyalties: Canadian Jewry, The King Government and the Refugee Dilemma." In *On Guard for Thee: War, Ethnicity, and the Canadian State, 1939–1945*, edited by Norman Hillmer, Bohdan Kordan, and Lubmyr Luciuk, 151–77.

– "Muses behind Barbed Wire." In *The Muses Flee Hitler: Cultural Transfer and Adaption, 1930–1945*, edited by Jarrell C. Jackman and Carla M. Borden, 271–82.

Düwell, Kurt, Angela Genger, Kerstin Griese, and Falk Wieseman, eds. *Vertreibung jüdischer Künstler und Wissenschaftler aus Düsseldorf 1933–1945*. Düsseldorf: Droste, 1998,

Eckhardt, Ferdinand. *Music from Within: A Biography of the Composer S C Eckhardt-Gramatté*. Edited by Gerald Bower. Winnipeg: University of Manitoba Press, 1985.

Eckhardt-Gramatté Gedenkschrift für das Familiengrab in Berlin-Wilhelmshagen. Winnipeg: D. Roger, 2000.

Elliot, Robin, and Gordon Smith, eds. *Istvan Anhalt: Pathways and Memory*. Montreal: McGill-Queen's University Press, 2001.

Engelmann, Frederick C., and Manfred Prokop. "Achievements and Contributions of Austrian-Canadians." In *A History of the Austrian Migration to Canada*, edited by Frederick C. Engelmann, Manfred Prokop, and Franz A.J. Szabo, 157–99.

Engelmann, Frederick C., Manfred Prokop, and Franz A.J. Szabo, eds. *A History of the Austrian Migration to Canada*. Ottawa: Carleton University Press, 1996.

Exilés et Émigrés: Les artistes européens qui ont fut Hitler. Exhibition catalogue, 14 June to 7 September 1997. Montréal Museum of Fine Arts.

Fermi, Laura. *Illustrious Immigrants: The Intellectual Migration from Europe, 1930–1941*. 2nd ed. Chicago: University of Chicago Press, 1971 [first published 1968].

Fleming, Donald, and Bailyn, Bernard. *The Intellectual Migration: Europe and America, 1930–1960*. Cambridge, Mass.: Belknap Press of Harvard University Press, 1969.

Flotzinger, Rudolf, ed. *Oesterreichisches Musiklexikon*. 5 vols. Vienna: Verlag der österreischische Akademie der Wissenschaften Wien, 2002– [available online at www.musiklexikon.ac.at].

Freise, Judith, and Joachim Martini. *Jüdische Musikerinnen und Musiker in Frankfurt, 1933–1942: Musik als Form geistigen Widerstandes. Eine Ausstellung von Judith Freise und Joachim Martini in der Paulskirche zu Frankfurt am Main vom 7 bis zum 25 November 1990*. Frankfurt: O. Lembeck, 1990.

Friedländer, Saul. *The Years of Persecution 1933–1939*. Vol. 1 of *Nazi Germany and the Jews*. 2 vols. New York: Harper Collins, 1997–2006.

Friesen, Astrid von. *Der lange Abschied: Psychische Spätfolgen für die 2. Generation deutscher Vertriebener*. Gießen: Psychosozial Verlag, 2000.

Frost, Stanley Brice. *McGill University for the Advancement of Learning*. 2 vols. Montreal: McGill-Queen's University Press, 1980–1994.

– "A Short Account of the History of the Faculty of Music." Paper Presented to the James McGill Society, 7 December 1978. Typescript. MGill University Archives, Reference Files, "Stanley Frost."

Gaub, Albrecht. "From Swastika to Maple Leaf: Refugee Musicians from Nazi Germany and Austria in Canada." Paper delivered at Dalhousie University, 13 October 2000.

– "Karl Steiner: Canadian Apostle of the Second Viennese School." *Institute for Canadian Music Newsletter* 1, no. 2 (May 2003): 3–7 (available at http://www.utoronto.ca/icm/0102a.html).

– "Nördlich der Unbegrenzten Möglichkeiten: Von den Nationalsozialisten vertriebene Musiker im kanadischen Exil." *Das Orchester* 49, no. 3 (2001): 2–7.

Geschichte einer Ausstellung: Zwei Jahrtausende deutsch-jüdische Geschichte. Berlin: Stiftung Jüdisches Museum, 2001.

Giese, Rachel. *Friends of Chamber Music: A History of Twenty-Five Years, 1948–1973*. Vancouver: [Friends of Chamber Music], 1973 [typescript].

Gillman, Peter, and Leni Gillman. *"Collar the Lot!" How Britain Interned and Expelled its Wartime Refugees*: London: Quartet, 1980.

Godden, Reginald, and Austin Clarkson. *Reginald Godden Plays: The Musical Adventures of a Canadian Pianist*. Etobicoke: Soundway Press, 1990.

Goldsmith, Martin. *The Inextinguishable Symphony: A True Story of Music and Love in Nazi Germany*. New York: John Wiley, 2000.

Göpfert, Rebekka. *Der jüdische Kindertransport von Deutschland nach England 1938/39: Geschichte und Erinnerung*. Frankfurt and New York: Campus, 1999.

The New Grove Dictionary of Music and Musicians, ed. Stanley Sadie and John Tyrrell. 2nd ed. 29 vols. London and New York: MacMillan, 2001.

Gutman, Israel, ed. *Encyclopedia of the Holocaust*. 4 vols. New York: Macmillan, 1990.

Haendel, Ida. *Woman with Violin: The Autobiography of Ida Haendel*. London: Gollancz, 1970.

Haffner, Sebastian. *Geschichte eines Deutschen: Die Erinnerungen 1914–1933*. Munich: Deutsche Taschenbuch Verlag, 2002.

– *Von Bismarck zu Hitler: Ein Rückblick*. Munich: Knaur, 1987.

Hamann, Brigitte. *Winifred Wagner oder Hitlers Bayreuth*. Munich: Piper, 2002.

Harris, Mark Jonathan, and Deborah Oppenheimer. *Into the Arms of Strangers: Stories of the Kindertransport*. London: Bloomsbury, 2000.

Heilbut, Anthony. *Exiled in Paradise: German Refugees, Artists and Intellectuals in America from the 1930's to the Present*. New York: Viking, 1983.

Heister, Hanns-Werner, Claudia Maurer-Zenck, and Peter Petersen, eds. *Musik im Exil: Folgen des Nazismus für die internationale Musikkultur*. Frankfurt: Fischer, 1993.

Heister, Hanns-Werner, and Hans-Günter Klein. *Musik und Musikpolitik im faschistischen Deutschland*. Frankfurt: Fischer, 1984.

Helmer, Paul. "Ulrich Leupold." *Consensus: A Canadian Lutheran Journal of Theology* 32, no. 1 (2007): 73–8.

Hillmer, Norman, Bohdan Kordan, and Lubmyr Luciuk, eds. *On Guard for Thee: War, Ethnicity, and the Canadian State, 1939–1945*. Ottawa: Canadian Committee for the History of the Second World War, 1988.

Hirschfeld, Gerhard, ed. *Exile in Great Britain: Refugees from Hitler's Germany*. Leamington Spa, Warwickshire: Berg; Atlantic Highlands, New Jersey: Humanities Press, 1984. [English translation of *Exil in Großbritannien; Zur Emigration aus dem nationalsozialistischen Deutschland*. Publications of the German Historical Institute. Stuttgart: Klett-Cotta, 1983].

Hitler, Adolf. *Mein Kampf*. Munich: Franz Eher Nachfolger, 1934.

Hoffmann, Luwig, ed. *Exil in der Tschechoslowakei, in Großbritannien, Skandinavien und in Palästina*. Frankfurt am Main: Röderberg, 1981.

Holborn, Louise Wilhelmine. *The International Refugee Organizations: The History and Organization of a Specialized Agency*. New York: Oxford, 1956.

Hollfelder, Peter. *Geschichte der Klaviermusik*. 2 vols. Wilhelmshaven: Noetzel, 1988.

Hughes, H. Stuart. *The Sea Change: The Migration of Social Thought, 1930–1965*. New York: Harper & Row, 1975.

Iacovetta, Franca, Robert Perin, and, Angelo Principe, eds. *Enemies Within: Italian and other Internees in Canada and Abroad*. Toronto: University of Toronto Press, 2000.

Jackman, Jarrell C., and Carla M. Borden, eds. *The Muses Flee Hitler: Cultural Transfer and Adaption, 1930–1945*. Washington, DC: Smithsonian Institution Press, 1983.

Jay, Martin. *Permanent Exiles: Essays on the Intellectual Migration from Germany to America*. New York: Columbia University Press, 1985.

Jefferson, Alan. *Elisabeth Schwarzkopf*. London: Gollancz, 1996.

Jesse, Eckhard. "Der Reichstagsbrand: 70 Jahre danach." *Mut: Forum für Kultur Politik und Geschichte* 428 (April 2003): 32–3.

Jessup, Lynda, Andrew Nurse, and Gordon E Smith, eds. *Around and About Marius Barbeau: Modelling Twentieth-Century Culture*. Gatineau, Quebec: Canadian Museum of Civilization, 2008.

Jones, Ted. *Both Sides of the Wire: The Fredericton Internment Camp*. Fredericton, New Brunswick: New Ireland Press, 1988.

Josephson, David, "The Exile of European Music: Documentation of Upheaval and Immigration in the *New York Times*." In *Driven into Paradise: The Musical Migration from Nazi Germany to the United States*, edited by Reinhold Brinkmann and, Christoph Wolff.

Kallmann, Helmut. "Canadian Music as a Field for Research." *Toronto Conservatory of Music Bulletin* (March 1950).

– *A History of Music in Canada 1534–1914*. Rev. ed. Toronto: University of Toronto Press, 1987 [first edition, 1967].

– "Mapping Canada's Music: A Life's Task." In *Music in Canada / La musique au Canada: A Collection of Essays*, edited by G. Bimberg, 1: 11–34. Kanada-Studien 25. Bochum: Universitätsverlag Dr. N. Brockmeyer, 1997.

– "Music in the Internment Camps after World War II: John Newmark's Start on a Brilliant Canadian Career." *German-Canadian Yearbook* 14 (1995): 181–91.

Kallmann, Helmut, ed. *Catalogue of Canadian Composers*. Rev. and enlarged. Toronto: Canadian Broadcasting Corporation, 1952.

Kallmann, Helmut, Kenneth Winters, and Gilles Potvin, eds. *Encyclopedia of Music in Canada*. 2nd ed. Toronto: University of Toronto Press, 1992.

Kaptainis, Arthur. "Generation EX: German and Austrian Expatriates of the War Years Changed the Cultural Landscape of Canada." *The Gazette* (Montréal), 19 December, 1998, D1–2.

Kater, Michael. *Composers in the Third Reich*. New York: Oxford, 1999.

– *Different Drummers: Jazz in the Culture of Nazi Germany*. New York: Oxford, 1992.

– *The Twisted Muse: Musicians and Their Music in the Third Reich*. New York: Oxford, 1997.

Kaufman, Hans. "Behind Barbed Wire." Unpublished collection of camp chronicles, October 1940 to 1942.

Keer, Dawn L. "Helmut Kallmann: An Account of His Contributions to Music Librarianship and Scholarship in Canada," Masters thesis in Library Science, University of Alberta, 1991.
Keillor, Elaine. *Music in Canada: Capturing Landscape and Diversity.* Montreal: McGill-Queen's University Press, 2006.
– "Musical Activity in Canada's New Capital City in the 1870s." In *Musical Canada: Words and Music Honouring Helmut Kallmann,* edited by John Beckwith and Frederick A. Hall, 115–33.
Kent, Donald Peterson. *The Refugee Intellectual: The Americanization of the Immigrants of 1933–1941.* New York: Columbia University Press, 1953.
Kerr, Donald, and Deryck Holdsworth, eds. *Historical Atlas of Canada: Addressing the Twentieth Century,* vol. 3, 1891–1961. Toronto: University of Toronto Press, 1990.
Keyserlingk, Robert H. "Breaking the Nazi Plot: Canadian Government Attitudes towards German Canadians, 1939–1945." In *On Guard for Thee: War, Ethnicity, and the Canadian State, 1939–1945*, edited by Norman Hillmer, Bohdan Kordan, and Lubmyr Luciuk, 53–69.
Klemperer, Otto. *Klemperer on Music: Shavings from a Musician's Workbench.* Edited by Martin Anderson. London: Toccata, 1986.
Koch, Eric. *The Brothers Hambourg.* Toronto: Robin Brass Studio, 1997.
– *Deemed Suspect: A Wartime Blunder.* Toronto: Methuen, 1980.
Koepke, Wulf, and Michael Winkler, eds., *Deutschsprachige Exilliteratur: Studien zu ihrer bestimmung im Kontext der Epoche 1930 bis 1960.* Studien zur Literaur der Moderne Band 12. Bonn: Bouvier, 1984.
Kraus, Karl. *Die Fackel.* Vienna 1899–1936; reprint, Munich: Kösel, 1969–72.
Krawchuk, Peter. *Interned without Cause.* Translated by Pat Proko. Toronto: Kobzar Publishing, 1985.
Kreyszig, Walter Kurt, "Interkulturalität aus musikwissenschaftlicher Perspektive am Beispiel Kanada/Österreich." In *Kanada-Studien im Auftrag des Instituts für Kanada-Studien der Universität Augsburg,* 28:191–242. Hagen: ISL Verlag, 2000.
Krohn, Claus-Dieter, *Intellectuals in Exile: Refugee Scholars and the New School for Social Research.* Amherst: University of Massachusetts, 1993 [English translation of *Wissenschaft im Exil: deutsche Sozial- und Wirtschaftswissenschaftler in der USA und die New School for Social Research.* Frankfurt am Main: Campus, 1987].

Laplante, Louise, ed. *Compositeurs canadiens contemporains*. Translated by Véronique Robert. Montréal: Les presses de l'Université du Québec, 1977.

Lazarevich, Gordana. *The Musical World of Frances James and Murray Adaskin*. Toronto: University of Toronto Press, 1988.

Levi, Erik. "Carl Ebert, Glyndebourne and the Regeneration of British Opera." In *Theatre and Film in Exile: German Artists in Britain, 1933–45*, edited by Günter Berghaus, 179–88.

Lindt, Peter M., ed. *Schriftsteller im Exil; zwei Jahre deutsche literarische Sendung am Rundfunk in New York*. New York: Willard Publishing, 1944.

Locke, Hubert G., ed. *Exile in the Fatherland: Martin Niemöller's Letters from Prison*. Grand Rapids, Michigan: Eerdmans, 1986.

Macintosh, Robert Dale. *A Documentary History of Music in Victoria, British Columbia*. 2 vols. Vol. 1, Victoria: University of Victoria, 1981; vol. 2, Victoria: Beach Holme, 1994.

– *History of Music in British Columbia 1850–1950*. Victoria: Sono Nis Press, 1989.

MacKay, Donald. *The Square Mile: Merchant Princes of Montreal*. Vancouver: Douglas & McIntyre, 1987.

MacMillan, Ernest. "Emmy Heim." *Toronto Conservatory Bulletin* (November 1954): 2.

MacMillan, Ernest, ed. *Music in Canada*. Toronto: University of Toronto Press and Canadian Music Council, 1955.

MacMillan, Keith. "Ernest MacMillan: The Ruhleben Years." In *Musical Canada: Words and Music Honouring Helmut Kallmann*, edited by John Beckwith and Frederick A. Hall, 164–82.

MacMillan, Keith, and John Beckwith, eds. *Contemporary Canadian Composers*. Toronto: Oxford University Press, 1975.

Maheu, Renée. *Un piano sur la mer: John Newmark et son temps*. Montréal: Intouchables, 1997.

Mappin, John, and John Archer. *Bernard Amtmann, 1907–1979: A Personal Memoire*. Toronto: Amtmann Circle Publications, 1987.

Martin, Marko, "Als wäre ich nie gewesen oder kaum." *Mut: Forum für Kultur Politik und Geschichte* 417 (May 2002): 62–69.

– "Schatten der Vergangenheit." *Mut: Forum für Kultur, Politik und Geschichte* 484 (December 2007): 16–23.

Maurer Zenck, Claudia. *Ernst Krenek: Die amerikanischen Tagebücher, 1937–1942*. Dokumente aus dem Exil. Wien : Böhlau, 1992.

McCabe, Cynthia Jaffee. "Wanted by the Gestapo – Saved by America: Varian Fry and the Emergency Rescue Committee." In *The Muses Flee Hitler: Cultural Transfer and Adaption, 1930–1945*, edited by Jarrell C. Jackman and Carla M. Borden, 68–82.

McClatchie, Stephen. *The Gustav Mahler-Alfred Rosé Collection: An Inventory*. London: University of Western Ontario Library, 1996.

McIntyre, Paul, "The Empire Replanted: The Enrichment of Canada's Musical Life by Austrian Immigrants in the Twentieth Century." In *Austrian Immigration to Canada: Selected Essays,* edited by Franz A.J. Szabo, 113–26.

Medawar, Jean, and David Pyke. *Hitler's Gift: The True Story of the Scientists Expelled by the Nazi Regime*. New York: Arcade, 2001.

Melady, John. *Escape from Canada! The Untold Story of German POWs in Canada 1939–1945*. Toronto: Macmillan, 1981.

Meyer, Michael. *The Politics of Music in the Third Reich*. New York: Lang, 1991.

Middell, Eike. *Exil in den USA: Mit einem Bericht "Schanghai – Eine Emigration am Rande."* Kunst und Literatur im antifaschistischen Exil, 1933–1945, 3. Frankfurt am Main: Röderberg, 1980.

Mittenzwei, Werner. *Exil in der Schweiz*. Kunst und Literatur im antifaschistischen Exil, 1933–1945, 2. Frankfurt am Main: Röderberg, 1981.

Moore, Lindsay. "Herman Geiger-Torel, Nicholas Goldschmidt and Arnold Walter: Prophets in the Desert?" Paper delivered at CUMS Conference, Dalhousie University, 30 May 2003.

Musicians in Canada: A Bio-Bibliographical Finding List / Musiciens au Canada: bio-bibliographique. Edited by Kathleen M. Toomey and Stephen C. Willis. Ottawa: Canadian Association of Music Libraries 1981.

Musik in Geschichte und Gegenwart, Die: Allgemeine Enzyklopädie der Musik. Ed. Friedrich Blume. 17 vols. Kassel: Bärenreiter, 1986, Taschenbuchausgabe, 1989 (*MGG* 1); 2nd edition, ed. Ludwig Finscher. Kassel: Bärenreiter, 1994– (*MGG* 2).

New Cambridge Modern History Atlas, The. Edited by H.C. Darby and Harold Fullard. Cambridge: Cambridge University Press, 1970.

Newman, Richard, and Karen Kortley. *Alma Rosé: Vienna to Auschwitz*. Portland: Amadeus, 2000.

Nibelungenlied und seine Welt, Das. Darmstadt: Primus, 2003.

Palmier, Jean-Michel. *Weimar en exil: Le destin de l'émigration intellectuelle allemande antinazie en Europe et aux États-Unis*. Paris:

Payot, 1988. [tome 1: *Exil en Europe*; tome 2: *Exil en amérique, 1939–1945, de la seconde guerre mondiale au maccarthysme*].

Pass, Walter, Gerhard Scheit, and Wilhelm Svoboda. *Orpheus im Exil. Die Vertreibung der österreichischen Musik von 1938 bis 1945*. Vienna: Verlag für Gesellschaftskritik, 1995.

Peglar, Kenneth. "Opera and the University of Toronto, 1946–1971." Toronto: [1971].

Pfanner, Helmut F. *Exile in New York: German and Austrian Writers after 1933*. Detroit: Wayne State University Press, 1983.

Pichler, Anna Maria, and Gabrielle Tyrnauer. "Austrian Refugees of World War II." In *A History of the Austrian Migration to Canada*, edited by Frederick C. Engelmann, Manfred Prokop, and Franz A.J. Szabo, 75–99.

Potter, Pamela. *Most German of the Arts: Musicology and Society from the Weimar Republic to the End of Hitler's Reich*. New Haven: Yale University Press, 1998.

Prieberg, Fred. *Musik im NS-Staat*. Frankfurt: Fischer, 1982.

– *Trial of Strength: Wilhelm Furtwängler in the Third Reich*. Translated by Christopher Dolan. Boston: Northeastern University Press, 1994.

Pross, Helge. *Die deutsche akademische Emigration nach den Vereinigten Staaten, 1933–1941*. Berlin: Duncker und Humblot, 1955.

Puckhaber, Annette. "Ein Privileg für Wenige: Die deutschsprachige Migration nach Kanada im Schatten des Nationalsozialismus." PhD dissertation, University of Trier, 2001.

Raab Hansen, Jutta. *NS-verfolgte Musiker in England: Spuren deutscher und österreichischer Flüchtlinge in der britischen Musikkultur*. Hamburg: von Bockel, 1996.

Ramon, Esther. *The Homburger Family from Karlsruhe 1674–1990*. Jerusalem: Posnen, 1992.

Kennedy, Raymond. "A Bibliography of the Writings of Mieczyslaw Kolinski." *Current Musicology* 3 (Spring 1966): 99–103.

Ritchie, J.M. *German Exiles British Perspectives*. Exil Studien: Eine interdisziplinäre Buchreihe. New York: Peter Lang, 1997.

Robinson, Mark, ed. *Altogether Elsewhere: Writers on Exile*. Boston: Faber & Faber, 1994.

Röder, Werner, and Herbert A. Strauss. *International Biographical Dictionary of Central European Emigrés 1933–1945 / Biographisches Handbuch der deutschsprachigen Emigration nach 1933*. 4 vols. in 3. München and New York: K.G. Saur, 1980–1983. [Vol. 1: *Politik,*

Wirtschaft, Öffentliches Leben; Vol. 2: *The Arts, Sciences and Literature;*Vol. 3: *Index.*]

Sachs, Harvey. "She Shall Have Music." *Saturday Night* (July/August, 1994): 24–7, 60.

Sahl, Hans. *Die Wenigen und die Vielen*, Frankfurt am Main: Fischer, 1959. English translation, *The Few and the* Many. Translated by Richard and Clara Winston. New York: Harcourt, Brace & World, 1962.

– *Wir sind die Letzten: Gedichte.* Veröffentlichungen der Deutschen Akademie für Sprache und Dichtung Darmstadt 50. Heidelberg : L. Schneider, 1976.

Schabas, Ezra. *Sir Ernest Macmillan: The Importance of Being Canadian.* Toronto: University of Toronto Press, 1994.

– *There's Music in These Walls: A History of the Royal Conservatory of Music.* Toronto: Dundurn, 2005.

Schabas, Ezra, and Carl Morey. *Opera Viva – The Canadian Opera Company: The First Fifty Years.* Toronto: Dundurn, 2000.

Schall, Richard. *Verzeichnis deutschsprachiger musikwissenschaftlicher Dissertationen 1861–1960.* Kassel: Bärenreiter, 1963.

– *Verzeichnis deutschsprachiger musikwissenschaftlicher Dissertationen 1961–1970.* Kassel: Bärenreiter, 1974.

Schiller, Dieter. *Exil in Frankreich.* Kunst und Literatur im antifaschistischen Exil 1933–1945, 7. Frankfurt am Main: Röderberg, 1981.

Schindler, Agate. "Walter Kaufmann: A Forgotten Genius." In *Jewish Exile in India: 1933–1945*, edited by Anil Bhatti, 87–112.

Schoenberner, Gerhard, ed. *Künstler gegen Hitler: Verfolgung, Exil, Widerstand.* Bonn: Inter Nationes, 1984.

Schulman, Michael. "Kolinski's Music Affected by International Travelling." *Music Scene* 276 (Mar–Apr 1974): 8, 18.

Schutz, Alfred, and Aron Gurwitsch. *Philosophers in Exile: The Correspondence of Alfred Schutz and Aron Gurwitsch, 1939–1959.* Translated by J. Claude Evans. Bloomington: Indiana University Press, 1989.

Schwarz, Boris. *Music and Musical Life in Soviet Russia 1917–81.* Rev. 4th ed. New York: Norton, 1983 [first published 1972].

– "The Music World in Migration." In *The Muses Flee Hitler: Cultural Transfer and Adaption, 1930–1945*, edited by Jarrell C. Jackman and Carla M. Borden, 135–50.

Seiffert, Elaine B. "Arnold M. Walter: His Contribution to Music Education in Canada, 1946–1968." MA thesis, University of Western Ontario, 1980.

Setterfield, Gwenlyn. *Niki Goldschmidt: A Life in Canadian Music.* Toronto: University of Toronto Press, 2003.

Sinclair, Sonia. "No Ordinary Campers." *Maclean's* 113, no. 20 (15 May 2000): 24–5.

Slonimsky, Nicolas. *Music since 1900.* 4th ed., New York: Schirmer, 1971; 5th ed. New York: Schirmer, 1994.

Solti, George, and Harry Sachs. *Solti on Solti: A Memoir.* London: Chatto & Windus, 1997. German translation, *Solti über Solti.* Munich: Kindler, 1997.

Stadler, Friedrich, ed. *Vertriebene Vernunft: Emigration und Exil österreichischer Wissenschaft.* Veröffentlichungen des Ludwig-Boltzmann-Institutes für Geschichte der Gesellschaftswissenschaften. Vienna: Jugend und Volk, 1987.

Steinweis, Alan. *Art, Ideology and Economics in Nazi Germany: The Reich Chambers of Music, Theatre, and the Visual Arts.* Chapel Hill: University of North Carolina Press, 1993.

Stengel, Theophil. *Lexikon der Juden in der Musik,* bearbeitet von Dr Theo Stengel Referent in der Reichsmusikkammer in Verbindung mit Dr habil. Herbert Gerigk Leiter der Hauptstelle Musik beim Beauftragten des Führers für die Überwachung der gesamten geistigen und weltanschaulichen Schulung und Erziehung der NSDAP. Berlin: B. Hahnefeld 1940. In Weissweiler, Eva. *Ausgemertzt! Das Lexikon der Juden in der Musik und seine mörderischen Folgen.* Cologne: Dittrich, 1999.

Stent, Ronald. *A Bespattered Page? The Internment of "His Majesty's Most Loyal Enemy Aliens."* London: Andre Deutsch, 1980.

Stokes, Lawrence D. "Canada and an Academic Refugee from Nazi Germany: The Case of Gerhard Herzberg." *Canadian Historical Review* 57, no. 2 (1976): 150–70.

Stompor, Stephan. *Künstler im Exil: in Oper, Konzert, Operette, Tanztheater, Schauspiel, Kabarett, Rundfunk, Film, Musik- und Theaterwissenschaft sowie Ausbildung in 62 Ländern.* Frankfurt am Main: Lang, 1994.

Streseman, Wolfgang. *Wie könnte es geschehen? Hitlers Aufstieg in der Erinnerung eines Zeitzeugen.* Berlin: Ullstein, 1987.

– *Zeiten und Klänge: Ein Leben zwischen Musik und Politik.* Berlin: Ullstein, 1997.

Struber, Ilja, ed. *Exil, Wissenschaft, Identität: Die Emigration deutscher Sozialwissenschaftler, 1933–45*. Frankfurt am Main: Suhrkamp, 1988.

Stubley, Eleanor, ed. *Compositional Crossroads: Music, McGill, Montréal*. Montreal: McGill-Queens University Press, 2008.

Suchy, Barbara. "Otto Joachim." In *Vertreibung jüdischer Künstler und Wissenschaftler aus Düsseldorf 1933–1945*, edited by Kurt Düwell et al., 123–132; 138–140.

Szabo, Franz A.J. *Austrian Immigration to Canada: Selected Essays*. Ottawa: Carleton University Press, 1996.

Tembeck, Iro. *Dancing in Montreal: Seeds of a Choreographic History*. Studies in Dance History, vol. 5, no. 4. Madison, WI: Society of Dance History Scholars, 1994.

Thirty-four Biographies of Canadian Composers / Trent-quatre Biographies de compositeurs canadiens. Montréal: CBC, 1964; reprint St. Clair, Mich.: Scholarly Press, 1972.

Troper, Harold. "Canada." In *Encyclopedia of the Holocaust*, edited by Israel Gutman, I: 275–7.

Unger, Heinz, and Naomi Walford. *Hammer, Sickle, and Baton: The Soviet Memoires of a Musician*. London: Cresset Press, 1939.

Vinci, Tom. "A Remembrance of Ellen Vinci and a Reflection on her Life," 3 October 2003, [typescript].

Vries, Willem de. *Sonderstab Musik: Music Confiscations by the Einsatzstab Reichsleiter Rosenberg under the Nazi Occupation of Western Europe*. Amsterdam: Amsterdam University Press, 1996.

Wagner, Richard. "Das Judenthum in der Musik." In *Gesammelte Schriften und Dichtungen*, 4th edited by Leipzig: Siegel, 1907, 5: 66–85.

Walter, Arnold. "A Composer's Story." *Canadian Composer* 77 (February 1973): 4–13.

– "Education in Music:" In *Music in Canada*, edited by Ernest MacMillan, 133–45.

– "The Growth of Music Education." In *Aspects of Music in Canada*, edited by A. Walter, 247–87.

– "Introduction." In *Aspects of Music in Canada*, edited by A. Walter, 3–25.

– "*Music and the Common Understanding*." Lecture 9. Saskatoon: University of Saskatchewan, 1966.

– "Musikorganisation und Staat," *Melos* 12 (1933): 61–64.

– "Was heißt und zu welchem Ende studiert man Musiksoziologie?" *Melos* 11 (1932): 191–5.

Walter, Arnold, ed. *Aspects of Music in Canada*. Toronto: University of Toronto Press, 1969.

Walter, Bruno. *Briefe, 1894–1962*. Edited by Lotte Walter Lindt. Frankfurt am Main: S. Fischer, 1969.

– *Theme and Variations: An Autobiography*. Translated by James A. Galston. London: Hamish Hamilton, 1947 [First published in German as *Erinnerungen und Gedanken*].

Walter, Hans-Albert. *Bedrohung und Verfolgung bis 1933*. Vol. 1 of *Deutsche Exilliteratur 1933–1950*. Darmstadt: Luchterhand, 1972

– *Europäisches Appeasement und überseeische Asylpraxis*. Vol. 2 of *Deutsche Exilliteratur 1933–1950*. Stuttgart: J.B.Metzler, 1984.

– *Exilpresse*. Vol. 4 of *Deutsche Exilliteratur 1933–1950*. Stuttgart: Metzler, 1978

– *Internierung, Flucht und Lebensbedingungen im zweiten Weltkrieg*. Vol. 3 of *Deutsche Exilliteratur 1933–1950*. Stuttgart: Metzler, 1988

Wanka, Willi. *Opfer des Friedens: die Sudetensiedlungen in Kanada*. München: Langen Müller, 1988.

Warren, Richard. *It Begins with the Oboe: A History of the Toronto Symphony Orchestra*. Toronto: University of Toronto Press, 2002.

Weber, Horst, ed. *Musik in der Emigration, 1933–45: Verfolgung, Vertreibung, Rückwirkung*. Stuttgart: Metzler, 1994.

Wegner, Matthias. *Exil und Literatur: deutsche Schriftsteller im Ausland*. 2nd ed. Frankfurt am Main: Athenäum, 1967.

Weissweiler, Eva. *Ausgemerzt!: Das Lexikon der Juden in der Musik und seine mörderischen Folgen*. Köln : Dittrich-Verlag, 1999. [includes a facsimile of Theophil Stengel's *Lexikon der Juden in der Musik*, published in Berlin, 1940].

Werth, Alexander. *Russia at War, 1941–1945*. London: Barrie and Rockliff, 1964.

Wolters-Fredlund, Benita. "Music, Culture, Ethnicity and Nationalism: The Toronto Jewish Folk Choir and Conceptions of Canadian Multiculturalism." Paper delivered at CUMS Conference, Dalhousie University, 30 May 2003.

Zweig, Stefan. *Die Welt von Gestern; Erinnerungen eines Europäers*. Berlin: [n.p.], 1958.

LIBRARIES AND ARCHIVES

Acadia University Archives, Wolfville, NS, http://library.acadiau.ca/archives

British Columbia Archives, Victoria, www.bcarchives.gov.bc.ca

Canadian Jewish Congress Archives and Resource Centre, Montreal, www.cjccc.ca/national_archives

Gustav Mahler-Alfred Rosé Collection, Univ. of Western Ontario, London, www.lib.uwo.ca/music/gmar.html

Joan Baillie Archives, Archives of the Joey and Toby Tanenbaum Opera Centre. Toronto, www.coc.ca/company/tanenbaum_archives.html

Marvin Duchow Music Library, McGill University, Montreal, http://www.mcgill.ca/music-library

McGill University Archives, McLennan Library, Montreal, http://www.archives.mcgill.ca/resources/guide/vol1/rg39.htm

New Brunswick Archives, Fredericton, www.archives.gnb.ca

Library and Archives Canada, Ottawa, www.lac-bac.gc.ca; the LAC MUS fonds are held in the Music Section, Library and Archives Canada, Gatineau, QC

Nova Scotia Archives, Halifax, www.gov.ns.ca/nsarm

Simon Fraser University Archives, Vancouver, www.sfu.ca/archives

University of British Columbia Archives, Vancouver, www.library.ubc.ca/archives

Upper Canada College Archives, Toronto, www.ucc.on.ca

University of Toronto Archives, Robarts Library, Toronto, www.library.utoronto.ca/utarms/archives/holdings.html

University of Toronto Music Library, www.music.utoronto.ca/library.htm

University of Western Ontario Library, London, www.lib.uwo.ca/music

York University Archives, Toronto

Index